THE FUTURE OF
GAY RIGHTS
IN AMERICA

THE FUTURE OF
GAY RIGHTS
IN AMERICA

EDITED BY H.N. HIRSCH

Routledge
Taylor & Francis Group
New York London

Published in 2005 by
Routledge
Taylor & Francis Group
270 Madison Avenue
New York, NY 10016

Published in Great Britain by
Routledge
Taylor & Francis Group
2 Park Square
Milton Park, Abingdon
Oxon OX14 4RN

Printed in the United States of America on acid-free paper
10 9 8 7 6 5 4 3 2 1

International Standard Book Number-10: 0-415-95077-5 (Hardcover) 0-415-95078-3 (Softcover)
International Standard Book Number-13: 978-0-415-95077-0 (Hardcover) 978-0-415-95078-7 (Softcover)
Library of Congress Card Number 2005002937

Library of Congress Cataloging-in-Publication Data

The future of gay rights in America / edited by H.N. Hirsch.
    p. cm.
  Includes bibliographical references and index.
  ISBN 0-415-95077-5 (hb : alk. paper) -- ISBN 0-415-95078-3 (pb : alk. paper)
  1. Gay rights--United States. 2. Gays--Legal status, laws, etc.--United States. I. Hirsch, H. N.

KF4754.5.F88 2005
342.7308'7--dc22
                                                   2005002937

Taylor & Francis Group
is the Academic Division of T&F Informa plc.

Visit the Taylor & Francis Web site at
http://www.taylorandfrancis.com

and the Routledge Web site at
http://www.routledge-ny.com

Contents

Acknowledgments

The editor would like to thank Chris Jozwiak for his able research assistance and Rob Tempio at Routledge for his support.

Introduction

H. N. HIRSCH

The closing years of the twentieth century and the opening years of the twenty-first will be remembered in American history as (among other things) the era of gay rights.[1] A stunning federal Supreme Court decision— *Lawrence v. Texas*[2]—overturned state sodomy laws, the principal legal tool used for decades to outlaw same-sex intimacy and to excuse and justify other forms of discrimination against those engaging in same-sex intimate behavior. In short order, the Massachusetts Supreme Judicial Court, drawing on the reasoning of *Lawrence* as well as state constitutional provisions, allowed same-sex marriage for the first time, at least in that state[3]—catapulting the issue of gay marriage, and gay rights more generally, to the center of national political consciousness.

These two court decisions (even allowing for the backlash that the election of 2004 may have represented[4]) would have been considered a utopian gay fantasy a mere ten years ago. The social changes these decisions reflect are equally profound. For we must recall that early in the lifetime of many living gay Americans, we were routinely jailed, defined as mentally ill, denied employment, housing and other basic civil rights, and subjected to appalling levels of violence. By the millions, we led constricted, closeted lives. Although conditions remain shockingly similar for some, particularly in some parts of the nation—gay teenagers continue to commit suicide at rates much higher than those of their straight peers,[5] and, as the murder of

Matthew Shepard in 1998 made abundantly clear, hate crimes continue to be committed everywhere[6]—we are nevertheless, without question—and despite any backlash—living through a period of revolutionary change, especially at the level of legal and constitutional rights.

It is, of course, a truism that virtually all major political and moral issues in America are, ultimately, settled by constitutional decision. Civil rights for African Americans, women's rights, the rights of aliens and immigrants, the right to life, the right to die—all of these issues have been, and will continue to be, tested against the Constitution's purposely vague guarantees of equal protection, due process, and liberty.[7]

The same is true of gay rights. In *Lawrence*, the Court overturned all remaining state sodomy laws.[8] That, by itself, was revolutionary—but the Court did not merely act; it acted boldly. Its decision was broadly based, not narrow or technical. The Court made it clear that a state ban on same-sex intimacy denied fundamental constitutional rights—specifically, the Constitution's fundamental guarantee of liberty—and, going even further, strongly implied that such laws violated fundamental human rights, rights recognized by other countries.[9] And the Court, in doing so, did not merely sidestep, but without apology overturned its own relatively recent precedent, *Bowers v. Hardwick*, a 1986 case that had sustained state laws such as those at issue in *Lawrence*, and had done so in language reeking of homophobia.[10] For all of these reasons, *Lawrence* can be considered extraordinary.[11]

When the Supreme Court comes to consider the issue of gay marriage, as it almost certainly will, in one form or another—perhaps when a married same-sex couple from Massachusetts moves to a state that has outlawed such marriages, or perhaps when the constitutionality of state bans against same-sex marriage are challenged on federal constitutional grounds—it will draw upon the reasoning announced with surprising clarity in *Lawrence*. Or, perhaps, if President Bush is able to reshape the Supreme Court quickly—a distinct possibility—and if his nominees act as he hopes (which might be more difficult to predict), a new Court may quickly and stunningly overturn *Lawrence*, and return us, for a time, to *Bowers*. Whatever may happen from this point forward—and there will, undoubtedly, be twists and turns that we cannot at this moment anticipate—the Supreme Court will play a central role. Just as we cannot understand the modern movement for African-American civil rights without a thorough understanding of *Brown v. Board of Education*,[12] and just as we cannot understand the history of modern feminism without understanding *Roe v. Wade*,[13] we will not be able to understand the modern movement for gay rights without out a thorough understanding of *Lawrence v. Texas* and its aftermath.[14]

The chapters in this volume consider and, in some cases, critique various aspects of *Lawrence* and its conceptualization of gay rights, as well as the decision's historical, political, and philosophical context, and its implications for the future, particularly for the issue of gay marriage.

In section I, we begin with an essay by distinguished historian John D'Emilio, who places *Lawrence* in context. D'Emilio first looks backward, arguing that the decision "closes a very long chapter in the history of sexuality," and that the concept of criminality now will no longer shape gay lives. He sees the decision as one that reflects a distinctively modern understanding of sexuality, and that places same-sex desire within the context of human rights. D'Emilio then looks forward, arguing that *Lawrence* does not pave the way for judicial endorsement of gay marriage, and further argues that gay advocates should fear, rather than welcome, a consideration of the marriage question by the Supreme Court in the near future.

Next, David Erdos examines and critiques one of the chief philosophical weapons deployed by those who argue against gay rights: Natural Law. Erdos demonstrates that, even by their own internal principles, these arguments do not stand up. Although the arguments examined by Erdos may seem quaint to some, there is no question that the philosophical doctrine of Natural Law has been taken up with great fervor by, for example, both Catholic and Evangelical Protestant opponents of gay rights, and that, both in general and with specific reference to gay issues, these doctrines continue to have a powerful influence shaping American politics—as exemplified by the recent debate about whether the Democratic party lost the 2004 election because it did not pay sufficient attention to the opinions of religious Americans.[15]

Next, three chapters examine the empirical evidence concerning the place of gay issues in recent American elections. Sean Cahill demonstrates that gay issues have been central to every federal election campaign since 1992, and disputes the conventional wisdom concerning the role of gay issues in 2004, as do Ken Sherrill and Ethel Klein in their contributions. Sherrill looks closely at the attributes of the 2004 gay vote and the anti-gay vote, and Klein looks at the methodological errors of those claiming decisive importance for gay marriage in the presidential outcome.

The chapters in section II all consider some aspect of the Supreme Court's decision in *Lawrence v. Texas*. John Brigham discusses the institutional, personal, and political context of the decision and looks at some of its participants. Dale Carpenter examines the background facts of the case, many of which were "lost" to the actual Supreme Court decision, and presents a fascinating glimpse of the human realities of the case, and of the contrast between human reality and legal doctrine. Andrew Koppelman asks the important question, exactly what rule of law does *Lawrence* establish, and then goes on to examine the implications of the decision for the future, including the issue of gay marriage in the states. Koppelman, unlike

D'Emilio, is somewhat optimistic about the implications of *Lawrence* for the recognition of marriage in states other than Massachusetts. Joe Rollins, Anna Marie Smith, and Jo Ann Citron and Molly Shanley all offer a critique of some facet of the Court's decision. Rollins examines the implications of the decision for the conceptualization of "the Homosexual subject," and the implications of this for the question of marriage. Smith examines the ins and outs of basing such decisions on a concept of individual rights, and the political implications of such conceptualization. Both Rollins and Smith could be said to offer a "queer" critique of *Lawrence*.[16] Citron and Shanley read the majority opinion in *Lawrence* as normalizing homosexual sex in what they characterize as a respectful manner and make an important distinction between what the case *holds* and what it *means*. They argue that the legal analysis of the majority opinion has broad implications including, potentially, positive implications for the recognition of same-sex marriage and for other forms of relationship beyond marriage.

Two chapters then offer disciplinary perspectives on *Lawrence*. First, political scientist Ron Kahn places *Lawrence* in its jurisprudential context. Calling the decision "transformational" and optimistic about its implications for the future, Kahn explains why the decision could not have been anticipated by today's dominant mode of legal reasoning—legal realism. Kahn considers the relation of the decision to jurisprudential issues such as "originalism"—the theory that the Constitution should be interpreted to mean only what the framers intended it to mean—and, at the same time, uses *Lawrence* to critique the work of one of the most widely quoted contemporary legal scholars, Cass Sunstein. Legal scholar Sanford Levinson then examines one of the most unusual aspects of the *Lawrence* decision, its citation of legal precedent from outside of the United States.

In chapter 14, I examine the question of gay marriage from a theoretical perspective, and examine its place in recent debates within the gay community; I then offer some empirical evidence concerning public opinion about marriage within the gay community. Finally, Keith Bybee offers some thoughts on the relationship between politics and manners, and the relation of both to gay equality in general and same-sex marriage in particular. Like D'Emilio, Bybee suggests that the expansion of *Lawrence* to cover same-sex marriage may take considerable time.

These chapters do not of course exhaust the issues raised by *Lawrence*, by the 2004 election, or by gay rights, but they will, we hope, offer a starting point for analysis and discussion as this issue continues to unfold.

In his monumental play *Angels in America*, which took the world by storm in the early nineties, Tony Kushner has his gay protagonist Prior Walter make a seemingly simple statement as the long and complex drama draws to a close: "We will be citizens." Understood at the time, perhaps, as a plaintive demand, Prior was more prescient than anyone could have guessed just a few short years ago.

Notes

1. It is considered politically incorrect in some quarters to use the word "gay" to signify the members of all sexual minority communities. However, I have chosen to use the word in this introduction, and in the title of this volume, because of the incompleteness of the phrase "gay and lesbian"—which leaves out, for example, bisexuals and the transgendered—and because of the infelicity of the acronym "LGBT" (which is also considered incomplete by some, for example, Native Americans who recognize the "Two-Spirited"). This position on the word "gay" is mine alone and should not be attributed to any of the contributors to this book.
2. *Lawrence v. Texas*, 539 U.S. 558 (2003).
3. *Goodridge v. Department of Public Health*, 798 N.E.2d 941, Mass., Nov. 18, 2003.
4. According to quick and, we argue, inaccurate analyses, opposition to same-sex marriage may have tilted the 2004 presidential election to the Republican incumbent, George Bush; see chapters 3, 4, and 5. In that election, a number of states passed laws and constitutional amendments designed to halt the spread of gay marriage.
5. Mike U. Smith and Mary Ann Drake, "Suicide and Homosexual Teens," March 1, 2001, http://www.glsen.org/cgi-bin/iowa/all/library/record/532.html (accessed January 13, 2005).
6. Human Rights Campaign, "Alarming Rates of Hate Crimes Reported by FBI: Sexual Orientation-Based Crimes Now Second-Highest Category of Reported Hate Offenses" (November 23, 2004), http://www.hrc.org/Template.cfm?Section=Search&CONTEN-TID=24206&TEMPLATE (accessed January 13, 2005).
7. For an interpretation of this purposeful vagueness, see H. N. Hirsch, *A Theory of Liberty: The Constitution and Minorities* (New York: Routledge, 1992).
8. *Lawrence v. Texas*, 539 U.S. 558, 559 (2003). Highlighting the fact that, at the time of the decision, only thirteen states had laws prohibiting sodomy, and that in four of those states, the laws were only enforced against homosexual conduct.
9. See chapter 13.
10. See chapter 10.
11. Although the authors in this volume agree that *Lawrence* recognizes a fundamental constitutional right, that conclusion is not universally accepted. For the contrary view, see Randy Barnett, "Justice Kennedy's Libertarian Revolution: *Lawrence v. Texas*," in CATO SUP. CT. REV. 2002–2002 21 (Jane L. Swanson, ed. 2003) and Pamela Karlan, "Foreword: Loving Lawrence," Mich. L. Rev. 102 (2003): 1450. For the argument that *Lawrence* does, indeed, recognize a fundamental right, see Dale Carpenter, "Is Lawrence Libertarian?", Minn. L. Rev. 88 (2004) 1140.
12. *Brown v. Board of Educ*ation, 347 U.S. 483 (1954).
13. *Roe v. Wade*, 410 U.S. 113 (1973).
14. Although our emphasis in this book is on the legal and constitutional process, and the ultimate recognition of rights in that process, it should be noted that many victories have also been gained in local and state legislatures, and in private industry, on such issues as domestic partnership benefits. For a complete discussion, consult William N. Eskridge Jr. and Nan D. Hunter, *Sexuality, Gender, and the Law* (New York: Foundation Press, 2004), esp. chapters 6–9.
15. Adam Nagourney, "The Nation: Democrats Entangled; So What Happened in That Election, Anyhow?" *New York Times*, January 2, 2005, http://www.nytimes.com/2005/01/02/weekinreview/02nago.html?8hpib=&pagewanted=print&position (accessed January 13, 2005).
16. Joe Rollins and H. N. Hirsch, "Sexual Identities and Political Engagements: A Queer Survey," *Social Politics* 10, no. 3 (2003): 290–313. Includes a definition and discussion of queer theory.

PART **I**
Context

CHAPTER 1

Some Lessons from *Lawrence*[1]

JOHN D'EMILIO

Any right-thinking person ought to be thrilled by the *Lawrence v. Texas* decision. The highest court of a nation that claims to have been conceived in liberty and sees itself as the birthplace of freedom in the modern world declared that sodomy laws have no place in a free society. According to Justice Anthony Kennedy, author of the majority opinion, the case of John Lawrence and Tyrone Garner, arrested for having sex together in the privacy of Lawrence's home, involved "transcendent dimensions" of personal liberty. Criminalizing same-sex acts, Kennedy declared, "demeans the lives of homosexual persons."[2] This bracing judicial rhetoric was inspiring to the gay men and lesbians sitting in the courtroom that morning. Linda Greenhouse, the constitutional law reporter for *The New York Times*, observed that "several were weeping, silently but openly," as Kennedy read the opinion.[3] But anyone who values personal freedom and the right of individuals to control their own body ought to have cheered as well. As William Brown, a Londoner, put it when he was arrested almost 300 years ago on the charge of sodomy, "I think there is no crime in making what use I please of my own body."[4] Who would argue with that?

A wide range of commentators have made bold claims about the decision's significance. David Garrow, a Pulitzer Prize-winning historian who writes about both civil rights and sexuality, called it "one of the two most important opinions of the last 100 years."[5] Carolyn Lochhead, the Washington-based reporter for the *San Francisco Chronicle*, described it as "a watershed" in the history of the gay rights movement.[6] The opinion "sent shock waves around the country," according to *The Advocate*, a national gay magazine.[7] Lawyers involved in the gay rights movement were especially effusive in their praise. Ruth Harlow, legal director of Lambda Legal, the largest litigation group of its kind, characterized *Lawrence* as "a historic, transformative decision."[8] Jon Davidson, another Lambda lawyer, said it was "monumental … a day of liberation."[9] Across the country, queer activists hailed it as the gay community's equivalent of *Brown v. Board of Education of Topeka, Kansas*, the 1954 Supreme Court case that ruled racially segregated public schools to be inherently unequal and hence unconstitutional.

Nor were detractors any less restrained in their views. Cultural conservatives predicted all sorts of dire consequences. Scott Lively, director of the American Family Association of California, declared that *Lawrence* "puts a stamp of approval on anything-goes sexuality."[10] The case opened up "a complete Pandora's box," according to Sandy Rios, president of Concerned Women for America. Americans were facing a "moral Armageddon," she proclaimed.[11] The country was now on "a slippery slope" of moral decline, said the president of one Christian evangelical seminary.[12] Employing the imagery of the war on terrorism, Reverend Lou Sheldon of the Traditional Values Coalition referred to Kennedy's opinion as "a 9/11 major wake-up call that the enemy is at our doorsteps."[13] In a passionately worded dissent, Justice Antonin Scalia forecast "a massive disruption of the current social order." Judicial approval of bigamy, incest, and bestiality were next, he predicted.[14]

Most strikingly, both sides in America's much-hyped "culture war" saw *Lawrence* as clearing the path to same-sex marriage. *Newsweek*'s cover about the case ignored sodomy laws altogether and simply asked "Is Gay Marriage Next?"[15] Evan Wolfson, a lawyer who has made same-sex marriage his life's work, claimed that prohibitions against it were now on "very shaky grounds."[16] Lawrence Tribe, a Harvard University legal scholar called laws against same-sex marriage "constitutionally suspect."[17] Patricia Logue, one of Lambda's attorneys, forecast that gay marriage was "inevitable now," while Chai Feldblum, a Georgetown law professor active in lesbian and gay rights efforts, saw it happening "in the next decade."[18] Despite the fact that Justice Kennedy stated that the case "does not involve" same-sex marriage, Justice Scalia countered: "Do not believe it. … Today's opinion dismantles the structure of constitutional law that has permitted a distinction to be made between heterosexual and homosexual unions." In the wake of *Lawrence*, Scalia asserted, "what justification could there possibly be for denying the benefits of marriage to homosexual couples?"[19]

Most of these pronouncements miss the mark badly. As I will argue in this chapter, the *Lawrence* case is important and it does have much to teach us. The lessons it offers are especially vital to grasp if one is interested in understanding how to make change in the United States. But its significance, though great, is both more modest and more sobering than some of the viewpoints expressed afterward seem to suggest.

In the remainder of this chapter, I will elaborate three lessons that we can extract from *Lawrence*:

1. Intellectual work can be a force for change in society.
2. Despite how little same-sex sodomy laws have touched the lives of gay men and lesbians in the early twenty-first century, declaring them unconstitutional will make a difference. But precisely what kind of difference remains an open question, and it is a difference that will grow in importance as time passes.
3. Significant as Supreme Court decisions have been in American history, the nation's highest court is not generally at the cutting edge of progressive social change. Rather than lead, the Supreme Court most often follows. In other words, its decisions matter, but not in the inflated way that contemporary spin—from activists, the media, or disgruntled justices—would have us believe.

At first blush, these lessons may seem contradictory. For instance, if the Court follows rather than leads, how much can its decisions actually matter? Yet I believe these points to be consistent with one another. Nor am I claiming that these are the only lessons one can extract from the case. But understanding these three points allows us to absorb *Lawrence* in ways that can help us make sense both of history and of events since the decision.

Intellectual Work Can Be a Force for Change

In *Lawrence*, the Supreme Court did something highly unusual: It overturned one of its previous decisions. Just seventeen years earlier, in *Bowers v. Hardwick*, a divided court had let stand a Georgia sodomy statute. *Lawrence* was not the first instance in which the Court had done this. Perhaps the most famous example was the school desegregation case of *Brown*. There the Court reversed a position it took in 1896 in *Plessy v. Ferguson*, when it affirmed the constitutionality of segregation laws. But the principle of *stare decisis*—to stand by what has already been decided—has by and large characterized the history of the federal courts.

The reasons should be obvious. A common practice of reversing itself would subject the Court to a charge of capriciousness. In what sense are we governed by the Constitution if a high court can rule first this way and then that way, according to the views of its changing membership? In what sense does the Constitution matter if a court can change its mind in response to shifts in public opinion? Wouldn't this bring us the judge-made law against which conservatives so frequently rail? Isn't it the responsibility of the legislative, not the judicial, branch of government to remain accountable to the popular will? As Justice Kennedy put it in his opinion in the *Lawrence* case, "The doctrine of *stare decisis* is essential to the respect accorded to the judgments of the Court and to the stability of the law."[20]

Notwithstanding this principle, Kennedy also unambiguously declared, "*Bowers* was not correct when it was decided, and it is not correct today."[21] What would allow him to reject so forthrightly the opinion of a previous Court, especially when two of his colleagues had participated in the earlier decision? The concise answer is "history."

As is generally true in important cases, interested parties on both sides of the question submitted *amicus curiae* ["friend of the court"] briefs. One of these came from a group of historians, of whom I was one. Since sodomy statutes have a long history, it made sense for scholars who study the past to express their views. Indeed, in two earlier challenges to state sodomy laws, I had been asked to submit an affidavit.

In *Lawrence*, the need to bring historical perspective to bear was especially relevant because the 1986 *Bowers* decision had been so heavily laden with references to history. Writing for the majority, Justice Byron White declared in *Bowers* that "proscriptions against that conduct have ancient roots."[22] In a concurring opinion, Chief Justice Warren Burger was more expansive. "Decisions of individuals relating to homosexual conduct," he proclaimed, "have been subject to state intervention throughout the history of Western civilization. Condemnation of those practices is firmly rooted in Judeao-Christian moral and ethical standards. ... To hold that the act of homosexual sodomy is somehow protected as a fundamental right would be to cast aside millennia of moral teaching."[23]

We historians offered a different view of the past. Our brief put forward two propositions: "no consistent historical practice singles out same-sex behavior as 'sodomy' subject to proscription," and "the governmental policy of classifying and discriminating against certain citizens on the basis of their homosexual status is an unprecedented project of the twentieth century."[24] In other words, we took a point of view defying the conventional wisdom that, until recently, homosexuality was roundly proscribed and vilified.

In arguing the first proposition, the brief was not claiming that the prohibition of same-sex acts was new. Rather, it asserted that the prohibitions "have varied enormously," that the laws covered a wide range of acts, and that, for the most part, the state has only haphazardly enforced these laws. Drawing on the contrast between acts and identities, a distinction common in the historical literature, the brief pointedly stated that "the phrase 'homosexual sodomy' would have been literally incomprehensible to the Framers of the Constitution, for the very concept of homosexuality as a discrete psychological condition and source of personal identity was not available until the late 1800s."[25]

Building on this first point, the brief then went on to argue that specifically anti-gay policies and laws were very much products of the relatively recent past, that they had a short half-life rather than a long pedigree. The document charted the surge of police activity against gays in the middle decades of the twentieth century, the codifying of discriminatory policies by the federal government, and the rise of "new demonic stereotypes of homosexuals."[26] In the end, rather than the ancient roots or the millennia of moral teaching that *Bowers* called forth, the historians transformed same-sex sodomy laws into a method invented in the twentieth century by a powerful state to target a class of its citizens for cruel, blatant oppression.

In his opinion for the majority in *Lawrence*, Justice Anthony Kennedy leaned heavily on the argument presented by the historians. *Bowers*, he effectively said, got its history wrong. "There is no longstanding history in this country of laws directed at homosexual conduct as a distinct matter," he wrote.[27] Kennedy's opinion went on to discuss history at some length, incorporating not only the argument in the historians' brief, but also citing and independently quoting a number of the works of historical scholarship noted in the brief. Kennedy offered a history of sexuality that one might reasonably label a "social construction" perspective. This viewpoint, that the meaning of human sexual behavior varies profoundly over time and across cultures, allowed him to propound a view at odds with the majority's presumptions in *Bowers*. Sodomy laws may go back centuries, but criminalizing a group of citizens because of their intimate lives and then denying them basic rights in the public sphere because of their sexual identity were not deeply rooted in the nation's past.

Why was Justice Kennedy able to argue this so confidently in 2003 whereas his predecessors, seventeen years earlier, were equally assured that the record of the past was unambiguously hostile to homosexual expression? Was Kennedy simply wiser than they? The key reason is that the historical scholarship from which he drew did not exist when the opinion in *Bowers* was written. Check the references in both the historians' brief and Kennedy's opinion. The overwhelming majority of the works of history cited were published from the mid-1980s onward. Whatever Kennedy's views of the Fourteenth Amendment and the Due Process Clause might be, he needed back up to discard so recent a contrary decision. This is what the historians offered.

The academic inquiry that both feminism and gay liberation have opened up since the 1970s, their belief that sexuality is historical and cultural and that it helps structure social inequality, made the rewriting of constitutional jurisprudence in *Lawrence* possible. History has never simply been the unadorned story of what happened in the past. For the most part, history is composed of the stories that the winners tell about the past. Contesting this version of the past, as historians of race, gender, and sexuality have done in the last generation, is an important part of the work of creating a more egalitarian society, grounded in principles of social justice. *Lawrence* shows us that intellectual work does matter, that ideas can be a force for change.

Lawrence Will Make a Difference—But Later, Not Now

From a certain angle, one could reasonably argue that the *Lawrence* case hardly makes a difference at all. Compare it, for instance, to two earlier cases that are widely recognized as historic: *Brown v. Board of Education* and *Roe v. Wade*, the 1973 decision that declared that most laws criminalizing abortion were unconstitutional.

In 1954, when the Court decided *Brown*, the law in seventeen states mandated racially segregated public schools. A majority of African Americans lived in these states. Jim Crow laws separated blacks and whites in everyday life—in restaurants, movie theaters, public parks, highway rest stops, swimming pools, beaches, and countless other places. *Brown* was an invaluable asset that led, over the next decade or so, to the dismantling of the legal structure of racial segregation.

In 1973, when the Court's decision in *Roe v. Wade* overturned state antiabortion laws, abortion was a crime in almost every state. Each year, several hundred thousand women and many medical practitioners braved arrest, conviction, and imprisonment as they went in search of, or performed, abortions. With *Roe*, abortion almost immediately became widely available, and the impact was dramatically and quickly felt by large numbers of women and men.

In 2003, the Court issued *Lawrence* and almost nothing changed. The number of states with sodomy laws had been steadily declining since 1960, when all fifty states still had these laws, to the time of *Bowers* in 1986 when only twenty-four states retained them, to 2003 when the number had dwindled to thirteen. Even in these thirteen states, sodomy laws were rarely enforced. Hardly any gay men and virtually no lesbians were being arrested for same-sex acts in private with a consenting adult. In Harris County, Texas, where John Lawrence and Tyrone Garner were arrested, there hadn't been a sodomy prosecution in the previous twenty-two years. More to the point, the laws under which police did make arrests—ordinances against public lewdness, vagrancy, and disorderly conduct—remained on the books, still available for use by law enforcement officials with homophobic inclinations. It is safe to say that, a month or even a year after *Lawrence*, it would be hard to fill a modest-sized living room with gay men, lesbians, or bisexuals who could point to changes in their everyday lives because of the case.

Nonetheless, the case will make a difference, even if that difference needs to be measured in ways other than by its immediate impact. Let me put it this way: If new interpretations of history played a role in making the *Lawrence* decision possible, *Lawrence* in turn matters because of how it will change even further the history of same-sex relations.

One way in which *Lawrence* is important is that it closes a very long chapter in the history of sexuality. Even though the impact of sodomy laws was different in seventeenth-century British North America than in Texas in 2003, the laws that *Lawrence* invalidated were nonetheless part of a history of criminalizing same-sex acts that stretched back uninterruptedly for centuries. This continuity has now been broken. As years pass by, the shadow cast by sodomy laws will recede farther and farther away. Criminality will no longer shape how gay men, lesbians, and bisexuals live now and instead will become part of a past untethered to daily life. Over time, this will make a difference.

The effects of criminal status over the last few generations have been profound. Even if rarely enforced, sodomy statutes rationalized the imposition of a broad range of other penalties. How can persons whose deepest emotional yearnings make them prone to criminal activity be allowed to occupy a position of public trust? Sodomy laws served as a self-evident reason to bar gay men, lesbians, and bisexuals from government employment. They justified exclusion from professions such as law, medicine, and teaching in which moral character figured prominently. A propensity to commit crime served as grounds for denying lesbian and gay parents custody of their children or visitation rights. For decades, sodomy laws were the unanswerable response as to why gay bars should be raided and shut down: They were sites that existed only to facilitate illegal sexual activities. While most of these practices have been fading in recent decades, the continuing existence of sodomy laws was a link to this past. These statutes kept the stigma alive, making it available for deployment by the family court judge, the vice cop, or the school principal in charge of hiring. With *Lawrence*, this history is now over. *Lawrence* detached homosexuality from a criminalized past.

A second way *Lawrence* is important is that it has now attached same-sex relations to quite a different history, one that situates sexual expression within the realm of expanding personal liberty. In the eighteenth century, when the Constitution was written and ratified, sexuality in the United States was normatively contained for whites within a marital reproductive framework. Over the last two centuries, more and more Americans have voted with their desire and transformed sexual expression into something intended to bring intimacy, happiness, and pleasure. Two hundred years ago, the average number of children to which a white American woman gave birth was seven. Today the fertility of American women hovers around two. Although the timing and rate of decline has varied, this reproductive revolution has cut across all groups of women born in the United States. Race, religion, region, ethnicity, educational level, and economic status: These characteristics have affected when the decline in fertility set in and how quickly it happened, but not whether it has occurred. Sexuality has increasingly entered the realm of personal choice, the sphere of individual liberty.

Over the last half century, the Supreme Court finally began to recognize this *de facto* revolution in the sexual lives of Americans. It has brought this new meaning of sex into the sphere of constitutional jurisprudence. One set of decisions did not involve sexual behavior directly but rather the cultural representation of sexuality. Beginning in 1957 with the *Roth* case, a long series of challenges to federal and state obscenity statutes came before the Supreme Court. Enforcement of these laws placed powerful constraints on the depiction of human sexuality in the public sphere, whether in news media, film, television, the performing arts, or literature. The Supreme Court never went as far as to declare these statutes unconstitutional. But by narrowing considerably the operation of these laws, it opened up to view not only a world of pornography but also more mundane forms of sexual expression. Much of the gay and lesbian literature and a good deal of the queer press of the post-Stonewall decades would not have passed muster under the obscenity standards of the pre-*Roth* era. It would be impossible to overstate how important these rulings on obscenity were.

Although these decisions fell under the rubric of free speech and the First Amendment, underlying the Court's approach was a view of sexuality that was distinctively modern. Delivering the majority opinion in *Roth*, Justice William Brennan described sex as "a great and mysterious motive force in human life ... one of the vital problems of human interest."[28] Can one imagine a major public official in the United States a century or more earlier speaking about sex with those phrases?

A second set of cases addressed sexuality in the context of reproduction. In *Griswold v. Connecticut*, the Court struck down a Connecticut law that restricted access by married couples to contraceptives; in *Eisenstadt v. Baird*, a Massachusetts law that restricted access by the unmarried to contraceptives; and in *Roe v. Wade*, any state laws that prohibited abortions in the first two trimesters of a pregnancy. Through these, the Court constructed what it termed a "zone of privacy" rooted in constitutional notions of liberty. In *Griswold* the Justices applied to the marriage relationship language that invested it with great power: "a right of privacy older than the Bill of Rights ... intimate to the degree of being sacred ... as old and as fundamental as our entire civilization."[29] In *Eisenstadt* the Court notably extended this right to privacy beyond the framework of the couple. "The marital couple is not an independent entity with a mind and heart of its own," Justice Brennan wrote, "but an association of two individuals ... If the right to privacy means anything, it is the right of the individual, married or single, to be free from unwarranted governmental intrusion."[30]

On the surface these decisions, including *Roe*, appear to be about reproduction, not sexuality. Yet in sustaining the right of individuals to choose not to have a child, the Court was simultaneously affirming their right to have sex without procreative intent. These decisions elevated sexual expression—or, more precisely, non-procreative heterosexual acts in private between consenting adults—to the status of a protected liberty that the U.S. Constitution guaranteed.

The importance of *Lawrence* lies in the way it explicitly drew homosexual acts between consenting adults in private into this framework of constitutional rights. "Liberty presumes an autonomy of self," Kennedy declared near the beginning of his opinion. Calling *Griswold* "the most pertinent beginning point in our decision," he described "an emerging awareness" over the past half century that "liberty gives substantial protection to adult persons in deciding how to conduct their private lives in matters pertaining to sex." This right, he wrote, "extends beyond the marital relationship."[31] Unlike any other Supreme Court case in history, *Lawrence* placed the intimate lives of homosexuals within the realm of human rights. This certainly deserves to be called important.

Still, it is worth reiterating that the importance of *Lawrence* does not lie in what it offers now. Closing the door on a long history of criminality simply confirms what was almost universal practice in the United States already. Placing the expression of same-sex desire within the context of human rights and personal liberty implies a promise, though it leaves unspecified the content of the promise or a timetable for delivering on it. But, while *Lawrence* barely matters at all today, the difference it makes will grow in significance with the passage of time. As the stigma of criminality fades into the more distant past, the notion that sexual expression is a human right will ineluctably become incorporated into our understanding of what freedom entails. Over a generation or two, this shift in perspective will have an impact whose force no one can yet measure.

The Supreme Court Follows Rather Than Leads

What about marriage? Isn't a constitutional ruling in favor of same-sex marriage the promise that *Lawrence* tantalizingly extends? And won't this promise be delivered sooner rather than later? From Justice Scalia and religious conservatives to gay and lesbian activists to the editorial writers of many newspapers, commentators across the political and social spectrum drew the same conclusion: *Lawrence* paves the way for judicial endorsement of gay marriage.

There is very little reason to take this claim seriously. If *Lawrence* teaches us anything, it is that the Supreme Court follows rather than leads. Rather than chart brand new directions for society, it tends instead to confirm change that has already occurred. Its rulings bring law into alignment with shifting values and social norms. The Court consolidates an emerging consensus; it does not launch novel social experiments.

The *Lawrence* opinion itself substantiates the claim that the Supreme Court follows along paths that have already been laid out instead of leading society into unexplored territory. Justice Kennedy repeatedly emphasized how uncontroversial the elimination of sodomy laws was. As early as 1955, he wrote, the model penal code of the American Law Institute called for the decriminalization of all sexual acts between consenting adults in private. He cited the British Wolfenden Report of 1957 recommending the same thing. Kennedy called attention to the many states that had already eliminated sodomy statutes. He highlighted the 1981 decision of the European Court of Human Rights that sodomy laws were a violation of basic human rights. He pointed to the "substantial and continuing" criticism that the *Bowers* decision elicited for upholding these laws.[32] All of these references serve a single rhetorical purpose. They emphasize that the judicial elimination of sodomy laws is not a big deal. Kennedy is trying to tell his audience that striking down a few remaining sodomy laws simply flows with the stream of history. It does not impose an untested social policy upon Americans.

Viewed in this light, the content and structure of Kennedy's opinion in *Lawrence* can be seen as evidence that a pro-same-sex marriage decision will not be emanating from the Court any time soon. There are a number of reasons for adducing this. First, Justice Kennedy tells us so. Near the end of his opinion, he goes out of his way to comment that extending notions of personal liberty to the intimate lives of homosexual persons has no implications for the issue of same-sex marriage. "The present case," he wrote, "does not involve whether the government must give formal recognition to any relationship that homosexual persons seek to enter."[33]

Second, whereas Kennedy used a historical rationale to support his constitutional judgment about sodomy laws, no such rationale is available on behalf of same-sex marriage. Historians were able to construct a powerful case about sodomy statutes that allowed Kennedy to claim that history was on his side. By contrast, despite a huge historical literature on marriage produced by feminist historians, it would be implausible to argue that anything other than the union of a man and a woman was ever understood in the United States to constitute a marriage. Yes, there have been significant restrictions on the right to marry, most notably involving race. Yes, a few groups—like nineteenth-century Mormons and some small utopian communities—practiced plural marriage. But nowhere in the current historical literature is there any substantial support for a right to marry a person of the same sex.

Third, Kennedy justified his decision through reference to an "emerging awareness" in the recent past that individuals should be free to conduct their private sexual lives as they see fit. Where is this emerging awareness around same-sex marriage? In the last decade, four courts have found state constitutional grounds to support recognition of same-sex unions; of these, only the court in Massachusetts was uncompromising in declaring that same-sex couples must be given access to marriage. By contrast, overwhelming majorities in the U.S. Senate and House of Representatives have supported legislation declaring that, for the purpose of federal law, marriage shall only be understood to be the union of a man and a woman. In the last decade or so, the legislatures of thirty-seven states have similarly passed legislation affirming that marriage is the union of a man and a woman. In thirteen states, a substantial majority of voters have approved referenda declaring the same thing. More of these are on the way. Nowhere is there evidence that a newly emerging consensus is forming in support of same-sex marriage. If anything, a huge preponderance of evidence from our democratically constituted political system suggests a powerful consensus against it.

The argument that *Lawrence* paves the way for same-sex marriage is a self-serving one. It serves the interests of religious opponents of marriage in that the claim works as a call-to-arms to mobilize the troops against this new social experiment. It serves the interests of political conservatives within the Republican Party in that it gives credence to their charge that a liberal activist judiciary is creating judge-made law. And it serves the interests of those within the gay and lesbian movement who have staked their reputations on the marriage fight in that it gives credence to their claim that this goal is within reach and hence should be prioritized.

If *Lawrence* tells us anything about the marriage battle, it is that the last thing proponents of same-sex marriage should be hoping for is a Supreme Court case on the issue, since it is unlikely to result in a favorable ruling. The Court eliminated sodomy laws when there were almost no sodomy laws left and almost no support for those laws and their enforcement. When same-sex marriage becomes as commonplace as sodomy laws were rare, maybe then we will see the Supreme Court offering its constitutional blessing. Just don't expect that to happen any time soon.

Notes

1. This chapter began as a talk presented on a panel at the University of Illinois at Chicago, October 29, 2003. My thanks to Timothy Murphy for organizing the panel, and to the other panelists, Judith Gardiner, Jaime Hovey, Sharon Holland, and Murphy himself.
2. *Lawrence v. Texas*, 539 U.S. 558 (2003).
3. *New York Times*, June 27, 2003, 1.
4. Alan Bray, *Homosexuality in Renaissance England* (London: Gay Men's Press, 1982), 114.
5. Evan Thomas, "The War Over Gay Marriage," *Newsweek*, July 7, 2003, 38–45.
6. *San Francisco Chronicle*, June 29, 2003, A4.
7. Chad Graham, "Changing History," *The Advocate*, January 20, 2004, 36–39.
8. Lisa Leff, "Gays Joyful, Relieved Over Court Ruling," Associated Press, June 26, 2003, as distributed over http://www.lgbt-politics@yahoogroups.com/ (accessed June 26, 2003).
9. *Los Angeles Times*, June 27, 2003, A31.
10. Ibid.
11. Thomas, "The War Over Gay Marriage."
12. Ted Olson and Todd Hertz, "Opinion Roundup: Does *Lawrence v. Texas* Signal the End of the American Family," *Christianity Today*, June 30, 2003, http://www.christianitytoday.com/ct/2003/126/11.0html.
13. Quoted in National Gay and Lesbian Task Force, "Know Thy Enemy: A Compendium of Recent Quotes about the Supreme Court Sodomy Ruling and the Same-Sex Marriage Backlash," July 29, 2003, http://www.thetaskforce.org/media/release.cfm?releaseID=562.
14. *Lawrence v. Texas*.
15. *Newsweek*, July 7, 2003.
16. Graham, "Changing History."
17. *New York Times*, November 19, 2003, A24.
18. *Los Angeles Times*, June 28, 2003, A21.
19. *Lawrence v. Texas*.
20. Ibid.
21. Ibid.
22. *Bowers v. Hardwick*, 478 U.S. 186 (1986).
23. Ibid.
24. The "Brief of Professors of History" may be found under the title "The Historians Case against Discrimination," http://hnn.us/articles/1539.html.
25. Ibid.
26. Ibid.
27. *Lawrence v. Texas*.
28. *Roth v. United States*, 354 U.S. 476 (1957).
29. *Griswold v. Connecticut*, 381 U.S. 479 (1965).
30. *Eisenstadt v. Baird*, 405 U.S. 438 (1972).
31. *Lawrence v. Texas*.
32. Ibid.
33. Ibid.

CHAPTER 2

Questions of Tolerance and Fairness

DAVID O. ERDOS

"New natural law"[1] arguments continue to be deployed in public and legal debate by those opposed to moves to display tolerance toward and secure greater civil equality for homosexuals and their relationships. For example, during the *Lawrence* litigation,[2] major religious right groupings such as Focus on the Family and the Family Research Council utilized new natural law arguments in moral and legal defense of Texas's erstwhile "homosexual conduct" law.[3] The aim of this paper is to subject such arguments to an immanent critique. Thus, for the sake of argument, the basic sexual understandings of the new natural law will not be questioned.[4] However, I will argue that, even if one accepted the validity of these understandings, such arguments cannot provide a reasonable justification either for the Texas law struck down in the *Lawrence* litigation or for most (if not all) of the forms of discrimination faced by homosexual people today. Two principal arguments will be advanced to support these conclusions. First, it will be argued that "homosexual conduct" laws seek to regulate the intimate lives of individuals in a way strongly incompatible with the tolerance required in a free society. Second, most (if not all) of the legal disadvantages suffered by those in homosexual relationships are not imposed on heterosexual relationships which the new natural law considers to be equally (if not more) "immoral." For example, the pre-*Lawrence* Texas legal framework criminalized the sexual conduct of homosexuals while leaving a whole slew of purportedly equally immoral sexual conduct committed by heterosexuals unregulated by the criminal law. Similarly, homosexuals are excluded from the institution of civil marriage in the United States and elsewhere while the supposedly equally "nonmarital"[5] relationships of many heterosexuals (e.g., divorcees) are not so excluded. The legal treatment of homosexual relationships is, therefore, unfair even within the perspective of new natural law. Theoretically, this situation of unfairness could be rectified either by subjecting a very large number of heterosexual relationships to the same disadvantages as homosexual relationships or by releasing homosexual relationships from these disadvantages. However, there are good reasons to think that the effect in practice of the application of this principle of fairness would be to reduce substantially the extent to which homosexual relationships are placed at a disadvantage.

This chapter is structured into four sections. Section one lays out the basics of new natural law theory including how this theory understands sexual morality. It also provides a brief summary of the critique which has been offered against these understandings. In particular, it will be pointed out that many have argued that new natural law arguments in the area of sexual ethics amount to little more than the assertion of certain religious or sectarian understandings dressed up in a philosophical garb.[6] However, the main purpose of this chapter is not to contribute to this (radical) critique. The next two sections focus on the more immanent arguments that are at the heart of my thesis. Section two puts forward a principle of tolerance which, it will be argued, defeats new natural law arguments for invasive laws such as the erstwhile Texas "homosexual conduct" law. Section three will put forward a principle of fairness which, it will be argued, should lead somebody committed to new natural law understandings of sexual morality to oppose most (if not all) forms of discrimination faced by homosexual people and their relationships. Section four draws these arguments together.

Sexual Morality, New Natural Law Theory, and the Liberal Critique

New natural law theory proceeds on the premise that fully reasonable action actualizes basic, pre-moral goods. These goods, according to new natural lawyer Robert George are "ends or purposes that have their intelligibility not merely as means to other ends, but as intrinsic aspects of well-being and fulfillment."[7] Morality is introduced in this scheme by the condition of "practical reasonableness." Not having a coherent plan of life, having arbitrary preferences for some of the basic human goods rather than others, being selfish, failing to respect the basic human goods in all of your actions, not following your conscience, and failing to foster the common good of your community are all held to demonstrate a lack of "practical reasonableness." It is such a failure which makes one's conduct immoral.

In the area of sexual ethics, new natural law theory has been somewhat confused. In his article of 1970, John Finnis posits the existence of a basic good of "procreation" and uses this, together with the value of "practical reasonableness," to build a theory of sexual morality. All "anti-procreative [sexual] choices" (p. 387) (including contracepted sex and masturbation) are held immoral since they go against this basic good. Furthermore, Finnis derives a need for any sexual union to be lifelong and exclusive from the consideration that

> what is demanded in procreation is not just *esse* but *bene esse*, not a spawning, but the bringing in of the child into a community of love which will provide the substance of his education into a loving ability to realize all the human values.[8]

Thus, the only form of sexual activity that is permissible is sexual union of the procreative-type in an indissoluble and exclusive marriage between husband and wife. Toward the end of his article, Finnis briefly suggests the existence of another basic good, which he labels "friendship," and suggests that establishing a practicably reasonable attitude toward this good can also be important in ensuring moral action in the area of sexual conduct. For example, he invokes the good of friendship in an argument against sexual harassment within marriage:

> It is wrong to force sexual attentions on one's spouse, indifferent to her state or her wishes[9]—not for any special sexual reason, but because it is contrary to the demands of the basic value of friendship (p. 387).

Finnis's 1980 treatise on natural law does not deal with sexual morality at length, although, to the extent that it does, it follows a similar argument to Finnis's 1970 article. Sexual activity is seen as legitimate only to the extent that it actualizes and participates in the goods of procreation (now renamed "life") and friendship.[10]

The conclusions Finnis derived from this understanding can and have been attacked from a number of angles. First, it has been argued that his understanding of what constitutes a "procreative" sex act is confused and inconsistent. Finnis argues that uncontracepted sex between married heterosexual couples who are infertile is still, as behavior, "procreative." Stephen Macedo, however, suggests such a claim is no more plausible than arguing that pointing a gun at somebody's head and pulling the trigger is, "as behavior," an act orientated to murder even when that gun is (and is known to be) unloaded.[11] Thus, Macedo argues that a consistent application of the new natural law's rejection of "non-procreative" sex would also have to condemn all sex between infertile different-sex couples. On a more radical level, many have argued that this understanding of human sexuality discounts the good that romantic friendship and union can play in many human lives even when procreation is unavailable.[12] Also, many have criticized the inability of new natural law to recognize pleasure as a basic human good. It has been argued that this closure to the possibility of human pleasure being a good in and of itself imposes unreasonable restrictions on human happiness.[13]

While the natural lawyers have stuck to their understanding that pleasure is not a basic good, their writings at least from the 1990s onward have attempted to package their understanding of human sexuality somewhat differently. Rather than focusing on sexual morality as consisting of respect for the two goods of procreation and friendship, new natural lawyers now argue that there is a self-evident basic good of "two-in-one-flesh" marital communion and that sexual activity must actualize and participate in this good or be held immoral. "Two-in-one-flesh" marital communion is defined as an indissoluble and exclusive union between a man and a women joined together through acts of uncontracepted penile-vaginal union.[14] Sex which "embodies" this "marital communion" is held intrinsically valuable since it actualizes this basic good. All other forms of sexual communion are immoral since they involve the "instrumentalizing of the body for the sake of an illusory experience or fantasy of marital union."[15] Finnis, focusing on homosexual relationships, sees the situation thus:

> Reality is known in judgment, not in emotion, and *in reality,* whatever the generous hopes and dreams and thoughts of giving which some same-sex partners may surround their sexual acts, those acts cannot express or do more than what is expressed or done if two strangers engage in such activity to give each other pleasure, or a prostitute pleasures a client to give him pleasure in return for money, or (say) a man masturbates to give himself pleasure and a fantasy of more human relationships after a grueling day on the assembly line. This is, I believe, the substance of Plato's judgment—at that moment in the *Gorgias* which is also decisive for the moral and philosophical critique of hedonism—that there is no important distinction in essential moral worthlessness between solitary masturbation, being sodomized as a prostitute and being sodomized for the pleasure of it. Sexual acts cannot *in reality* be self-giving unless there are acts

by which a man and a women actualize and experience sexually the real giving of themselves to each other—in biological, affective and volitional union in mutual commitment, both open-ended and exclusive—which like Plato and Aristotle and most peoples we call marriages.[16]

The claim here appears to be that all sexual activity which is not of a very narrow type ("two-in-one-flesh" marital communion) involves an instrumentalizing of the body no different from the instrumentalizing of the body in prostitution. All these very diverse sexual acts are dismissed as examples of hedonism which cannot actualize or participate in any value more noble than the pursuit of raw pleasure. This closure to the possibility of genuine unitive potential in sexual relationships where there is either an inability or a lack of desire to perform acts of "two-in-one-flesh" marital communion[17] has led many commentators to argue that new natural law theory can only be understood on a sectarian or religious basis.[18] Thus, Nicholas Bamforth argues that

> Finnis's claims make little or no analytical sense unless Catholic teachings are first taken into account; his claims are, on their own, little more than unsupported assertions—statements with little or nothing to back them up.[19]

Similarly, David Richards has argued that

> Finnis's [and thus new natural law's] perfectionism is not the reasonable working out of his abstract premises, for these premises could, with more justice be worked out to quite different effect (for example, identifying homosexual relations as one way of achieving the general good of friendship and love). Rather, Finnis fills out these vaguely appealing abstract premises from a point of view not reasonably shared at large. His theory of universal reasonableness is, on examination, a sectarian sham.[20]

Issues of Tolerance

This chapter is not mainly concerned with reviewing arguments for and against the reasonableness of new natural law understandings of human sexuality, but rather with addressing the issue of justice regarding the treatment of homosexuals and their relationships vis-à-vis heterosexuals, if it were taken (for the purposes of argument) that the new natural law understanding of human sexuality was correct. It should be clear that such a presumption does not in itself determine what is or is not just when it comes to how the state treats homosexuals and their relationships.

In fact, the new natural lawyers disagree among themselves on this very issue. John Finnis, for example, argues for a doctrine of tolerance derived from his understanding of the nature of the political common good as elaborated by the Catholic Church's Second Vatican Council (Vatican II). Vatican II postulated that the common good of the political community was instrumental rather than basic. As such, the legitimate power of the political community was limited. For example, the Council settled that the state may not legitimately intervene "coercively in people's search for true religious beliefs, or in people's expression of the beliefs they suppose true".[21] This, for Finnis, is because

> it will harm those people and violate their dignity even when its intervention is based on the correct premise that their search has been negligently conducted and/or has led them into false beliefs. Religious acts, according to the Council [Vatican II], "transcend" the sphere which is proper to government; government is to care for the temporal common good.[22]

Government, he states, may only restrict religious freedom when necessary for the protection of the rights of others, the securing of public peace, and the upholding of public morality. However, it may not restrict religious liberty for the sake of securing religious salvation itself. Finnis argues for similar reasons that the state may only legislate for the purposes of securing "public morality" and not for the purposes of repressing private immorality as such and for its own sake. Thus, the state involves itself in an injustice if it sets about to "make even secret and truly consensual adult acts of vice a punishable offence against the state's laws".[23] Finnis thus argues for a tolerance of all forms of "secret, adult, consensual sexual activity."[24] Other natural lawyers such as Robert George and Gerard Bradley disagree. For example, Robert George, while agreeing with Finnis that the political common good is instrumental rather than basic, argues that

> it does not follow, or so it seems to me, from the instrumental nature of the political common good that moral paternalism, where it can be effective is beyond the scope of that good.[25]

Thus, George considers that, in and of itself, laws criminalizing masturbation, contracepted marital sex, fornication, and all forms of homosexual sex may be perfectly just.[26] It is unclear, however, on what ground of principle this leaves Finnis's argument for external religious freedom such as freedom to observe one's own religious festivals and freedom from being forced to attend religious events. We should remember that Finnis's argument for such external religious freedom is also justified on the strictly limited nature of the political community. If the political community is not in fact as limited as Finnis thinks, then it seems unclear what ground of principle would stop the state from using arguments of paternalism to intervene in people's religious lives so long as (a) it didn't attempt to interfere with internal religious freedom (i.e., privately held religious beliefs) and (b) it was "based on the correct premise that their search [for religious belief] had been negligently conducted and/or had led them into false beliefs" (Finnis 1994, p. 1073).[27] It should be noted that the Vatican document *Persona Humana* (1975),[28] which puts forward the same conception of sexuality as that defended by Finnis and George, quotes St. Paul in Ephesians 5:4, where he implies that the principle moral wrong of engaging in sexual acts which contradict Christian teaching is that this involves the "worshipping of a false god."

> For you can be quite certain that nobody who actually indulges in fornication or impurity or promiscuity—which is worshipping of a false god—can inherit anything of the Kingdom of God.

However, just as Holy See doctrine post-Vatican II does not seek to abolish the religious freedom of non-Catholics, *Persona Humana* does not suggest that private, consensual sexuality between adults should be subject to criminal persecution.

Finnis is right to perceive a common basis between freedom of religion and the freedom of romantic and sexual expression (although, as will be argued below, his strong antipathy toward "wrongful" sexual activity prevents him from taking this commonality to its logical conclusion). The important relationship between these freedoms rests, at root, in the fact that both human sexual expression and human religious expression are deeply meaningful practices for many individuals. Indeed, as such practices generally involve the reaching for deep personal meaning either individually or in voluntary communion with others, human sexual expression and human religious expression can both be considered specific forms of a more general cateogory, namely, intimate self-expression.

As H. L. A. Hart noted over forty years ago, in the area of sexuality, intimate self-expression may be absolutely central to "emotional life, happiness, and personality."[29] Invasive laws in such areas are, therefore, likely to cause immense psychological pain since they involve

> the infliction of a special form of suffering—often very acute—on those whose desires are frustrated by the fear of punishment. This is of particular importance in the case of laws enforcing a sexual morality. They may create misery of a quite special degree. For both the difficulties involved in the repression of sexual impulses and the consequences of repression are quite different from those involved

in the abstention from "ordinary" crime. Unlike sexual impulses, the impulse to steal or to wound or even kill is not, except in a minority of mentally abnormal cases, a recurrent and insistent part of daily life. Resistance to the temptation to commit these crimes is not often, as the suppression of sexual impulses generally is, something which affects the development or balance of the individual's emotional life, happiness, and personality.[30]

Evidence indicates that a significant group of people experience an exclusive, unchosen congenital and irreversible orientation toward members of the same sex.[31] Thus, laws against private homosexual expression seek to deprive such a sexual and romantically intimate life to a whole class of persons.

A free society is based fundamentally on the idea that deeply personally meaningful activities such as religious expression[32] or sexual expression may only be curtailed when justifiable by compelling social needs. It is certainly possible to imagine cases where criminal prohibition in both such areas is justified. For example, take the issue of (heterosexual or homosexual) pedophilia. Here the child is properly considered incapable of consenting to sexual conduct and the interest of the child in remaining unmolested massively outweighs any other interest present.[33] Similarly religious practices or requirements (whether practiced in the historical period or currently) such as human sacrifice or the punishment of apostasy, blasphemy, or witchcraft may (indeed must) similarly be prohibited in a free society. These types of practices, however, cannot be considered intimate self-expression since they do not involve the voluntary coming together of persons to share in a deeply meaningful activity but, instead, rest on coercion of one individual for the benefit of another. In the vast majority of cases, however, a person can experience a religious life and a sexual or romantic life in a purely intimate fashion. In a free society, and given the importance of such expression to many individuals, a person's right to such a religious or sexual life cannot be extinguished or heavily curtailed if respect for the principle of human autonomy is to be upheld. Certainly, there can be no justification in a free society for attempts to prohibit or heavily regulate sexual and romantic relationships between homosexuals which, as George and Bradley note, "typically involve ... little or no injustice."[34, 35]

As this discussion has shown, state attempts to extinguish a person's rights to an intimate sexual life rest, not on a judgment about the morality of such a sexual life, but rather on a perfectionist understanding of the state which in its logic undermines not only sexual freedom but also other freedoms including religious freedom. George's argument that the criminalization of homosexual practices may be perfectly just constitutes a grave departure from the principles of tolerance and respect for human autonomy upon which a free society is ultimately based. To his credit, Finnis does acknowledge both the injustice of such criminalization and the fact that its injustice principally rests on the fact that such regulation "transcends" the appropriate limited role of the secular state in a similar way that criminalizing "wrong" but non-coercive religious practices does. However, Finnis's account becomes unreasonable by his introduction of a requirement that "wrong" sexual activity remain "secret."[36] This heavy regulation of sexual and romantic self-expression is not argued for or justified and, moreover, no such requirement is required by Finnis in the case of "wrong" religious practice. As has been argued, respect both for intimate religious practice and for intimate sexual practice both rest on an acknowledgement of the deeply meaningful place which such practices play in many individuals' lives. Once this is recognized, it becomes clear that just as heavy curtailment of a person's intimate religious life is rarely if ever justifiable, heavy curtailment of a person's right to intimate sexual self-expression such as contemplated in Finnis's secrecy requirements is similarly unjustifiable.

Issues of Fairness

New natural law theory condemns not only all homosexual acts but also a great number of acts committed by heterosexuals, including marital contracepted sex, adultery, divorce, fornication, oral sex, anal sex, and masturbation. However, in popular debate and in the laws of many jurisdictions, homosexuality is often singled out. For example, the State of Texas pre-*Lawrence*[37] criminalized homosexual sexual conduct while leaving virtually all forms of private, noncommercial, heterosexual conduct (including, rather oddly, bestiality) untouched. In the area of marriage and partnership law, both divorce and adultery are legally possible in most states whilst only a few states recognize same-sex marriage. Can new natural law provide a principled defense of the distinctions the law is making in these cases?

Fairness and the Criminal Prohibition of Homosexual Conduct: A Consideration of the Lawrence Litigation

> Insofar as this politics [prohibitionism] is effective, it is unreasoned; insofar as it is reasoned, it is increasingly marginal.[38]

Key proponents of new natural law theory mischaracterize what was at stake in the *Lawrence* "homosexual conduct" case in a way that is unfair (even within natural law theory itself) to gays and lesbians and their relationships. For example, in an article published shortly before the *Lawrence* decision was announced, Robert George opined that the Supreme Court should not find in favor of the plaintiffs. To do so, he argued, would for the first time grant constitutional protection to a form of "sexual misconduct."[39] However, from the perspective of the new natural law, this is simply incorrect. As far back as 1965 the Supreme Court, in *Griswold*,[40] legalized contraceptive intercourse within civil marriage and thus provided protection for what the new natural law would consider "sexual misconduct"—namely contracepted sex. Robert George on previous occasions has been quite clear that all contracepted sex, no matter in what context it takes places, is a "nonreproductive sex act":

> Nobody, we believe, performs a reproductive-type act when he or she deliberately thwarts that act's reproductive potential.[41]

Moreover, as has been previously noted, new natural law condemns all nonreproductive-type sex acts as immoral due to their failure to actualize "two-in-one-flesh communion" and thus their "instrumentalizing" of the self:

> sexual acts are such that either they embody a marital communion— a communion that is only possible in *reproductive-type acts* between a man and a woman, in a marital relationship—or they involve instrumentalizing the body for the sake of an illusory experience or fantasy of marital union, an illusion or fantasy that is especially inappropriate with children, one's parents and so on.[42]

Thus, it was certainly not accurate to state that, before the *Lawrence* decision the Court had provided no constitutional protection to acts which the new natural law considered "sexual misconduct." However, George presented an additional argument for not providing protection for "homosexual conduct"—namely, that to do so would, for the first time "grant constitutional protection to a type of nonmarital sex act (indeed, in this case, an intrinsically nonmarital act)."[43] Interpreted literally it is clear that this statement was no more valid than the previous statement about "sexual misconduct." As we have already seen, contracepted sex is held to be "sexual misconduct" in new natural law precisely because it is held to be a "nonmarital" (indeed an "intrinsically nonmarital") act. However, it might be that George was meaning to refer less to the specific act being protected and more to the relationship within which these acts (in themselves perhaps "intrinsically nonmarital") were occurring. Perhaps he was attempting to argue that success for the plaintiffs in the *Lawrence* decision would introduce a new zone of sexual privacy to those in "nonmarital" sexual relationships. Does this distinction between "marital" and "nonmarital" sex provide a genuine distinction between *Lawrence* and previous constitutional privacy cases? It does not. To realize why, one has to look at the meaning of "marriage" within George's article and other writings. For example, what does George mean when he states that homosexual sex is an "intrinsically nonmarital sex act"? It is clear here that George is not using the word "marital" in a positivistic sense. If that was the case, then a same-sex couple who was legally married in, say, Canada or Belgium, and who then had sex together would clearly be performing a marital sex act. However, by using the word "intrinsically nonmarital" George is clearly excluding this as a possibility. It is, therefore, clear that George is using the words "marriage" and "marital" not in a positivistic sense but in a deeply normative one—not surprising given that he is attempting to present a moral argument against providing protection for homosexual sexual activity. The problem, however, with using "marriage" in this sense is that it is clearly untrue that the *Griswold* decision only provided sexual privacy protection to relationships which were "marital" in this sense. *Griswold*, in fact, provided sexual privacy protection to couples who were "intrinsically" incapable of having a marital relationship according to new natural law standards. This is because it provided protection not only to couples who had only been married once, but also to the sexual activity of couples who had previously been married but had been (civilly) divorced and then had (civilly) remarried. As has previously been elaborated, new natural law doesn't believe that such a "divorce" is a moral possibility. As Grisez states, "Marriage as such, not only Christian marriage, is inherently indissoluble."[44] This is true no matter what the previously married couple may wish:

> Nothing they [the married couple] subsequently choose or do will be able to divide them from each other and/or unite them simultaneously in a similar union with somebody else.[45]

Thus, a person who marries and then civilly divorces and civilly remarries will, in the eyes of new natural law, remain married to their previous spouse. Any sex in their new marriage will constitute adultery since, as Grisez states, "remarriage after divorce [is] adultery."[46] Their relationship will be "intrinsically" adulterous since new natural law states that a genuine "two-in-one-flesh" marriage can never be dissolved.[47] Thus, it can be seen that the *Griswold* court provided a realm of sexual privacy not only to those in genuine "two-in-one-flesh" marriages but also to those in relationships which, according to the new natural law, were intrinsically nonmarital, immoral, and even adulterous. Later, in *Eisenstadt*[48] the Court granted a right to contraception to couples who were not even civilly married. Thus, contrary to George's article, it was not the case that, from the perspective of the new natural law, success by the plaintiffs in the *Lawrence* decision would (or did) cause a radical break in American constitutional law by providing protection either for intrinsically "nonmarital" sexual acts or even for sexual acts committed in intrinsically "nonmarital" relationships. Both of these accomplishments, in fact, occurred over thirty years earlier in the *Griswold* decision. In failing to state this reality, George singles out homosexuals and their relationships as uniquely incapable of "moral"/"marital" sexual conduct in a way which not even his new natural law theory would appear to allow.

George's argument only seems initially plausible because it illegitimately elides two senses of the word "marital." What needs to be but is not distinguished in his article is the important distinction between "marriage" as a positive, legal reality and "marriage" as a normative "two-in-one-flesh" reality within new natural law. This illegitimate elision is, in fact, a common trope within a great deal of the writing of the new natural lawyers on the subject of marriage and sexual morality. For example, one can see further evidence for such an elision in the *amicus curiae* brief submitted by George and Gerard Bradley on behalf of the Family Research Council and Focus on the Family to the Supreme Court in the *Lawrence* case.[49] The George-Bradley brief argued that the erstwhile Texas "homosexual conduct" law should be seen as a reasonable way "to prudently protect and promote marriage"[50] and should not be considered a reflection of "*animus* toward homosexuals and lesbians."[51] This was despite the fact that Texas, while criminalizing homosexual sexual conduct, left unregulated virtually every other form of noncommercial, "nonmarital" sexuality (including bestiality and adultery without spousal consent). According to Bradley and George's brief, the reason for the "reasonableness" of this highly divergent treatment lay in the fact that "same sex deviate acts can never occur within marriage, during an engagement to marry, or within any relationship that could ever lead to marriage,"[52] whereas all of the other forms of sexuality left unregulated by Texas had the potential for just this sort of relationship with "marriage." In fact, this was incorrect, even taking this argument as referring to marriage in a positivistic sense.[53] For example, solitary masturbation was perfectly legal in Texas previous to the *Lawrence* litigation even though it clearly did not have the capacity to take place in a relationship which could or will lead to "marriage."[54] The same clearly applies to sex between a human being and an animal which (rather bizarrely) was also legal within the pre-*Lawrence* Texas regime. However, another and important difficulty with Bradley and George's argument is that they are clearly not using the term "marriage" in a positivistic sense, but in a distinctively normative one. Thus, for example, they argue that *animus* against homosexuals (and thus the illegitimacy of the Texas law) would be proved if the Texas legislature had decriminalized prostitution between men and women while retaining criminal prohibition against same-sex prostitution. This is because, according to the George-Bradley brief, it is inconceivable that sexual activity (even between different-sex persons) that was provided for money could over time blossom into a marital relationship. However, in a strictly positivistic sense, it is entirely possible for just such a transformation to take place. The inability of George and Bradley to envisage such a possibility indicates the presence of normative argument. Thus, their claim on prostitution and marriage should properly be read as stating that a relationship born out of prostitution is incapable of becoming "marital" in a "two-in-one-flesh" sense. Thus, the criminalization of both homosexual and heterosexual prostitution can count as evidence that the State of Texas pre-*Lawrence* was following its moral vision of protecting and promoting "two-in-one-flesh" marital union and was thus being "reasonable." However, as the George-Bradley brief states Texas could not be reasonably basing its public policy on such "two-in-one-flesh" concerns rather than *animus* toward homosexuals if (say) only same-sex prostitution was criminalized. The problem, however, is that looked at comprehensively the pre-*Lawrence* Texas legal framework was clearly failing to pay much heed to these "reasonable" new natural law concerns. As already noted, masturbation and bestiality, while legal in Texas pre-*Lawrence*, fail even to link to a positivistic definition of marriage. Moreover, many other acts were perfectly legal, which were highly incompatible with the notion that Texas's legal framework was a prudent means to promote a "two-in-one-flesh" conception of marriage. For example, adultery was perfectly legal even though such an act is seen in a new natural law setting not only to be "nonmarital" (i.e., outside the covenant of marriage which new natural law advocates) but directly "antimarital" (i.e., a clear violation of that covenant).[55] The same was also true of divorce and remarriage.[56] Moreover, any prudential reasons against enacting laws against divorce, remarriage, and adultery (particularly adultery without spousal consent) would not have appeared especially strong. Cases of adultery, for example, could clearly be distinguished from other "sexual vices" and there are no reasons to think that prosecution would be especially difficult. However, divorce, remarriage, and adultery (with or without spousal consent) were perfectly legal in Texas prior to the *Lawrence* decision.

Thus, there is abundant evidence that the Texas legal framework was not based on a fairly and equally applied new natural law theory of human sexuality. Instead, one small and insular minority of the population (i.e., homosexuals) was being singled out for draconian treatment that the heterosexual majority was totally unwilling to impose on themselves. The law in Texas pre-*Lawrence* manifested, even within the paradigm of new natural law, a complete failure to treat similar cases alike. This was a clear violation of the principle of fairness that has been at the heart of theories of justice since at least the time of Aristotle. The attempt by new natural lawyers such as Robert George and Gerard Bradley to justify such distinctions as "reasonable" seriously draws into question the ability of new natural legal theorists to apply their own philosophy fairly and in a way that does not advocate or justify disparate and unjust treatment toward a marginalized section of the population.[57]

Fairness and Civil Marriage

It is not only in their justification of criminal prohibitions on "homosexual conduct" where new natural lawyers seem to apply double standards in their treatment of homosexual as opposed to heterosexual relationships. Their writings on proposals to give same-sex couples a legal right to civil marriage betray this difficulty as well. As has already been mentioned, for the new natural lawyers, true marriage is an indissoluble and exclusive union between a man and a woman where the means of sexual expression is exclusively of the procreative type (i.e., uncontracepted penile-vaginal union). This "two-in-one-flesh" conception of marriage is quite distinct from the civil marriage that is now recognized in the jurisdictions of most modern democratic states. These states generally allow divorce, remarriage, adultery, and contraception. Few, if any, such states recognize uncontracepted penile-vaginal union as necessary to make a marriage valid. Thus, the sort of marriage which the new natural lawyers recognize is not (and has not for a long time been) the same as the one generally recognized in the laws of the democratic world. "Two-in-one-flesh" marriage does not have an existence as a civil, as opposed to religious, reality in these countries. For example, no one in America can currently consider themselves to be married in a "two-in-one-flesh" sense merely as a result of contracting a civil marriage, since all civil marriages hold out the availability of divorce.[58] Grisez goes as far as to state that anyone getting married who holds (even as a remote possibility) the idea that they wish to retain the option of getting divorced at a future date is not properly married.[59] Moreover, a very large number of marriages (namely those contracted by divorced people) are "intrinsically nonmarital" from the perspective of new natural law and, in fact, amount to a form of adultery. This huge divergence between marriage as a current legal reality in the West and the new natural law's "two-in-one-flesh" concept of marriage appears to pass the new natural lawyers by when writing on the "threat" posed by same-sex marriage. According to them, the law currently is based on their understanding of "two-in-one-flesh" marriage:

> Marriage as embodied in our customs, laws, and public policies, is intelligible and defensible as a one-flesh union whose character and value give a man and a woman moral reasons (going beyond mere subjective preferences or sentimental motivations) to pledge sexual exclusivity, fidelity, and permanence of commitment.[60]

Any attempt, however, to extend marriage to same-sex couples would simply "abolish marriage":[61]

> Thoughtful people on both sides of the debate recognize this. It is evident, then, that legal recognition of same-sex marriages, far from making marriage more widely available (as well-intentioned but misguided conservative advocates of same-sex marriage say they want to do) would in effect abolish the institution, by collapsing the moral principles at its foundation.[62]

Therefore, according to their analysis, "[a]t stake is the intelligibility of marriage as we have, from time immemorial, understood it."[63] The new natural lawyers further claim that if the benefits of marriage were extended to same-sex couples "there would, then, be no non-arbitrary basis whatsoever upon which monogamy could be legally maintained."[64] Thus it can be seen that, when debating same-sex marriage, the new natural lawyers advance two invalid claims. First, they argue that current civil marriage is equivalent to "two-in-one-flesh" marriage. Second, they posit an intrinsic link between the issue of whether to allow same-sex couples to marry and the issue of monogamy within marriage.

Looking at the first of these arguments, it is clear that the new natural lawyers appear to ignore the fact that the definition of civil marriage in the Western world has not been static over time but has actually changed greatly over the years. The changes wrought by the abolition of gender inequalities within heterosexual marriage and the legalization of contraception and divorce (and then remarriage) have massively changed the nature of marriage away from being orientated toward "two-in-one-flesh" union and toward a focus on a type of romantic love most realizable in a monogamous setting. A move to allow same-sex marriage might involve the abolition of "two-in-one-flesh" marriage as a legal reality were it not for the fact that these other developments have already done the job. The current conception of marriage in the attitudes and in the law of the West is far more accommodating of the potential for same-sex couples to marry than the new natural lawyers care to admit. Language suggesting that such a change would "abolish marriage" smacks of an unfair attempt to demonize homosexual relationships and to wrongly suggest that they do not have important resemblances to many heterosexual relationships currently recognized in the law as marriages.

It is also untrue that there is no nonarbitrary legal principle that could extend marriage to homosexual couples that would not, at the same time, undermine the principle of monogamy at the heart of civil marriage. The two issues are, in fact, logically separate. It can be quite rationally argued that the type of romantic love between equals which modern marriage attempts to protect is only possible in a monogamous setting, while at the same time seeing the exclusion of a distinct group of people from this institution (i.e., homosexuals) as a grave injustice. It is totally unclear why such an argument for same-sex marriage and for monogamy would be an "arbitrary" one.

Conclusion

This chapter has argued that even if, for the sake of argument, one accepted the new natural law theory of sexual conduct, it does not provide a justification for either the criminalization of homosexuality or for the other disadvantages that homosexual persons and their relationships currently face. Two types of argument have been put forward to support this conclusion. First, it has been argued that attempts to criminalize seemingly harmless, private, consensual, noncommercial, intimate conduct such as homosexual acts constitute a grave departure from the respect for individual freedom and dignity that is at the heart of a free society. Such a conception of human personhood is properly recognized in the law of America and elsewhere as "implicit in the concept of ordered liberty."[65] Second, laws against homosexual sexual conduct are doubly suspect, when (as in the Texas case) they single out homosexual acts for criminal sanction while imposing no such restraint on a whole slew of purportedly equally "immoral" acts and relationships that involve the heterosexual majority. No new natural law argument can justify such a situation and thus a fundamental principle of fairness is violated. New natural law theory similarly fails to provide a reasonable justification for the exclusion of same-sex couples from civil marriage. Since civil marriage law generally already recognizes many marriages which new natural law would not recognize as legitimate "two-in-one-flesh" relationships, no principle within new natural law can reasonably support the exclusion of the homosexual minority from such a civil institution. Thus, it can be argued that, if new natural lawyers applied their theory fairly, then they would have to stop opposing attempts to redress discrimination faced by homosexual people and their relationships and actually argue in favor of these changes. Based on past performance, however, it seems highly unlikely (to put it mildly) that such an outcome will eventuate.

Notes

1. The branch of contemporary Thomist-based philosophy that this chapter critiques is known as the "new natural law" since it attempts to justify traditional Catholic morality through an analysis that starts by positing pre-moral basic human goods. From these goods and a claim about practical reasonableness, an attempt is made to derive moral conclusions. In this two-step approach it differs from the "old natural law" that starts with the positing of "obvious"

moral truths. New natural law theory was originally developed by Catholic theologian Germain Grisez, and it is on his basic moral writings that the new natural lawyers base their concepts. Of course, it should be noted that there is no logical reason why "natural law" need be hostile to lesbian and gay rights. Indeed, some writers whose metaphysical understandings might be considered to be within the paradigm of "natural law" (or at least "natural right") have actively embraced the defense of such rights. See, for example, Ronald Dworkin, *Taking Rights Seriously* (Cambridge: Harvard, 1977).

2. See *Lawrence v. Texas*, 539 U.S. 558 (2003). The Texas "homosexual conduct" law was eventually struck down in a 6–3 decision. Justice Kennedy delivered the opinion of the Court and was joined by Justices Stevens, Souter, Ginsburg, and Greyer. The opinion struck down the Texan law as a violation of "liberty" as protected in the due process clause of the Fourteenth Amendment. Justice O'Connor filed a concurring judgment, which labeled the law classbased legislation in both its effect and application and struck it down on equal protection grounds. She left open the issue of whether the law also violated the substantive "liberty" component of the due process clause. Justice Scalia filed a dissenting brief which Chief Justice Rehnquist and Justice Thomas joined. Justice Thomas signed his own dissenting opinion in which he stated that the law, while in his opinion constitutional, was also "uncommonly silly." Similar decisions finding that laws against homosexual conduct violate fundamental human rights have been made by the European Court of Human Rights (*Dudgeon v. United Kingdom*, 45 Eur. Ct. H. R. [ser. A] [1981]) and by the United Nations Human Rights Committee (*Toonen v. Australia*, U.N. Doc. CCPR/C/50/D/488/1992 [Mar. 31, 1994]).

3. During the *Lawrence* litigation, the Family Research Council and Focus on the Family argued through an *amicus brief* presented by new natural lawyers Robert P. George and Gerard Bradley for the upholding of the Texas law as a "reasonable means of protecting and promoting marriage" (George and Bradley, 2003, 5). See George and Bradley, *Amicus Curiae* brief of the Family Research Council, Inc. and Focus on the Family in support of the respondent, *Lawrence. v. Texas* (02-102) (2003) (Herein referred to as the George-Bradley brief).

4. Those interested in a more radical critique of the new natural law should particularly refer to the work of Gareth Moore, *A Question of Truth: Christianity and Homosexuality.* (London: Continuum, 2003; principally chapter 9). Also useful are the works by David Richards, "Kantian Ethics and the Harm Principle: A Reply to John Finnis," *Columbia Law Review* 87 (1987): 437–71; Stephen Macedo, "Homosexuality and the Conservative Mind" and "A Reply to Critics," *Georgetown Law Journal* 84(2) (Dec. 1995): 261–300, 433–56; and Nicholas Bamforth, *Sexuality, Morals and Justice: A Theory of Lesbian and Gay Rights Law* (London: Cassell, 1997; principally chapter 5).

5. "Nonmarital" from the perspective of new natural law.

6. Richards, "Kantian Ethics and the Harm Principle: A Reply to John Finnis," 437–71; Bamforth, *Sexuality, Morals and Justice: A Theory of Lesbian and Gay Rights Law.*

7. Robert P. George, *The Clash of Orthodoxies: Law, Religion and Morality in Crisis* (Wilmington, DE: ISI Books, 2001), 267.

8. John Finnis, "Natural Law and Unnatural Acts." *The Heythrop Journal* XI (1970): 365–87, 384.

9. I think the use of gender is significant here. One has a keen sense in much of new natural law literature that man is considered naturally the "active" and woman the "passive" force within sexual encounters.

10. John Finnis, *Natural Law and Natural Rights* (Oxford: Clarendon Press, 1980).

11. Macedo, "Homosexuality and the Conservative Mind," 261–300, 280.

12. Ibid., 281–285.

13. "Many will find deeply unreasonable, as well, the judgment that pleasure is not in and of itself a good" (Ibid., 282).

14. Grisez argues that the moral reality of gender differentiation in genuine "two-in-one-flesh" marriage leads to a rejection not only of certain kinds of sexual entanglements but also different-sex marital relationships which fail to allocate the correct roles to the man and the woman in the marriage and, in particular, which fail to give the "father-husband" "a special role in decision-making" (Germain Grisez, *The Way of the Lord Jesus, Vol. 2: Living a Christian Life* (Wuincy, IL: Fransiscan Press, 1993), 553–4. Grisez argues:

> By differentiating the sexes, God plainly intends to differentiate the spouses' roles; and because this natural differentiation serves the good of marriage and family, it should be endorsed willingly, not resisted and limited as much as possible. (627)

32 • David O. Erdos

Thus, this gendered view of moral reality is at profound odds not only with increasing acceptance of same-sex relationships but also with moves to secure social equality to women within the basic institutions of society including marriage. For a pertinent analysis of gender justice in the family see Susan Okin, *Justice, Gender and the Family* (New York: Basic Books, 1991).

15. Robert P. George, *In Defense of Natural Law* (Oxford: Clarendon Press 1999), 180.
16. John Finnis, "Law, Morality and Sexual Orientation," *Notre Dame Law Journal* 69 (1994): 1049–76, 1067. Needless to say, Finnis's attempts to co-opt, in support of "two-in-one-flesh" understandings of sexual morality, the outlooks of "most people" and, in particular, the outlook of classical thinkers such as Plato and Aristotle that have been subject to a great deal of attack. See Martha C. Nussbaum, "Platonic Law and Colorado Law: The Relevance of Ancient Greek Norms to Modern Sexual Controversies." *Virginia Law Review* 80 (1994): 1515–1651.
17. This includes not only sexual and romantic relationships between same-sex couples but also relationships of many heterosexuals who may, for example, be unable to perform acts of penile-vaginal union due to some form of disability or may wish to experience sexual union but avoid the prospect of conception.
18. It should be noted that the new natural lawyers, while purportedly advancing secular arguments for their positions, openly rely on a theory of sexual morality developed within a Catholic orthodox context by theologian Germain Grisez. For example, Finnis states that his legal understanding of sexual relations "is an application of the theory of morality and natural law developed over the past thirty years by Germain Grisez and others. A fuller exposition can be found in the chapter on marriage, sexual acts, and family life in the new second volume of Grisez's great work on moral theology" (Finnis 1994, 1063). Similarly, Robert George frequently cites Grisez's understanding of sex and marriage in his work. For example, in an article published with Patrick Lee he states that his view of sexual morality is based on "a natural law argument for the proposition that sexual acts are morally right only within marriage, an argument first developed in detail by Germain Grisez, and subsequently presented by others influenced by his thought" (George 1999, 161). For a detailed exposition by Grisez of his theory of sexual morality see Grisez 1993, ch. 9.
19. Bamforth, *Sexuality, Morals and Justice: A Theory of Lesbian and Gay Rights Law,* 167.
20. Richards, "Kantian Ethics and the Harm Principle: A Reply to John Finnis," 469.
21. Finnis, "Law, Morality and 'Sexual Orientation,'" 1049–76, 1072.
22. Ibid., 1074.
23. Finnis, "Law, Morality and 'Sexual Orientation,'" 1049–76, 1076.
24. Ibid. It is of historical interest to note that David Richards pointed out the tension between religious freedom and perfectionist understandings of the role of the state at a conference with John Finnis in 1987. As he stated:

> Surely it is not more "self-stultifying" to coerce authentic religious conscience in the interests of [alleged] religious truth than to criminalize authentic feelings of homosexual love in the interests of the [alleged] truth of marital friendship. In both cases, a perfectionist concern for human goods might require coercion in the interest of better incentives to the pursuit of those goods. We reject such perfectionism in religion for the same reason we should reject it in the area of homosexuality: it enforces a sectarian conception of human goods instead of a minimal conception of ethical reasonableness and thus flouts the reasonable moral freedom that is the inalienable right of a self-governing people. (Richards, "Kantian Ethics and the Harm Principle: A Reply to John Finnis," 470)

In 1987 Finnis appeared to completely reject any linkage between religious freedom and other freedoms. See John Finnis, "Legal enforcement of 'duties to oneself': Kant v. Neo-Kantians," *Columbia Law Review,* 87 (1987): 433–456.

25. Robert P. George, "The Concept of Public Morality," *American Journal of Jurisprudence* 45 (2000): 17–32, 30.
26. "For the sake of setting a moral standard, George would leave state laws prohibiting adultery, fornication and sodomy on the books, even while acknowledging the difficulty and wisdom of enforcing them," J. I. Meritt, "Heretic in the Temple," *Princeton Alumni Weekly,* October 8, 2003.

27. One might think that the new natural law could argue for a "double standard" between matters of sexuality and matters of religion on the basis of the following argument. First, religious belief is a matter of "faith" (i.e., there can be no reason given to a nonbeliever in favor of the religious propositions the new natural lawyers favor) while the sexual understandings of the new natural law can be proved by "reasons" and thus can constitute knowledge (i.e., justified true belief). Second, coercion to enforce "knowledge" is justifiable in a way that the enforcement of a religious orthodoxy based on "faith" (even if true) is not. The advancement of such an argument fails, however, since the new natural lawyers do believe (however implausibly) that many of their religious beliefs do constitute real knowledge and are susceptible of proof. Thus, George and Wolfe maintain that a proof can be provided for the existence of a providential God and, therefore, that it is possible to have "knowledge" of such a God's existence. As they state:

> Most Americans believe in God, though few could get very far with, say, an unbelieving professor from their state university in arguing on the subject. We would nonetheless contend that they possess genuine knowledge. Their views are, to be sure, less sophisticated than the views of professional academics or other intellectuals, but they possess the considerable virtue of being true. Is the existence of a providential God (i.e., a God who creates and attends to his Creation), therefore, "publicly accessible" and thus defensible at the bar of public reason (broadly and properly defined—not Rawlsian public reason)? We, like virtually all of the founders of American government, think it is. (Robert P. George and Christopher Wolfe, Eds., *Natural Law and Public Reason*. Washington, D.C.: Georgetown University Press, 2000, 68–9).

This understanding conflicts with the religious practices of those who reject such a God including those who don't believe a God external to human experience and those who have a poly rather than monotheistic understanding of reality.

28. Congregation for the Doctrine of the Faith, *Persona Humana* (1975).
29. H. L. A. Hart, *Law, Liberty and Morality*. (Oxford: Oxford University Press, 1962), 22.
30. Ibid., 22.
31. Richard A. Posner, *Sex and Reason*. (Cambridge: Harvard University Press, 1992), 296–7.
32. Including practices associated with belief systems such as humanism and some forms of Unitarianism which, while sharing with traditional religion a search for the fundamental reality of human existence and a working out of how we are to live, do not involve a belief in an external God or gods.
33. This would be so even if it were established that an inclination to pedophilia was an immutable characteristic of some people.
34. Gerard V. Bradley and Robert P. George, "Marriage and the Liberal Imagination," *Georgetown Law Journal* 84 (2) (1995): 301–320, 320.
35. There are important reasons why the principle upon which the legalization of homosexual conduct rests does not reach to such offenses as incest, bestiality, and prostitution. Prostitution is not an expression of human sexuality that is truly "intimate" and, therefore, cannot form a part of "intimate life." Bestiality is held illegal and immoral, in part, since it violates the principle of consent that is properly at the heart of all sexual morality. Finally, as Steven Macedo notes, states have a special reason to be concerned with even adult incest since the legalization of any incest would:

> undermine many of the goods of family life: it would lead to a horrible and revolting form of vulnerability for children. (Macedo 1995, 287)

Furthermore, while there is good evidence that substantial numbers of people exhibit an exclusive, congenital, and irreversible orientation toward members of the same sex, no such evidence exists of people exhibiting such an orientation toward close members of their family, animals, etc. Thus, the degree of denial of liberty in such cases is similar to forms of peripheral sexual regulation such as the prohibition of sexual relations between members of the armed forces or the police, etc. It is, however, not qualitatively similar to the denial resulting from the criminalization of homosexual conduct and, therefore, the burden on the state to prove the rationality of such legislation is justifiably lower. It should be noted that laws criminalizing masturbation or fornication between heterosexuals do severely restrict the right to an intimate life and, moreover, there are no pressing public reasons justifying such restrictions. Thus, such laws, along with laws against homosexual conduct, should also be struck down as being in violation of the principles underlying a free society.

36. John Finnis, "Law, Morality and 'Sexual Orientation'," 1049–76, 1076.
37. *Lawrence v. Texas* No. 02-102 (decided June 26, 2003).
38. Andrew Sullivan, *Virtually Normal: An Argument about Homosexuality.* (London: Picador, 1995), 55.
39. Robert P. George, "Rick Sanotorum Is Right: Where Will the Court Go after Marriage?" National Review Online, May 25, 2003, http://www.nationalreview.com/comment/comment-george052703.asp.
40. Evidence indicates that a significant group of people experience an exclusive, unchosen, congenital, and irreversible orientation toward members of the same sex. See Posner 1992, 296–7.
41. Gerard V. Bradley and Robert P. George, "Marriage and the Liberal Imagination" *Georgetown Law Journal* 84 (2) (1995): 301–20, 310 (note 30).
42. George (ed.), *In Defense of Natural Law,* 180 (emphasis added).
43. George, "Rick Santorum Is Right: Where Will the Court Go after Marriage?"
44. Grisez, *The Way of the Lord Jesus, Vol. 2: Living a Christian Life,* 591.
45. Ibid., 579.
46. Ibid., 644.
47. According to the new natural law, not even adultery can justify divorce from a genuine "two-in-one-flesh" marriage and remarriage of even the "innocent" party is, therefore, impermissible (Grisez 1993, 588–590). A firm line is thus placed between the impossibility of divorce and the possibility of annulment. This is because "annulment is not a form of divorce but a judgment that a particular marriage never existed" (Grisez 1993, 553). Since an annulled marriage literally never existed, it would appear that sex which took place within this "marriage" could not in a normative sense be considered "marital" within new natural law. Indeed, it would appear that this sex would have amounted to no more than fornication and thus would be "instrumentalizing" rather than capable of actualizing a basic good. Moreover, if one of the parties to the "marriage" was aware that their marriage was not in fact "genuine" (e.g., due to a lack of correct intention at the time of the marriage), then it would seem that the instrumental and fornicatory nature of these sexual acts would be culpable.
48. *Eisenstadt v. Baird* 405 U.S. 438 (1972).
49. Robert P. George and Gerard Bradley, *Amicus Curiae* brief of the Family Research Council, Inc. and Focus on the Family in support of the respondent, *Lawrence v. Texas* (02-102) (2003).
50. Ibid., 4.
51. Ibid., 25.
52. Ibid., 3.
53. Another major problem with arguing that criminalizing homosexual sex but not heterosexual nonmarital sex is a "reasonable" way to "promote [heterosexual] marriage" is that it is unclear how criminalizing all sexual conduct for a group of the population that is incapable of heterosexual marriage (i.e., homosexuals) can have any relationship to be the "promotion" of heterosexual marriage at all. On the other hand, criminalizing heterosexual nonmarital intercourse clearly could have such a promotional affect by giving heterosexuals a clear choice either to remain sexually abstinent or to marry. Thus, it would appear that whereas Bradley and George's argument might work if heterosexual "nonmarital" intercourse but not homosexual "nonmarital" intercourse were criminalized, it fails to provide a reasonable, non-*animus* related basis for the reverse.
54. Aquinas himself took the purported immorality of masturbation extremely seriously, considering it worse than rape because it was not in keeping with the idea of sexuality as linked with procreation (*Summa Theologica* II-II, 154, 12).
55. "Adultery is an injustice. He who commits adultery fails in his commitment. He does injury to the sign of the covenant which the marriage bond is, transgresses the rights of the other spouse, and undermines the institution of marriage by breaking the contract on which it is based. He compromises the good of human generation and the welfare of children who

need their parents' stable union." Catholic Church, *Catechism of the Catholic Church*, London: *Geoffrey Chapman* (2nd ed.) (1999), 510.

56. "Divorce is a grave offence against natural law. It claims to break the contract, to which the spouses freely consented, to live with each other till death. Divorce does injury to the covenant of salvation, of which sacramental marriage is the sign. Contracting a new union, even if it is recognized by the civil law, adds gravity to the rupture. The remarried spouse is then in a situation of public and permanent adultery[.]", Catholic Church, *Catechism of the Catholic Church*, 510–11.

57. Indeed, even the arguments used by Bradley and George that attempt to provide a distinction between "acts" and "relationships" are in fact unknown within new natural law. New natural law theory, as developed by Grisez, has traditionally condemned all "nonmarital" acts as intrinsically equally immoral whatever the context of the relationship: "Heterosexual activities deliberately not open to new life provide nothing better than a similar experience of intimacy without any real communion of person. Thus, such heterosexual activities—including contracepted intercourse, without or outside marriage—are morally similar to sodomy" (Grisez 1993, 654). Furthermore, Grisez has argued that all sexual acts taking place between fertile heterosexuals outside "two-in-one-flesh" marriage are clearly objectively more immoral than any homosexual acts since they involve the possible "injustice" of bringing illegitimate children into the world: "Any illicit sexual intercourse that could result in conception involves readiness to do injustice to the possible child" (Grisez 1993, 655). Here again we see a new natural law argument for criminalizing heterosexual "nonmarital" acts but not homosexual "nonmarital" acts and certainly no argument or warrant for doing the reverse.

58. Indeed, in all of the states in America it is possible as a heterosexual couple to procure a "no-fault" divorce.

59. "If they [the couple getting married] anticipate that they might intentionally attempt to separate from each other, they either must be prepared to cause the trauma divorce would involve or must will to limit their unity in order to avoid that trauma. But doing either is at odds with conjugal love. If, therefore, in attempting to marry the parties reserve the right to divorce, they act inconsistently with the conjugal love necessary for marriage" (Grisez 1993, 577–8).

60. Robert P. George, "The 28th Amendment: It Is Time to Protect Marriage and Democracy in America," *National Review*, July 23, 2001.

61. Robert P. George and Gerard Bradley, *Amicus Curiae* brief of the Family Research Council, Inc. and Focus on the Family in support of the respondent, *Lawrence v. Texas* (02-102) (2003), 17.

62. George, "The 28th Amendment: It Is Time to Protect Marriage and Democracy in America."

63. George and Bradley, *Amicus Curiae* brief of the Family Research Council, Inc. and Focus on the Family in support of the respondent, *Lawrence v. Texas* (02-102) (2003), 20.

64. Ibid., 19.

65. *Palko v. Connecticut*, 302 U.S. 319, 58 S. Ct. 149 (1937).

CHAPTER 3

Same-Sex Marriage, Civil Unions, and the 2004 Presidential Vote[1]

KENNETH SHERRILL

In the 2004 presidential election, 60 percent of the voters said that they supported same-sex marriage or civil unions and 37 percent opposed any form of legal recognition for same-sex relationships. Under normal circumstances in U.S. politics, a 60–37 percent margin would be considered to be a stunning victory. Instead, the notion that the issue of same-sex marriage cost the Democratic Party the election has been uncritically accepted as the common wisdom. In fact, majority opposition to legalize same-sex relationships was limited to members of a relatively small number of overlapping analytic categories, and virtually all of these are among the core supporters of the Republican Party—people who are not likely to vote Democratic under almost any condition.

Here are the fourteen groups in which a majority opposed legal recognition of same-sex relationships:

1. Those who believe that abortion should be illegal in all cases (16 percent of all voters): 74 percent oppose legal recognition of same-sex relationships.
2. Those who believe that abortion should be illegal in most cases (26 percent of all voters): 52 percent oppose.

3. Those who attend religious services more than once a week (16 percent of all voters): 68 percent oppose.
4. Protestants who attend services weekly (16 percent of all voters): 62 percent oppose.
5. Born-again or evangelical Christians (36 percent of all voters): 61 percent oppose.
6. Those who say they are "enthusiastic" about the Bush administration (22 percent of all voters): 58 percent oppose.
7. Voters who were contacted by phone or in person by the Bush campaign but not by the Kerry campaign (10 percent of all voters): 53 percent oppose.
8. Those who are "not at all concerned" by the availability and cost of health care (2 percent of all voters): 68 percent oppose.
9. Those who usually think of themselves as Republicans (37 percent of all voters): 51 percent oppose.
10. Those who think of themselves as conservatives (31 percent of all voters): 60 percent oppose.
11. Those who voted for George Bush in 2004 (51 percent of all voters): 51 percent oppose.
12. People who are Mormons or members of the Church of Latter Day Saints (2 percent of all voters): 61 percent oppose.
13. Those who voted for George Bush in 2000 (44 percent of all voters): 50 percent oppose.
14. White Protestant conservatives (16 percent of all voters): 64 percent oppose.

These data show that even among these groups of core Republican voters, opposition to legal recognition of same-sex relationships is rarely overwhelming. In fact, opposition to any legal recognition of same-sex relationships by more than a two-thirds majority is found in only two groups: those voters who oppose abortion in all cases (74 percent oppose) and those voters who attend religious services more than once a week (68 percent oppose). These two groups have many overlapping members as well.

Some will argue that while the issue of same-sex marriage did not affect the direction of the vote, it did affect turnout: Those who opposed it were more likely to vote, particularly in "battleground" states. This might be the case, but the election returns indicate that President Bush did less well—in terms of the margin of his victory and in terms of the increase in his percent of the vote—in these states than in states that did not have referenda on same-sex marriage; it also begs the question of why the Democratic Party, the Kerry campaign, and their affiliated interest groups were unable to find a way to mobilize their core constituents. We cannot eliminate organizational failure on the part of the Democratic campaign to generate comparable turnout among their core constituents as a more likely explanation of the Republican victory. Recent analyses of exit polls and of aggregate data indicate that Bush's victory is best explained in terms of voter concerns about terrorism and in terms of his increased support among married women. These studies also conclude that the issue of same-sex marriage had a negligible impact on the outcome—if it had any impact at all.

Why should same-sex marriage motivate turnout more effectively than unemployment in a state like Ohio? Is it possible that Republicans were more likely to get voters out because they relied on in-state volunteers, while Democrats relied on paid workers and out-of-state volunteers? Did the declining power of industrial labor unions in Ohio have an impact on the ability of Democrats to get out the vote? Any politician can tell you that local organization matters in a get-out-the-vote effort. The Democratic leadership's placing of the blame for their loss on same-sex marriage may reflect nothing more than an inability to face the party's organizational failures—or it may reflect a felt need for a scapegoat. The data provide scant, if any, evidence that the issue of same-sex marriage had a significant effect on the presidential election. Far from it, our data indicate that less than 40 percent of the American voters supported denying legal recognition to same-sex couples.

The interesting story about the increased turnout in 2004 was that a rising tide lifted all boats. While all groups increased in the number of voters, the relative percentages of the groups remained constant so there was no net effect. Analyzing turnout data and county-level data, Simon Jackman, a Stanford political scientist, found that the same-sex marriage initiatives in eleven states boosted turnout by about 3.3 percent in those states. Looking across the electorate, all groups remained roughly constant since 2000, including lesbian, gay, and bisexual (LGB) voters at 4 percent. Jackman found that the marriage initiative seems to have boosted turnout and the intensity of opinion, but there was no relationship between the change in support for Bush and the change in turnout. In fact, the six states in which Bush had the greatest increase in his share of the vote did not have a same-sex marriage initiative on the ballot, while two of the states that did have an initiative were among the five in which Bush's percentage changed the least. On average, Bush went up 2.8 percent in states that had no marriage initiative and 2.5 percent in those that did. Jackman looked at Ohio's eighty-eight counties in detail and found no relationship between an increase in turnout and support for a same-sex marriage initiative.

The data indicate that same-sex marriage had little net effect on the outcome of the election. Those in favor of civil unions split 52 percent to 47 percent for Bush over Kerry, mirroring the national outcome. Among the 25 percent who favored same-sex marriage, Bush got 22 percent of the vote—or about 5.5 percent of the total. Among the 37 percent who opposed all legal recognition of same-sex relationships, Kerry got 29 percent of the vote—or about 11 percent of the total. Kerry, in fact, got more votes from opponents of legalized recognition than Bush got from supporters of same-sex marriage, so the issue's net effect may have been to benefit Kerry rather than hurt him.

The growth in support for civil unions is astounding. Just five years ago, legislators in Vermont feared that their careers were over as a result of voting to enact a system of civil unions. Today, the public clearly views civil unions to be a viable alternative. On average, 35 percent of all voters in the 2004 election supported civil unions, and the support is broad-based. Thirty-four percent of Kerry voters and 36 percent of Bush voters supported civil unions, while 40 percent of Kerry voters supported same-sex marriage and 51 percent of Bush voters opposed any legal recognition of same-sex relationships.

Four groups offer majority support for same-sex marriage. Jewish voters are most likely to support same-sex marriage, with 64 percent in favor, 28 percent supporting civil unions, and only 4 percent opposed to any legal recognition of same-sex marriages. They're followed by liberals (54 percent), those who believe abortion should be legal at all times (52 percent), and LGB voters (51 percent).

The fact remains that, on average, only one-quarter of the voters supported same-sex marriage. This accounts for the success of the referenda defining marriage as being between one man and one woman in thirteen states this year. When the issue is framed as a yes-or-no question, same-sex marriage is defeated. Surveys can provide voters with a greater range of choices and thus produce more nuanced results. Only three voters in eight opposed providing legal recognition to same-sex relationships when provided with the alternative of civil unions.

Differences between LGB Voters and All Voters in 2004

The following table is based on a sample of 3,220 respondents, of which 4 percent ($n = 126$) reported that they were LGB. Note that in a subsample of this size, the margin of error (two standard deviations) is 9 percent for items that are around 50 percent. It is 5 percent for items that are around 10 percent.

TABLE 3.1 Responses of LGB Voters Versus All Voters in the 2004 Presidential Election

Item	Percent of LGB Voters	Percent of All Other Voters
Age		
18–29	28	17
30–44	34	29
45–59	21	30
60 or over	17	24
How often do you attend religious services?		
More than once a week	15	16
Once a week	15	26
A few times a month	13	13
A few times a year	29	28
Never	29	15
Which characterizes your feelings toward the Bush administration?		
Angry	46	22
Enthusiastic	9	23
(Other categories omitted.)		
Who would you trust to handle the economy?		
Bush/neither	21	55
Kerry/neither	68	49
Do you have any children under 18 living in your household?		
Yes	26	36
How confident are you that votes in your state will be counted accurately?		
Very	38	51
Not very	19	7
(Other categories omitted.)		
Is your opinion of George W. Bush:		
Favorable	23	54
Unfavorable	71	45
Is your opinion of John Kerry:		
Favorable	74	46
Unfavorable	25	52

(*Continued*)

TABLE 3.1 Responses of LGB Voters Versus All Voters in the 2004 Presidential Election (*Continued*)

Item	Percent of LGB Voters	Percent of All Other Voters
Which comes closest to your view of gay and lesbian couples?		
They should be allowed to legally marry	51	25
They should be allowed to legally form civil unions (but should not get married)	31	35
There should be no legal recognition of their relationships	17	38
Did anyone call you or talk to you in person on behalf of either major presidential campaign about coming out to vote?		
Yes, for Kerry	15	11
Yes, for Bush	8	10
Yes, for both	14	13
No	62	65
Do you or does someone in your home own a gun?		
Yes	46	42
No	54	58
2003 total family income		
Under $15,000	12	9
$15,000–$29,999	16	14
$30,000–$49,999	23	22
$50,000–$74,999	16	23
$75,000–$99,999	13	14
$100,000–$149,999	9	11
$150,000–$199,999	5	4
$200,000 or more	5	4
Do you think the war with Iraq has improved the long-term security of the United States?		
Yes	25	47
No	72	51
Compared to four years ago, is the job situation in your area:		
Better today	10	24
Worse today	60	42
About the same	30	34

(*Continued*)

TABLE 3.1 Responses of LGB Voters Versus All Voters in the 2004 Presidential Election (*Continued*)

Item	Percent of LGB Voters	Percent of All Other Voters
Have you or someone in your household lost a job in the last four years?		
Yes, I have	19	14
Yes, someone else has	27	15
Yes, I have and someone else has	3	3
No one has	51	68
Married with children under eighteen		
Yes	13	28
Women with children	14	20
Currently married		
Yes	30	64
State of the national economy		
Excellent/good	27	48
Not so good/poor	66	51
Do you think of yourself as a:		
Democrat	54	36
Republican	18	38
Independent	20	23
Something else	8	4
On most political matters, do you consider yourself:		
Liberal	47	20
Moderate	32	46
Conservative	21	33
In today's election for President, did you vote for:		
John Kerry	77	46
George W. Bush	23	53
Other	0	1
Are you:		
White	80	80
Black	14	11
Hispanic/Latino	6	6
Asian	1	2
Other	2	2

(*Continued*)

TABLE 3.1 Responses of LGB Voters Versus All Voters in the 2004 Presidential Election (*Continued*)

Item	Percent of LGB Voters	Percent of All Other Voters
National Region		
East	19*	22
Midwest	20	25
South	35*	32
West	26	21
Religion (combining Protestant and other Christian):		
Protestant/Other Christian	49	54
Catholic	23	27
Jewish	4	3
Something else	9	6
None	14	10
Are you:		
Male	47	45
Female	53	55
Population of area:		
Over 500,000	15	11
50 to 500,000	18	19
Suburbs	45	45
Small City and Rural	22	25
Do you think that things in this country are generally going in the:		
Right direction	26	51
Wrong direction	68	45
Omit	7	3
Union Household?		
Yes	36	24
No	64	76
Did you vote in the presidential election in 2000?		
No, did not vote	17	17
Yes, for Al Gore	58	36
Yes, for George W. Bush**	25	44

Note: * These data indicate a shift of LGB voters away from the East and a surprisingly high percentage in the South.
** People generally over-report having voted for the winner.

Note

1. This manuscript is drawn from work originally done for the National Gay and Lesbian Task Force Policy Institute, analyzing available exit poll data. A subsequent version was published in *Gay and Lesbian Review* and now has been revised for this book. I would like to thank the NGLTF Policy Institute and *GLR* for their encouragement and Arthur J. Weiss for his comments on earlier versions of this manuscript.

CHAPTER 4

The Symbolic Centrality of Gay Marriage in the 2004 Presidential Election[1]

SEAN CAHILL

Introduction

Barbara Babcock notes that often groups of people or phenomena that are demographically or socially peripheral become symbolically central.[2] Peter Stallybrass and Allon White note that this is true of "the gypsy," or Roma people, in European culture.[3] Jews were a small minority in Germany, but the Nazis portrayed them as a vast threat to the German "volk." In the late 1960s most young Americans did not have long hair, but "hippies" became emblematic of their generation. Welfare mothers were symbolically central in the early years of the Reagan Administration, and again in the mid-1990s, even though they were a small minority of the population and welfare spending represented a small percentage of the total federal budget. Today gay people are probably no more than 5 percent of the U.S. population, and the number of gay and lesbian couples seeking to marry represents an even smaller percentage than that. Yet gay people, and especially their quest for marriage equality, have become symbolically central in U.S. politics.

This symbolic centrality is certainly linked to the dramatic upsurge in visibility of gay people in television shows like *Queer Eye for the Straight Guy* and *Playing It Straight*. It also reflects the fact that more gay, lesbian, bisexual, and transgender people are "out" and demanding equal treatment under the law (gay and lesbian couples have been suing for the right to marry since 1971). But it is also due to the fact that anti-gay organizations have constructed gays as the antithesis of all that is good in American society—a threat to family, children, religion and religious freedom, health, and even national security.

In 2003, the debate over whether to allow same-sex couples access to the institution of civil marriage emerged as a major political issue in the United States. This resulted from three landmark court decisions: the June 10, 2003 ruling by Ontario's high court that same-sex couples should have the right to marry under the nation's charter of rights;[4] the U.S. Supreme Court ruling a week later in *Lawrence v. Texas* that anti-gay sodomy laws violated the U.S. Constitution's right to privacy;[5] and the November 2003 Massachusetts Supreme Judicial Court ruling that denying marriage to same-sex couples violates that state's constitutional guarantees of equal protection and due process.[6]

Following the June high court rulings in Ontario and the United States, anti-gay activists and politicians announced their support for the Federal Marriage Amendment (FMA), introduced in May 2003 by Rep. Marilyn Musgrave (R-CO), which would ban same-sex marriage and restrict states' ability to offer more limited forms of partner recognition, such as domestic partnership and civil unions. Religious right groups warned that the U.S. Supreme Court's striking down of sodomy laws in *Lawrence v. Texas* would lead to gay marriage, even though Justice Kennedy, writing for the majority, and Justice O'Connor, in her concurring opinion, explicitly stated that what was at stake in *Lawrence* was the right to engage in private intimacy, not same-sex partner recognition. By the end of 2003, more than 100 U.S. Representatives and four U.S. Senators had signed on as cosponsors to the FMA.

In February 2004, San Francisco hosted a "winter of love" when its newly elected mayor started issuing marriage licenses to gay and lesbian couples. Soon several thousand people, both locals and couples from around the country, were wed at San Francisco City Hall. The first couple to tie the knot, Del Martin, 83, and Phyllis Lyon, 79, are founders of the Daughters of Bilitis, are co-founders of the modern U.S. gay rights movement, and have been partners for more than fifty years. Sandoval County, New Mexico, followed San Francisco's lead and issued a few dozen marriage licenses, and the mayors of Salt Lake City, Chicago, and other cities announced their support of marriage equality for same-sex couples.[7] Even before San Francisco's move, hundreds, perhaps thousands of American same-sex couples had traveled to Canada to legally wed.

After hinting at backing the anti-gay FMA for months and repeatedly stating his opposition to gay marriage, President Bush endorsed a federal anti-gay marriage amendment on February 24, 2004. The crowded Democratic field of presidential candidates was repeatedly queried on the topic. The leading candidates said they opposed gay marriage but also opposed the FMA, accusing the president of political gay-bashing for electoral gain. Frontrunner John Kerry endorsed state anti-gay marriage amendments in Massachusetts and Missouri, however, adding to the confusion.

The 2004 election marks the fourth presidential election in a row in which gay issues played a significant role. Pat Buchanan denounced gay marriage and legal protections for gay people at the 1992 Republican convention; six other speakers also denounced gay people and/or legal protections for gay people. In 1996, Republican candidates criticized efforts by same-sex couples to gain access to the institution of civil marriage, and Congress debated and passed the anti-gay Defense of Marriage Act. In 1999 and 2000, Republican candidates denounced the Vermont high court ruling in support of equal benefits for gay couples, and then Governor George W. Bush announced his opposition to sexual orientation nondiscrimination laws, which he portrayed as "special protections." Once again, in 2003–2004, gay issues played a prominent role in the elections, with nearly a dozen Democratic candidates articulating the most pro-gay positions ever in a presidential campaign. The Bush-Cheney campaign and the Republican National Committee made opposition to gay marriage and alleged "activist judges" a central issue. And anti-gay, religious right groups like Focus on the Family and the Traditional Values Coalition succeeded in getting state constitutional amendments placed on the ballot in thirteen states in 2004. Nine of these thirteen amendments went beyond banning marriage, threatening more limited partner protections such as domestic partner health insurance. And many of these amendments made thousands of cohabiting, unmarried opposite-sex couple families ineligible for benefits, along with same-sex couples and their children. All of these amendments passed by overwhelming margins. As this book went to press, anti-family state constitutional amendments were expected in dozens more states, and federal anti-gay family bills were expected to be reintroduced in Congress in the 109th Congress of 2005–2006.

The Impact of Lawrence and Other Court Rulings on the Marriage Debate

The attention paid to same-sex marriage and gay people resulted from three landmark court decisions in 2003.

June 10, 2003: Ontario's High Court Rules that Same-Sex Couples Should Have the Right to Marry under the Nation's Charter of Rights.[8]

On June 10, 2003, an Ontario appeals court ruled unanimously that seven same-sex couples had the right to marry. The three judge panel ruled unanimously that Canada's Charter of Rights and Freedoms—"Canada's version of the Bill of Rights," according to the *New York Times*[9]—mandated equal access to civil marriage for gay and lesbian couples. "Same-sex couples are capable of forming long, lasting, loving and intimate relationships," the court ruled, arguing further that extending the right to marry to gay couples would cause no harm to the rest of the community.[10] Canada's Prime Minister Jean Chretien quickly endorsed the ruling and introduced a bill into Parliament to nationalize the impact of the ruling.[11]

One month later, British Columbia's appeals court issued a similar ruling.[12] Among those flocking to Toronto and Vancouver to wed were hundreds of American gay couples. In March 2004, Quebec followed suit, meaning that three-quarters of Canadians now lived in a province that allows gay marriage.[13] (By the end of 2004 three additional provinces and one territory—the Yukon—had followed suit, meaning that 85 percent of Canadians (27 million people) lived in a province or territory in which gay couples could marry.[14] On December 9, 2004, Canada's highest court ruled in favor of marriage equality, clearing the way for the passage of a bill through Canada's Parliament).[15]

June 26, 2003: The U.S. Supreme Court Rules that Anti-Gay Sodomy Laws Violate the U.S. Constitution's Right to Privacy.[16]

In June 2003, the U.S. Supreme Court struck down archaic laws in thirteen states banning private, consensual sexual intimacy. (The impact of sodomy laws in two additional states, Massachusetts and Michigan, was in dispute at the time of the ruling.) Widely known as "sodomy laws," nine of these thirteen laws banned certain practices regardless of whether the couple engaging in them was heterosexual or homosexual.[17] The other four states' laws banned certain sexual practices only for homosexual couples. But even in the nine states where laws targeted both opposite-sex and same-sex couples, in practice the laws were disproportionately deployed against gay couples.

The court's 6–3 ruling that such laws violated the Constitution's privacy provision did not directly address the issue of state recognition of same-sex marriages. However, language in the majority decision was interpreted by both gay rights proponents and opponents as hinting at future support for marriage equality. Justice Anthony Kennedy, writing for the majority, ruled that the state cannot single out gay people for harassment and discriminatory treatment simply because of "moral disapproval" of homosexuality.[18] Kennedy wrote of "respect" for gay couples and warned that "the state cannot demean their existence …" The court also described gay relationships as a "personal bond" involving much more than just sex.[19] Kennedy said that reducing gay couples to "sex partners," as anti-gay organizations and supporters of sodomy laws often do, is offensive in the same way that describing a husband and wife as nothing more than sex partners would be offensive. However, apparently cognizant of the marriage challenges pending in New Jersey and Massachusetts, and that some might interpret the *Lawrence* ruling as supporting marriage equality for gay couples, Kennedy made a point of noting that the case against the Texas sodomy law "does not involve whether the government must give formal recognition to any relationship homosexual persons seek to enter." In her concurrence, Justice Sandra Day O'Connor said that the "traditional institution of marriage" was not at issue.[20]

Despite these majority caveats, Justice Scalia angrily argued just the opposite in his dissent, in which he was joined by Chief Justice Rehnquist: "Today's opinion dismantles the structure of constitutional law that has permitted a distinction to be made between heterosexual and homosexual unions, insofar as formal recognition in marriage is concerned."[21] Anti-gay activists and politicians vocally agreed. Quickly, the *Lawrence* decision repealing archaic, often colonial-era sodomy laws in thirteen states became increasingly portrayed in the mainstream media as a precursor to legalization of gay marriage. Rev. Jerry Falwell warned that "it's a capitulation to the gay and lesbian agenda whose ultimate goal is the legalization of same-sex marriages."[22] Republican Senator Rick Santorum of Pennsylvania warned that "the greatest near-term consequence of the *Lawrence v. Texas* anti-sodomy ruling could be the legalization of homosexual marriage."[23] (In April 2003, Santorum had cautioned that if anti-gay sex laws were struck down, then there would be no way to prohibit "man on child, man on dog" sex; he also described cases of Catholic priests abusing children as "a basic homosexual relationship."[24])

Gay rights activists found themselves in the unusual position of agreeing with Falwell, Scalia, and Santorum in terms of the implications of *Lawrence* for marriage equality. "I think it's inevitable now," said Lambda Legal Defense and Education Fund's Patricia Logue, co-counsel in the *Lawrence* case, of legalized same-sex marriage. "In what time frame, we don't know."[25] *Lawrence* lead attorney Ruth Harlow, also with Lambda, said, "The ruling makes it much harder for society to continue banning gay marriages."[26]

November 18, 2003: The Massachusetts Supreme Judicial Court Rules that Denying Marriage to Same-Sex Couples Violates that State's Constitutional Guarantees of Equal Protection and Due Process.[27]

On November 18, 2003, the Massachusetts' Supreme Judicial Court declared that marriage is a civil right and that gays and lesbians have a constitutional right, under the due process and equal protection provisions of the

Massachusetts Constitution, to marry the person of their choice: "Limiting the protections, benefits, and obligations of civil marriage to opposite-sex couples violates the basic premises of individual liberty and equality under law protected by the Massachusetts Constitution."[28]

"We construe civil marriage to mean the voluntary union of two persons as spouses, to the exclusion of all others," the 4–3 majority wrote. "This reformulation redresses the plaintiffs' constitutional injury, and furthers the aim of marriage to promote stable, exclusive relationships." The court rejected claims by some opposed to same-sex marriage that allowing gay and lesbian couples to marry would undermine the institution of marriage: "Extending civil marriage to same-sex couples reinforces the importance of marriage to individuals and communities. [The fact] [t]hat same-sex couples are willing to embrace marriage's solemn obligations of exclusivity, mutual support, and commitment to one another is a testament to the enduring place of marriage in our laws and in the human spirit."

In its decision, the court distinguished between civil and religious marriage, noting that "civil unions" for same-sex couples were a separate and unequal, unsatisfactory option, and argued that children, as well as their parents, suffered from the inability to marry.

In the wake of the Massachusetts high court ruling in late 2003, Massachusetts state legislators asked whether civil unions, which afford nearly all of the benefits of marriage at the level of state policy (but none of the 1,138 federal benefits, and are not portable), would suffice to meet the court's ruling. In February 2004, the court answered that civil unions would not suffice, as they would continue "to relegate same-sex couples to … second-class status." The court noted that "the history of our nation has demonstrated that separate is seldom, if ever, equal."[29] This second ruling reaffirmed the right of same-sex couples to marry.

Weeks after the November 2004 presidential election, the U.S. Supreme Court declined to consider a legal challenge to the *Goodridge v. DPH* decision by the Massachusetts-based Catholic Action League and eleven state legislators who charged that *Goodridge* usurped legislative power by expanding the institution of civil marriage to include same-sex couples.[30]

Recent Historical Context: The Emergence of Marriage as a Central Political Issue in the 1990s

The *Lawrence* decision, as well as the court rulings in Canada and Massachusetts in favor of marriage equality, were of course welcomed by advocates for equal rights for lesbian, gay, bisexual, and transgender (LGBT) people. They were also denounced by anti-gay politicians and organizations, including the leading groups of the religious right. Conservatives and would-be theocrats joined together to mobilize resentment and reaction against the *Lawrence* and *Goodridge* rulings, in particular, promoting dozens of state anti-gay family laws and amendments as well as two federal initiatives: the Federal Marriage Amendment (FMA) and the Marriage Protection Act (MPA), a bill that would strip federal courts of the power to rule on the issue of same-sex marriage. The MPA would undermine the principle of judicial review established in *Marbury v. Madison* (1803). By early 2005, when in the wake of Terri Schiavo's death rhetorical attacks on the judiciary reached a crescendo, it became clear that the MPA was part of a broader assault on the judiciary by the religious right and its allies in Congress, such as House Majority Leader Tom DeLay. The FMA and MPA represent just the latest round of a concerted, decade-long campaign to ban marriage for same-sex couples in state and federal law. The broader anti-gay movement has been around for almost as long as the modern gay rights movement: The first anti-gay ballot measure repealed a sexual orientation nondiscrimination law in Boulder, Colorado, in 1974.

The first ballot measure to target marriage for same-sex couples was proposed in Idaho in 1994. The Idaho initiative would have banned marriage for gay couples as well as many other legal protections, such as sexual orientation nondiscrimination laws. It was narrowly defeated. While the anti-gay movement—comprised of conservative religious groups such as Focus on the Family, Concerned Women for America, and the Traditional Values Coalition—has promoted anti-gay ballot measures as an organizing and fundraising strategy for three decades, it was not until the mid-1990s that they started promoting anti-gay marriage and other anti-family ballot questions.

Hostility toward gays was a central theme of the Republican Convention in August 1992. Gay rights and AIDS activists clashed with conservative activists and police outside the Houston Astrodome. Inside, Pat Buchanan denounced "the amoral idea that gay and lesbian couples should have the same standing in law as married men and women." He also ridiculed Clinton's support for gay equality to a receptive crowd, many of whom held signs reading "Family Values Forever, Gay Rights Never." Buchanan advocated a "cultural war" against secular humanism and those advocating tolerance for various differences. Among at least six other speakers who echoed Buchanan's call was Education Secretary William Bennett, who devalued gay people and spoke against gay marriage. "Within very broad limits people may live as they wish," Bennett said. "And yet we believe that some ways of living are better than others—better because they bring more meaning to our lives; to the lives of others; and to our fragile, fallible human condition. Marriage must be upheld because in marriage between husband and wife— and in fatherhood and motherhood—come blessings that cannot be won in any other way."[31] Vice President Dan Quayle alluded to gays in his acceptance speech: "Americans try to raise their children to understand right and wrong, only to be told that every so-called 'lifestyle' is morally equivalent. That is wrong."[32] Finally, Republican National Committee Chairman Rich Bond explained to the press, "We are America. These other people are not America."[33]

The Republicans' strategy failed, however. A *New York Times* poll right after the convention found that only 23 percent of voters considered homosexuality an important election issue.[34] Bill Clinton's mantra, "It's the economy, stupid," was a better indicator of the sentiment of voters still trying to escape the depths of a recession. Despite the desire of many in the Republican Party to make Clinton's support for lifting the military ban a campaign issue, campaign aides resisted this, fearing further backlash like that evoked by the rhetorical excesses of the Houston convention.[35] In the end, Clinton won primarily due to economic discontent and a desire for new leadership. Lesbians and gays raised more than $3 million for Clinton-Gore, one-eighth of the total $25 million raised by the ticket, and were a key component of his electoral coalition. Three in four gays voted Democratic, and only 14 percent for President Bush.[36]

The 1996 Election and the Federal Defense of Marriage Act (DOMA)

In 1993, the Hawaii Supreme Court launched an important and ongoing international debate when it ruled that it was impermissible gender discrimination under the state constitution to deny three lesbian and gay couples the right to obtain a marriage license.[37] This decision stated that Hawaii could only deny the marriage licenses if it could indicate a compelling reason to do so. In 1996, a Hawaii trial court found that the state had failed to justify its denial with a compelling reason and so the couples did have the right to marry under civil law.

In reaction to these developments in Hawaii, anti-gay activists and politicians made gay marriage a central issue in the 1996 presidential campaign. In January, activists held a rally denouncing same-sex marriage just before the Iowa caucuses, the first primary election event. Nearly every Republican candidate attended and signed a pledge to "defend" heterosexual marriage against the threat allegedly posed by three same-sex couples in Hawaii who had sued the state for the right to marry. The presidential candidates' anti-gay rhetoric quickly transformed mainstream state and national politics. By April 1996, the *Los Angeles Times* observed that "homosexual marriage has abruptly emerged as an emotional flashpoint in the debate about America's cultural mores."[38]

Anti-gay groups like Concerned Women for America (CWA) joined the fray. CWA's Beverly LaHaye falsely claimed that the legalization of same-sex marriage would force churches to marry gay couples. She warned that "every local, state and federal law will be changed to accommodate homosexual 'marriage.'" LaHaye also warned that "homosexual 'marriage' would cause massive financial, legal and social upheaval as laws are revised to include same-sex partners ... our entire system of government will be overhauled to include homosexuality as an approved and legal lifestyle."[39] (Two years later, when President Clinton issued an executive order banning sexual orientation-based discrimination, LaHaye denounced that action as well.) Throughout 1996, newspapers and talk radio hosts railed against gay marriage—even liberal editorial boards like that of the *Boston Globe*. Six in ten Americans polled expressed disapproval of same-sex marriage.[40]

Against this backdrop, in 1996 Congress passed the Defense of Marriage Act, which defined marriage in federal law as a "legal union between one man and one woman," thereby restricting federal benefits, such as Social Security survivor benefits, to heterosexual couples. The bills also told states they did not have to recognize same-sex marriages should another state legalize such marriages.[41] The bill's twenty-two conservative Republican sponsors titled it the Defense of Marriage Act (DOMA), implying that the desire of gay and lesbian couples to marry constitutes an aggression against the traditional heterosexual institution of marriage. Before he resigned his Senate seat to run for president, Republican Bob Dole (R-KS) became the lead Senate sponsor of the bill. After it passed Congress, President Clinton not only signed the bill, he also bragged about doing so in ads run on Christian radio stations. Dole also returned a $10,000 donation from the Log Cabin Republicans, a gay Republican organization. President Bill Clinton's expression of opposition to lesbian and gay marriage, and his decision to sign DOMA into law in October 1996, prevented same-sex marriage from becoming a major campaign issue in the final weeks of the 1996 presidential campaign.

A total of fifteen state legislatures passed anti-gay marriage statutes by the end of 1996. Anti-gay marriage bills were defeated or withdrawn in twenty other states. Only thirteen states reported no anti-gay marriage legislative activity in 1996.[42] Another fifteen states adopted anti-gay marriage statutes in 1997 and 1998.[43] Hawaii and Alaska also passed anti-marriage constitutional amendments in 1998, reversing earlier state court victories for marriage equality.

Vermont's High Court Ruling and the 2000 Election Campaign

Throughout the primary race for the 2000 nomination, which started in mid-1999, all ten of the Republican candidates opposed any form of legal protection for gay people, such as nondiscrimination laws. A few said they would appoint people to their administration regardless of sexual orientation.

Echoing the 1996 anti-marriage rally on the eve of the Iowa caucuses, in August 1999, six of the Republican candidates signed an anti-gay pledge on the eve of the Iowa straw poll, pledging to oppose domestic partner benefits, education to fight anti-gay harassment and violence in the schools, adoption by gay people, and other issues. Significantly, Governor George W. Bush and Senator John McCain did not sign on, though Bush's spokesperson said this was because Bush had a policy against signing pledges.[44]

In the latter half of 1999, a slew of articles appeared in the mainstream press describing a more gay-friendly mainstream Republicanism.[45] Within the Republican Party, the most anti-gay, conservative candidates faded early on, while those who rose to the top tier—McCain and Bush—espoused more subtle anti-gay politics. McCain in particular called for a more inclusive Republican Party, and said he was "proud" to meet with Log Cabin Republicans; nonetheless, McCain voted against the Employment Nondiscrimination Act in 1996.

In December 1999, the marriage issue arose again in the wake of the Vermont Supreme Court's ruling that the state must provide to same-sex couples every benefit and protection it provides to married heterosexual couples. Democratic candidates Bill Bradley and Al Gore, who sought the gay community's vote, applauded the decision, while the Republican candidates denounced it. Christian right activist Gary Bauer called the ruling "worse than terrorism."[46]

Throughout 2000, Governor Bush continued to articulate anti-gay positions when asked. In South Carolina, he told a Christian radio station that he probably wouldn't appoint gays to his administration because "[a]n openly known homosexual is somebody who probably wouldn't share my philosophy."[47] When first elected governor of Texas, Bush made a similar statement. There were no openly gay or lesbian members of his administration, and during his term, Bush defended Texas's sodomy law as "a symbolic gesture of traditional values,"[48] opposed sex education, and sought to tax condoms as a vice.[49] Throughout 1999 and 2000, Bush spoke out against gay adoption, same-sex marriage, hate crimes legislation, nondiscrimination laws, and sex education. Despite this, the Log Cabin Republicans, a gay group, reportedly spent $500,000 campaigning for Bush's election in 2000.

Vice presidential nominee Dick Cheney—who had an extremely conservative voting record while a Congressman in the 1970s and 1980s, including votes against AIDS funding and the gathering of hate crimes statistics (not to mention votes against Head Start and against sanctions toward the apartheid regime in South Africa)—pleasantly surprised many when he said in a debate with Democratic Senator Joseph Lieberman that same-sex partners should be able to enter into relationships and that states should be able to decide whether to recognize such relationships.[50] Such states' rights—usually a core tenet of conservative philosophy—were restricted by the federal Defense of Marriage Act (DOMA), which Cheney and Bush supported.

Despite Bush and Cheney's bottom-line adherence to anti-gay policy positions, the 2000 Republican Convention set a markedly different tone from its predecessors. A racially diverse array of speakers addressed an overwhelmingly white crowd of delegates. Among the only notes of discord came when gay Congressman Jim Kolbe spoke on international trade, and some delegates bowed their heads to pray for Kolbe's soul. Also, despite the efforts of Wisconsin Governor Tommy Thompson, anti-gay language was kept in the Republican Party Platform. This language opposed marriage and other forms of partner recognition for gay couples, military service, as well as sexual orientation nondiscrimination laws.

Marriage and the 2004 Election

On the eve of the 2004 presidential election, thirty-nine states had anti-gay marriage statutes; six of these statutes went beyond banning marriage and threatened other, more limited forms of partner recognition. Four states had anti-marriage constitutional amendments; Hawaii and Alaska passed amendments in 1998, Nebraska in 2000, and Nevada in 2002. Nebraska's amendment banned marriage and other forms of family protections for same-sex couples. State anti-gay family laws have implications that figure in a variety of cases. For example, in 2002, a Pennsylvania court cited the state's anti-marriage statute to block a second-parent adoption by a same-sex partner. A higher court later reversed the ruling.[51]

The Federal Marriage Amendment

On May 21, 2003, Rep. Marilyn Musgrave (R-CO) introduced H.J. Resolution 56 to amend the U.S. Constitution to define marriage as between a man and a woman, and to prevent legislatures or courts from mandating more limited benefits, such as civil unions or domestic partnerships. By December 2003, there were 107 bipartisan cosponsors in the U.S. House of Representatives. On November 25, 2003, Senator Wayne Allard (R-CO) introduced S. J. Resolution 26 as a companion bill with four Republican cosponsors.

The Federal Marriage Amendment (FMA) would short-circuit state efforts to legalize marriage for same-sex couples by banning same-sex marriage and prohibiting courts and legislatures from citing state or federal law, or state or federal constitutions, to mandate more limited forms of recognition, such as hospital visitation rights, domestic partner health benefits, and second-parent adoption. When first introduced in 2003, it read:

> Marriage in the United States shall consist only of the union of a
> man and a woman. Neither this Constitution nor the Constitution

of any State, nor State or Federal law, shall be construed to require that marital status or the legal incidents thereof be conferred upon unmarried couples or groups.[52]

The proposed constitutional amendment would not just ban civil marriage for same-sex couples. By prohibiting the conferral of "marital status or the legal incidents thereof" on same-sex couples based on an interpretation of the federal Constitution, state constitutions, or state or federal law, the FMA could jeopardize hard-won domestic partner health benefits and registries offered in nearly a dozen states and hundreds of municipalities as well as by thousands of private employers. Civil unions, which afford most of the obligations, responsibilities, and recognitions of marriage to Vermont gay couples at the level of state policy, could also be jeopardized.

While anti-gay groups say the FMA would allow legislatures to pass domestic partner and civil union policies, these same groups regularly challenge more limited forms of same-sex partner recognition.[53] The American Center for Law and Justice, founded by the Christian Coalition's Rev. Pat Robertson, filed a lawsuit on behalf of the Catholic Action League of Massachusetts to strike down Boston's municipal domestic partnership policy in 1998–1999.[54] The Center for Marriage Law and the Alliance Defense Fund filed a similar lawsuit against domestic partnership benefits in Portland, Maine.[55] The proposed Federal Marriage Amendment could embolden such challenges and could deter state and local governments from offering domestic partner health insurance to their employees or registries for resident gay couples.

In March 2004, the FMA's lead sponsors amended the proposal's language slightly, removing the phrase "nor State or Federal law" from the second sentence. It now reads:

Marriage in the United States shall consist only of the union of a man and a woman. Neither this Constitution [n]or the Constitution of any State shall be construed to require that marital status or the legal incidents thereof be conferred upon unmarried couples or groups.[56]

While this change might allow a court to interpret a state nondiscrimination law to require marriage equality, it would still undercut the state constitutional basis for Vermont's 1999 high court ruling that led to civil unions, or for Massachusetts' high court ruling in favor of marriage rights for same-sex couples. Any future rulings in support of protections for gay couples, even short of marriage, based on the equality provisions of the state or federal constitutions would be precluded by the revised FMA.

Amending the U.S. Constitution is very unusual and has only been done to address great public policy need. In 214 years, our Constitution has only been amended seventeen times since the original Bill of Rights in 1791. Amendments historically have been used to protect or clarify the rights and liberties of the American people. The FMA would represent the first time a restriction of the rights of a group of people was written into our Constitution since it was ratified in Philadelphia in 1789. (At that time it contained the notorious "three-fifths" clause, which counted slaves as three-fifths of a person for the purposes of allotting electoral votes. It also excluded women and nonproperty-owners from basic rights.) The FMA would set a significant precedent that would have an enormous impact on the tradition of American justice.

The 2004 Democratic Presidential Candidates: The Most Pro-Gay Field Ever

The ten Democratic presidential candidates who ran in 2003 and 2004 were by far the most pro-gay field of candidates ever. All of the Democrats supported most of the key issues of concern to lesbian, gay, bisexual, and transgender (LGBT) people: sexual orientation nondiscrimination laws, HIV/AIDS prevention and treatment, lifting the military ban, hate crimes laws, domestic partnership, and gay-supportive education policy.[57] The few differences among the candidates were regarding marriage and civil unions.

Three of the ten candidates—former U.S. Senator and Ambassador Carol Moseley Braun (IL), Congressman Dennis Kucinich (OH), and the Rev. Al Sharpton—supported full marriage equality for same-sex couples. The other seven candidates did not unequivocally support marriage equality. Five of these—Senator John Edwards (NC), Representative Dick Gephardt (MO), Senator John Kerry (MA), Senator Joseph Lieberman (CT), and Senator Bob Graham (FL)—repeatedly expressed their opposition to marriage for same-sex couples. At the same time, most spoke out against the Federal Marriage Amendment (FMA), and made supportive comments in the wake of the Massachusetts court ruling. Democratic nominees Kerry and Edwards both spoke out against the FMA; when it came up for a vote in July 2004 just before the Democratic National Convention, they skipped the vote, but said they would have voted against it had they been present.

The other two candidates, retired General Wesley Clark and former Vermont Governor Howard Dean, did not say they opposed marriage for gay couples. However, on numerous occasions, when asked if they supported marriage, they answered that they supported civil unions. They also expressed support for the recent Massachusetts ruling in favor of marriage equality, saying it reflected concern for "rights" (Clark) and "equality" (Dean) for all Americans regardless of sexual orientation.[58]

Senator John Kerry (D-MA), the 2004 Democratic candidate, opposed marriage and supported civil unions. He frequently stated his opposition to the FMA but also expressed support for anti-gay marriage constitutional amendments being considered in Massachusetts and Missouri. The amendment introduced in the Massachusetts legislature was a "super-DOMA," a state "Defense of Marriage Act" that would not only ban marriage, but also threaten more limited forms of recognition such as domestic partnership. In March 2004, this amendment was rejected by the Massachusetts legislature in favor of a different amendment that would ban marriage but legalize civil unions. Kerry announced his support for the Massachusetts constitutional amendment while campaigning in Ohio, which had just passed a super-DOMA law weeks earlier, becoming the thirty-eighth state to ban gay marriage and the fifth state to ban other forms of partner recognition as well. Kerry's position was therefore inconsistent, in that he opposed such a measure in the U.S. Congress, where he sits, but supported such a measure in the Massachusetts legislature. Kerry later expressed support for the anti-marriage amendment passed overwhelmingly by voters in Missouri in August 2004.

The Bush-Cheney Administration's Record on Gay Issues Leading Up to the 2004 Election

Under the banner of "compassionate conservatism," President George W. Bush successfully positioned himself and his administration as moderate on a number of issues, including issues of concern to lesbians and gay men. President Bush often cultivates an image of tolerance, or at least makes it hard to accurately characterize his position, by offering contradictory statements on particular issues. For example, on October 3, 2003, Bush signed an official proclamation designating the week of October 12 through October 18, 2003 as "Marriage Protection Week," declaring, "Marriage is a sacred institution, and its protection is essential to the continued strength of our society. ... Marriage is a union between a man and a woman."[59] But during the same week that President Bush endorsed the anti-gay Marriage Protection Week, he sent congratulations to the gay Metropolitan Community Church (MCC) on the occasion of the congregation's thirty-fifth anniversary. Nationwide, MCC churches perform more than 6,000 same-sex weddings annually.[60] However, Bush's largely anti-gay policy record is clear:

- He opposes marriage equality for same-sex couples and supports amending the U.S. Constitution to define marriage as only between a man and a woman.[61]
- He opposes the adoption of children by gay and lesbian families,[62] and his promotion of heterosexual marriage and fatherhood as solutions to child poverty sends the message that only heterosexual married couples are fully suited for raising children.[63]

- He opposes nondiscrimination laws[64] and hate crimes legislation[65] that include sexual orientation and gender identity.
- He continues to support the military's "Don't Ask, Don't Tell" policy, which prohibits lesbian, gay, and bisexual people from serving openly in the U.S. armed forces.[66]
- He opposes age-appropriate, research-based sex education, and has dramatically increased funding for abstinence-only-until-marriage sex education. These programs teach that sex outside the context of marriage is inherently dangerous, both physically and psychologically, and essentially tell gay and lesbian people that they should remain abstinent throughout their lives, since they cannot get married in forty-nine states.[67]
- He has nominated numerous anti-gay judges, and has appointed federal officials who are openly hostile to gay people.[68]
- He has advocated allowing faith-based service providers to ignore local and state nondiscrimination laws that include sexual orientation or gender identity when hiring for positions paid for with federal funds.[69]
- The Bush Administration has conducted costly and time-consuming audits of AIDS service organizations.[70] In 2003, National Institutes of Health (NIH) staff warned researchers to avoid certain terms connected with homosexuality in federal grant proposals to avoid extra scrutiny.[71] And, in October 2003, the Traditional Values Coalition, an anti-gay, right-wing religious organization, prompted the U.S. Department of Health and Human Services to audit 250 research projects funded by NIH that involved issues related to sex or sexuality.[72]

Bush on Marriage Equality

For much of 2003 and into early 2004, Bush sent mixed messages about the Federal Marriage Amendment (FMA). Supporters of marriage equality for same-sex couples were somewhat buoyed when, on July 2, 2003, Bush said of the FMA, "I don't know if it's necessary yet ... what I do support is a notion that marriage is between a man and a woman."[73] However, at a press conference in late July 2003, in which he was asked about the misleading and inaccurate statement in his State of the Union Address that Iraq had tried to purchase yellowcake uranium in Africa, Bush also announced his intention to introduce legislation that would further codify the ban on same-sex marriage.[74]

Bush has repeatedly denounced the November 2003 Massachusetts Supreme Judicial Court ruling legalizing marriage for same-sex couples,[75] for example, in his January 2004 State of the Union address.[76] After the Massachusetts Supreme Judicial Court ruled February 4, 2004 that civil unions would not provide equality to same-sex couples, and reaffirmed the right of gay couples to marry under the Massachusetts Constitution's equality and due process guarantees, Bush called the ruling "deeply troubling" and reiterated his statement from the State of the Union Address.[77] Later that month he called gay marriages in San Francisco "troubling."[78] Finally, in late February 2004, Bush officially endorsed an anti-gay marriage amendment, calling on Congress to quickly pass such a measure.

Bush on More Limited Forms of Partner Recognition

In 2000, Bush said, "In the private sector [domestic partner benefits] are perfectly fine." On the governmental level, he said, the decision should be left up to cities and states.[79] However, as Governor of Texas, Bush took no initiative to offer domestic partner benefits to state employees, or to create a domestic partner registry for Texas residents. Bush has not indicated whether he supports domestic partner benefits for same-sex partners of federal employees. Such a bill was introduced into the Republican-controlled Congress in 2003, cosponsored by conservative Democratic Senator Joseph Lieberman (D-CT), but Bush has not done anything to help move it toward passage.[80]

Civil unions were first created in Vermont in 2000. They provide equal benefits under state law to same-sex couples living in that state. However, they offer no federal protections and are not portable to other states, although, generally marriages are portable as couples move from one state to another. Without portability, when a couple that has a civil union in Vermont moves out of state, they are legal strangers in that new state. While the federal government currently does not recognize same-sex marriages from Massachusetts, it is possible that a different administration would direct federal agencies to recognize marriages of same-sex couples from Massachusetts and elsewhere, and provide access to the 1,138 federal protections that are contingent upon marital status. This would also require the repeal or striking down of the Federal Defense of Marriage Act.

When White House Press Secretary Scott McClellan was asked how the President feels about the "concept of civil unions as an alternative to gay marriage," McClellan responded that Bush supports the Defense of Marriage Act (DOMA), which "states that other states don't have to recognize the civil unions or same-sex marriages of other states. So his position is very clear in support of that."[81] Texas, which Bush used to lead as governor, does not offer civil unions to same-sex couples. And Bush endorsed Marriage Protection Week in October 2003, during which elected officials were asked to sign a pledge opposing not only marriage but also domestic partnership and civil unions for gay couples.

Yet a week before the November 2004 election, Bush said he supported civil unions. This monumental "flip-flop" reversed Bush's earlier endorsement of

Marriage Protection Week and the federal amendment, which both sought to ban civil unions. Yet the media failed to note this glaring inconsistency and Bush came across as moderate and reasonable on gay issues.

In the 2000 debate with Senator Joseph Lieberman, Vice President Dick Cheney defended the right of gay couples to protect their relationships and defended states' rights to devise whatever form of partner recognition they might choose. However, in early 2004, Cheney reversed this position and endorsed President Bush's call for a constitutional amendment banning same-sex marriage. The existing Federal Marriage Amendment (FMA) would also prevent court rulings like that in Vermont that prompted the state legislature to create civil unions. Then in August 2004, Cheney yet again reversed himself, saying that he personally thought individual states should be able to grant whatever recognition they deemed appropriate to same-sex couples. He said that he personally disagreed with the President's support for the FMA. Incredibly, in a campaign in which Senator Kerry was harshly denounced as a "flip-flopper," complete with Bush supporters appearing at rallies dressed as dolphins and wielding beach sandals, no mainstream media outlet or pundit pointed out the inconsistency of both Bush and Cheney's positions on same-sex partner recognition.

The Bush Administration has not taken a clear stance on the provision of Social Security survivor and spousal benefits for same-sex couples. However, the Bush-Cheney Administration's support for the FMA would preempt any court ruling in favor of equal treatment of same-sex couples under Social Security policy. On June 24, 2002, President Bush signed the Mychal Judge Act, named after the New York City Fire Department chaplain who was killed during the September 11, 2001 terrorist attacks.[82] The bill allows same-sex partners of public safety officers killed in the line of duty to receive federally guaranteed life insurance benefits as long as the same-sex partners were designated as beneficiaries by their partners. The bill, however, is only retroactive to September 11, 2001.[83]

The White House Defends Its Position: "Judicial Tyranny"

In his 2004 State of the Union address, President Bush portrayed the Massachusetts Supreme Judicial Court as an anti-democratic rogue elephant run amok: "Activist judges ... have begun redefining marriage by court order, without regard for the will of the people and their elected officials ... the people's voice must be heard. If judges insist on forcing their arbitrary will upon the people, the only alternative left to the people would be the constitutional process."[84] When announcing his support for a constitutional amendment banning gay marriage a month later, Bush denounced "activist judges ... [who] have made an aggressive attempt to redefine marriage."[85]

Bush's denunciation of activist judges is ironic given the role a bitterly divided U.S. Supreme Court played in his ascendancy to office. The 5–4 *Bush v. Gore* ruling of December 2000 ignored the will of the American people as expressed in the popular vote, and, many would argue, possibly the will of Florida voters and thereby the Electoral College. Bush's charge of judicial tyranny in the Bay State also echoes a broader theme that recurs frequently in discourse related to marriage for same-sex couples. The day after Massachusetts' high court legalized marriage for gay couples, U.S. House Majority Leader Tom DeLay pushed the U.S. Constitutional ban, arguing that it's the only option "[w]hen you have a runaway judiciary that has no consideration of the Constitution of the United States."[86] Other conservative politicians and activists have echoed these claims. Family Research Council President Tony Perkins calls allegedly activist judges "the black plague."[87]

Following the 6–3 *Lawrence v. Texas* ruling striking down sodomy laws, one conservative columnist called for the impeachment of "the Sodomy 6."[88] In November 2003, the Catholic Action League called on the Massachusetts state legislature to impeach and convict for "abuse of office" the four justices who voted for marriage equality for same-sex couples, so the Governor could appoint new justices "who will respect their oath of office."[89] In the wake of the *Lawrence* and *Goodridge* decisions, as well as the federal court-ordered removal of a monument of the Ten Commandments from Alabama's Supreme Court, the Traditional Values Coalition issued "A Call to End Judicial Tyranny!" This call urged Congress to cut the salaries of "renegade judges and their staffs," impeach them or abolish their positions, replace appointed state judiciaries with elected ones, and pass a law prohibiting the U.S. Supreme Court from ruling on homosexuality, abortion, and other right-wing policy priorities.[90] Bills restricting courts from ruling in certain areas have already been introduced in some state legislatures. The Marriage Protection Act, a court-stripping bill that would ban federal courts from ruling on cases involving same-sex marriage, passed the U.S. House of Representatives in July 2004. Such proposals would overturn the principle of judicial review established two centuries ago in *Marbury v. Madison*.

In fact, six of the seven Massachusetts Supreme Judicial Court judges, and three of the four so-called renegade judges in the majority, were appointed by Republican governors. Seven of the nine U.S. Supreme Court justices were appointed by Republican presidents. Of thirteen federal appeals courts, nine have majorities of Republican appointees, two have majorities of Democratic appointees, and two are split evenly between Republican and Democratic appointees. Courts have also struck down environmental regulations, campaign finance restrictions, gun control, and even parts of the Violence against Women Act, all policies that enjoy strong public support. Court rulings often go against public opinion.

"Let the People Decide"

Anti-gay groups appeal to populist sentiment when they say that the people should be able to decide whether to grant gay people rights through an up or down vote on a ballot question. However, it runs counter to America's founding principles to suggest that majorities should be able to mete out or withhold rights to members of a stigmatized minority through a secret ballot vote. Founding father James Madison warned that "measures are too often decided, not according to the rules of justice and the rights of the minor party, but by the superior force of an interested and overbearing majority."[91] In other words, majority rule, unchecked, can lapse into majority tyranny. Many developments we look back upon as historical advances—such as court rulings against segregation or bans on interracial marriage—would likely not have been passed by a majority of voters had they been put up to a popular vote at the time. In November 2004, Alabama voters narrowly rejected an attempt to remove segregationist language from their state constitution. A majority of Alabama voters chose to keep language banning school desegregation and mandating discriminatory poll taxes, half a century after the U.S. Supreme Court had ruled such racist policies unconstitutional and forty years after the Civil Rights Act banned them.[92]

Prejudice or ignorance should never determine public policy. Anti-gay ballot measures such as the thirteen passed in 2004—in which whether to grant or withhold individual rights would be decided by the majority in a secret ballot—violate this fundamental principle. Imagine the outcome if a simple majority vote could decide the rights of individuals with disabilities, or immigrants, or women, or members of religious or racial minorities, or people who don't own property. Many other basic rights—such as freedom of the press, church-state separation, and Miranda rights—would perhaps not win majority support if put up for a popular vote, particularly in some conservative states.

Courts play a crucial role in countering the potential tyranny of the majority by focusing on basic rights protected by state and federal constitutions, regardless of the political ramifications or the prejudices of the day. Courts defend justice when they courageously stick with constitutional principles—as the Massachusetts' high court did in the marriage case—without regard to the politics or the popularity of their decision. This is the American system of government at its best.

The 2004 Republican and Democratic Platforms on Marriage and Same-Sex Couples

While there are many key issues on which the two major parties disagree, their attitudes toward policy issues affecting lesbian and gay people represent one of the most striking areas of disagreement. Since 1980, the two parties have headed in sharply divergent directions in terms of platform language regarding gay issues. This is in large part because gays became an integral part of the Democratic Party base, while anti-gay religious right activists became ascendant in the Republican Party, particularly following the creation of the Christian Coalition following Rev. Pat Robertson's failed run for the presidency in 1988.

The 2004 Republican and Democratic platforms differed sharply on gay issues, including whether to offer legal protections to lesbian and gay couples. The Republican platform opposed any benefits for same-sex couples, supported the Federal Marriage Amendment (FMA) and the court-stripping Marriage Protection Act, and claimed that being raised by heterosexual, married parents was essential to the "well-being" of children. It also denounced "judges with activist backgrounds in the hard-left" who "threaten America's dearest institutions and our very way of life."[93] While the Democratic Party platform did not take an explicit position on the issue of marriage for same-sex couples, it did call for "full inclusion of gay and lesbian families in the life of our nation" and "equal responsibilities, benefits, and protections for these families." The Democrats denounced "President Bush's divisive effort to politicize the Constitution by pursuing a 'Federal Marriage Amendment'" and said states should be able to "define" marriage, as they had for two centuries.[94]

The Mary Cheney Brouhaha

While there were significant differences between candidates Kerry and Bush on gay rights concerns (for example, Kerry supports nondiscrimination laws, while Bush opposes them as "special rights") and marriage, these were largely played down during the campaign. While Kerry made veiled references to Bush's support for the Federal Marriage Amendment (FMA) and Bush made more explicit and frequent references to Kerry's vote against the Defense of Marriage Act (DOMA) in 1996, in general gay issues did not emerge as a major point of differentiation between the two candidates. And while thirteen states voted on anti-gay marriage amendments in the summer and fall of 2004, perhaps the most bizarre development in the 2004 presidential election campaign was the reaction to Senator Kerry's noting of Mary Cheney's homosexuality during the third and final presidential debate. In response to a question about whether homosexuality was a choice (which Bush, in a nod to his Christian right base, declined to answer), Kerry spoke of the Cheney family's acceptance of their openly gay daughter, Mary. Following the debate, Republican spinmeisters and mainstream journalists pounced on Kerry's remarks as inappropriate. A media firestorm ensued for days. This reaction struck many gay activists, however, as bizarre, for the following reasons:

1. Mary Cheney had been an openly gay spokesperson for years in two capacities, as gay liaison for Coors Brewing Company, and as a leader of the Republican Unity Coalition, a pro-gay Republican group founded during the 2000 election.[95]
2. Mary Cheney had repeatedly spoken out on gay issues.[96]
3. Mary Cheney's sexuality had been publicly acknowledged by mainstream politicians and media outlets, pro- and anti-gay activists, as well as by her father, the vice president.[97]
4. Mary Cheney, as an openly gay person, helped raise significant amounts of money to elect an anti-gay Republican Congress and to help re-elect an anti-gay administration.[98]

Anti-Gay Marriage Amendments to State Constitutions

On November 2, 2004, eleven states passed anti-gay marriage amendments, eight of which also threatened more limited partner benefits for both gay and straight couples. Margins of victory ranged from Mississippi's overwhelming approval of an amendment by 82–18 percent to Oregon's more narrow margin of 57–43 percent. Voters in Missouri and Louisiana also approved anti-marriage amendments in August and September of 2004.

According to 2000 U.S. Census data on same-sex and unmarried opposite-sex couple families, at least 2.2 million residents in thirteen states are likely to lose the right to provide legal protections for their families as a result of the passage of anti-family state constitutional amendments there in 2004.[99] Nine of the thirteen state amendments go beyond banning marriage and also ban or threaten any form of partner recognition, such as domestic partner health insurance, civil unions, inheritance rights, and second-parent adoption. This means that thousands of same-sex partners and opposite-sex unmarried partners may be stripped of their domestic partner benefits, including health coverage. In Georgia, domestic partner health coverage offered by Atlanta, Decatur, and Dekalb County are in peril. In Ohio, gay and straight employees of Ohio University, Ohio State, Cleveland State, and Youngstown State could lose partner health coverage and other employer-provided benefits. The same goes for employees at the University of Michigan, Michigan State, and the University of Utah. In late 2004, Michigan Governor Jennifer Granholm stripped state employees of domestic partner health insurance, claiming that she was forced to make this move because Michigan voters approved an amendment stating that "the union of one man and one woman in marriage shall be the only agreement recognized as a marriage or similar union for any purpose."[100]

In Ohio, nearly 48,000 men, women, and children in gay and lesbian families, including 10,048 children, are now ineligible for the most basic family protections. In addition, because the amendment appears to ban any of the benefits of married couples for unmarried couples, gay or straight, more than 200,000 straight unmarried couples are now ineligible for family protections. Some 45 percent of these straight unmarried couples in Ohio are raising children.

Even though eight states passed bans on marriage that threaten civil unions, the National Election Poll taken on November 2, 2004 indicated that 60 percent of Americans support either marriage (25 percent) or civil unions (35 percent) for gay couples. Only 35 percent of Americans oppose any legal protections for gay couples.[101] So even though they passed by a wide margin, what these amendments actually do to American families is not something most American voters say they support. In a country in which 45 million Americans lack health coverage and costs are skyrocketing, the last thing we should be doing is stripping people of employer-provided health coverage. Unfortunately, that's what most of these amendments do.

As of the end of 2004, forty states banned marriage for same-sex couples. Fifteen states have adopted broader anti-gay family measures that may ban more limited protections like civil union domestic partnership, for both gay and straight couples. Seven states have passed constitutional amendments banning marriage, while ten more passed amendments banning marriage and threatening other forms of partner recognition. Some states have both an anti-marriage law and an amendment. Dozens more states are considering anti-gay family amendments in the 2005–2006 legislative session.

Supporters of Marriage Equality Re-Elected in Massachusetts   Despite efforts by Massachusetts Republican Governor Mitt Romney to make same-sex marriage a wedge issue in the Massachusetts state legislative elections, all of the incumbent state legislators in Massachusetts who supported equality for same-sex couples and voted against an anti-gay marriage amendment in early 2004 were re-elected on November 2, 2004. In addition, of eight open legislative seats where a pro-equality candidate faced an anti-gay candidate, six of the eight seats were won by the pro-equality candidates. The Republican Party lost three seats in the state legislature, one of its seven State Senate seats (out of forty), and two of its twenty-two House seats (out of 160). The state GOP spent about $3 million on the legislative races.

Incumbent State Senator Marion Walsh—a supporter of gay marriage who represents a heavily Catholic and socially conservative district in Boston and some western suburbs—beat back a challenge by a candidate who made his opposition to marriage equality his major issue. "I acknowledged straight on that I'm not going to take people's civil rights away," Walsh said, "that I'm not going to change the constitution." Walsh received nearly 65 percent of the vote in November 2004, according to the *Boston Globe*.

While no anti-equality incumbents were defeated in the Massachusetts legislative elections in November 2004, two incumbents who supported the anti-gay marriage amendment were defeated in the Democratic primaries in September 2004. Carl Sciortino, an openly gay challenger who defeated incumbent Democrat Representative Vincent Ciampa in the primary, beat back a write-in campaign by Ciampa by a two-to-one margin. Ciampa's write-in campaign included extreme anti-gay and xenophobic mailings and claims. Ciampa voted for the anti-gay amendment, despite having many gay and progressive constituents. In addition, Steven Canessa defeated anti-gay incumbent Rep. Mark Howland in September. Several anti-marriage incumbents, including Rep. Shirley Gomes of Cape Cod and Sen. Scott Brown, who represents a district south of Boston, barely won re-election over pro-equality challengers.

These election results demonstrate that support for equal treatment of same-sex couples need not be an election liability, and that constituents will re-elect pro-marriage incumbents. They also make it more likely that legislators will reject, in the 2005–2006 session, efforts to reverse the Massachusetts Supreme Judicial Court ruling in support of marriage equality for same-sex couples.

Post-Election Scapegoating   In the wake of President Bush's close re-election over Senator Kerry in November 2004, and the election of an even more anti-gay Congress, a new conventional wisdom emerged, holding that John Kerry lost the 2004 presidential election because of gay marriage, particularly because of an anti-marriage amendment on the Ohio ballot. Newsweek reported that Bill Clinton warned Kerry to come out strongly in favor of the anti-family amendments on the ballot in eleven states on November 2.[102] On the Sunday morning talk shows on November 14, 2004, Clinton called the anti-marriage amendments "an overwhelming factor" in Kerry's loss.

While gay marriage was an issue in the 2004 elections, it was only one of many concerns motivating voters. It is a gross overstatement to say that Kerry lost because of gay marriage. Here are some facts that complicate this simple calculus:

- Eight of the eleven states with anti-gay marriage amendments on the ballot have gone Republican in most or all of the recent presidential elections.
- Three battleground states had anti-family amendments. Kerry won two of these—Michigan and Oregon—even as voters there approved anti-gay marriage amendments. Kerry won Oregon 51 to 47 percent, while Gore barely carried it 47 to 47 percent. Kerry matched Gore's share of the Michigan vote—51 percent—but won 288,513 more votes than Gore did there in 2000.

- The third battleground state with an anti-marriage amendment, Ohio, went Republican in four of the last six elections. Since 1980, only Bill Clinton has been able to win Ohio for the Democrats. Going into the 2004 election, Ohio was "leaning Republican."
- Kerry won 473,474 more votes in Ohio than Al Gore did in 2000. Bush won 444,938 more votes in Ohio in 2004 than he did in 2000, when he carried the state. In other words, Kerry picked up 28,536 more votes over Gore's showing than Bush increased *his* showing by. Kerry's Ohio vote was 22 percent higher than what Gore got in 2000; Bush increased his 2004 vote by only 19 percent over his 2000 vote count there. But because Bush won the state in 2000 and was starting from a higher base of Republican votes, this 28,536 vote deficit didn't matter and Bush won the state.
- Like President Bush, Kerry and his running mate, Senator John Edwards, frequently voiced their opposition to gay marriage. Kerry endorsed anti-marriage amendments in his home state of Massachusetts and in Missouri.

The "Moral Values" Vote   In the weeks following Bush's close victory over Kerry, much was made of the so-called "moral values" voters. According to the National Election Pool, 22 percent of voters said that their choice for president was motivated by a concern for "moral values" more than any other issue. Eighty percent of these voters broke overwhelmingly for Bush. Some 20 percent of voters said "the economy/jobs" was the deciding issue, 19 percent said "terrorism," 15 percent said "Iraq," and smaller percentages chose other issues.

Television news reporters seized upon this datum to claim that Bush won because of moral values, read as opposition to gay marriage and abortion rights. Dan Rather called it "the decisive issue in the election." Anderson Cooper said, "Moral values ruled this election." Bill Plante said, "In the end, it was not the Iraq war or the economy, the two issues most often mentioned as voters' biggest concerns, but moral values, which were the biggest factor in motivating people to go to the polls."[103]

An in-depth analysis of responses to this exit poll question conducted by political scientist Ken Sherrill of Hunter College finds that moral values is less of an explanation or a cause of voting behavior, and more a correlate and/or consequence of liking President Bush and supporting his policies.[104] Sherrill found that those who said that moral values drove their choice of a presidential candidate were also much more likely to attend religious services once a week or more, much more likely to describe themselves as born-again or evangelical Christians, more likely to approve of Bush's handling of the presidency, more likely to approve the decision to invade Iraq, and more likely to think things are going very well or somewhat well in Iraq. Of those who said the Iraq war was going "very well," 35 percent said they chose their presidential candidate because of "moral values." Of those who said the war was going "somewhat well," 32 percent said "moral values" motivated their vote. But of those who said the war was going "very badly," only 10 percent said they voted based on concerns about "moral values." Those who pointed to "moral values" to explain their vote were also much more likely to report that their family's financial situation is better today than four years ago. Of those who said they were "better today" financially, 31 percent said "moral values" determined their vote for president, but only 11 percent said "the economy/jobs" was the decisive factor. Of those who said they were "worse off" today financially, 33 percent cast their presidential vote based on "the economy/jobs," while only 12 percent cast their vote based on "moral values." Only 10 percent of those voting for Democratic Congressional candidates said they voted for president based on "moral values," but 34 percent of those voting for Republican Congressional candidates said "moral values" drove their presidential choice.

What all of this means is that those likely to say they voted for president based on "moral values" also share a general constellation of values and political beliefs that aligns closely with those of the Republican Party and President Bush. "Moral values" may be their top choice as an explanation of their general political perspective from among the seven choices offered on the National Election Poll, but this does not mean that "moral values" *caused* them to vote for Bush.

Another important caveat was offered by Andrew Kohut of the Pew Research Center on *The News Hour with Jim Lehrer* just days after the election: For many religious conservatives, who usually vote Republican, there is a "social desirability" factor involved. If "moral values" is on a list of seven possible choices, many religious conservatives—who think of themselves as moral people with values—feel compelled to choose that option.

In a national poll of 1,000 voters conducted November 1–2, 2004 by Lake, Snell, Perry & Associates, only 2 percent said that "gay and lesbian rights issues" were the most important issues to them in deciding for whom to vote. The top issue was "jobs and the economy" (23 percent), followed by "homeland security and terrorism" (19 percent), and "Iraq" (13 percent). Only 10 percent cited "moral values" as their chief concern.[105]

To say that the anti-family amendments on the ballot in eleven states cost Senator Kerry the election is simplistic and not warranted by the exit poll data. The anti-gay/anti-family amendments—which will deny health coverage to thousands of American families, gay and straight, many with children—were a factor in the outcome in Ohio, but not in Oregon,

Michigan, or the other eight states. Even in Ohio, the anti-marriage amendment was only one of many factors in a close election.

Conclusion

Marriage equality for same-sex couples emerged as a central political issue
in the 2004 presidential election as a result of a number of court rulings
in the U.S. and Canada in 2003, some about marriage and some—such as
Lawrence v. Texas—not. It also emerged as a central wedge issue because
anti-gay activists and Republican Party leaders sought to make it a central
issue, through events like the October 2003 Marriage Protection Week,
through Congress's scheduling of debates and votes on the Federal Marriage
Amendment and Marriage Protection Act in July 2004, just prior to the
Democratic National Convention, and through Bush's frequent references
to the issue on the campaign trail. The 2004 election was the fourth presidential election in which gay rights controversies became central. Despite
the right's clear attempts to use marriage as a wedge issue, the ten Democratic presidential candidates were collectively the most pro-gay ever, and
while few were affirmatively for marriage equality, most spoke out against
efforts to ban marriage for gay couples through an amendment to the U.S.
Constitution. While the Bush-Cheney Administration opposes most forms
of legal equality for gay people, Bush's announcement a week before the
election that he had no objections to civil unions, in contradiction of his
own party platform, reassured the socially moderate "soccer mom" vote that
Bush was not a hater. And although most voters said they supported allowing gay couples to marry or form civil unions, overwhelming majorities in
nine states passed amendments in summer and fall 2004 that threaten or
prohibit civil unions. In the wake of the passage of eleven anti-marriage
amendments on election day, many pundits blamed gay marriage for
Kerry's loss, even though there are many indicators that complicate this
simple calculus.

The U.S. Constitution guarantees "equal protection of the laws" for all
Americans—not just for heterosexual Americans, and not just for those
who can win a popularity contest. Putting basic rights up for a majority vote
is neither moral nor in the best traditions of this country. Denying loving
and committed couples equal legal protections for their relationships and
their children is not moral. There are many basic rights that, if put up for
a popular vote, would not win majority support. Many of the most basic
freedoms critical to our political system—church-state separation, Miranda
rights, freedom of the press—would not necessarily win majority approval
in many parts of the country. For example, while racial equality is now a
mainstream American value (in polite company at least), voters in Alabama

voted against it on November 2, 2004. An amendment that would have removed segregationist language from the Alabama constitution was narrowly defeated by Alabama voters that day; the amendment would have removed language calling for segregated schools and requiring a poll tax, which prevented nearly all Black Alabamans from voting prior to the passage of the Civil Rights Act and Voting Rights Act in the mid-1960s.[106]

The reaction against marriage equality for same-sex couples will continue for the foreseeable future, but already about 5,000 lesbian and gay couples have married in Massachusetts, and the sky has not fallen there. Activists are preparing for a likely ballot fight to protect the right to marry in Massachusetts, and will continue to fight against anti-family amendments across the country. Meanwhile, given the centrality of gay rights controversies in the 2004 election and the three previous presidential contests, it is likely that marriage and other legal controversies will remain a central fault line in U.S. politics for years to come.

Notes

1. Portions of this chapter are based on material first published in Sean Cahill, *Same-Sex Marriage in the United States: Focus on the Facts* (New York: Lexington Books, 2004).
2. Barbara Babcock, *The Reversible World: Symbolic Inversion in Art and Society* (Ithaca, NY: Cornell University Press, 1978), 32. Cited in Peter Stallybrass and Allon White, *The Politics and Poetics of Transgression* (Ithaca, NY: Cornell University Press, 1986), 20.
3. Stallybrass and White, 20.
4. C. McClelland, "Same-Sex Marriage Endorsed in Canada; Government Will Act to Change Law," *Washington Post*, June 18, 2003, A22.
5. P. Dvorak, "Gay Community Hails a 'New Day;' Ruling on Sodomy Law Celebrated," *Washington Post*, June 27, 2003, B01.
6. P. Belluck, "Marriage by Gays Gains Big Victory in Massachusetts; Legislature Told to Clear Way—Court Cites State Constitution," *New York Times*, November 19, 2003, A1, A24.
7. S. Bryan, "New Mexico County Begins Issuing Marriage Licenses to Gay Couples," *Associated Press*, February 21, 2004.
8. McClelland.
9. C. Krauss, "Gay Canadians' Quest for Marriage Seems Near Victory," *New York Times*, June 15, 2003.
10. Ibid.
11. McClelland.
12. "Second Canadian province legalizes gay marriage," *Sydney Morning Herald*, July 10, 2003.
13. Rex Wockner, "Quebec legalizes same-sex marriage," March 22, 2004 (gay wire service).
14. Wikipedia, "Same Sex Marriage in Canada," December 3, 2004, http://en.wikipedia.org/wiki/Same-sex_marriage_in_Canada (accessed December 7, 2004).
15. Associated Press, "Canada Court Approves Gay Marriage," CNN.com, (accessed December 9, 2004).
16. Dvorak.
17. In addition to the laws still in effect in thirteen states, sodomy laws were also still on the books in Michigan and Massachusetts as of June 2003, but their status was in dispute as court rulings had limited their reach.
18. D. Savage, "Ruling Seen as Precursor to Same-Sex Marriages; Supporters and Foes of Gay Civil Rights Say the Court's Overturning of Sodomy Laws Could Lead to Gay Unions," *Los Angeles Times*, June 28, 2003, http://www.latimes.com (accessed June 29, 2003).
19. Ibid.
20. Ibid.

21. A. Gearan, "Scalia Blasts Court on Sodomy Ruling," *Associated Press*, June 26, 2003 (accessed June 27, 2003).

22. N. Lewis, "Conservatives Furious over Court's Direction," *New York Times*, http://www.nytimes.com, June 27, 2003 (accessed June 28, 2003).

23. Rick Santorum, "Americans Must Preserve the Institution of Marriage," *USA Today*, July 9, 2003.

24. Associated Press interview, April 7, 2003. Reprinted in "National Gay and Lesbian Task Force slams Santorum's bigoted language," New York: National Gay and Lesbian Task Force, April 23, 2003, http://www.thetaskforce.org/media/release.cfm?print=1&releaseID=534 (accessed January 13, 2005).

25. Savage.

26. Ruth Harlow cited in Santorum, July 9, 2003.

27. Belluck.

28. *Goodridge v. Department of Public Health*, 440 Mass. 309, 342 (2003).

29. R. Lewis, "SJC affirms gay marriage," *Boston Globe*, February 5, 2004, www.boston.com (accessed June 13, 2004).

30. Yvonne Abraham, "No Court Ruling on Same-Sex Marriage; US Justices Won't Hear Mass. Case," *Boston Globe*, November 30, 2004.

31. Chris Bull and J. Gallagher, *Perfect Enemies: The Religious Right, the Gay Movement, and the Politics of the 1990s* (New York: Crown, 1996), 91–92.

32. Ibid., 94.

33. Robert McElvaine, "GOP 'Values'? Read Their Lip Service," *Los Angeles Times*, October 12, 1992; Chip Berlet and Margaret Quigley, "Theocracy and White Supremacy: Behind the Culture War to Restore Traditional Values," in *Eyes Right: Challenging the Right-Wing Backlash*, ed. Chip Berlet, (Boston: South End Press, 1995), 15.

34. Bull and Gallagher, 94.

35. Ibid., 129.

36. H. Rhoads, "Cruel Crusade: The Holy War against Lesbians and Gays," The Progressive, 53:7, March 1993, 18; Bull and Gallagher, 95; Robert Bailey, *Out and Voting II: The Gay, Lesbian, and Bisexual Vote in Congressional Elections, 1990–1998* (New York: Policy Institute of the National Gay and Lesbian Task Force, 2000).

37. Baehr v. Lewin, 852 P.2d 44 (Haw. 1993) (plurality).

38. *Boston Globe* (April 14, 1996).

39. Ibid.

40. *Boston Globe* (September 11, 1996).

41. "No State … shall be required to give effect to any public act, record, or judicial proceeding of any other State … respecting a relationship between persons of the same sex that is treated as a marriage under the laws of such other State … or a right or claim arising from such a relationship." Defense of Marriage Act of 1996, Pub. L. No. 104–199, 110 Stat. 2419 (1996). Cited in Gregory Lewis and Jonathan Edelson, "DOMA and ENDA: Congress Votes on Gay Rights," in *The Politics of Gay Rights*, eds. Craig Rimmerman, Kenneth Wald, and Clyde Wilcox (Chicago: University of Chicago Press, 2000), 212–213.

42. National Gay and Lesbian Task Force Policy Institute, Capital Gains and Losses: A State by State Review of Gay-Related Legislation in 1996 (Washington, D.C.: NGLTF, 1996), http://www.thetaskforce.org/downloads/cgal96.pdf (accessed February 5, 2004).

43. National Gay and Lesbian Task Force Policy Institute (1998), Capital Gains and Losses: A State by State Review of Gay, Lesbian, Bisexual, Transgender, and HIV/AIDS-Related Legislation in 1998 (Washington, D.C.: NGLTF, 1998), 13, http://www.thetaskforce.org/downloads/cgal98.pdf (accessed February 5, 2004); Missouri's Supreme Court overturned its 1996 anti-gay marriage law in May 1998, but the legislature passed another anti-marriage law two years later.

44. *Des Moines Register*, August 13, 1999.

45. Mark Sandalow, "McCain Welcomes Support of Gays in GOP; Candidate Meets with Log Cabin Group," *San Francisco Chronicle*, November 9, 1999.

46. H. Ramer, "Bauer: Gay Marriage is Worse than Terrorism," *Associated Press*, December 27, 1999.

47. Lisa Keen, "An About Face for Bush? Opinion on Appointing Gays Remains Murky," *Washington Blade*, October 15, 1999.

48. "A Sodomy Law's Last Stand," *The Advocate*, July 18, 2000. Then-Governor Bush was originally quoted by David Elliot, *Austin-American Statesman*, January 22, 1994.

49. Sean Cahill and Erik Ludwig, *Courting the Vote: The 2000 Presidential Candidates on Gay, Lesbian, Bisexual and Transgender Issues*, (New York: National Gay and Lesbian Task Force Policy Institute, 1999).

50. National Gay and Lesbian Task Force, "Election Center 2000: VP Candidate Profile Richard 'Dick' Cheney" (New York: NGLTF, 2000), http://www.ngltf.org/elections/cheney.htm (accessed January 8, 2004).

51. L. Kirchner, "State Court Called Gay Adoption Ban 'Absurd'," *Pittsburgh's Out*, October 2002, 3.

52. H.J. Resolution 56, introduced May 21, 2003.

53. Such challenges have overturned domestic partner policies in Atlanta, GA; Minneapolis, MN; Arlington County, VA; and Massachusetts (all final) as well as Philadelphia (on appeal). Ten other legal challenges were unsuccessful. Source: Charles Gossett, "Dillon Goes to Court: Legal Challenges to Local Ordinances Providing Domestic Partnership Benefits," paper presented to the annual meeting of the American Political Science Association, Atlanta, GA, September 4, 1999. Updated in personal communication with Charles Gossett, October 2002.

54. C. Barillas, "Mass. High Court Repeals Boston DP Ordinance," *Data Lounge*, July 9, 1999, http://www.datalounge.com/datalounge/news/record.html?record=4439 (accessed March 8, 2004).

55. WorldNet Daily, "City Sued Over Domestic Partnerships," August 13, 2003, http://www.inthedays.com/articles.php?articleId=619 (accessed March 8, 2004).

56. C. Curtis, "New Wording Proposed for Marriage Ban," PlanetOut.com, March 22, 2004 (accessed March 23, 2004).

57. Sean Cahill et al., *The 2004 Democratic Presidential Candidates on Gay, Lesbian, Bisexual, and Transgender Issues* (New York: National Gay and Lesbian Task Force Policy Institute, 2003); National Gay and Lesbian Task Force, *The Presidential Candidates' Positions on LGBT issues* (New York: National Gay and Lesbian Task Force Policy Institute, January 2004), http://www.ngltf.org/electioncenter/SummaryComparison.pdf (accessed January 30, 2004).

58. Alain Dang, *The Democratic Presidential Candidates on Marriage Equality for Same-Sex Couples* (New York: NGLTF Policy Institute, 2004), http://www.ngltf.org/electioncenter/DemsMarriage.pdf (accessed January 30, 2004).

59. President George W. Bush, "Marriage Protection Week, 2003, by the President of the United States of America: A Proclamation," October 3, 2003, http://www.whitehouse.gov/news/releases/2003/10/print/20031003-12.html (accessed January 13, 2004).

60. City News Service, "Gay Church Group Announces National 'Freedom to Marry Week' Actions," January 8, 2004.

61. Remarks by the President, The White House, Office of the Press Secretary, February 24, 2004.

62. W. Slater, "Bush Opposes Adoption by Gays," *Dallas Morning News*, March 23, 1999.

63. T. Zeller, "Two Fronts: Promoting Marriage, Fighting Poverty," *New York Times*, January 18, 2004, WK3.

64. Press briefing by Ari Fleischer, April 25, 2003, http://www.whitehouse.gov/news/releases/2003/04/20030425-4.html (accessed July 9, 2003); "The 2000 Campaign; 2nd Presidential Debate between Gov. Bush and Vice President Gore," *New York Times*, October 12, 2000, A22.

65. Slater; P. Burka, "James Byrd, Jr: Law's Latest Symbol," *Texas Monthly*, September 1999, http://www.texasmonthly.com/mag/1999/sep/byrd.php (accessed July 9, 2003).

66. C. Connolly, "Gore's Vews on Gays in Military Get Public Voice," *Washington Post*, December 15, 1999, A6; "Excerpts from debate among G.O.P candidates," *New York Times*, January 7, 2000, A15.

67. Kaiser Family Foundation, Daily HIV/AIDS report, March 25, 2003, http://www.kaisernetwork.org/daily_reports/rep_index.cfm?hint=1&DR_ID=16743 (accessed July 9, 2003).

68. For example see J. S. Bybee, "The Equal Protection Clause: A Note on the (Non)relationship between *Romer v. Evans* and *Hunter v. Erickson*," 6 WM. & MARY BILL RTS. J. 201, 224 (1997); Timothy M. Tymkovich, John Daniel Dailey, Paul Farley, "Gay Rights and the Courts: The Amendment 2 controversy: A tale of three theories: Reason and prejudice in the battle over Amendment 2," 68 U. COLO. L. REV. 287 (1997); Among Bush's anti-gay cabinet members

are Attorney General John Ashcroft, who opposed James Hormel's nomination to become Ambassador to Luxembourg because Hormel is gay, and Interior Secretary Gail Norton, who invited discredited psychologist Paul Cameron to testify in support of Colorado's anti-gay Amendment Two, which was found unconstitutional by the U.S. Supreme Court in *Romer v. Evans*, 1996.

69. Jim Towey, *Protecting the civil rights and religious liberty of faith-based organizations: Why religious hiring rights must be preserved* (Washington, D.C.: White House Office of Faith-Based and Community Initiatives, no date), http://www.whitehouse.gov/government/fbci/booklet.pdf (accessed January 6, 2004). This memo was sent to Congress from the White House in late June 2003.

70. S. Russell, "Funds for S.F. AIDS Program in Peril; CDC Threatens to Pull Money for 'Obscene' Campaign," *San Francisco Chronicle*, June 14, 2003, A1.

71. J. Kaiser, "Politics and Biomedicine: Studies of Gay Men, Prostitutes Come under Scrutiny," *Science*, June 9, 2003, 300–403; "Politicizing Science," *Bangor Daily News*, June 9, 2003, A8.

72. J. Radow, "Researcher 'Hit List' Undermines NIH Peer-Review Process, Charges Rep. Waxman," *Washington Fax*, October 28, 2003; B. Herbert, "The Big Chill at the Lab," *New York Times*, November 3, 2003, A19. As NIH Director Elias A. Zerhouni, M.D., pointed out, some of these studies examine male sexual dysfunction and impotence, which is a major cause of marital relationship dissatisfaction and divorce. The Traditional Values Coalition is opposing research that could help solve sexual dysfunction, which is a major source of familial stress and dissolution.

73. N. Anderson, "Candidates Leery of Gay Marriage Debate," *Los Angeles Times*. July 3, 2003, http://www.latimes.com/news/nationworld/politics/la-na-marriage3jul03001429,0,2329538.story?coll=la-news-politics-national (accessed July 9, 2003).

74. "President Bush Discusses Top Priorities for the U.S.," July 30, 2003. http://www.whitehouse.gov/news/releases/2003/07/20030730-1.html (accessed July 31, 2003).

75. George W. Bush, "President Defends the Sanctity of Marriage: Statement by the President," November 18, 2003, http://www.whitehouse.gov/news/releases/2003/11/20031118-4.html (accessed December 17, 2003).

76. S. Jones, "Bush's Comments on Marriage Draw Praise, Criticism," Cybercast News Service, January 21, 2004, http://www.CNSNews.com/html (accessed January 21, 2004).

77. M. Dobbin, "Enraged Foes of Gay Marriage Gear Up for Fight; Massachusetts Ruling Energizes Drive for a Constitutional Ban on Same-Sex Wedlock," *Sacramento Bee*, February 6, 2004.

78. W. Washington, "Bush 'Troubled' by Gay Marriage, but is Quiet on Amendment Plans," *Boston Globe*, February 19, 2004.

79. A. Mitchell, "Bush Talks to Gays and Calls it Beneficial," *New York Times*, April 14, 2000, A26.

80. Domestic Partners Benefits and Obligations Act, H.R. 638, 107th Cong. (2003).

81. Press briefing by Scott McClellan, July 30, 2003, http://www.whitehouse.gov/news/releases/2003/07/20030731-9.html (accessed August 1, 2003).

82. Mychal Judge Police and Fire Chaplains Public Safety Officers' Benefit Act of 2002, Pub. L. No. 107–196, 116 Stat. 719. Codified at 42 U.S.C. § 3796 (2002).

83. Susan J. Becker, "Tumbling Towers as Turning Points: Will 9/11 Usher in a New Civil Rghts Era for Gay Men and Lesbians in the United States?" *William & Mary Journal of Women and Law*, 9 (2003): 207–253.

84. Ann Kornblut, "Bush Demonstrates Willingness to Tackle Divisive Cultural Issues," *Boston Globe*, January 21, 2004.

85. "Remarks by the President," Washington, D.C.: The White House, Office of the Press Secretary, February 24, 2004.

86. J. Mason, "Texans Urge Ban on Gay Unions," *Houston Chronicle*, November 19, 2003.

87. B. Fancher and J. Parker, "Pro-Family Leaders Speak up for 'Marriage Protection Week,'" Agape Press/crosswalk.com, July 7, 2003, http://www.crosswalk.com/news/1225015.html (accessed January 24, 2004).

88. J. Farah, "Impeach the 'Sodomy 6,'" July 7, 2003, http://www.worldnetdaily.com/news/article.asp?ARTICLE-ID=33447 (accessed January 24, 2004).

89. Catholic Action League, "Catholic Action League Condemns SJC Decision on Same-Sex Marriage," November 18, 2003, http://www.frmcgivneyassembly.org/CatholicActionLeague.html (accessed December 1, 2003).

90. Traditional Values Coalition Special Report, "Judges: Our Robed masters; A Call to End Judicial Tyranny!" (Washington, D.C.: TVC, no date), http://www.traditionalvalues.org (accessed January 22, 2004).

91. James Madison, "Federalist 10," *The Federalist Papers* (New York: Penguin Classics, 1987).

92. Associated Press, "Alabama segregation amendment unchanged," December 3, 2004, http://www.cnn.com/2004/ALLPOLITICS/12/03/segregation.amendment.ap/index.html (accessed December 7, 2004).

93. http://www.gop.com/media/2004platform.pdf (accessed November 10, 2004).

94. http://www.democrats.org/pdfs/2004platform.pdf (accessed November 10, 2004).

95. Mary Cheney "has been openly lesbian for years," according to an article in *The Advocate*, a gay newsweekly, from early 2004. "Mary Cheney Gets the Dr. Laura Treatment by Gay Rights Group," *The Advocate*, February 18, 2004, http:// www.advocate.com/new_news.asp?ID=11347&sd=02/18/04 (accessed October 15, 2004.) According to an article posted on the Republican Unity Coalition (RUC) website, Mary Cheney served as the lesbian and gay liaison for Coors Beer. Hastings Wyman, "Charles Francis, A New Kid on the Block," Washington, D.C.: Republican Unity Coalition, no date. http://www.republicanunity.com/artcl/ttc.htm (accessed October 15, 2004). A Coors spokesperson would not disclose when Cheney held this position. *Southern Political Report* writer Hastings Wyman, the author of the article posted on the RUC website, thinks Cheney stopped working for Coors in 2000 when her father was chosen as Bush's running mate. A Salon.com report states that Cheney worked for Coors in this capacity from at least 1999 through mid-2000. D. Cullen, "All in the Family," July 29, 2000, http://dir.salon.com/politics/feature/2000/07/29/mary/index.html (accessed October 15, 2004). Mary Cheney served on the board of the RUC, a pro-gay group aimed at "creating a gay-straight alliance within the Republican Party ... [and] making being gay or lesbian a non-issue in the Republican Party ..." from April 2002 to June 2003. C. Lochhead and Z. Coile, "How Gay GOP Group Lost its Faith in Bush; High Hopes in 2000 Dissolve in Dispute over Marriage Ban," *San Francisco Chronicle*, October 10, 2004; "Mary Cheney Leaves Gay GOP Group as David Rockefeller Signs On," *Washington Blade*, June 13, 2003. Reprinted on RUC website, http://www.republicanunity.com/archive/2003_07_06_archive.htm (accessed October 15, 2004).
This was widely reported in both the mainstream and gay press, and criticized by anti-gay groups, such as Concerned Women for America. "Mary Cheney joins homosexual activist group," *Culture and Family Institute Report*, Washington, D.C.: Concerned Women for America, April 25, 2002, http://www.cwfa.org/articles/468/CFI/cfreport/ (accessed October 15, 2004).

96. When Mary Cheney joined the RUC, she said in a statement, "Working together we can expand the Republican Party's outreach to non-traditional Republicans. We can make sexual orientation a non-issue for the Republican Party, and we can help achieve equality for all gay and lesbian Americans." (L. Grove, "The Reliable Source," *Washington Post*, April 23, 2002.) Tim Russert, speaking on the NBC-TV *Today* show after Senator Rick Santorum made anti-gay comments regarding the *Lawrence v. Texas* sodomy law case pending before the U.S. Supreme Court, said that the RUC was "headed by former President Gerry Ford and Mary Cheney." Russert noted that the RUC had called on Senator Santorum to apologize for comparing homosexuality to pedophilia and "man on dog" bestiality. ("Interview: Tim Russert discusses Senator Rick Santorum's anti-gay remarks and Bush's tax cut proposal," NBC News: Today, April 24, 2003.) Bill Press, on MSNBC's Buchanan and Press, said, "Mary Cheney's group [the RUC] attacked Rick Santorum and said his comments were indefensible" (MSNBC, Buchanan and Press, May 2, 2003).

97. At a January 2001 RUC breakfast held to coincide with the inauguration of George Bush and Dick Cheney, former Republican U.S. Senator Alan Simpson of Wyoming "spoke of having known Vice President Dick Cheney for more than 35 years, and of having watched his lesbian daughter Mary group up to be 'one of the most remarkable women.'" (Bob Roehr, "GOP group forms: Republican unity Coalition seeks to 'build bridges,'" *Windy City Times*, January 24, 2001.) *Newsweek* reported that, at the January 2001 RUC inaugural breakfast, "[Former U.S. Senator Alan] Simpson went out of his way to introduce everyone to Mary Cheney and her partner." (M. Brant, "A new GOP? Prominent gay Republicans look to make sexual orientation a non-issue. And the Bush administration is listening—quietly," *Newsweek* Web Exclusive, December 13, 2001 (accessed October 15, 2004). Concerned Women for

America reported on April 25, 2002, that "Mary Cheney, the lesbian daughter of Vice President Dick Cheney, has joined the board of a homosexual activist Republican group that seeks to make homosexuality a 'non-issue' in the GOP" ("Mary Cheney joins homosexual activist group," Culture and Family Institute Report (Washington, D.C.: Concerned Women for America, April 25, 2002), http://http://www.cwfa.org/articles/468/CFI/cfreport/ (accessed October 15, 2004). On September 5, 2002, the *San Francisco Chronicle*, reporting on an RUC fundraising dinner in Los Angeles, called Mary Cheney "the vice president's gay daughter." (J. Wildermuth and C. Marinucci, "Simon Blames Staff for Fiasco on Gay Survey; Candidate Now Insists He Never Saw Questionnaire," *San Francisco Chronicle*, September 5, 2002.) On May 2, 2003, Bill Press of MSNBC's *Buchanan and Press* asked anti-gay activist Peter LaBarbera "… can [Republican National Committee Chair] Marc Racicot meet with Mary Cheney, Dick Cheney's daughter? … Is she welcome in the Republican Party, the vice president's daughter under your rules? … She's an active lesbian; she's proud of it. Is she welcome?" (LaBarbera said his objection was to Mary Cheney's gay activism, not the fact that she is gay; *Buchanan and Press*, May 2, 2003.) Finally, Vice President Dick Cheney acknowledged his daughter is gay during a campaign appearance in Davenport, Iowa, in August 2004. Asked about gay marriage, Cheney responded: "Lynne and I have a gay daughter, so it's an issue our family is very familiar with." ("Campaign Feud Continues over Cheney's daughter: Mary Cheney Finds Herself in Eye of Political Storm," *Associated Press*, October 15, 2004.)

98. From the day Bush and Cheney were sworn in January 20, 2001 to mid-2003, Mary Cheney spoke at prominent fundraising breakfasts and dinners for the RUC and other Republican Party causes. (P. Morrison, "Inside Politics: Also-Ran in Diddlys: Does it Get Any Worse?" *Los Angeles Times*, September 9, 2002.) During the 2002 mid-term election cycle, the RUC "provided record-setting support for the Republican Party, with $50,000 RUC checks each to the National Republican Senatorial Committee and the National Republican Congressional Committee." This included a fundraiser attended by Mary Cheney at the home of Arizona Republican Tom Synhorst. "Republican Unity Coalition," *Dysinfopedia: An Encyclopedia of People, Issues and Groups Shaping the Political Agenda*. Center for Media and Democracy, no date, http://www.dysinfopedia.org (accessed October 15, 2004). The RUC set a goal of raising $1 million for the 2002 Congressional elections. E. Werner, "GOP Group Drops Simon from Lineup of Speakers," *San Jose Mercury News*, September 4, 2002; Hastings Wyman, "Charles Francis, a New Kid on the Block," RUC website, no date, http:// www.republicanunity.com/artcl/ttc.htm (accessed October 15, 2004). In 2003–2004, the Republican Congress, Mary Cheney, and the RUC helped elect, then proceeded to promote and vote in favor of the anti-gay Federal Marriage Amendment (FMA) and the Marriage Protection Act, a court-stripping bill. It also increased spending on abstinence-only-until-marriage education and sought to defund AIDS service providers and research on health issues affecting lesbian, gay, bisexual, and transgender people. In 2004, Mary Cheney was a paid staffer of the Bush-Cheney re-election campaign, earning a $100,000-a-year salary. "Mary Cheney Gets the Dr. Laura Treatment by Gay Rights Group," *The Advocate*, February 18, 2004, http:// www.advocate.com/new_news.asp?ID=11347&sd=02/18/04 (accessed October 15, 2004). The Bush-Cheney Administration was, in mid-2004, the most anti-gay in modern history. It opposes nondiscrimination laws, hate crimes laws, partner recognition, marriage, adoption, and sex education. Its faith-based initiative has sought an explicit right to discriminate against gay people in social service employment with federal tax dollars. It has appointed numerous anti-gay judges and refused to speak up for gay rights in international fora. Jason Cianciotto and Roddrick Colvin, *The Bush-Cheney Administration on 12 Key Issues of Concern to Lesbian, Gay, Bisexual and Transgender People*, New York: Policy Institute of the National Gay and Lesbian Task Force, 2004, http:// www.thetaskforce.org (accessed October 15, 2004).

99. This figure is derived from an analysis of U.S. Census data on same-sex partner households and unmarried opposite-sex partner households by researcher Gary Gates for the National Gay and Lesbian Task Force. "Number of same-sex couples and opposite-sex unmarried couples affected by anti-gay marriage ballot initiatives," New York: National Gay and Lesbian Task Force Policy Institute, no date, http://www.thetaskforce.org/downloads/couplesaffected.pdf (accessed November 29, 2004).

100. Associated Press, "Michigan Governor Pulls Same-Sex Benefits," *The Bakersfield Californian*, December 1, 2004.
101. Ken Sherrill, "Same-Sex Marriage, Civil Unions, and the 2004 Election," New York: National Gay and Lesbian Task Force Policy Institute, November 2004.
102. "How he won it," *Newsweek*, November 15, 2004.
103. *CBS Evening News*, November 3, 2004; CNN, *Anderson Cooper 360*, November 3, 2004; CBS, *The Early Show*, November 4, 2004.
104. Ken Sherrill, "Moral Values and the 2004 Election," New York: National Gay and Lesbian Task Force, November 2004.
105. Poll conducted for National Gay and Lesbian Task Force. Lake Snell Perry and Associates (November 1–2, 2004). *Election Eve 2004 Omnibus Survey*. Washington, D.C.: Lake Snell Perry and Associates.
106. Associated Press. "Alabama Segregation Amendment Unchanged," December 3, 2004, http://www.cnn.com/2004/ALLPOLITICS/12/03/segregation.amendment.ap/index.html (accessed December 7, 2004).

CHAPTER **5**

The Anti-Gay Backlash?

ETHEL D. KLEIN

Images of thousands of gay and lesbian weddings at San Francisco City Hall are purported to have enraged the evangelical community, propelling to the polls many Christian conservatives who failed to vote last time and who, but for gay marriage, would not have voted this time. "Moral values" voters were anointed the force that determined the election; gay marriage was blamed for triggering this movement, as evidenced by the anti-gay marriage amendments that were resoundingly passed in the eleven states where they were on the ballot. Simply put, gay marriage cost John Kerry the election.

This simple explanation became conventional wisdom overnight. It rang true, reinforcing many people's political predispositions. Democrats had feared the ballot initiatives would cost them the election and Republicans had counted on opposition to same-sex marriage to bring out their troops. As with many simple explanations for complex phenomena, the catchy headlines and snappy sound bites provided by the gay marriage story came at the expense of accurate analysis.

The moral values analysis of the 2004 election rests on three claims. First, this election year was historic in the upsurge of values voters rushing to the polls. Second, anti-marriage initiatives led to higher turnout among Christian conservatives. Third, Bush performed especially well where gay marriage was on the ballot. These assumptions do not hold up under empirical scrutiny. Moral values mattered at the margin, but not substantially more than they did in 2000. And there is very little evidence at all that, among moral values issues, gay rights played a particular mobilizing role. Opposition to abortion was, and is, a much more important core issue to moral values voters.

No Upsurge of a Moral Values Constituency

Moral values voters are not a new phenomenon. There were about as many such voters this year as in other recent presidential elections. An analysis of national exit polls conducted by the *Los Angeles Times* indicates that 24 percent of voters chose moral/ethical values as one of their two most important issues in the 1992 presidential campaign. That figure jumped to 40 percent in 1996, dipped slightly to 35 percent in 2000, and rebounded back to 40 percent in 2004. The evidence suggests no significant increase in the percentage of values from voters committed to the President in 2004 than in 2000. Seventy percent of those who chose "moral/ethical values" voted for Bush in 2004 compared to 74 percent in 2000.[1]

Abortion, gay rights, and stem cell research are the specific issues most often associated with the moral values agenda. Exit polls conducted by Edison Media Research/Mitofsky International of over 13,000 voters (see Table 5.1) as they left their polling places found there was no increase in the percentage of pro-life voters—16 percent of voters believed abortion should be illegal in all cases and another 26 percent believed it should be illegal in most cases, for an aggregate 42 percent of the 2004 electorate that is distinctly pro-life. The 2000 numbers (from the Voter News Service exit polls) are quite similar: 13 percent of the 2000 electorate believed abortion should always be illegal and 27 percent believed it should be illegal in most cases, for a pro-life aggregate of 40 percent of the electorate. The 2004 electorate took a middle ground on gay rights, with 37 percent arguing for no legal recognition of gay and lesbian couples, 35 percent supporting civil unions but not marriage, and 25 percent favoring marriage. Only 14 percent of Bush voters said they cast their ballot for the President because he has strong religious faith. Significantly more of Bush's supporters mentioned leadership (29 percent) and a clear stance on the issues (27 percent) as the candidate qualities that mattered most.

The mythic importance of the moral values vote was spurred by an exit poll question media analysts interpreted as showing that moral values—not the economy or the Iraq war or terrorism—was *the* most important issue determining how Americans voted. This over-interpretation of a modest exit poll question led to bold headlines. Commentators, both

TABLE 5.1 Voter Survey on Abortion

The question: Which of the following comes closest to your position? Abortion should be	Percent of all voters 2004	Percent of all voters 2000	Percent of Bush voters 2004	Percent of Bush voters 2000
Legal in all cases	21	23	25	25
Legal in most cases	34	33	38	38
Illegal in most cases	26	27	73	69
Illegal in all cases	16	13	77	74

Source: 2004 National Election Pool (NEP). Surveys conducted for The Associated Press and television networks by Edison Media Research/Mitofsky International among 13,660 voters nationwide. 2000 results from Voter News Service (VNS) based on 13,130 respondents.

Democrats and Republicans, declared moral values as the ascendant political force capturing the hearts and minds of American voters.

Republicans claimed moral values voters as their base. Democrats fought over how to capture this vote. Rethinking the push for gay marriage in order to appeal to moral values voters was on the top of most lists. California Senator Diane Feinstein expressed the views of many Democrats when she lamented, "The whole issue has been too much too fast, too soon. People aren't ready for it."[2] Hilary Rosen of the Human Rights Campaign worried that this election "may have shown us that the change agents for gay marriage are looking too much like a noisy red Ferrari speeding down quiet Main Street."[3]

The exit poll question that caused this hubbub is methodologically flawed, and the use of the question as the linchpin for explaining the changing tides of American politics suggests it served an ideological agenda or a need to tell a new story more than an analytic assessment. In reality, the percentage differences in what voters claimed shaped their choice are tiny, and the result was further skewed by the pollsters' choice of which issues to aggregate and which to present separately.

Asked which one issue mattered most in deciding their vote (see Table 5.2), 22 precent checked off moral values, 20 percent picked jobs and the economy, followed by 19 percent choosing terrorism, and 15 percent citing the war in Iraq. Substantively, there was not a significant difference in the percentage of the electorate picking moral values relative to the economy and terrorism. Much has been made of the fact that 80 percent of the voters who cited moral values voted for Bush. One can make the case that the economy was equally important, given that 80 percent of economy-driven voters cast their ballots for Kerry.

TABLE 5.2 Voter Survey on Issues

The question: Which one issue mattered most in deciding how you voted for president? (Check only one)	Percent of all voters	Percent of Kerry voters*	Percent of Bush voters*
Taxes	5	43	57
Education	4	73	26
Iraq	15	73	26
Terrorism	19	14	86
Economy/jobs	20	80	18
Moral values	22	18	80
Health care	8	77	23
Moral values	22		
Domestic issues	37		
National security	34		

Source: National Election Pool (NEP). Surveys conducted for The Associated Press and television networks by Edison Media Research/Mitofsky International among 13,660 voters nationwide.
*Moral values, domestic issues and national security values not available to the author.

The over-interpretation of this poll question goes beyond the common media mistake of aggrandizing small differences that do not have statistical or substantive significance. There is a serious methodological flaw in the writing of the exit poll question as well; when asking voters to choose only one issue that mattered most to them in deciding how to vote, it is important to have consistency in the choices offered.

"Moral values" represents a constellation of concerns, not one specific issue. Had the wording of the question clustered Iraq and terrorism under national security, mentioned by 34 percent of the electorate, or collected specific policies under domestic issues, mentioned by 37 percent of voters, the conversation about electoral outcomes would be very different. So, too, if the question had disaggregated moral values into separate policy issues such as abortion, stem cell research, and gay rights, past polls consistently show that very few voters pick these issues as being decisive to their choice for president.

Gary Langer, the ABC News Polling director, pointed out the methodological problems with the "choose one issue" question in a *New York Times* opinion piece after the election, underscoring that this "poorly devised exit poll question and a dose of spin are threatening to undermine our understanding of the 2004 presidential election." Langer clarified that while morals and values are critical in informing political judgments, they tap into personal characteristics that capture a different dimension of the vote decision rather than a discrete political issue such as the economy or terrorism; he concluded that "conflating the two distorts the story of Tuesday's election."[4]

A follow-up study by the Pew Research Center for the People and the Press illustrates the way in which this question wording created response bias. Pew conducted a post-election survey November 5–8, 2004 among 1,209 voters who were originally interviewed in October. The survey finds that when moral values is pitted against issues like the Iraq war and terrorism as was the case in the exit poll, a plurality of voters (27 percent) cited moral values as most important to their vote, followed by the war in Iraq (22 percent), the economy (21 percent), and terrorism (14 percent). When a separate group of voters was asked an open-ended question about their top issue, the war in Iraq and the economy moved past moral values. The war in Iraq was picked by 27 percent, the economy by 14 percent, and moral values tied with terrorism at 9 percent.

The Pew survey followed up with participants who volunteered moral values as a deciding factor, by asking, "What comes to mind when you think about moral values?" Just over four in ten of those who picked moral values from the list mentioned issues like gay marriage and abortion (less than 4 percent of the electorate). Others talked about qualities like religion, helping the poor, and the candidates' honesty and strength of leadership. Andrew Kohut, director of the Pew Research Center, concluded that social conservative issues like abortion, gay rights, and stem cell research were not anywhere near as important as the economy and the war in Iraq.[5]

Gay marriage never emerged as a very important electoral issue relative to other items on the political agenda. Prior to the election, when registered voters were asked to rate the importance of specific policies in helping determine their vote, they consistently rated the economy, terrorism, jobs, and the war in Iraq as the most important concerns. In open-ended questions, gay marriage never reached double digits. When voters were asked to rank its importance, same-sex marriage rated relatively unimportant in comparison to economic issues, national security, health care, or education.

In a mid-October Pew survey, respondents were asked how important a whole host of issues were in deciding how to cast their vote (see Table 5.3): very important, somewhat important, not too important, or not important at all. The usual suspects topped the very important list—the economy (78 percent), terrorism (77 percent), jobs (76 percent), education (75 percent), war in Iraq (74 percent), and health care (73 percent). Moral values, with myriad meanings, was selected as very important by 63 percent. The specific issues tied to that agenda were ranked at the bottom of most important concerns and gay marriage was at the very bottom of the list. Abortion was rated as very important to their vote decision by 47 percent of voters,

TABLE 5.3 Voter Decisions Based on Issues (Listed by Percent)

The question: In making your decision about whom to vote for, will the issue of (insert item) be very important, somewhat important, not too important, or not at all important?	Very important	Somewhat important	Not too important	Not at all important
The economy	78	18	3	1
Terrorism	77	17	3	2
Jobs*	76	19	4	1
Education*	75	20	3	2
Iraq	74	20	3	2
Health care*	73	22	4	1
Social Security*	65	27	6	2
Moral values	63	23	8	4
Taxes*	59	31	7	2
The federal budget*	57	32	7	3
Abortion	47	27	12	11
Gun control	45	31	14	8
Stem cell research	43	31	14	7
Gay marriage	32	22	19	24

Source: Pew Research Center for the People and the Press. October 15–19, 2004 (N = 1,307 Registered Voters). * Only asked of half the sample.

followed by gun control (45 percent), stem cell research (43 percent), and gay marriage (32 percent). Forty-three percent of voters said gay marriage was not particularly important to how they were voting, higher than any other issue on the list.

Marriage Bans Did Not Result in Higher Turnout among Christian Conservatives

Compared with 2000, the 2004 turnout brought no increase whatsoever in the portion of the voting electorate who attend church on a weekly or more frequent basis—42 percent of all voters in 2000 were weekly churchgoers, and 42 percent of this year's voters were weekly churchgoers. Moreover, President Bush's share of the vote among weekly churchgoers was not significantly higher in 2004 than it was in 2000. If anything, his support grew among people who do not attend church frequently (see Table 5.4).

TABLE 5.4 Church Attendance and Voter Preference

The question: How often do you attend religious services?	Percent of all voters 2004	Percent of all voters 2000	Percent of Bush voters 2004	Percent of Bush voters 2000
More than once a week	16	14	64	63
Once a week	26	28	58	57
A few times a month	14	14	50	46
A few times a year	28	28	45	42
Never	15	14	36	32

Source: 2004 National Election Pool (NEP). Surveys conducted for The Associated Press and television networks by Edison Media Research/Mitofsky International among 13,660 voters nationwide. 2000 results from Voter News Service (VNS) based on 13,130 respondents.

There is no evidence that evangelicals constituted a larger share of the vote in 2004. However, there is evidence that the electorate was more conservative than in 2000. The percentage of voters who said they considered themselves conservative on political matters increased from 30 percent in 2000 to 34 percent in 2004. These conservative gains, however, were virtually the same among less frequent churchgoers as among those who attend church at least once a week. Similarly, turnout among Republicans who do not attend religious services regularly was up at least as much as among those who are regular churchgoers.

Actual turnout figures provide little conclusive evidence that having a gay-marriage ban on the ballot increased turnout. Marriage ban states did see higher turnouts than states without such measures, but the differences are relatively small—59.9 percent turnout in marriage-ban states compared to 59.1 percent turnout elsewhere. Moreover, this difference in turnout was largely a function of the fact that three of the initiative states were also highly contested battleground states. Turnout in battleground states was 7.5 percent higher than in less-competitive states.[6]

Bush Did Not Perform Especially Well Where Gay Marriage Was on the Ballot

The President's vote share averaged seven points higher in gay marriage-banning states than in other states (57.9 percent vs. 50.9 percent).[7] This is attributed to the fact that eight of the eleven states (Arkansas, Georgia, Kentucky, Mississippi, Montana, North Dakota, Oklahoma, and Utah) have voted Republican in most of the recent presidential elections. Four years earlier, when gay marriage was not on the agenda in these same states, his share was 7.3 percent higher than in other states.

Overall, the mean increase in Bush support was 2.8 percent in states without gay marriage amendments compared to 2.5 percent in states with ballot initiatives, a difference that is not statistically significant.[8] None of the six states in which Bush's share of the vote increased the most from 2000 to 2004 (Hawaii, Rhode Island, New Jersey, Alabama, Tennessee, Connecticut) had anti-same-sex marriage initiatives on the ballot. Three of the ten states where Bush's share of the vote increased the least did have same-sex marriage initiatives on the ballot—Montana, Oregon, and Ohio.

Contrary to conventional wisdom, Bush did less well in battleground states with anti-same-sex marriage initiatives than in battleground states that did not have these ballot measures. Michigan and Oregon voters passed anti-gay marriage initiatives but gave the presidential race to Kerry. Bush won Ohio, but Kerry ran substantially better there in 2004 than Gore did in 2000, winning 48.5 percent of the vote compared to Gore's 46.5 percent. A preliminary analysis of voter turnout across all eighty-eight Ohio counties concluded that mobilization for the same-sex marriage initiative had no net effect on the outcome of the presidential election in Ohio.[9]

Gay Marriage and the Future of Gay Rights

This is not to suggest that the public supports gay marriage. It does not, as clearly demonstrated by the passage of anti-same-sex marriage initiatives in thirteen states during the past election year. Marriage is the cutting edge issue facing the long, hard-fought movement for gay rights. It marks an effort to advance beyond tolerance of private sexual behavior to acceptance through publicly sanctioned institutions.

Current mobilization in opposition to gay marriage is reminiscent of the furor around President Clinton's decision to drop the ban on gays in the military that led to the compromising "Don't Ask, Don't Tell" policy. Nearly six in ten Americans opposed allowing openly gay men and lesbians to serve in the military. Clinton's 58 percent job approval after inauguration dropped to 37 percent according to Gallup polls. The debate raged on for six months, as powerful military and congressional opposition to lifting the ban was spearheaded by Gen. Colin Powell, then-chairman of the Joint Chiefs of Staff, and former Sen. Sam Nunn (D, Ga.), chairman of the Senate Armed Services Committee. The hearings were televised; anti-gay sentiments ran high.

The "Don't Ask, Don't Tell" debate over gays in the military opened a new public conversation around gay rights, albeit at the high cost of many people's careers. In the decade since the Clinton Administration adopted "Don't Ask, Don't Tell," public support for allowing openly gay men and women to serve in the military has increased from 40 percent in the 1993

NBC/*Wall Street Journal* survey to 63 percent in the November 2004 CNN/ *USA Today*/Gallup poll.[10] In this same period, Gallup reported the number of people saying homosexuality is an acceptable lifestyle increased from 38 percent in 1992 to 54 percent in 2004. A majority of Americans (52 percent) currently believe sex between two consenting adults of the same sex should be legal, up from 32 percent in 1986.[11]

A similar pattern is emerging around the debate over gay marriage, with civil unions currently being promoted as the middle ground in much the same way that "Don't Ask, Don't Tell" served as the compromise position on lifting the ban on gays in the military. While a majority of voters remain opposed to gay marriage, Gallup reports showed an increase in public acceptance of marriage in recent years. The number of Americans who believe marriage between homosexuals should be recognized by law as valid, with the same rights as traditional marriage, increased from 27 percent in 1996 to 42 percent in 2004. When asked to choose among favoring legal marriage for homosexuals, favoring civil unions but not marriage, or being opposed to any legal recognition of gay relationships, most polls show majority support for some form of recognition (combining legal and civil union). In the latest CBS News/*New York Times* poll taken mid-November 2004, 53 percent favored recognition (21 percent favored legal marriage, 32 percent said civil unions), whereas 44 percent opposed any legal recognition of same sex relationships (see Table 5.5).

TABLE 5.5 Voter Views on Gay Unions (Listed by Percent)

The question: Which comes closest to your view? Gay couples should be allowed to legally marry. Gay couples should be allowed to form civil unions but not legally marry. There should be no legal recognition of a gay couple's relationship.	Legal Marriage	Civil Unions	No Legal Recognition	Unsure
ALL VOTERS	21	32	44	3
Republicans	9	36	54	1
Democrats	31	30	36	3
Independents	21	32	43	4
Trend				
7/11–15/04	28	31	38	3
5/20–23/04	28	29	40	3
3/10-14/04	22	33	40	5

Source: CBS News/*New York Times* Poll. Nov. 18–21, 2004. $N = 885$ adults nationwide. MoE ± 3 (for all adults).

Conclusion

Political parties win elections. Political factions fight over the interpretation of that victory and the manipulation of its meaning, what is commonly referred to as "spin." It is not the purpose of this chapter to suggest that moral values had no impact on the 2004 presidential election. Rather, this chapter challenges the assertion that moral values in general, and gay marriage in particular, was the driving force behind President Bush's victory. To the contrary, the evidence suggests that gay marriage and the presence of anti-same-sex marriage initiatives had almost no impact on turnout or on the election results.

This disconnect between perception and reality raises a larger question of why this emphasis on moral values became, and continues to be, the dominant strategic lesson of this election campaign? Part of the answer is the pressures, no doubt, surrounding political reporting, finding something new and newsworthy to say. Part of the answer is also that victors write history, and Karl Rove won. But another significant part of the answer remains a reflection of individual personal values. There is a great deal more tolerance of gays and lesbians in America today than there was a decade ago, but we have not yet reached acceptance. The public's readiness to latch on to the moral values explanation is a reflection of its discomfort with public debates about moral values.

Elections are rarely decided by one factor. A multivariate analysis of the roots of the Bush vote is likely to shed some much-needed light on the subject. That analysis, however, must wait until raw data from the exit polls are made publicly available or until the release of the National Election Studies conducted by the University of Michigan. Only then will political scientists have the opportunity to take a rigorous look at the 2004 decision-making process. Unfortunately, by then the election story will have been long written, political strategies will be in place, and there will be little public interest in revisiting the past.

Notes

1. Christopher Muste, "Hidden in Plain Sight," *Washington Post*, December 12, 2004; B04.
2. "Same-Sex Marriage Issue Key to Some G.O.P. Races," *New York Times*, November 14, 2004; Section P, 4.
3. Ellen Goodman, "Must Gay Rights Wait for Our 'Comfort'?" *Boston Globe*, December 16, 2004.
4. Gary Langer, "A Question of Values," *New York Times*, November 6, 2004.
5. "Survey: Format Influenced Voter Priorities," *USA Today*, November 12, 2004.
6. Paul Freedman, "The Gay Marriage Myth," *Slate*, November 5, 2004.
7. Ibid.
8. Simon Jackman, "Same Sex Marriage Ballot Initiatives and Conservative Mobilization in the 2004 Election." Presentation at Institute for Research in the Social Sciences (IRiSS), Stanford University, November 9, 2004.

9. Ibid.

10. Heather Mason, "Gays in Military: Public Says Go Ahead and Tell," Gallup News Service, December 21, 2004.

11. The Gallup Organization Trends: Homosexual Relations 1977–May 2005 (http://www.gallup.com/poll/content/default.aspx?ci=1651).

CHAPTER 6

Some Thoughts on Institutional Life and "The Rest of the Closet"

JOHN BRIGHAM

This chapter is about the Supreme Court learning what it means to be gay. The time period is between the Court's rulings in *Bowers v. Hardwick* (1986) and *Lawrence* (2003). Oral argument is placed at the center of this process. Argument is the visible expression of ongoing relationships that constitute the institutional life of the Court. Standing before the bench in *Lawrence* was attorney Paul M. Smith who argued against the constitutionality of the Texas sodomy law. Smith, described as openly gay, had been at the Court as a law clerk to Supreme Court Justice Lewis Powell in 1980–1981. Powell's highly publicized reassessment of his vote to uphold the Georgia law in *Bowers* laid the foundation for *Lawrence*. I will examine the significance of the Court's public embrace of Smith's sexual orientation against the backdrop of denial and homophobia that surrounded *Bowers*.

First, some background. On December 4, 2002, a few days after the Supreme Court decided to hear the gay rights case of *Lawrence v. Texas* and the affirmative action cases from Michigan that would define the Court's 2002–2003 term, Linda Greenhouse speculated in the *New York Times* on the impact that a justice's personal life has on his opinions.[1] In particular she considered the significance for the *Bowers* decision of Justice Lewis F.

Powell, Jr.'s purported lack of experience with homosexuals, or, in the words
of the *Lawrence* argument, persons who have intimate same-sex relationships. This was an extraordinary rumination by the nation's most authoritative news source. According to scholars consulted by Greenhouse, this
acknowledged lack of familiarity with gays and lesbians extended beyond
Justice Powell to the whole Supreme Court of the 1980s. Greenhouse's
account of the gap between what it meant to be homosexual and the
justices' understanding of this sexual orientation during Powell's tenure on
the Court is important because it changed in twenty years. The account of
this aspect of the high court by the senior correspondent for the *New York
Times* was prescient, prophetic, and, because it was the "*Times,*" perhaps
also determinative for *Lawrence*. This chapter addresses what that article
broached but could only suggest—the understanding of intimacy and sexual
orientation at the Court.

As it turned out, the *Lawrence* opinion revealed a noticeable shift in the
Court's sensitivity to homosexuality. This leads some to speculate that in
the period since *Bowers* the Supreme Court had been transformed and that
the familiarity is institutional. It was now comfortable with—some would
even say sensitive to—the gay community. This chapter examines the institutional dimensions of what seems like a sort of institutional gaydar.

Ultimately, Paul M. Smith argued *Lawrence*. Smith is a former clerk to
Justice Powell. He was at the Court in the *Bowers* era. He is an experienced
appellate advocate and is openly gay. What it means for the Court to recognize homosexuality as a part of its institutional life reverses "the classic
coming out narrative".[2] The transformation for the Supreme Court is, in
fact, more like the institutional acquisition of gaydar. Awareness comes from
being around clerks like Paul Smith and knowing they are gay. This institutional gaydar comes from the intimate relations that are legal. These are
the struggles over meaning, policy, and law that form the basis for life as
a law student, a clerk, or an appellate advocate. These struggles are intertwined with knowledge of social life, including sexual orientation.

The Court and the Closet

Ms. Greenhouse told her readers, with the gay rights cases of *Bowers v.
Hardwick* and *Lawrence v. Texas* in mind, that we should draw "lessons on
how life informs" opinions from recent history, particularly the life history
of Justice Powell.[3] This was an uncompromising reflection on judicial
motivation from perhaps the most influential source for what the Supreme
Court is doing. But, Greenhouse also left a bit to the imagination with
regard to what the newspaper's and her own motivation was; therefore, the
meaning of the article was a bit cryptic.

The article was thoughtful. It incorporated commentary from recent scholarship on the Court and its members. It reflected upon the enduring question of how free the justices can be from their bodies. The article also played on the lore of the institution. This included the robing closet that sits just behind the courtroom where oral arguments are held. The closet is the place where the justices have traditionally shaken each other by the hand before going into public to hear arguments on the great constitutional issues of the day. It is the closet that they come out of when they part the purple curtain and take their seats behind the bench in the courtroom. While they did not come out of that closet for *Lawrence,* they did learn to recognize others coming out. This was sometime after they had worked in the Marble Temple.

Between *Bowers* and *Lawrence,* scholars Joyce Murdoch and Deb Price published an important book. Their *Courting Justice*[4] chronicles the relationship between the Court and the gay community as an increasingly open engagement. Their story begins in what they call the "hyper-closeted days" of the 1950s and traces the interaction of the gay and lesbian community with the Court, a place they say "eventually" comes to terms with the forces that blow through American society.[5] They trace the homosexual cases from Justice Frank Murphy's tortured relationships with women and Justice Tom Clark's tortured handling of *Rosenberg v. Fleuti* in 1963 to *Bowers, Boy Scouts v. Dale,* and *Romer v. Evans.* They make it almost to *Lawrence,* as it turns out. The authors have the Court reacting to the growing legitimacy of legal claims brought by the gay and lesbian community.[6] These legal scholars investigate the institutional life of the Court as they report on twenty-two homosexual former Supreme Court clerks, eighteen gay men and four lesbians.

Rethinking *Bowers*

In her article, Greenhouse was addressing, specifically, how Justice Lewis Powell had dealt with the issue of same-sex intimacy himself after participating in the decision of *Bowers v. Hardwick.* Powell came to the Court in 1972, an appointee of President Richard M. Nixon. He participated in more than two dozen homosexual cases by the time the Court considered *Bowers.* He retired at the end of the 1986–1987 term, a year after *Bowers* and a few days after participating in the gay Olympics decision.[7]

According to biographer and former clerk, John C. Jefferies, Jr., Powell had remarked that he had never known a homosexual.[8] Greenhouse quotes Powell as saying, "I don't believe I've ever met a homosexual."[9] Justice Powell told this to one of his clerks while the *Bowers* case was pending before the Court. The clerk, who was gay, replied, "Certainly you have, but you just don't know that they are."[10]

A few years after he retired, on October 18, 1990, in the question period following the James Madison Lecture at New York University Law School, Powell had been asked about his decision in *Bowers* and he famously commented to the effect that he had made a mistake in that case. Asked about reconciling his *Bowers* and his *Roe* opinions he said about *Bowers*, "I think I probably made a mistake on that one."[11] Jefferies reports that Lawrence Tribe tried to get Powell to put it in writing, but the Justice declined.

Murdoch and Price's *Courting Justice* came out a decade later and the impact of openly gay and lesbian lawyers was part of a politics of transformation that led to this extraordinary book. Like Bob Woodward and Scott Armstrong's *The Brethren* and Edward Lazarus' *Closed Chambers*[12] before it, the book is full of insider information drawn from interviews with clerks to the Supreme Court's justices. And like books such as David Garrow's *Liberty and Sexuality*,[13] *Courting Justice* is attentive to the interplay of personal relations, political interests, and legal thought that leads to the development of constitutional doctrine.

Addressing the matter of Justice Powell's contact with the gay community, Murdoch and Price state that in each of six consecutive terms in the 1980s one of Justice Powell's four law clerks was gay. But they adhere to the notion that Powell did not acknowledge homosexuality, that is, he did not recognize homosexuality as a practice. Murdoch and Price describe a situation later in Powell's life when one of his former clerks died of AIDS. They indicate that Powell, though he was compassionate, would not face the disease and its implications.[14] Jefferies also examines Powell's understanding of homosexuality. He distinguishes between Powell knowing homosexuals with a vague awareness of what their lifestyle entailed, and acknowledging them as homosexuals. The distinction is one in the meaning we accord to experience. In Powell's case, perhaps like the Court in *Bowers*, the experience of homosexuality was only minimally developed. In the practices by which Powell lived, homosexuality did not have a place. This is the sort of distinction that is at the heart of the institutional shift from the denial in *Bowers* to the acknowledgement if not embrace of homosexuality in *Lawrence*.[15]

What can we say about presenting the experience of being gay, or the human quality of homosexuality, to the Supreme Court (and about how the Court responds)? Necessarily the institution rather than the individual justices becomes the relevant context. The analytic issue is how Justices, clerks, secretaries, and institutional hangers-on convey the message of gayness and what it means for the institution to acknowledge the practice. It becomes a matter, in this sense, of how the Court comes in contact with the culture. It is a sort of ontology of the closet.[16] Rumors of Justice Frank Murphy's homosexuality or those that have swirled around the bachelorhood of Justice David Souter do not constitute the orientation of the Court. But how the rumors are treated and whether they are acknowledged becomes important. Ultimately, it is institutional practice that is relevant.

Murdoch and Price's reporting is framed by institutional analysis. Much of the discussion calls attention to individual predispositions in a fashion similar to that suggested by Greenhouse. For instance, *Courting Justice* has an extensive discussion of Justice Tom Clark's treatment of homosexuality in *Boutilier v. INS*, in which he wrote the majority opinion.[17] This was a 1966 case that considered the constitutionality of a federal statute that barred homosexuals from admission to the United States. Clark coined the phrase "afflicted with homosexuality" to uphold the statute. Murdoch and Price draw on interviews with Clark's children, including former Attorney General Ramsey Clark, to demonstrate that Tom Clark personally was aware of homosexuality and supportive of a much-loved nephew who was gay.[18]

The buzz around Paul M. Smith incorporated being gay and being a distinguished advocate. The totality was significant by the time he stood up before the bench in 2003. But when we say or others have said that the gayness of attorney Paul Smith reached the Justices, we start with the fact that the Court, as an institution, knew Paul Smith. Here, the institutional gaydar is tempered with the rarefied experiences and personal connections that characterize this elite institution. The culture had shifted and Smith was part of the shift. It wasn't only at the fringes of sexuality that people could tell who was gay. Even the Supreme Court could tell, and this was without the drama of coming out directly to the Justices.

Smith graduated from Amherst College in 1976 and received his law degree from Yale Law School in 1979. After graduation from law school, Smith became a clerk for James L. Oakes of the Second Circuit. Oakes' clerkships, in rustic Brattleboro, Vermont, have long been an entrée to the Supreme Court. They are also famously intimate in the relationships established between the clerks, Judge Oakes, and his family. After his year with Oakes, Smith became a clerk at the Supreme Court for the 1980–1981 term. This was five years before *Bowers*, so it's pretty clear that Smith was not out to Justice Powell, whom he served, but who said even years after that he had not met a gay person.

As an openly gay lawyer, Smith came out at some point after he left the Court and came back to argue the case as a gay man. He was described at a Stonewall Bar dinner as an "openly gay partner" at Jenner and Block.

For the Court or even a few of the Justices to know the advocate is certainly an asset in any oral argument before the Supreme Court. Familiarity is what gives celebrity its buzz and movie stars their cache. In the case of the Court the unknown attorney presenting before the bench is not without precedent. In many cases, the prestige of an appearance before the Court pushes attorneys to accept the assignment of this most rarefied form of advocacy when more experienced attorneys would jump at the chance. The results are mixed. The Justices often complain about the quality of advocacy before them. Yet Sarah Weddington, who argued *Roe,* was unknown and quite young when she stood before the bench. She famously held onto the job when others would eagerly have bumped her for the prestigious assignment.[19]

Oral Argument

Oral argument, though often of interest to the public, has not been a focus of much scholarly attention because, in general, the arguments have not been readily available and they are not part of the formal, official record of the cases.[20] There are exceptions. David O'Brien quotes Chief Justice Hughes and Justice Brennan on how much argument meant to them. He mentions that arguments come at a crucial time and "focus the minds of the justices and present the possibility for fresh perspectives on a case."[21] He also says that arguments were more important in the nineteenth century when they were more extensive and the amount of printed submission was quite a bit less voluminous. I have examined the institutional practices that constitute what I called "the Cult of the Court,"[22] and discussed the unique public phenomenon of oral argument. Later, in 1994, after legal historian Peter Irons had made materials on many of the greatest Supreme Court arguments available, in spite of the preferences of the Court,[23] social science scholars held a panel on oral argument at the Political Science Meeting in New York City in which we discussed ethnographic considerations.

At the very formal and outwardly staid Supreme Court, the justices engage in behavior during oral argument that, in most contexts, would simply seem rude.[24] Attorneys making the most important appearances of their career are routinely and mercilessly interrupted as they argue their side in the dispute. Attorneys before the Court are well aware of the tradition, although some seem inadequately prepared. The attorneys must shift focus and build on interests expressed by the justices in brief but pithy exchanges. This makes the experience not only intense because of its magnitude but tricky because of the spontaneity involved. This rewards experienced practitioners and the best make a great deal of money for their few minutes before the bench. Indeed, as I argued in *The Cult of the Court,* "practices like oral argument … determine more than who wins and who loses. They affect the substance and the quality of the Court's work, and … what we take to be the law."[25]

Court arguments are spontaneous and interactive. I think of them as improvisations.[26] The arguments are sometimes funny and often engaging. There is always an element of theater. But, this is a theater of law and the drama is a function of the stakes and the setting. It is not dramatic in the sense of a Broadway play, and the relationship between the Justices and the audience seems to be entirely different. The humor is sometimes intentional but often arises from mistakes. The spontaneity is a function of the practice of proceeding more like a seminar than a lecture. This is important to those who wish the law to be rooted in academic practice or at least to those for whom academic practice is related to inquiry and intelligence. It is also interesting because this somewhat arcane discursive practice has a bearing on the issue of broadcasting these arguments.

Jefferies examined the argument in *Bowers* carefully and was puzzled by the institutional response to the case, and Powell's place in it.[27] Jefferies felt that *Bowers* might have been a replay of *Bakke* with Justice Powell playing a pivotal role balancing the poles of opinion on the Court, except that Powell joined the majority opinion. Although Jefferies calls this move by Powell "the greatest mystery of his career,"[28] the mystery is relatively easy to solve given the failure to acknowledge homosexuality.

There is considerable debate currently as to whether oral arguments should be televised. The full blown visual performance is not available because the justices have not wanted it to be. My analysis of the performance of oral argument suggests that it shouldn't be televised. However, with available technology and access, you can hear the justices talking about law during arguments.[29] The qualities of law as a linguistic activity are more precisely and unmitigatedly evident during oral argument than they are in the written opinions. Argument serves today the way the presentation of opinion in open court did years ago. It links the Justices to the ideas and concepts of the law. There is an element of performance but, unlike in the theater, the Justices are not directly appealing to the audience in the room. The audience appears to be the other Justices and the attorneys as in a conversation. This is why it makes such little sense to televise the proceedings.

In thinking about televising the proceeding and why the Court resists, the distinctive character of this activity deserves note.[30] Like athletics, where the outcome is not known prior to playing the game and like talk shows where unscripted things are meant to happen, argument before the Court takes form as improvisation. There is a tradition at the Court closely related to that of improvisational theater.[31] The huge difference is that the audience, in the traditional sense, has relatively little influence on the proceedings and huge significance for future events. Argument is more like a rehearsal or even a script conference. Some of the commentary that is to follow will address how the Court improvises with reference to the nature of debate on the Constitution and the implications for more media attention to this part of the governing process.

The oral argument in *Lawrence* took place March 26, 2003. Paul M. Smith argued for the petitioner John Lawrence and Charles A. Rosenthal presented the case for Texas.[32] The selections that follow are chosen with an eye on the issue of coming out to the Court, of representing sexual orientation to the Justices so that they might know someone who is gay.[33]

> Mr. Smith: The one thing, that I submit the court, the state should not be able to come in to say is: We are going to permit ourselves, the majority of people in our society, full and free rein to make these decisions for ourselves, but there's one minority of people [who] don't get that decision and the only reason we're going to give you is we want it that way. We want them to be unequal in their choices and their freedoms, because we think we should have the right to commit adultery, to commit fornication, to commit sodomy. And the state should have no basis for intruding into our lives, but we don't want those people over there to have the same right.

In one sense, the subtlety of Smith's use of terms relating to sex, particularly who is doing it, is significant for what he presents to the Justices. Smith is comfortable with the terms, or seems to be. The Justices, for the most part, are less engaged here and most of them might be expected to discuss them with some awkwardness. Justice Scalia, on the other hand, just weighs in, showing a zest for the delicate give and take.

> Justice Antonin Scalia: So the same-sex/other-sex aspect doesn't come into it ...
> Mr. Smith: I think it does come into it, because if you are going to suggest that the state of the law on the books in the nineteenth century is the touchstone you have to take into account that in the nineteenth century at least on the face of the law married couples were regulated in terms of their forms of sexual intimacy that were created for them.

In dealing with Justice Scalia there is evidence of the tradition that the argument is focused at the center of the Court. That framework taken in the context of the issue here suggests that Smith might be less interested in coming out to Justice Scalia, though sometimes to be subject to his assaults can win favor in other corners. This seemed to be true when Justice Ginsburg followed the above exchange with a very supportive intervention of her own.

Of course, in most places in the argument, attorney Smith is not representing gayness. He is demonstrating legal expertise. He is very good at putting a social and political discussion into the language of constitutional rights, but this is the point about how the institution confronts homosexuality in the context of oral argument and the institutional engagement for which it is the centerpiece. For instance, early in the argument Smith had this exchange.

> Justice Scalia: These moral judgments. You can make it sound very puritanical, the, you know, the laws against bigamy. I mean, who are you to tell me that I can't have more than one wife, you blue-nose bigot? Sure, you can make it sound that way, but these are laws dealing with public morality. They've always been on the book; nobody has ever told them they're unconstitutional simply because there are moral perceptions behind them. Why is this different from bigamy?
> Mr. Smith: First of all, the first law that's appeared on the books in the states of this country that singles out only same-sex sodomy appeared in the 60's and the 70's, and it did not—and it does not—go way back, this kind of discrimination.
>
> Now, bigamy involves protection of an institution that the state creates for its own purposes, and there are all sorts of potential justifications about the need to protect the institution of marriage that are different in kind from the justifications that could be offered here involving merely a criminal statute that says we're going to regulate these people's behaviors, we include a criminal law which is where the most heightened form of people protection analysis ought to apply.
>
> This case is very much like McLaughlin, Your Honor, where you have a statute that said, we're going to give a specially heightened penalty to cohabitation, but only when it involves a white person with a black person. That interracial cohabitation is different, and the state there made the argument, we're merely regulating a particular form of conduct, and that's a different form of conduct than interracial cohabitation. And this court very clearly said, No, you're classifying people; and that classification has to be justified.
>
> And this court at many times said a merely disapproval of one group of people, whether it be the hippy communes in Moreno or the mentally retarded in Cleburne, or indeed gay people.... .

It is unusual for Justice Scalia to listen this patiently to this during oral argument once he has engaged with an attorney on a point of law. In general, Scalia represents the old view of homosexuality as outside the social realm of the Court, though you get this sense that this is a political commitment rather than lack of knowledge or interest. While what turns out to be the Court's view depends on how much or how little Scalia influences his colleagues, the prospect of a political position is based on a different awareness than that of the *Bowers* Court.

> Justice Scalia: A justification is the same that's alluded to here, disapproval of homosexuality.
> Mr. Smith: Well, I think it would be highly problematic, such a custody case.
> Justice Scalia: Yes, it would?

Mr. Smith: If that were the only justification that could be offered, there was not some showing that there would be any more concrete harm to the children in the school. ...[34]

Smith's expertise in privacy law and the ways of the Supreme Court appear to have overshadowed his representativeness as a gay lawyer. Because of the context—his representation for the Lambda Legal Defense Fund— Smith did not have to say anything that did not directly contribute to his legal position in the case. He succeeded in making homosexuality a legitimate sexual orientation by his own skill in appellate advocacy. He did not so much fail to make his sexuality explicit as succeed in presenting himself as part of the Court's institutional life. Before the Court, Smith was not simply a gay advocate; he was a distinguished practitioner, one of the elite lawyers who practice regularly before the Supreme Court. In the same term, Smith also argued the important case pitting the American Library Association against federal law requiring filtering access to the Internet in libraries that received federal funds. The following term, in the fall of 2003, Smith argued the political gerrymandering case—one of the year's most important—*Vieth v. Jubelier.*

The result is an opinion by Justice Anthony Kennedy of California that demonstrates considerable sensitivity in returning to *Bowers*, reinvigorating the value of privacy in the Constitution, and elevating the status of homosexuality to protected class. It speaks with a concern about the constitutional value that is driven by a sense that privacy had been improperly denied to homosexuals nearly twenty years before.[35]

It concludes with the manifesto, "times can blind us to certain truths and later generations can see that laws once thought necessary and proper in fact serve only to oppress. As the Constitution endures, persons in every generation can invoke its principles in their own search for greater meaning."[36] This is a long way from Justice White's denial of protection to homosexuals in *Bowers* to which Powell regrettably added his name.

In April of 2003, a few weeks after the argument in *Lawrence* and partly in response to the case, Pennsylvania Republican Senator Rick Santorum compared homosexuality to incest, bigamy, and adultery, saying, "If you have a right to homosexual sex in your home ... you have a right to anything." The comments have become known more for the outrage they produced than the credibility or stature of Santorum's position.[37] In defending his statement he commented, "I have no problem with homosexuality. I have a problem with homosexual acts." While suggesting some confusion about the nature of homosexuality, the comment revealed a world divided in new ways. The activity that had once been closeted and could be ignored by a justice such as Lewis Powell, and indeed the Court itself, had now become contested terrain, out there and challenging to those who defined their lives in opposition. In the controversy over Santorum's remarks his defenders would try and distinguish between acts and the sexuality defined by them.[38] By recognizing the sexuality as part of its institutional life, the Supreme Court saw the acts as protected.

Conclusion

In this collection, others will comment in greater depth on the opinion handed down on sodomy and privacy at the end of June 2003, but the tone much spoken about in Justice Kennedy's majority opinion and cited above reflects a change in the Court's position that can be attributed to sensitivities developed in the Court. That change is exemplified in the evolution of Justice Powell's thinking and the elevation of Paul M. Smith to accomplished advocate before the bench. It is also the product of an evolution reflected in the out-of-body collective expression that is a ruling of the Court written, in this case, by Justice Kennedy.

Notes

1. Linda Greenhouse, "Black Robes Don't Make the Justice, but the Rest of the Closet Just Might," *New York Times*, December 4, 2002, A23.
2. See Susan Burgess, "Did the Supreme Court Come Out in *Bush v. Gore*? Queer Theory on the Performance of the Politics of Shame," forthcoming in *Differences: A Journal of Feminist Cultural Studies*, Spring 2005.
3. Greenhouse.
4. Joyce Murdoch and Deb Price, *Courting Justice: Gay Men and Lesbians v. the Supreme Court* (New York: Basic Books, 2001): 23.
5. Ibid., 6.
6. Eighty-seven cases with some bearing on the interaction between gay men and lesbians and the Supreme Court.
7. *SFAA v. USOC*, June 25, 1987.
8. John C. Jefferies, Jr. *Justice Lewis F. Powell, Jr.* (New York: Charles Scribner's Sons, 1994): 528.
9. Greenhouse.
10. Ibid.
11. Jefferies, 530.
12. Bob Woodward and Scott Armstrong (New York: Simon and Schuster, 1979); Edward Lazarus, *Closed Chambers: The Rise, Fall, and Future of the Modern Supreme Court* (New York: Penguin Books, 1999).
13. *Liberty and Sexuality: The Right to Privacy and the Making of Roe v. Wade* (New York: Lisa Drew Books, 1994).
14. Murdoch and Price, 343.
15. Ibid., 528.
16. See Eve Sedgwick, *The Epistemology of the Closet* (Berkeley: University of California Press, 1990).
17. Decided May 22, 1967.
18. The authors of *Courting Justice* also note that Justice Fortas used the oral argument in *Boutilier* to try and educate the Court that homosexuality was not a disease (110–111) and they characterize Justice William O. Douglas, who dissented, as "completely comfortable with homosexuality" according to his wife (122).

19. In her case the juxtaposition of the young woman against the crusty male attorney representing Texas came to personify the case.
20. John R. Schmidhauser, *The Supreme Court: Its Politics, Personalities, and Procedures* (New York: Holt, Rinehart and Winston, 1963). This is an early discussion of procedures that opened the Court to scholars but had little to say about argument.
21. David M. O'Brien, *Storm Center: The Supreme Court in American Politics* (New York: Norton, 2003): 249.
22. John Brigham, *The Cult of the Court* (Philadelphia: Temple University Press, 1987).
23. Stephanie Guitton and Peter H. Irons, *May It Please the Court* (New York: The New Press, 1994).
24. Some time ago, I organized a panel on oral argument. The proceedings were published in *Law and Courts*, the newsletter of the Law and Courts Section of the American Political Science Association.
25. Brigham,176.
26. John Brigham, "Improv at the Supreme Court: The Affirmative Action Cases," Law and Society Association Meeting, Pittsburgh, June 2003.
27. Jefferies, 515.
28. Ibid., 526
29. Brigham, *Cult of the Court*, 183.
30. Erin Jackson, Honors Thesis, University of Massachusetts, Amherst.
31. See note 26.
32. Excerpts as recorded by the Alderson Reporting Company, Washington, D.C.
33. The issue arose for me in a presentation by Professor Jennifer Levi of Western New England College of Law and the Lambda Legal Defense Fund when she said Smith's advocacy brought gayness to the Court. When asked how this worked Professor Levi seemed vague. I think this vagueness arose from the mix of sensitive issues and complex institutional life that constitute this issue. Jennifer Levi, "The Court and Civil Rights: Strange Classmates, Stranger Bedfellows," Supreme Court Review Conference, Western New England College of Law, Springfield, MA, October 18, 2003.
34. A report on the oral argument by Gay & Lesbian Activists Alliance Secretary Barrett L. Brick does not mention Smith identifying himself to the Court as being gay, http://www.glaa.org/ archive/2003/ brickonlawrencevtexasorals0326.shtml.
35. Justice Kennedy writes, "In summary, the historical grounds relied upon in *Bowers* are more complex than the majority opinion and the concurring opinion by Chief Justice Burger indicate. Their historical premises are not without doubt and, at the very least, are overstated." 539 U.S. ____(2003): 10.
36. Ibid.,18.
37. Associated Press interview published April 21, 2003 (accessed at www.sfgate.com).
38. In the Massachusetts legislature's debate over how to respond to the state Supreme Court's 2003 ruling that homosexuals must be given the opportunity to marry, February 9–13, 2004, state representative Shaun Kelly personalizes his argument with "Liz, this is for you," for his colleague Elizabeth Malia who had spoken of the challenges she would face as a lesbian if her partner of thirty years were to die. Yvonne Abraham, "Debate Humanized Issue," *The Boston Sunday Globe*, February 15, 2004, B6.

CHAPTER 7

Lawrence Past[1]

DALE CARPENTER

You don't have any right to be here.[2]

Why are we all down on our knees thanking them for giving us something they should never have taken away?[3]

On the night of September 17, 1998, someone called police to report that a man was going crazy with a gun inside a Houston apartment. When Harris County sheriff's deputies entered the apartment they did not find anybody with a gun but did witness John Lawrence and Tyron Garner having sex. This violated the Texas Homosexual Conduct law, and the deputies hauled them off to jail for the night. Lawyers took the men's case to the Supreme Court and won a huge victory for gay rights.

So goes the legend of *Lawrence v. Texas.[4]* Do not believe it. In every important respect it is terribly incomplete or very questionable. It flattens into two dimensions or simply erases a rich, complex, and tangled web of emotions, frustrations, motives, deceptions, jealousies, accidents, civil disobedience, serendipitous events, heroic acts, stirring pleas, and deep prejudices. It ignores the elements of race and class present in the case. It naively accepts the word of law enforcement authorities who harshly (and perhaps corruptly) enforced a purposeless law that was lying on the state criminal code like an unused whip. It omits the role the closet played in bringing the arrest out of the closet. It ignores the bravery of a single clerk for a lowly judge. It forgets the bartender *cum* activist who had come out of his own closet, saw a moment, seized it, and made it history. It is a lie.

A number of mysteries lie at the heart of this most important gay civil rights case yet decided by the United States Supreme Court. What were the defendants actually doing when sheriff's deputies entered John Lawrence's apartment? Did the deputies really see them having sex? Was the case a set-up by gay rights activists to challenge the constitutionality of the Texas sodomy law, as some conservative groups have charged? How did the arrest of these two previously unknown men wind up in the nation's highest court instead of dying a shame-faced and anonymous death, as so many prior sodomy prosecutions had? This chapter, drawing from original interviews of people close to the case from its inception, and including much information not previously disclosed to the public, attempts to answer those questions.

Posing as Somdomites[5]: John Lawrence and Tyron Garner

Little is known publicly about the men whose arrest led to the most important gay civil rights decision in American history. According to Mitchell Katine, the Houston attorney who handled the case at the trial court level, "They're not out to be any more famous than they accidentally came to be. They're private people, and they are very happy this law has been changed, but they are just regular people."[6] "These are not professional civil rights people," says Katine.[7]

Indeed, the lawyers representing Lawrence and Garner have consistently shielded the men from public scrutiny, declining media requests (and my request) for interviews.[8] Lane Lewis, the first person known to have talked to Lawrence about the arrest shortly after he was released from his overnight stay in jail, served as the men's informal public relations manager for a time after they were arrested.[9] "My job the first couple of years was keeping the media away from these boys," says Lewis, now thirty-six years old, a gay civil rights activist, and a bartender in a Houston gay dance club.[10] Lewis instructed Lawrence and Garner not to discuss the case with any media and to refer all questions to their attorneys or to Lewis himself.[11] Some information about the men can be gleaned, however, from newspaper accounts, interviews, and the informational intake worksheets prepared by the Harris County Sheriff's Department the night Lawrence and Garner were arrested.

John Geddes Lawrence, whose apartment was entered by sheriff's deputies, was born in Beaumont, Texas, in 1943. He is white and was 55 years old at the time of the arrest.[12] One observer has described his demeanor as "more like a small-town banker than a social activist."[13] Katine describes both Lawrence and Garner as "on the quiet side, passive-type individuals."[14] At the time of the arrest, Lawrence lived on the second floor of a small Houston apartment complex. For more than a decade prior to the arrest, he worked as a medical technologist at a nearby medical center.[15] Lawrence had no prior involvement in either the gay civil rights movement or in any gay rights groups.[16]

Tyron Garner was born in Houston in 1967. He is black and was 31 years old at the time of the arrest.[17] Garner was unemployed and a Houston resident at the time.[18] He has had no steady employment since the arrest, either, working occasionally as a waiter in restaurants.[19] The sheriff's department intake worksheet for Garner lists his religious preference as Baptist.[20] Like Lawrence, he had no prior involvement in the gay civil rights movement or in any gay rights groups.[21]

Both men had had run-ins with the criminal law before. Lawrence had twice been arrested for driving while intoxicated, once in 1978 and again in 1988.[22] Garner's prior criminal record was more extensive and more serious. It included arrests for possession of marijuana and aggravated assault on a police officer in 1986, driving while intoxicated in 1990, and assault involving bodily injury in 1995.[23] Garner's prior arrests, in particular, may well have played a role in the events leading up to the encounter with the sheriff's deputies.

Nothing is known publicly about their relationship. They have consistently refused to discuss the nature of their relationship at the time of the arrest or since. For example, it is not known publicly whether they are/were committed partners, occasional sexual partners, or one-time sexual partners.[24] Katine says that the two men had known each other, at least as friends, for many years before the arrests.[25] They had been introduced to each other by Robert Royce Eubanks (now deceased), with whom Garner was romantically involved at the time of the arrest.[26] Based on his personal conversations with the men, Lewis believes that Lawrence and Garner may have been occasional sexual partners, but were not in a long-term, committed relationship when they were arrested.[27]

The Arrest: The Deputies' Version

Lawrence began with an uncommon—and unusual—police intrusion into the bedroom. The events of that night are to this day cloaked in mystery and some secrecy. They may never be known completely.

It is generally agreed the events began with a reported weapons disturbance at Lawrence's apartment shortly before 10:30 P.M. on September 17, 1998.[28] The report came from a man, later determined to be the then-41-year-old

Eubanks,[29] who likely called the Harris County Sheriff's Department from somewhere near Lawrence's apartment complex.[30] Eubanks told the dispatcher, according to the Probable Cause Affidavit filed the night of the arrest, that "a black male was going crazy in the apartment and he was armed with a gun."[31] Based on his personal contacts with Eubanks, Lewis believes it is quite likely he used a racial slur—rather than "black male"—to describe the supposed armed man. Lewis describes Royce as a "gun-totin', beer-swillin', Gilley's kickin' bubba from Pasadena [Texas]."[32]

Deputy Joseph Rich Quinn was the first to arrive[33] within minutes of getting the dispatch,[34] followed shortly thereafter by deputies William D. Lilly, Donald ("Donnie") Tipps, and Kenneth Landry.[35] According to standard procedure, Quinn took the lead because he was the first deputy on the scene. The deputies saw Eubanks at the foot of the stairs to the second-floor apartments. Eubanks motioned to Quinn and said, "Over here! Over here!" Quinn approached him and noticed he was "highly upset, shaking, and crying a little." Quinn asked, "Where is the man with the gun?" Eubanks pointed to Lawrence's second-floor apartment.[36]

Quinn, Lilly, Tipps, and Landry headed up the stairwell, guns drawn, in what is known as a "tactical stack," one deputy right behind the other. Quinn was in the lead position. When they reached the apartment Quinn saw that the door was mostly closed, but not pulled completely shut. It was resting against the doorjamb, slightly ajar, but offered no view into the apartment. Quinn checked the door knob and determined it was unlocked. He knocked on the door, which had the effect of pushing it open slightly. The light was on. Quinn then pushed the door completely open. The deputies were quiet up to this point, not announcing their presence.[37]

From this point in the story, the accounts of the deputies diverge in ways small and large. Quinn's account, coming from the lead officer on the scene and the one responsible for filing the complaints against Lawrence and Garner, is the most richly detailed.

Lilly, the only deputy besides Quinn who claims to have seen Lawrence and Garner having sex, was reluctant to talk about the case at all, and offered me only a brief, bare-bones account. He declined to answer detailed questions and deferred any further interview until he received the approval of his superiors to do so. On August 25, 2003, I was informed that the department would not allow Lilly to discuss the case further. No explanation for this decision was given.[38]

Tipps played a smaller role at the scene, but I include his account based on my interview with him. I was unsuccessful in securing an interview with Landry who, in any event, appears to have played a similarly subordinate role.

What follows is a summary of what each deputy told me in interviews about what happened after they opened the door to Lawrence's apartment. I present these summaries of my interviews of the deputies to let the reader decide their credibility. Subsequent to my interviews with each man, I sent each of them a summary by e-mail asking for clarifications and corrections. I have noted these requested clarifications and corrections, if any, in the summaries.

The Quinn Account[39]

At first Quinn saw only a normal living room area with a couch and chairs. Nobody was in the living room. No television or radio was playing and no other sound was heard. Quinn could see a kitchen area off to the right. To the left there was a bedroom. Quinn shouted, "Sheriff's Deputies!" twice, loud enough for anyone inside the apartment to hear. There was no response. As the deputies entered the living room, they began a "peel off" maneuver where deputies go in different directions to secure the area. One deputy peeled off toward the left to investigate the bedroom. The door to that bedroom was open and nobody was inside.

Quinn peeled off to the right, toward the kitchen area. There, Quinn saw a fully clothed man ("Man #4") standing beside the refrigerator, talking on the phone. Quinn could not initially remember his name, but believes the man was Hispanic and in his thirties.[40] Quinn told the man, "Do not move! Let me see your hands." The deputies frisked and handcuffed the man to secure him while they continued to search the apartment for the reported armed intruder.

Still the deputies heard no noises in the apartment. They noticed there was another bedroom behind the kitchen area. The door to this bedroom was wide open, but the light was off inside the room, so its contents were not completely visible. The deputies again formed a tactical stack, with Lilly taking the lead this time and Quinn right behind him, guns still drawn.

Slowly, Lilly and Quinn approached the bedroom. With the help of the lights that were on in the kitchen and living room Lilly could make out two naked men having anal sex, one on the bed (Garner) and the other standing behind him at the side of the bed (Lawrence). "It actually startled him [Lilly], what they were doing," says Quinn, "and he lurched back."

At this point, Quinn, who had not yet seen the men having sex, guessed that Lilly must have been surprised by seeing the reported gunman. Quinn came around low on Lilly's right side and entered the bedroom, in a crouched position, with his gun pointed straight ahead. Quinn's finger was on the trigger of his gun, ready to fire. A deputy turned the bedroom light on and the deputies clearly saw Lawrence and Garner having anal sex. With the deputies' guns pointed straight at the two men, Quinn yelled "Stop!" to them and "Step back!" to Lawrence. Despite these orders, the men continued to have sex. In fact, "Lawrence looked eye-to-eye at me," but kept having sex. Quinn repeated his instructions two or three more times. But the men continued to have sex for what Quinn says was "well in excess of a minute." Finally, Lilly and Tipps pulled Lawrence away from Garner.

Quinn believes there is no way the men did not hear him when he announced, "Sheriff's Deputies!" twice. The door to the bedroom was wide open, there was no other sound in the apartment, and the distance between where Quinn made the announcement and the bedroom door was only about twenty to twenty-one feet. Further, Lawrence and Garner should have heard Quinn tell Man #4 to put up his hands, since the distance from where Quinn stood at that point and the bedroom door was a mere three feet. Quinn estimates that the time between the announcement and the moment he entered Lawrence's bedroom was just under a minute, more than enough time for the men to stop having sex.

Quinn also cannot understand why Lawrence and Garner did not stop having sex when it was obvious the deputies were in the room, had turned on the light, had their guns aimed directly at them, and were shouting at them to stop. "Most people who have any self-dignity would stop," says Quinn. "Have some courtesy for me and stop doing that," he adds. Quinn initially did not recall that the men were intoxicated or high on drugs. However, the Offense Report for the sheriff's department filed that night by Quinn indicates that Lawrence, Garner, and Eubanks were "extremely intoxicated."[41] "I thought afterwards it was a set-up," says Quinn, meaning that Lawrence and Garner wanted to be caught in the act in order to be arrested and then to challenge the sodomy law.

After Lawrence was forcibly separated from Garner, the two men were handcuffed. Lawrence became angry and belligerent. "What the fuck are ya'll doing?" he shouted at the deputies. "You don't have any right to be here," Lawrence protested. Lawrence refused to put on any underwear and was led into the living room handcuffed and naked.

Once back in the living room, deputies sat Lawrence, Garner, and Man #4 on the couch. They were soon joined by Eubanks. Man #4 told the deputies he was a friend visiting Lawrence. Eubanks confessed that he had invented the story about an armed intruder in order to get back at Lawrence and Garner. Eubanks was angry and jealous that his current lover, Garner, was cheating on him with his ex-lover, Lawrence. At one point Eubanks became so agitated that he stood up, shouting at Garner, and had to be forced to sit back down.

Quinn was angry that Lawrence and Garner had not stopped having sex when the deputies entered the apartment and announced their presence.

He said, "Do you realize that not once but twice we called out?" Quinn told them, "You were close to being shot." Lawrence remained angry, calling the deputies "gestapo" and "storm troopers" and "jack-booted thugs."[42] Lawrence said the deputies were "harassing" them because they were homosexuals. Quinn responded, "I don't know you. And I don't know your sexual orientation. So how can I be harassing you because you're homosexual other than that I caught you in the act?"

By now, several other sheriff's department officers had arrived, including Sgt. Kenneth O. Adams. (Adams retired in 2002.) Quinn discussed with Adams what to do about Lawrence and Garner. Because homosexual conduct was a Class C misdemeanor (like a traffic ticket), punishable by fine but not prison, Quinn knew that the deputies had the option simply to issue a citation without actually taking them to jail. Quinn recommended that the men be charged with violating the homosexual conduct law and be taken to jail.

Quinn explains his recommendation (1) to cite the men and (2) to jail them, "I think the totality of the circumstances where I think there's a guy with a gun and I almost have to shoot, that it warranted me giving them a citation. It was a lovers' triangle that could have got somebody hurt. I could have killed these guys over having sex.[43] They were stupid enough to let it go that far."

Adams agreed with Quinn and it was decided to call the assistant district attorney on duty (there is a D.A. available twenty-four hours a day, offering legal counsel to the deputies in the field) to get approval for the citation and arrest. Quinn asked the assistant D.A. if it mattered, under the homosexual conduct law, whether the conduct was in a home or a public place. The D.A. looked at the statute and said it did not matter where the offense occurred.

While on the scene, the deputies noted numerous pornographic gay magazines and videotapes inside the apartment. "The apartment was loaded with pornography," says Quinn. "Everywhere you looked there was some kind." In particular, deputies noted "two pencil sketchings of James Dean, naked with an extremely oversized penis on him." The sketches "were hung up like regular pictures," says Quinn. Quinn and Tipps laughed about the Dean etchings, sarcastically joking, "This is the kind of thing I would have in my house!"

As deputies prepared to leave the scene, Quinn advised them to wash their hands. "You have to wonder," says Quinn, "'What have we touched? Have we come into contact with any fluids?'" Quinn recalls that, "I made sure I doused myself with sanitizer" that he kept handy in his patrol car.

Eubanks was charged with filing a false report, a Class B misdemeanor punishable by a short jail term, and was taken to jail. Man #4 was allowed to go free.

Lawrence refused to put on more than his underwear for his trip to jail. He also refused to be taken from his home and had to be physically carried to a patrol car by deputies, including Tipps. During the trip downstairs, Lawrence sustained minor scrapes on his legs (that bled a little), but he was not abused. Quinn says that Lawrence could have been cited for resisting transport while under arrest. But Quinn did not cite him because Lawrence "was doing all this to entice me to do something that could show I hated homosexuals."

Lawrence, Garner, and Eubanks were led away to the station in separate patrol cars. Eubanks rode with Quinn. Lawrence continued to be angry and uncooperative throughout the standard intake procedures. Garner was quiet and cooperative.

In his arrest report filed that night, Quinn recounted the events as follows:

> Officers dispatched to [Lawrence's address][44] reference to a weapons disturbance. The reportee advised dispatch a black male was going crazy in the apartment and he was armed with a gun.
>
> Officers met the reportee who directed officers to the upstairs apartment. Upon entering the apartment and conducting a search for the armed suspect, officers observed the defendant engaged in deviate sexual conduct namely, anal sex, with another man.[45]

Quinn filed an identical affidavit regarding Garner.[46] Both documents listed Lilly, and only Lilly, as a witness to the crime. Both were notarized by Kenneth Adams. The formal complaint against the men, signed by Quinn and notarized the same night by Adams, indicates that Quinn "has reason to believe and does believe that" each man "engage[d] in deviate sexual intercourse, namely anal sex, with member of the same sex (man)."[47]

In addition to his affidavit and formal complaint, Quinn also wrote up an offense report, a more detailed narrative of the night's events for internal department use. It was filed with the sheriff's department a few hours after the arrest, at 3:22 A.M. on September 18, 1998. Part of the offense report simply lists the officers who were involved, the witnesses, and addresses for each person. Interestingly, the offense report indicates that Eubanks lived at Lawrence's address, indicating that they may have been roommates at the time.

Part of the offense report includes an "investigative narrative" that describes the events. It is made public here for the first time. I have preserved the original punctuation, and all-capital letters form, but have deleted personal identifying information for those involved:

INVESTIGATIVE NARRATIVE:[48]

OFFICERS DISPATCHED TO [Lawrence's address] REFERNCE [sic] TO A WEAPONS DISTURBANCE. UPON ARRIVAL OFFICERS WERE SUMMONED AND DIRECTED TO THE UPSTAIRS APARTMENT BY THE REPORTEE WHO WAS LATER IDENTIFIED AS ROBERT ROYCE EUBANKS W/M 7-22-58.

OFFICERS VERIFIED THE REPORT VERBALLY AND MR. EUBANKS REPLIED, "YES HE IS IN THAT APARTMENT UP THERE AND HE HAS A GUN."

OFFICERS KNOCKED ON THE DOOR AND ENTERED UPON FINDING IT UNLOCKED. OFFICERS BEGAN AN ARMED BUILDING SEARCH FOR THE SUSPECT WITH A WEAPON. OFFICERS FIRST OBSERVED A HISPANIC MALE LATER IDENTIFIED AS RAMON PELAYO-VELEZ 7-2-62 IN THE KITCHEN AREA TALKING ON THE TELEPHONE. OFFICERS SECURED THE FRONT BEDROOM AND PROCEEDED TO THE BACK BEDROOM OF THE FIVE ROOM APARTMENT.

OFFICERS UPON ENTERING THE BACK BEDROOM FOUND THE BLACK MALE AND A WHITE MALE ENGAGED IN DEVIATE SEXUAL INTERCOURSE NAMELY ANAL SEX. THE MALES WERE SEPARATED. THE BLACK MALE WAS IDENTIFIED BY TEXAS ID CARD [I.D. card number here] AS TYRON GARNER DOB 7-10-67. THE WHITE MALE WAS IDENTIFIED AS JOHN GEDDES LAWRENCE DOB 8-2-43. ALL PARTIES INVOLVED HAD BEEN DRINKING, AND WITH THE EXCEPTION OF MR. PELAYO-VELEZ, WERE EXTREMELY INTOXICATED.

OFFICER SEARCHED THE APARTMENT FOR THE ALLEGED GUN AND FOUND NO FIREARMS INSIDE. OFFICERS IN THE INVESTIGATION LEARNED THAT IT WAS AN APPARENT LOVE TRIANGLE AND MR EUBANKS CALLED BECAUSE HE WAS UPSET THAT MR GARNER AND MR LAWRENCE WERE HAVING SEX. MR EUBANKS IN HIS INTOXICATED STATE DENIED HAVING BEEN OUTSIDE THE APARTMENT AS OFFICERS ARRIVED.

OFFICER CONTACTED THE DISTRICT ATTORNEYS OFFICE AND SPOKE TO ADA[49] WILLIFORD. MS WILLIFORD WAS ADVISED OF THE CIRCUMSTANCES AND ACCEPTED A CHARGE OF FALSE REPORT TO A POLICE OFFICER ON MR. EUBANKS. OFFICER CONFIRMED WITH MS. WILLIFORD

THAT ELEMENTS OF HOMOSEXUAL CONDUCT DID NOT REQUIRE THE ACT TO OCCUR IN A PUBLIC PLACE. MS. WILLIFORD AGREED THE ELEMENTS OF THE OFFENSE WERE MET.

OFFICER FILED A CLASS C CHARGE OF HOMOSEXUAL CONDUCT ON MR GARNER AND MR. LAWRENCE IN JUSTICE OF THE PEACE PRECINCT THREE POSITION ONE JUDGE MIKE PARROTT'S OFFICE.

ALL SUSPECTS WERE TAKEN INTO CUSTODY AND TRANSPORTED TO THE WALLISVILLE ANNEX FOR FILING OF CHARGES. MR LAWRENCE RESISTED BEING HANDCUFFED AND HAD TO BE FORCIBLY RESTRAINED. MR. LAWRENCE REFUSED TO COOPERATE AND WALK UNDER HIS OWN POWER. MR LAWRENCE WAS CARRIED TO THE PATROL CAR. MR LAWRENCE DRAGGED HIS LEGS AND FEET AS OFFICERS CARRIED HIM DOWN THE STAIRS AND ALONG THE SIDEWALK.

MR. EUBAMKS [sic] WAS EXTREMELY BELLIGERENT AND VERBALLY ABUSIVE. MR EUBANKS HAD TO BE FORCIBLY REMOVED FROM THE PATROL CAR AT THE STATION. MR. EUBANKS FELL TO THE GROUND CLAIMING OFFICERS ASSAULTED HIM AND HAD TO BE PICKED UP AND CARRIED A PORTION OF THE WAY INTO THE STATION. HE THEN BEGAN WALKING UNDER HIS OWN POWER. MR. EUBANLS [sic] CLAIMED TO HAVE HIV, HEART PROBLEMS, EPILEPSY, AND ASTHMA. DUE TO HIS COMPLAINTS AND MR. LAWRENCE RECEIVING ABRASIONS TO HIS LEGS WHILE BEING CARRIED, OFFICER CALLED NORTH CHANNEL EMS. NORTH CHANNEL EMS ARRIVED AT THE STATION TO CHECK BOTH MR LAWRENCE AND MR EUBANKS. BOTH INDIVIDUALS REFUSED TREATMENT. ALL SUSPECTS WERE LATER TRANSPORTED TO IPC.

NO ADDITIONAL SUSPECT OR WITNESS INFORMATION AVAILABLE.

Quinn has no regrets about his actions, including his decision to issue the citations to Lawrence and Garner and to take them to jail: "When we review the entire record, the circumstances warranted what I did." And as for the notion he sometimes hears that "his case" ultimately lost, Quinn says, "I don't really look at it as my case." Quinn adds, "I don't regret it. I did what I had to do. And I filed the charge."

The Lilly Account[50]

The deputies went into the apartment, with guns drawn, looking for the reported armed man. When the deputies entered the apartment, they announced their presence loud enough for anyone in the apartment to hear. There was a man ("Man #4") standing in the kitchen when the deputies entered.

After Man #4 was secured, the officers went into the bedroom where they saw Lawrence and Garner having sex. Lilly personally saw Lawrence and Garner having sex. Lilly says that Lawrence and Garner stopped having sex as soon as the deputies entered the bedroom.

The Tipps Account[51]

When the deputies arrived at the door, it was slightly open. The deputies entered, guns drawn, and announced "Sheriff's Deputies!" loud enough for anyone inside to hear. The light was on in the living room, but there was nobody in the room. Tipps could not hear any sounds, such as from a TV or stereo.

Straight ahead there was a bedroom door, which was slightly open and the lights appeared to be on inside. That bedroom was approximately thirty to forty feet from where the deputies stood when they announced their presence.

Tipps and Landry broke off to the left to investigate a bedroom. They found nobody inside that bedroom. Meanwhile, Quinn and Lilly went toward the bedroom straight ahead. Tipps heard Lilly and Quinn giving orders to persons inside the bedroom, such as "Let me see your hands." When Tipps and Landry heard this they went immediately to the other bedroom. They were there within seconds. Tipps estimates about thirty seconds passed between the time the deputies announced their presence and the time he first heard Lilly and Quinn giving orders to the men in the other bedroom. Inside the bedroom, Tipps and Landry saw two naked men, one white and the other black. Tipps and Landry did not see the men actually having sex. Only Quinn and Lilly would have been in a position to see that. Tipps did not pull the men away from each other to make them stop having sex. As far as Tipps knows, they had stopped voluntarily.

While Garner was compliant, Lawrence was uncooperative, refusing to put on his clothes and demanding to see his lawyer. Tipps asked Quinn, "Did you see anyone with a gun?" Quinn replied, "No, but you ain't gonna believe this. Those guys were having sex." "Really?" asked Tipps. "Yep," said Quinn. Lilly told Tipps he had seen the men having sex through the door and was so startled he backed up. "Better ya'll than me" to see that, Tipps told Quinn and Lilly. Tipps says he cannot remember having seen another person in the apartment.

Tipps believes the men were cited and taken to jail for two reasons. First, because of the false weapons disturbance report. Second, because Lawrence was so uncooperative. These factors frustrated and angered Quinn and the other deputies.[52]

Tipps does not know why Lawrence and Garner would not have stopped having sex when the police entered the apartment and loudly announced their presence. "Maybe they didn't hear. Maybe they were too into what they were doing," he says. He does not believe that either Lawrence or Garner were drunk or high on drugs. He says that Lawrence and Garner did not protest their innocence to him. "They probably didn't think they were doing anything wrong," Tipps says. This was the first and only time Tipps has been involved in an arrest for homosexual conduct.

As for his place in history, Tipps observes, "I was hired to do a job and I'm going to do my job regardless. I was either at the right place at the right time or at the wrong place at the wrong time."

The Arrest: Lewis's Version

The only other account of September 17, 1998, from a person close to the events comes from Lane Lewis, the first person to get into contact with Lawrence about the case after the arrests. Lewis currently works as a bartender at a Houston gay dance club. Lewis has been involved in gay civil rights organizations and causes for more than a decade. He served as president of the Houston Gay & Lesbian Political Caucus, which vets and endorses candidates for public office. He has a license in social work from the state of Texas. In the years leading up to September 1998, Lewis made contacts with people who worked in the JP courts in Harris County because he knew that any sodomy case would go there first, and he wanted to be contacted if someone were arrested. The discussion that follows is based on my interviews with Lewis, recounting his knowledge of the facts as he learned them from Garner and especially Lawrence.[53] It is, of course, hearsay, but it is the closest thing we now have to Lawrence and Garner's own version of what happened.

When Lewis learned about the arrest, he called Lawrence. In this first telephone conversation, and in subsequent conversations, Lawrence explained what happened the night of the arrest. Lawrence said that he, Garner, and Robert Royce were all in Lawrence's apartment the night of the arrest. (Royce is now deceased.) There was no other person in the apartment that night, according to Lawrence. Lawrence thinks the police may have gotten the idea of a fourth person from a man they saw walking up the stairs, but he does not know. Royce was a sexual partner/boyfriend of Garner's at the time. The three men had known each other for some time.

Eubanks is the person who called the police to Lawrence's apartment. Eubanks may have called from inside the apartment or from a pay phone, but Lewis is unsure about this. Lawrence told Lewis that Eubanks made the call because he was jealous of the time Lawrence and Garner spent together watching TV and movies and drinking. Also, Eubanks was "drunk" at the time. Eubanks had never been involved in gay rights causes or gay organizations.

When the police arrived, Eubanks answered the door and let them in. Eubanks was fully clothed. There were pornographic gay movies and gay magazines visible to the police in the living room.

Lawrence told Lewis that he and Garner were not having sex when the deputies entered the apartment. In fact, Lawrence said that he and Garner were in separate rooms when the deputies arrived—Lawrence in the bedroom and Garner in the living room. Lawrence and Garner had never been sexually involved with each other, according to Lawrence. At the time of the arrests, Garner and Eubanks were boyfriends. Lawrence has since repeated this version of events to Lewis, including as recently as September 2003.

Lawrence and Garner were arrested and taken out of the apartment, according to what Lawrence told Lewis, "in their underwear and no shoes." Lewis says there is no validity to claims that the arrest was a set-up to test the law.

The Arrest: A Reasonable Doubt about the Deputies' Version

Based on the information we now have, it is uncertain whether Lawrence and Garner were having sex when sheriff's deputies entered Lawrence's apartment. Even if they were having sex at the moment the deputies opened Lawrence's front door and announced their presence, I believe it is unlikely sheriff's deputies actually saw Lawrence and Garner having anal sex. This conclusion is based on several considerations, which I outline next. They are arranged from most persuasive and probative to least. Perhaps no single one of them is persuasive by itself, but collectively they raise a serious question about whether the deputies actually witnessed Lawrence and Garner having sex. At a hypothetical criminal trial, under admittedly lax rules of evidence, lawyers for Lawrence and Garner challenging the factual basis for their arrests could, at the very least, use the considerations below to raise a reasonable doubt about whether their clients were actually guilty.

The Improbability of the Deputies' Accounts

Only two deputies claim to have actually seen Lawrence and Garner having sex. One is Quinn and the other is Lilly. Neither of the deputies' accounts is credible; Quinn's is almost comically incredible in parts. This does not mean either man is consciously lying, but it does seriously undermine their claims to have seen Lawrence and Garner having sex.

To accept Quinn's account, we have to believe that Lawrence and Garner (a) were having sex and continued to have sex after sheriff's deputies entered Lawrence's apartment and announced their presence twice so loudly that anyone in the apartment could easily hear, (b) with the door to the bedroom open about twenty feet away and lights on in the house; (c) with no interfering sounds such as a TV or stereo to cover the deputies' announcement; (d) then continued to have sex while Quinn and Lilly discovered a person standing in the kitchen near the bedroom, told him to put his hands up, and secured him, all within three feet of the bedroom door; (e) then continued to have sex as deputies approached the bedroom with the door open; (f) then continued to have sex after deputies turned on the bedroom light; (g) then continued to have sex while the deputies' guns were pointed at them and the deputies repeatedly shouted at them to stop and to step back; (h) then continued to have sex as Lawrence looked "eye-to-eye" directly at Quinn; (i) then continued to have sex for "well in excess of a minute" overall, until (j) deputies literally had to pull them apart from each other.[54]

This account is so fantastic it cannot be taken at face value. It defies common experience and common sense. Perhaps parts of it could be passed over as the consequence of a failing memory of an event that occurred five years ago. Perhaps what seemed to a shocked Quinn like "well in excess of a minute" during which he viewed live homosexual anal sex was really no more than a few seconds.

But parts of Quinn's account are very difficult to explain by fading memory. It is not credible to claim that deputies literally pulled one man off of the other, for example. Lilly's account disputes this, as does Tipps's account. Tipps and Lilly would surely remember if they had been obliged to pry apart two men having anal sex. This part of the story seems like a conscious embellishment, designed to put Lawrence and Garner in the worst possible light. If Quinn is capable of concocting such a lurid detail, what other parts of his story must be questioned?

Yet Lilly's truncated account is not much more believable, consisting as it does of elements (a) through (e) above. The only significant differences between Quinn's account and Lilly's are that Lilly claims the men immediately stopped having sex when the deputies entered the bedroom and that deputies did not have to pull them apart. Both of these differences make Lilly's account more credible than Quinn's. But that still leaves Lawrence and Garner having sex after the deputies loudly announce their presence from a distance of about twenty to thirty feet and continuing to do so while

Quinn and Lilly secure Man #4, just three feet away from Lawrence's open bedroom door, all with the lights on in the adjacent rooms and no other sound in the apartment.

I am not the first to note the improbability of this story. One source familiar with the case inside the Harris County judicial system told me her reaction when she first heard of the deputies' account: "My first thought was, 'That's a lie.' I don't care whether you're homosexual or heterosexual or like doing it with little puppies, when those deputies enter the apartment it's over."[55] A prosecutor involved in the case has also expressed incredulity that Lawrence and Garner would continue to have sex when sheriff's deputies entered, although he reaches the conclusion that Lawrence and Garner may have been part of a set-up to test the constitutionality of the state sodomy law.[56]

There are four possible ways to understand the deputies' accounts. The first three—attempting to defend the truthfulness of the deputies' account— are possible, but not probable explanations. The fourth, which suggests Lilly and especially Quinn are not telling the truth about actually seeing Lawrence and Garner having sex, is more probable.

The Obliviousness Explanation

The first explanation for Quinn's and Lilly's strange account is that perhaps Lawrence and Garner *did* continue to have sex after the deputies entered the apartment and announced their presence because Lawrence and Garner were oblivious to the announcement and the deputies' other activities.[57] This is unlikely, since all of the officers said that they announced their presence loud enough for anyone in the apartment to hear, there was no other sound in the apartment to cover the deputies' announcement, the door to the bedroom was open, and there is no indication that Lawrence and Garner are deaf or hearing impaired.

On the other hand, Quinn wrote in his offense report filed the night of the arrest that the men were "extremely intoxicated."[58] If true, this makes the obliviousness explanation slightly more plausible, since alcohol may have so impaired the men's judgment that they did not care who else was present in the apartment. However, the claim is not supported by any other officer at the scene and is directly contradicted by Tipps. Even if the men were intoxicated, the Quinn account is still dubious. Not one but both men would have had to be so alcohol-impaired that they were unable to respond as a rational person would by ceasing any sexual activity. There was more than enough time to do so, even for two very drunk people.

There is, in short, no credible evidence of anything that might have impaired the ability of the two men to hear the deputies' announcement and subsequent activities within the apartment, and then cease any sexual activity that might have been occurring.

The Moment-of-Passion Explanation

The second explanation for Quinn's and Lilly's strange account is that perhaps Lawrence and Garner *did* continue to have sex after the deputies entered the apartment and announced their presence because they were caught up in a moment of passion and could not stop themselves.[59] This assumes a degree of animalistic passion that seems highly improbable. Whatever passion Lawrence and Garner were enjoying at the moment was surely drained by the sound of a loud male voice announcing the presence of "Sheriff's Deputies" and by the activities and words accompanying the arrest of Man #4. Moreover, the time that must have elapsed between the announcement and the moment the deputies actually entered the bedroom (just under a minute, according to Quinn) would have allowed passions to cool considerably.

The Tipps account suggests a more plausible theory in support of the deputies' version of events than either the Quinn or Lilly account. Tipps indicates that about thirty seconds passed between the time the deputies announced their presence (presumably, the moment when Lawrence and Garner would have realized the police were present) and the time Lawrence and Garner were observed having sex. If, consistent with the Tipps version, Quinn and Lilly maintained that they went straight to Lawrence's bedroom upon announcing their presence, they would be more believable. But that is not the account they, the only two eyewitnesses, have offered. And even the Tipps estimate of thirty seconds seems like a stretch as a support for the deputies' story. Thirty seconds, while brief in absolute terms, can be an eternity in real life. It is more than enough time for two people, engaged in sexual activity, and suddenly conscious of loud voices twenty to thirty feet away, to stop what they are doing. Further, the Tipps estimate of thirty seconds is very difficult to square with Lilly's and Quinn's memory of confronting and securing a fourth man in the apartment *before* seeing Lawrence and Garner *in flagrante delicto*. Although there may be reasons why they would make up a story about seeing Lawrence and Garner having sex, there is no obvious reason why Quinn or Lilly would fabricate the presence of a fourth man. Tipps's estimate of thirty seconds from announcement to apprehension therefore seems likely to be low. The actual elapsed time was probably closer to the minute Quinn estimates.

The Test-Case Explanation

The third explanation for Quinn's and Lilly's strange account is that perhaps Lawrence and Garner *did* continue to have sex after the deputies entered the apartment and announced their presence because Lawrence and Garner were part of an elaborate scheme to set up a test case to challenge the constitutionality of the Texas sodomy law. Under this scenario, Lawrence and Garner *wanted* to be seen having sex so that they would be arrested for violating the law.

There has been some speculation that *Lawrence* was a "cooked" case, meaning that the officers' intrusion into Lawrence's apartment was deliberately provoked by gay activists in order to test the validity of the Texas sodomy law. Bill Delmore, a Harris County prosecutor who handled the Lawrence case all the way to the Supreme Court, believes Lawrence and Garner may have helped set up a challenge to the Texas law. "I have suspected that from the beginning," he says. Delmore gives three reasons for believing the case might have been set up to challenge the law. First, "It is difficult to imagine circumstances in which people would continue engaging in the act with police in the apartment. Most people would discontinue any sexual activity."[60] He told one newspaper: "If the police knocked on the door—and one would assume that they did[61]—people would stop their sexual conduct. But they didn't."[62] Second, Delmore says that he has talked to numerous officers and asked them whether, under circumstances where they are looking for an armed suspect and happened upon two men having sex, they would charge the men with violating the state sodomy law. Not one of them, he reports, said that he would make an arrest under those circumstances. Instead, they would tell the men to stop what they were doing, instruct them to put their pants on, and then continue the search for the armed suspect.[63] "I can't imagine a police officer would care enough to file a charge," says Delmore, "unless something offended him or he was involved in the set-up." Since he does not believe Quinn would have been involved in a set-up to challenge the Texas sodomy law, he concludes Quinn must have been offended by something and that the defendants provoked this offense by their behavior.[64] Third, Delmore heard that there was open discussion of a test case on gay radio shows in the area. Delmore admits this is hearsay.[65]

Quinn also suspects this was a deliberate test case, based on the high-powered legal team brought in to defend the men. "I thought afterwards it was a set-up," says Quinn.[66]

The speculation about a set-up tends to minimize Lawrence and Garner's claims that the Texas sodomy law truly invaded their liberty or privacy as a practical matter. If the speculation is correct, they had to invite the invasion to be able to complain of it.

There is support for the cooked-case speculation in the sheer rarity of enforcement of sodomy laws against consensual, noncommercial adult sex that occurs in the privacy of the home. The state claimed (probably incorrectly) that the Texas sodomy law, at least prior to 1994, had never been enforced in those circumstances. There is also support for this cooked-case speculation in the frustration of gay legal advocates in Texas, whose earlier challenge to the law had been dismissed by the courts for lack of standing precisely because there had been no enforcement.

The more probable conclusion, however, is that *Lawrence* was not deliberately set up as a test case. It was simply one of those rare, chance examples of sodomy law enforcement, a bolt from the blue. There are several reasons to doubt the cooked-case hypothesis.

First, Lawrence, Garner, and their attorneys deny that they set up the unusual circumstances that led to their arrests in order to test the law,[67] as do gay activists closely associated with the case.[68]

Second, neither Lawrence nor Garner had any known record of involvement with gay civil rights causes prior to their arrests.[69] In other undoubted examples of set-up test cases, the parties involved have tended to be active in the reform movements with which their test case is associated. In *Griswold v. Connecticut*,[70] for example, the persons arrested for setting up a birth-control clinic, including Estelle Griswold, had long been active in the birth-control movement generally and with Planned Parenthood specifically.[71] Finding two anonymous people, not previously involved in gay rights activism who are willing to be initiated into activism by being intruded upon *in flagrante delicto* by the police, arrested and hauled off to jail, convicted of a sex offense, and then to pursue litigation for years, with all of the media exposure and the potential loss of privacy that entails, begs belief. It is possible, of course, but does not seem likely.

Third, the person who reported seeing an armed intruder enter Lawrence's apartment, Robert Eubanks,[72] would almost certainly have had to be part of any conspiracy to test the law. It was his telephone call, after all, that started the chain of events. Eubanks admitted to the deputies *at the scene* that he was lying about an armed intruder,[73] was later convicted of filing a false report, and spent at least two weeks in jail.[74] Eubanks, like Lawrence and Garner, had no prior involvement in gay rights causes or organizations.[75] It is unlikely a non-activist would have agreed to participate in such a way and undergo the penalty.[76] Moreover, even the deputies' accounts of the events suggest an "innocent" (i.e., non-test-case) motivation for filing a false report. Eubanks was jealous because his boyfriend was fraternizing with another man.[77]

Fourth, even if Lawrence and Garner managed to orchestrate a scenario in which Eubanks would call the sheriff's department with a false report and Lawrence and Garner would be having sex when the police arrived, they could never have been certain that the deputies would actually cite them and arrest them. If Harris County D.A. Bill Delmore is correct, very few if any officers would actually cite people for having sex under such circumstances.[78] A test-case scenario would have been a very dubious enterprise at best, further reducing the likelihood it is true.

Finally, had gay activists wanted to set up a test case, it is unlikely they would have chosen Lawrence and Garner as the defendants. Instead, they would likely have chosen two people in a committed and long-term relationship who could articulately plead their own case to the media. By all accounts, Lawrence and Garner do not meet these criteria.

The Fabrication Explanation

The fourth explanation for Quinn's and Lilly's strange account is that Quinn is not being truthful about what he saw and that Lilly passively acquiesced in the story. According to this explanation, whatever Lawrence and Garner were doing when the deputies entered the apartment and announced their presence, they were not having sex by the time the deputies saw them in the bedroom. Under this scenario, the most likely of the four in my view, the deputies simply are not telling the truth when they say they actually saw Lawrence and Garner having sex.

The problem with this scenario is that it means believing a law-enforcement official fabricated evidence to issue a citation and make an arrest. This may be less of a problem for the fabrication explanation than one might suppose:

> Cops throughout the United States have been caught fabricating, planting and manipulating evidence to obtain convictions where cases would otherwise be very weak. Some authorities regard police perjury as so rampant that it can be considered a "subcultural norm rather than an individual aberration" of police officers. Large-scale investigations of police units in virtually every major American city have documented massive evidence [of] tampering, abuse of the arresting power, and discriminatory enforcement of laws according to race, ethnicity, gender, and socioeconomic status.[79]

One does not have to accept the full force of this conclusion, as I do not, to agree that police fabrication of evidence is common enough to make it a plausible answer when no other theory appears to explain the alleged crime.[80]

Police misconduct against gay people specifically, including fabrication of evidence and entrapment of gay men for sex crimes, is also not unheard of in the annals of American law.[81] The Lawrence/Garner arrests may be just another episode in that sorry history. But we should be reluctant to reach that conclusion unless there is no other plausible one. Neither the obliviousness explanation, nor the moment-of-passion explanation, nor the test-case explanation offers a plausible story about why Lawrence and Garner would continue to have sex until at least the moment the deputies entered Lawrence's bedroom.

Delmore doubts the fabrication theory. "I can't imagine the officer making up the fact that he'd seen them having sex," says Delmore. "I don't have any reason to think it happened in this case." However, Delmore acknowledges that he has never spoken to the officers involved in the arrest. "I wanted to know only what was in the record" in order to preserve the state's argument that the record did not disclose whether the activity was truly in private, was consensual, was non-commercial, and so forth.[82]

Quinn dismisses speculation that Lawrence and Garner were not actually having sex when the deputies entered the apartment, but that the deputies arrested them anyway. He argues, "Why would I risk my career and reputation for that?" One answer is that, from the perspective of that night, it would have seemed unlikely that Quinn or Lilly were taking much of a chance on their reputations or careers by arresting these two men for homosexual conduct.

Lilly was taking almost no chance, since he was not the lead deputy, never signed an affidavit, and would not be called to testify. He would never have to make a false statement; only Quinn would.

Even for Quinn the risks would have seemed small. Homosexual conduct was a Class C misdemeanor in Texas, the equivalent of traffic ticket. It would be a deputy's word against theirs, and who were they? They were obviously not rich or famous men. Moreover, they were homosexuals, a despised class of persons, who would probably meekly plead out the way so many before them had. It probably seemed unlikely the two men would even get a lawyer, or challenge their citations, much less take their case to the U.S. Supreme Court. They were easy marks.

The Evidence of a Motive to Fabricate

To strengthen the fabrication explanation we need a reason why Quinn would make up a story about seeing Lawrence and Garner having sex, and why Lilly might have acquiesced in the story. We need not choose a single motive, of course, for more than one may have been at work.

I believe motives to fabricate can be found in the deputies' own accounts of what happened that night and in their expressed feelings about the events. In order of probability, here are three possible motives for fabrication.

The Anger and Frustration Motive

It is clear that the deputies, especially Quinn, were angry and frustrated that night. To begin with, they had to deal with a false report of a weapons disturbance, a potentially deadly situation for the officers and for anyone they encountered. Though Lawrence and Garner could not be blamed for the false report, they were part of the frivolous (to the deputies) "lovers' triangle" that led to it. Quinn acknowledges that the false report played a role in his decision to cite Lawrence and Garner and to take them to jail instead of simply issuing them a citation.

Further, by all accounts Lawrence did not go gently into that good night. He refused to cooperate in putting his clothes on, derided the deputies as "gestapo" and "jack-booted thugs," accused them of anti-gay harassment, and cussed at them. These acts were tantamount to civil disobedience on his part. Of course, if he was falsely charged with a crime, Lawrence's anger becomes even more understandable. Quinn acknowledges that Lawrence's uncooperative and belligerent actions and words also played a role in his decision to cite Lawrence and Garner and to take them to jail instead of simply issuing them a citation.[83]

From the deputies' point of view, they had been lied to, had put their lives and the lives of others at risk, and had been verbally abused for silly reasons. Their anger and frustration may have been taken out on Lawrence and Garner who, as homosexuals, could plausibly be charged with the crime of acting on their homosexuality. They had probably been engaged in some sexual activity anyway, Quinn could have reasoned, making them no less guilty than if he had seen the act. A citation and arrest, from the deputies' perspective, may have been just punishment for those shenanigans.

The Homophobic Motive

Interviews with the deputies reveal their overall discomfort with homosexuality. Both Quinn and Tipps made it clear in my interviews of them that they regard homosexual acts as morally wrong. Moreover, their objections to homosexuality appear to be visceral. Quinn's statements about the pornographic contents of Lawrence's home, including his derisive laughter at a sketch on Lawrence's wall, indicate great disdain for Lawrence's lifestyle. Quinn's fears about coming into contact with "fluids" from the men may reveal an irrational fear of their activity and perhaps of them as persons. Quinn's defensiveness about not wanting to give Lawrence room to claim anti-gay bias also reveals his distrust of gays as manipulative and conspiratorial.

Further, while it is difficult to accept that the deputies actually saw Lawrence and Garner engaged in sex, it is likely the men were still nude (perhaps hurriedly looking for their clothes) when Quinn and Lilly saw them. Whatever Lilly saw, it shocked him so much that he lurched back. The very shock of seeing two adult men in a bedroom together in the nude, with the light off, may have awakened homophobic feelings.

In fact, Quinn's account of the men as continuing to have sex for over a minute with deputies watching and shouting, guns aimed at them, and light turned on, plays into stereotypes of gay men as so sex-obsessed they are literally unable to control themselves. They are animals in their lust. Quinn's complaint that Lawrence and Garner lacked what he calls "self-dignity" is very telling in this regard. Quinn could have expected that his version would be believed, since these stereotypes of gay men as sex-obsessed are widely shared.

The perception of gay men as hypersexual is a defining characteristic of homophobia. As James Woods argued in his study of gay men in American corporations:

> Prevailing stereotypes about gay men (that they are hypersexual, promiscuous, indiscriminate) emphasize the sexual aspects of their lives. The result is a tendency to hypersexualize gay men, to allow their sexuality to eclipse all else about them, *even to see sexual motives or intentions where there are none.*[84]

From the deputies' perspective, then, it may have seemed obvious that Lawrence and Garner had been having sex, or were preparing to do so. Moreover, what they had been doing or were preparing to do was morally objectionable and repulsive to the deputies. The fact that the men had not actually been caught in the act was unimportant. They were as good as guilty.

Upon discovering the possibility of homosexual activity in their presence, the deputies may have suffered a moment of what Eve Kosofsky Sedgwick has called "homosexual panic," one's fear of one's own potential for homosexual desire. That is one way to understand Lilly's "lurch back" upon seeing Lawrence and Garner in the bedroom.

To be fair, both Quinn and Tipps are somewhat equivocal about the rights of homosexuals. For his part, Quinn says that he is of two minds about the result in the Supreme Court. One the one hand, "if you just look at the way it's written [the Equal Protection Clause], there is no equal protection here. They don't ban that activity for heterosexuals. It isolates the homosexual." On the other hand, "the states themselves should have the right to make their own laws." "But then again," he adds, "we are one nation governed by a Supreme Court so I have to live by it." He does think "it's unfortunate it had to happen over something stupid that could've cost them their lives."[85]

As for the Supreme Court's opinion, Tipps says, "I don't agree with it. I don't agree with homosexual conduct either. Nothing against homosexual *people*."[86] Asked about whether the men should be entitled to privacy, he says, "There are some things that don't need to be done in your home and this is one of them."[87]

The Racist Motive

Finally, it is possible that complex racial feelings—unstated and perhaps subconscious—entered the decision to cite the men and take them to jail. Race-consciousness was present at the start of the events, when the sheriff's department received a report that "a black male" was "going crazy" with a gun. In fact, it is possible Eubanks used a racial slur when he made the report.[88] Lawrence's apartment was in a lower-class area on the outskirts of Houston, an area that is very traditionalist in its attitude toward gays and not very enlightened in its attitudes about race. The Harris County Sheriff's Department can often reflect those attitudes.[89]

Lawrence is white and Garner is black. Few have commented on the fact that they were an interracial pair or on what role that might have played in the relatively harsh treatment they received. "It was not a gentle arrest," says Katine.[90] I asked one gay rights activist what might cause the deputies to fabricate a story about having seen sexual activity. His response was simple, "Black guy, white guy, apartment, naked. That's all you need."[91] This answer suggests that a mix of homophobia and racism may have been at work.

If racism was present, however, it was not as simple as white deputies inflicting their racist views on an interracial couple. Although Quinn is white, Lilly is black. It is possible that Lilly, coming from a socially conservative and religious community, was especially offended by the sight of a black man about to engage in a morally objectionable sexual act with a white man. This offense may have been heightened if he perceived the black man was playing the receptive (passive, subordinate, female) role to that white man during sex.[92] At the scene of the arrest, after all, Lawrence was aggressive and belligerent (masculine); Garner was passive and cooperative (feminine).

This is speculation. The deputies have not admitted that race played any role in the arrests, nor would they be expected to admit it if it had. We cannot know with any certainty what role race may have played in the arrest of Lawrence and Garner. The possibilities are intriguing but ultimately probably unknowable. If race played any role, that role was very complicated and is unlikely ever to be acknowledged explicitly by law enforcement authorities.

The Conflicting Account Offered by Lewis, Based on His Conversations with Lawrence

Throughout the litigation, and continuing to the present, Lawrence, Garner, and their attorneys have refused to present their version of what happened that night. Neither Lawrence nor Garner has publicly admitted even having sex. Neither was ever called to testify in the case, since no testimony was ever taken. There was never a trial. In their briefs, their attorneys have been careful only to recite the facts as alleged in the arrest reports and complaints against the defendants.

In my initial interview with him about the case, Lane Lewis was very forthcoming and detailed about a number of things heretofore publicly unknown, such as the relationship of the defendants to one another and the sequence of events that led to gay rights attorneys' involvement in the case. Lewis freely told me everything he knew and could remember about events leading right up to the moment when the deputies first encountered Lawrence and Garner, and everything he knew and could remember about what followed that initial encounter. But, following instructions from Mitchell Katine, Lewis was at first unwilling to discuss the initial encounter itself. Specifically, Lewis was unwilling to discuss on the record what Lawrence and Garner were doing when the police entered the apartment or whether police actually saw Lawrence and Garner having sex. I asked Lewis directly whether Lawrence and Garner were having sex when the police entered the apartment. His response during our first interview was, "That would be a legal question best directed toward Mitchell [Katine] or Lambda." Lewis also declined at first to provide me a copy of his handwritten notes of his initial telephone conversation with Lawrence, as they contain the sensitive information he had been instructed not to discuss.[93]

Lewis subsequently changed his mind, however, and provided the account I recited above, which he said was based on his first conversation with Lawrence by telephone after Lawrence left the jail. In brief, Lewis says that Lawrence denied that the two men were having sex when police entered the apartment. Lewis's handwritten notes from that conversation, which he has provided me, back up this claim.

The Unwillingness of the Defendants, Their Representatives, and Lawyers to Discuss What the Defendants Were Doing or What the Police Likely Saw

Katine likewise refused to discuss what Lawrence and Garner were actually doing or what the police actually witnessed or could have witnessed. "We don't discuss that because we feel it's irrelevant and an invasion of their privacy," says Katine. He also refused to grant an interview with Lawrence and Garner themselves.[94]

This reticence is strange and, I think, very suggestive. If Lawrence and Garner *were* having sex and the deputies *actually saw* them doing so, there would be no reason for the defendants and their attorneys not to confirm it publicly. It could not hurt their case in the courts, since their entire argument is built on a right, which was infringed by the deputies enforcing an unconstitutional law on men having sex, to make certain intimate choices. It could not hurt their case with the public, who already assumes the men were having sex. For the same reason, revealing the truth about what happened would be no greater invasion of Lawrence and Garner's privacy than has already occurred. All of this makes their silence on the issue bewildering and suspect.

The negative inference from the attorneys' silence is that they are loath to reveal a fact they believe might be unhelpful: that Lawrence and Garner were not actually having sex when the deputies saw them. Why might this fact be thought unhelpful to their cause?

Perhaps the attorneys fear that if it were learned Lawrence and Garner were not having sex it would undermine the factual basis for the Supreme Court's decision, and even the decision itself. If this is the fear, it is exaggerated. What difference would it make in the case to learn Quinn lied about what he saw? The Court is not going to withdraw its opinion at this point. It is certainly not going to do so based on the revelation of a possible fact—a false and abusive arrest—that makes the case for striking the law even more compelling than it already was.

Or perhaps the defendants' attorneys fear that their own ethics as attorneys might be called somehow into question if it were revealed they allowed the case to proceed on a false assumption about what happened. If this is the fear, it too seems exaggerated. As long as the defendants' attorneys never asserted the circumstances as true facts they knew to be untrue, they have probably not breached any ethical or professional obligations. Simply repeating the facts as asserted in the arrest reports and complaints against the defendants would not qualify. I have found nothing in the record of the case that would call into ethical question the attorneys' behavior or statements, even assuming the police never witnessed sexual conduct in Lawrence's apartment and even assuming the defendants' attorneys believed this to be true.

Even if the fabrication explanation is correct, that does not undermine the validity or good faith of the defendants' no contest pleas. If the defendants expect police perjury and expect it to be believed, they are better off pleading guilty. They avoid the expense of trial and the risk of future police retaliation. The Supreme Court has upheld the validity of a guilty plea when the defendant pleads guilty but simultaneously argues his factual innocence.[95] Lawrence and Garner—and by extension, their attorneys—were perfectly justified in defending the case based on their constitutional objections rather than defending it based on the facts.[96] The first may have seemed a far more promising route than the latter and is well within the range of zealous, ethical advocacy.

Katine has offered the view that to discuss what Lawrence and Garner were actually doing with each other, if anything, that night would constitute an invasion of their privacy.[97] Yet the defendants' privacy has already been invaded by the public allegation, lodged by the deputies, that they were having anal sex with each other. To dispute that public allegation negates the invasion of their privacy; it does not expand it.

Whatever the reason for silence on this issue by the defendants and their attorneys, the strong but not inescapable implication is that the defendants' attorneys believe the police did not actually witness a violation of the Texas sodomy law.

The "Not Guilty" Pleas after the Arrests

Lawrence and Garner were taken to jail the night they were arrested. They stayed in jail for approximately twenty-four hours.[98] The next evening, without counsel, they appeared before hearing officer Carol Carrier for the purpose of determining probable cause for the arrest and for the purpose of entering their pleas. At such arraignment hearings, a representative of the district attorney's office reads the arresting officer's sworn statement. The hearing officer then determines whether there is a technical fault in the charge. If probable cause exists based on the officer's statement the defendant is asked to plead "not guilty," "guilty," or "no contest." Most defendants in low-level misdemeanor cases plead guilty or no contest, pay their fines, and are done with the whole business. The process typically takes five minutes or fewer, since there are often dozens of defendants waiting to be arraigned on everything from simple theft to traffic violations.[99]

At their initial arraignment hearing, both Lawrence and Garner pleaded "not guilty." Lawrence asked for a trial by jury.[100] Garner requested a trial by judge.[101] Both were then released on personal recognizance, which allows defendants to be released without paying a bond if they agree to appear at a subsequent court date. That subsequent court date was set for October 5, 1998, just over two weeks away.[102]

There are many reasons why Lawrence and Garner might have pleaded "not guilty" the day after their arrests and before they had the benefit of counsel. Perhaps they believed this was the best way to preserve their case until they could contact a lawyer. Perhaps they believed they had done nothing wrong, or at least nothing that should be a crime.

The most obvious inference from a "not guilty" plea, however, is that Lawrence and Garner were *professing their innocence of the crime charged.* The arraignment may well have been the first time they heard Quinn's claim that they had engaged in anal sex, rather than the more nebulous "homo-sexual conduct." Later, represented by attorneys eager to challenge not the factual basis for the arrests but the constitutionality of the law, their pleas changed to "no contest."[103] But the earlier "not guilty" pleas are the closest thing we have to a statement from Lawrence and Garner, immediately after the arrests, about what actually happened. The fact that they pleaded not guilty does not establish their innocence, of course. Perhaps they had actually been caught in the act and were avoiding the truth. But this is one more bit of information that tends to undercut Quinn's account of what happened.

The Hearsay Denial from Garner

Finally, although we have no direct testimony from either Lawrence or Garner about their experience on the night of the arrests, we do have hear-say information from Garner. According to Ray Hill, Garner told him that when the police entered the apartment, he and Lawrence were not having sex and, in fact, were in different rooms of the apartment. As Garner alleg-edly described it to Hill, "We weren't doing anything. I was in the living room and he [Lawrence] was in the bedroom." Lawrence never told Hill what they were doing when the police arrived and Hill never asked Lawrence about it.[104]

As with the other bases for challenging the deputies' account of what happened, this one is also open to question. It is possible that Hill misun-derstood what Garner told him. It is possible that Hill simply has a bad memory about what Garner said. It is possible that Hill is lying, though he has no apparent interest in doing so. It is also possible that Hill accurately remembers what Garner said but that Garner himself was not telling Hill the truth. But again, the most obvious possibility is that Garner actually told Hill that he and Lawrence were not having sex when the deputies encoun-tered them and that he was telling the truth. This hearsay is corroborated, of course, by Garner's own plea of "not guilty" immediately following his arrest. The hearsay denial is hardly conclusive, but it tends to undercut the story told by the deputies.

The Arrest: The Most Likely Scenario

In this section I offer a chronological account of what most likely happened the night of the arrests. This account is pieced together from the most plau-sible parts of each of the interviews I have conducted of people who were actually there that night or are close to those who were. Where no direct evidence is available I offer what I believe is a reasonable inference from the facts we do know. While this reconstruction of the arrest is far richer than anything that has yet appeared in public about the case, it is no doubt mistaken in parts and far from complete in other parts. I do not offer it as the final word on what happened. It is based on the best information available so far. It is only a first stab at what must be a continuing effort to obtain the truth of what happened. But it is at least probably not far from that truth in most major respects.

John Lawrence, Tyron Garner, and Robert Eubanks spent part of the day on Thursday, September 17, 1998, together planning for the gift of some of Lawrence's furniture to Eubanks.[105] The three men had dinner together. Sometime in the evening, they were joined by Lawrence's friend Ramon Pelayo-Velez in Lawrence's home, a modest two-bedroom apartment on the second floor of a small complex in a lower-middle-class and crime-prone area of Houston. None of the men could be described as "A-list" gays, that is, wealthy, educated, well-groomed, and cultured. None were involved in gay rights activism. Lawrence, a quiet 55-year-old white man, worked as a medical technologist at a nearby clinic. It was a low-paying but steady job. He had only two minor brushes with the law on his record, both arrests for drunk driving that had occurred more than a decade before. Garner, a quiet 31-year-old black man, was unemployed at the time and had more serious and recent incidents on his record, including an arrest for assault. Eubanks, a 41-year-old white man, was the most combustible of the lot, prone to bouts of drunkenness, swearing, and even violence. He has been described as a "gun-totin', beer-swillin', Gilley's kickin' bubba from Pasadena [Texas]." He occasionally lived with Lawrence as a roommate. Pelayo-Velez, a 36-year-old Hispanic man, was a friend of Lawrence's. Eubanks was currently Garner's boyfriend.

The men drank alcohol during the evening. They became somewhat tipsy, but, with the exception of Eubanks, not extremely intoxicated. They did not use drugs. At some point, Eubanks grew jealous of the interest Lawrence and Garner were showing in one another, as evidenced by the time they spent together. An argument among the men ensued. Shortly before 10:30 P.M., Eubanks stormed out of the apartment, closing the door not quite completely behind him. Lawrence and Garner retired to Lawrence's bedroom, determined to ignore Eubanks's tantrum. Pelayo-Velez entertained himself in the living room and kitchen, drinking and telephoning friends.

Knowing that Garner had had prior problems with the law, Eubanks decided he would punish Garner by calling the police and getting him into trouble again. Crying and shaking with anger, he went to a pay phone near the apartment complex and looked up the number for the Harris County Sheriff's Department. When the dispatcher answered, Eubanks reported that there was "a nigger going crazy with a gun" in Lawrence's apartment. He gave the dispatcher the name of the apartment complex and Lawrence's apartment number and said he would wait for deputies to arrive.

Eubanks waited for the deputies at the bottom of the stairs leading to Lawrence's apartment. He didn't have to wait long. Deputy Joseph Quinn was on patrol nearby and arrived within minutes of the call. Quinn was the first deputy on the scene, followed shortly thereafter by deputies William D. Lilly, Donald Tipps, and Kenneth Landry. According to standard procedure, Quinn took the lead on the scene because he was the first deputy to arrive. The deputies, weapons drawn, began looking for the man who had called in the report and for the apartment containing the armed suspect. Eubanks saw the deputies and motioned toward them, saying, "Over here! Over here!" The deputies could tell that Eubanks was upset. Quinn asked, "Where is the man with the gun?" Eubanks pointed up the stairs toward Lawrence's apartment, saying, "He is in that apartment up there and he has a gun."

Quinn, Lilly, Tipps, and Landry headed up the stairwell in what is known as a "tactical stack," one deputy right behind the other, with Quinn at the front of the stack. When they reached the apartment Quinn saw that the door was mostly closed, but not pulled completely shut. It was resting against the door jam, slightly ajar, as Eubanks had left it. Quinn could not see into the apartment. He turned the door knob and determined it was unlocked. Quinn knocked on the door, which pushed it open slightly and allowed him to get a peek inside. The light was on, but no sound could be heard. Seeing no armed suspect or other person, Quinn pushed the door wide open into a standard living room. Still no one could be seen inside. Announcing "Sheriff's Deputies! Sheriff's Deputies!" in a loud voice, Quinn and the deputies quickly entered the apartment.

Inside Lawrence's bedroom, about twenty to thirty feet from where the deputies announced their presence, with the light off but the bedroom door at least partly open, Lawrence and Garner were nude and engaged in sexual play. They heard the announcement, "Sheriff's Deputies!", were startled, stopped what they were doing, and started fumbling around in the dark for their clothes.

Meanwhile, Tipps and Landry peeled off to the left to investigate a bedroom. The door to that bedroom was open and nobody was inside. At the same time, Quinn and Lilly went to the right, toward the kitchen area, where the light was on. There, Quinn saw Pelayo-Velez, fully clothed, standing by the refrigerator and talking on the phone. Standing just three feet away from Lawrence's open bedroom door, Quinn ordered the man, "Do not move! Let me see your hands." The deputies quickly frisked and handcuffed Pelayo-Velez to secure him while they continued to search the apartment for the reported armed intruder.

Guns still drawn, Quinn and Lilly moved toward Lawrence's bedroom. Lilly took the lead in approaching the bedroom, with Quinn right behind him. With the aid of the lights from other rooms Lilly made out the moving shapes of two nude men in the bedroom. Startled at the sight, he jumped back. Quinn, who had not yet seen the naked men, guessed that Lilly must have seen the reported gunman. In a crouched position, Quinn came around low on Lilly's right side with his gun pointed ahead. The deputies entered the room. The deputies' fingers were on the triggers of their guns, ready to fire. Lilly turned the bedroom light on and the two deputies saw Lawrence and Garner standing there in the nude, shocked looks on their faces. Quinn shouted at the men, "Let me see your hands!" Lawrence and Garner complied, raising their hands.

Hearing this, Tipps and Landry immediately came to see what was happening. The deputies ordered the men to put on their underwear, handcuffed them, and led them into the living room where they sat the three men down to figure out what was going on. Lawrence, genuinely upset and bewildered at the deputies' intrusion into his home, asked, "What the fuck are ya'll doing here? You don't have any right to be here." Quinn replied that they had every right to enter the apartment under the circumstances.

A deputy fetched Eubanks and brought him up to the apartment. The deputies quickly determined that Eubanks had lied about an armed black man because he was jealous of the attention Lawrence and Garner were paying to each other. At one point Eubanks became so angry he stood up, shouted at Garner, and had to be forced to sit back down. When the deputies learned the report had been false, their frustration and anger grew. From their perspective, the prank could easily have resulted in a fatal shooting. "Do you realize that not once but twice we called out?" Quinn told the men. "You were close to being shot." Lawrence remained angry, calling the deputies "gestapo" and "storm troopers" and "jack-booted thugs."

As the deputies looked around the apartment, they found stacks of gay pornography and explicit images hanging as art on the walls. "The apartment was loaded with pornography," says Quinn. "Everywhere you looked there was some kind." In particular, the deputies noticed "two pencil sketchings of James Dean, naked with an extremely oversized penis on him." The sketches "were hung up like regular pictures," says Quinn. Quinn and Tipps laughed about the Dean etchings, sarcastically joking, "This is the kind of thing I would have in my house!"

Tipps asked Quinn, "Did you see anyone with a gun?" Quinn, angry about the false report, shocked at seeing two nude men in a bedroom together, offended by the gay pornographic images in the apartment, and frustrated with Lawrence for being uncooperative and name-calling the deputies, glanced at Lilly and made a split-second decision to charge them with homosexual conduct, which Quinn knew was a crime in Texas. "No," he replied. "But you ain't gonna believe this. Those guys were having sex." "Really?" asked Tipps, incredulous. "Yep," responded Quinn, "we caught 'em in the act." Quinn figured he would teach Lawrence and Garner a lesson not to disrespect law enforcement authorities. He also had nothing to lose in citing them. They were obviously not rich or important men. They would probably just pay their fines and move on. Lilly remained quiet, figuring this was Quinn's show, and that he (Lilly) would not be filing the charges, and that Lawrence and Garner had probably been having sex at some point anyway. With the men caught naked and now sitting there in their underwear, Tipps and Landry had no reason to doubt Quinn's word.

Lawrence accused the deputies of "harassing" them because they were gay. Quinn responded: "I don't know you. And I don't know your sexual orientation. So how can I be harassing you because you're homosexual other than that I caught you in the act?" Lawrence and Garner understood that they were being charged with "homosexual conduct" which, for all they knew, included any gay sexual play.

By now, several other deputies had arrived, including Sgt. Kenneth O. Adams. Quinn discussed with Adams what to do about Lawrence and Garner. Because homosexual conduct was a Class C misdemeanor (like a traffic ticket), punishable in Texas by fine but not prison, Quinn knew that the deputies had the option to issue no citation, or issue a citation without actually taking the men to jail. But Quinn recommended that the men not only be charged with violating the homosexual conduct law but also be taken to prison. "I think the totality of the circumstances where I think there's a guy with a gun and I almost have to shoot, that it warranted me giving them a citation" and taking them to jail, Quinn says. "It was a lovers' triangle that could have got somebody hurt. I could have killed these guys over having sex. They were stupid enough to let it go that far."

Adams agreed with Quinn and it was decided to call the assistant D.A. on duty (there is a D.A. available twenty hours a day, offering legal counsel to the deputies in the field) to get approval for the citation and arrest. The D.A. on duty was Ira Jones. Quinn told Jones that he had seen Lawrence and Garner having anal sex and then asked Jones if it mattered, under the homosexual conduct law, whether the conduct occurred in a home or in a public place. Jones looked at the statute and confirmed it did not matter where the offense occurred.

Eubanks was charged with filing a false report, a more serious Class B misdemeanor. He later served more than two weeks in prison for it. Pelayo-Velez was allowed to go free.

Enraged by the deputies' intrusion into his home, their behavior, and the charge, Lawrence engaged in his own form of civil disobedience. He refused to put on more than his underwear for his trip to jail. He demanded to see a lawyer. He also refused to walk out of his home and was physically carried by the deputies down the stairs, in his underwear, to a patrol car. Lawrence's legs dragged on the ground as the deputies carried him down the stairs, resulting in minor cuts and bruises. Quinn says that Lawrence could have been cited for resisting transport while under arrest. But Quinn did not cite him because Lawrence "was doing all this to entice me to do something that could show I hated homosexuals."

As the deputies prepared to leave the scene, Quinn advised them to wash their hands. "You have to wonder," says Quinn, "'What have we touched? Have we come into contact with any fluids?'" Quinn recalls that "I made sure I doused myself with sanitizer" that he kept handy in his patrol car.

Lawrence, Garner, and Eubanks were led away to the station in separate patrol cars. Eubanks rode with Quinn. Once they arrived at the station, Lawrence continued to be angry and uncooperative throughout the standard intake procedures. By contrast, Garner was quiet and cooperative. Garner had had enough prior experience with the police to know better than to provoke them. Lawrence and Garner were given orange prisoners' jump-suits and spent the night in jail.

The next evening, September 18, Lawrence and Garner appeared before a hearing officer and pleaded "not guilty." Lawrence requested a trial by jury; Garner, a trial by judge. They were released on personal recognizance, with bond set at $200, the maximum fine allowed for violating the state sodomy law.

I should explain one choice in particular that I made in picking and choosing from among the often conflicting elements of the various accounts of what happened the night Lawrence and Garner were arrested. As laid out in the reconstruction above, I believe it likely that Lawrence and Garner were in Lawrence's bedroom together when the police arrived. I further believe it likely the two men were involved in some kind of sexual activity (possibly, though not necessarily, including prohibited anal sex) when the police arrived.

Thus, on the one hand, I do not believe a central contention of Quinn and Lilly's account. For reasons I gave above, I think it unlikely the deputies actually witnessed Lawrence and Garner having anal sex.

On the other hand, I also do not believe that Lawrence and Garner were in separate rooms when the deputies arrived at Lawrence's door. According to Lewis and Hill, the men both contend that when police arrived Lawrence was in his bedroom and Garner was in the living room. But that account is difficult to accept. According to each of the three law enforcement personnel I interviewed who were the first to enter the apartment (Quinn, Lilly, and Tipps), there was nobody in the living room. For Lawrence and Garner's hearsay version to be correct (separate rooms, no sexual activity), all three deputies would have to be lying about whether Garner was in the living room. That is possible, but harder to accept than my version of events above (same room, some sexual activity, but none seen by deputies), according to which we need to believe that one deputy is actively lying, one is passively going along with the story, and one is being truthful. Tipps, in particular, was very believable during our interview. His account of his role and what he saw that night was straightforward, logical, fits with common experience, and was unembellished with details seemingly calculated to put Lawrence and Garner in an unflattering light.

Further, the conclusion that Lawrence and Garner were engaged in some sexual activity is supported by the undisputed fact that they were naked or only partially dressed when the deputies arrived. Although Garner subsequently put his clothes on, it is undisputed that Lawrence was taken from the apartment in his underwear.

A remaining puzzle is why, even now, Lawrence and Garner would continue to deny (again, according to the intermediaries I spoke to) that they were engaged in some sexual activity when the deputies arrived. I can only speculate about the reason(s). Perhaps they denied from the start that they were having sex and do not want to be perceived as lying now. Perhaps they are embarrassed to admit what they were doing. Perhaps they think it's nobody's business what they were doing and that a denial is a way to avoid further intrusive questions.

Further, if Lawrence and Garner were indeed in separate rooms when the deputies arrived, and if I am wrong to conclude that the men were probably engaged in some kind of sexual activity when the deputies never actually saw, that fact would change none of the larger conclusions I draw below about the abuse of police power and discretion. The underlying factual conclusion would remain the same—the deputies did not witness the men having sex, yet charged and arrested them anyway. And the lessons from the episode would, if anything, be magnified.

The Road to *Lawrence*

At Lawrence and Garner's initial arraignment on September 18, 1998, the hearing officer set an arraignment in the court of Justice of the Peace Mike Parrott for October 5, just over two weeks away.[106] If their case was to go anywhere, the arrest of these two men with no connections to the gay civil rights movement would somehow have to be brought to the attention of gay advocates and then given over to lawyers equipped to handle it. If the case had made it to the JP Court without the guidance of gay rights lawyers, there was a very real chance it would have been dismissed and lost to history.[107] The story of how we got from an arrest on a Class C misdemeanor to the U.S. Supreme Court has been ignored until now.[108]

Lawrence at the Bar

In 1998, Lane Lewis was working as a bartender at Pacific Street, then a Houston gay bar. On the night of Friday, September 18,[109] a regular customer of the bar (Lewis declined to name him, so I will call him "Tom") approached him and said, "You're not going to believe this." Tom, who worked within the Harris County judicial system, then explained that he had overheard "someone high up in the Harris County judicial system" talking about the arrest of two men for violation of the sodomy law. Tom told Lewis that he had mentioned the arrest to his partner, who also worked within the Harris County judicial system (Lewis declined to name the second person, so I will call him "Harry"). Tom told Lewis that Harry had access to the men's arrest report. Lewis asked Tom to have Harry fax Lewis the arrest report at his home.[110]

When Lewis went home, the arrest report was waiting on his fax machine. It had been faxed by Harry. Lewis looked at it, and saw the names of John Lawrence and Tyron Garner, whom he had not known before the incident. Lewis realized the significance of this arrest and called Tom and Harry at their home, saying: "I think this may be a Supreme Court case."

Lewis tried to call the phone number given for Garner on the arrest report, but there was no answer at Garner's number. Lewis next called Lawrence's number. Lawrence answered the phone. Lewis took notes of his conversation on the faxed arrest report, as they spoke. Lewis introduced himself and explained that he had obtained the arrest report. A surprised Lawrence asked, "How did you get our arrest report?" Lewis replied, "I can't tell you." Lewis explained to Lawrence that he wanted to help him, that he was not an attorney, and that he could hang up if he wanted to. He offered to get Lawrence an attorney that would represent him free of charge and that his case could lead to a Supreme Court decision that would get rid of sodomy laws across the country. Lewis said that if Lawrence didn't like the first attorney Lewis could get another one.

Lewis describes Lawrence as being angry about the arrest.[111] Lawrence said to Lewis, "I am very mad that they came into my home and did this." Lewis warned Lawrence about the possibility of enormous media coverage. They then talked about what had happened the night of the arrests.

After his initial telephone call with Lawrence, Lewis immediately thought that Mitchell Katine would be the best attorney to handle the case. To get advice, Lewis next called three leaders of the Houston gay community: Annise Parker,[112] Grant Martin,[113] and Ray Hill. Each seemed to disbelieve Lewis at first. Once convinced that the arrest was real, all three agreed that Katine would be the best attorney to handle the case.

Lewis next called Katine and described what had happened. Katine was in disbelief. Lewis faxed the arrest report to him. When he had reviewed the report, Katine called Lewis back and said: "Lane, do you have any idea what you've got here?" Katine was, he recalls, "shocked and excited."[114] Katine immediately called Suzanne Goldberg, an attorney for Lambda Legal, a national gay legal advocacy group, to get Lambda's assistance.

The Speech

In late September or early October,[115] Lewis, Lawrence, Garner, and Eubanks went to Katine's office to meet with several lawyers and to discuss whether and how to proceed with the case. The lawyers explained what they would do for Lawrence and Garner to pursue a constitutional challenge to the sodomy law. After the lawyers' presentation, the lawyers left the conference room to allow Lawrence and Garner to make a decision about whether to challenge the law. Only Lawrence, Garner, Eubanks, and Lewis were left in the conference room. Of Eubanks, Lewis says, "I could smell bourbon on him across the room. Man, he made us nervous." Lewis and the attorneys involved believed Eubanks was a loose cannon.

Lewis spoke to the men for about fifteen minutes. He told Lawrence and Garner that what he was about to say might sound corny. He then quoted the famous line from John F. Kennedy's inaugural address, "Ask not what your country can do for you but what you can do for your country." Invoking the history of the gay civil rights movement and its early pioneers, he told Lawrence and Garner to "think about all the gay and lesbian people who stuck their necks out so you could enjoy whatever freedom you have." He told them about the Mattachine Society, one of the earliest gay rights organizations, and about Harry Hay, one of the movement's pioneers. He told them how they had hidden in basements to have meetings. He told them about the Stonewall riot in New York in 1969, the spark for the modern phase of the gay civil rights movement. He told them the story of Harvey Milk, the first openly gay elected official in San Francisco, who was gunned down by a homophobic colleague. "They went above and beyond the call of their duty and I'm asking you to go above and beyond the call of your duty," Lewis said. He continued, "Think how far we've come from all of that, but think how far that really is. You were dragged out of your home." Then he added, "You tell me to stop and I'll pull the plug." Lewis finally asked, "Is this something you would be willing to move forward on?" Lawrence and Garner looked at each other and said yes.

The attorneys came back in the room, Lewis informed them of Lawrence and Garner's decision to challenge the sodomy law, the attorneys were elated, and the case proceeded.

Throughout the early stages of the case, Lewis served as Lawrence and Garner's friend, confidant, informal public relations manager, and spokesperson. They both trusted him and generally followed his instructions. "My job the first couple of years was keeping the media away from these three boys," Lewis says, referring to Lawrence, Garner, and Eubanks. (Garner was subsequently arrested and charged with assaulting Eubanks.) The three men agreed not to speak to the media except through Lewis. Lewis gave them instructions that if any media called, they were to be directed to Lewis and/or the attorneys. "Once you start talking," Lewis warned them, "they will be at your house, at your job, and everywhere else." Despite the publicity, neither Lawrence nor Garner ever threatened to withdraw from the case.

A Little Harder, Please

At their arraignment before Justice of the Peace Mike Parrott on November 20, it was already obvious this would be a major case. The *Houston Chronicle* had broken the story in the mass media on November 5 and it had been picked up by newspapers around the state and around the country. The day of the arraignment, a large number of attorneys showed up for the defendants. Also, the D.A.'s office got involved for the prosecution, an unusual event, according to Judge Parrott. Large numbers of media, including half a dozen TV cameras, were outside the courtroom waiting to see what would happen.[116]

The defendants signed the plea form, pleading "no contest" to the charge of violating the homosexual conduct law and waiving a jury trial.[117] No testimony was taken, nor would testimony be taken at any stage of the case. Only Quinn's affidavit and the formal complaint against the men were entered in the record. The sparse information in these documents is all the Supreme Court was ever told about the facts of the case.

Parrott, of his own accord, then imposed a fine of $100 on each of them. Within a few minutes or so, attorneys for the defendants approached Parrott to say that the fine was too low because it did not meet the minimum necessary for an appeal to the Criminal Court. They requested Parrott to set aside the fine and enter a higher fine in order to meet the minimum. The D.A.'s office did not object to the change. Parrott set a higher fine of $125 necessary to meet the minimum for an appeal.[118] Court costs of $41.25 were added to each fine, for a total fine against each man of $166.25.[119]

After the arraignment, Parrott discussed the case with Deputy Quinn, who had appeared at the arraignment in case his testimony was needed. Speaking to Parrott, Quinn denied press reports that the police had "busted down" Lawrence's door to enter the apartment. According to Parrott, "Lawrence was the only one with forcible entry, if you know what I mean."[120]

Lawrence in a New Light

The factual material and suppositions contained here shine a light on the background of *Lawrence* that is only dimly lit in the Supreme Court's *Lawrence* opinion itself. This new material suggests that the state of affairs for gay men and women was both better and worse than the Court supposed; that the Court's opinion offers a portrait of gay life dipped in a single color, obscuring the *melange* beneath; and that *Lawrence* is in every respect a product of a rich gay past that keeps intruding upon the gay present and future.

The background facts of *Lawrence* are a mix of lies, alcohol, pornography, sexual free-wheeling, and jealousy. Lawrence and Garner were not in a long-term, committed relationship. Lawrence, Garner, and Eubanks were apparently caught up in a jumbled, complicated mix of sexuality, friendship, and enmity, in which the lines between friendship and sexuality were blurred. No single category seems adequate to define their relationships to each other. Even the deputies' description of the troika as being in a "lovers' triangle" does not seem adequate.

While Lawrence was gainfully employed, neither Garner nor Eubanks seem to have made much of their lives career-wise. Lawrence and Garner had had problems with the law. Neither man was highly educated or articulate. They were not involved politically.

The background facts do not, in other words, make for a neatly packaged story with idealized characters. This may help explain the decision of the men's lawyers to shield them so completely from media scrutiny. As Katine acknowledges, "They are not who you would select as your poster people for doing something of this magnitude."[121] The background does not make for very good public relations.

How could this jumble become the occasion for a sermon from Justice Kennedy on the "transcendent dimensions" of life,[122] "the most intimate and personal choices a person may make,"[123] "personal dignity,"[124] and the way the law "demean[ed] their existence"[125]? The immediate answer is that none of the background facts should make any difference to the constitutional claim made by Lawrence and Garner. Even if the Court had known everything we now know, the men nevertheless would have been entitled to make their own choices about their private sexual conduct. Liberty includes the freedom to make choices that the majority finds suboptimal or even distasteful, and it extends that freedom to people who did not attend Harvard.

The more fundamental answer, however, is that *Lawrence*, in all of its complexity and background unpleasantness, is nothing more than a mirror held up to all life. People lead complex lives. They fall in love. They cheat. They lie. They drink. They are weak. They are vindictive. None of this makes them any less entitled to "respect for their private lives."[126] If it were otherwise, there would be very few people—gay or straight—entitled to liberty.

Lane Lewis recalls that when the Houston rally following the Supreme Court's decision was about to begin, someone asked whether they should start with the Pledge of Allegiance. "I turned around and said, 'No!'" Lewis recalls. He explains his visceral reaction, "The Supreme Court never had the right or authority to take away my right to express love or sex through sodomy,[127] so we shouldn't validate the system that leads to that. Why are we all down on our knees thanking them for giving us something they should never have taken away?" Lewis says the politicians and dignitaries present ignored him and it was decided to begin the rally with the Pledge anyway.[128]

There is much to learn from the previously untold story behind the arrests that led to *Lawrence*. The case is connected umbilically to a rich gay past, including its complexity, its bars, its closetedness, its political liberation, its encounters with police repression and corruption, and its resistance to discrimination.

If anyone "set up" the events that led to *Lawrence*, it was not gay activists. It was very possibly the arresting cops. Since sodomy laws, like the one in Texas, were never really about sodomy, it is fitting that they got their come-uppance in a case in which there was quite possibly no sodomy, or at least no sodomy the police witnessed. A law rarely enforced was upended in a case of phantom enforcement. The laws that encouraged gays to lie about their identity ended in a web of untruths probably created by the very authorities charged with enforcing them. The laws that declared homosexuals had no privacy right heterosexuals were bound to respect died at the hands of homosexuals who had learned to master the sleight of hand, not bothering to deny what they had not in fact done. Sodomy laws were ultimately the victim of overzealous police who had been taught their zealotry by sodomy laws themselves.

Notes

1. I want to thank Don Dripps, Dan Farber, Brett McDonnell, David McGowan, and Paul Rubin for reading an early draft of this chapter and for offering helpful comments. I also want to thank Ryan Scott for research and citation assistance.
2. John Lawrence to Deputy Joseph Quinn, September 17, 1998. Telephone interview with Joseph Quinn, August 9 and 31, 2003.
3. Telephone interviews with Lane Lewis, August 7 and 8, 2003.
4. 123 S. Ct. 2472 (2003). The factual account given in the first paragraph closely follows the Supreme Court's own description of the facts. The lower court decisions, including the state intermediate appellate court panel and the *en banc* intermediate appellate court, offered very similar accounts.
5. The phrase, including the misspelling of the word "sodomite," comes from Lord Queensbury, the father of Lord Alfred Douglas, who used it to describe Oscar Wilde in a note to Wilde in February, 1895. "Oscar Wilde," in *Notable Historical Trials IV: Burke & Hare to Oscar Wilde* (London, Folio Society 1999), 485. I use the phrase because, on the best available evidence, it is unlikely the police witnessed an act of sodomy in Lawrence's apartment. Lawrence and Garner did not challenge the factual basis of their convictions and thus "posed" as sodomites for purposes of the litigation.
6. "Private Lives amid a Very Public Decision," *Los Angeles Times*, July 1, 2003, E1.
7. Telephone interview with Mitchell Katine, Sept. 8, 2003 (hereinafter Katine interview).
8. Katine interview.
9. Lewis interview. Lewis has been active in gay civil rights causes in Houston for more than a decade, serving among other things as president of the Houston Gay & Lesbian Political Caucus. He has a license in social work in Texas.
10. Ibid.
11. Ibid.
12. "Harris County Sheriff's Department; Inmate Processing—Warrant Pending—DIMS Worksheet" (Lawrence intake worksheet; DIMS is an acronym for Departmental Information Management System; on file with author); R. A. Dyer, "Two Men Charged under State's Sodomy Law," *Houston Chronicle*, November 5, 1998 (the first story about the arrests to appear in a newspaper).
13. *Los Angeles Times*, July 1, 2003; Lewis interview; Hill interview.
14. Katine interview.
15. Lawrence intake worksheet.
16. Hill interview; Lewis interview.
17. "Harris County Sheriff's Department; Inmate Processing—Warrant Pending—DIMS Worksheet" ("Garner intake worksheet") (on file with author). See also R. A. Dyer, "Two Men Charged under State's Sodomy Law," *Houston Chronicle*, November 5, 1998.

18. Garner intake worksheet.
19. Katine interview.
20. Ibid. The intake worksheet is blank regarding Lawrence's religious preference. Lawrence intake worksheet.
21. Hill interview; Lewis interview.
22. JIMS Booking Inquiry—LBKI (Lawrence; on file with author). JIMS is an acronym for Justice Information Management System.
23. JIMS Booking Inquiry—LBKI (Garner; on file with author).
24. Dyer, *Houston Chronicle*, November 5, 1998.
25. Katine interview.
26. Telephone interview with Mitchell Katine (Mar. 14, 2004; Katine interview 2).
27. Lewis interview.
28. Deputy Joseph Quinn arrived at the apartment complex at 10:30 P.M. Paul Duggan, "Texas Sodomy Arrest Opens Legal Battle for Gay Activists," *Washington Post*, November 29, 1998 (on file with author). According to the department's intake form, the arrests occurred at 11:10 P.M. DIMS Worksheet.
29. Lewis identifies him simply as Robert Royce. Lewis interview. Two accounts call him "Roger Nance." "Texas Sex Bust Sparks Challenge," NewsPlanet, November 7, 1998 (on file with author); Paul Duggan, "Texas Sodomy Arrest Opens Legal Battle for Gay Activists," *Washington Post*, November 29, 1998 (on file with author). I will identify the man as "Eubanks."
30. Lewis interview. Katine believes the call came from a nearby pay phone. Katine interview. According to one report, citing Lawrence and Garner's attorney at the time (David Jones), Eubanks was with Lawrence and Garner earlier in the evening. Bruce Nichols, "Houston case may test sodomy law," *Dallas Morning News*, November 7, 1998 (on file with author).
31. Probable Cause Affidavit (John Geddes Lawrence), September 17, 1998, filed by J. R. Quinn (on file with author).
32. Lewis interview. Pasadena, Texas, is a lower-middle-class suburb of Houston.
33. Quinn interview. Quinn was thirty-nine at the time and had been a deputy with the sheriff's department for thirteen years.
34. The offense report indicates Quinn was dispatched at 10:49 P.M. and arrived at 10:52 P.M. Offense report, p. 2.
35. Interview with William D. Lilly, August 12, 2003; Interview with Donald Tipps, August 15, 2003. Now a detective for the sheriff's department, Lilly at the time of the arrest was a deputy. Lilly interview. Tipps was thirty-two at the time and has been a deputy since 1991.
36. Quinn interview.
37. Ibid.
38. Interview with Captain Van Peltz, August 25, 2003.
39. The following is a narrative account based on my interviews with Joseph Quinn.
40. A narrative of the arrests filed that night by Quinn identifies Man #4 as Ramon Pelayo-Velez. Detail report for Harris County Law Enforcement, Sept. 18, 1998, 5 ("Offense report"; on file with author). Man #4 is not mentioned as a witness in the Probable Cause Affidavit Quinn filed that night. (Probable Cause Affidavit.) Nor does his name appear in any of the other court documents I have obtained. No media account mentions him. While Lilly confirms the presence of a fourth man, Tipps does not recall anyone but Lawrence and Garner being in the apartment. (Lilly interview; Tipps interview.) Through Lane Lewis, Lawrence denies that a fourth man was present. (Lewis interview.) Katine also denies that anyone besides Lawrence or Garner were in the apartment when the deputies entered. Katine interview. I have not been successful in tracking down Pelayo-Velez or in identifying anyone else who might have been Man #4.
41. Offense report, 5. The intake worksheet for both Lawrence and Garner indicates that they had been using alcohol, but not drugs. (Lawrence intake worksheet; Garner intake worksheet.)
42. Lawrence later publicly described the deputies' actions as "sort of Gestapo." Steve Brewer, "Texas Men Post Bonds, Challenge State's Sodomy Law," *New York Times News Service* (November 20, 1998; on file with author). The Associated Press quoted Garner as saying, "I feel like my civil rights were violated and I wasn't doing anything wrong." Terri Langford, "No Contest Plea in Texas Sodomy Case," Associated Press, November 20, 1998 (on file with author).

43. Quinn's expressed concern for the men's lives reminds me of the concern expressed by the lead officer of the raiding party at the Stonewall Inn bar in 1969, the event that sparked a riot and the modern phase of the gay civil rights movement. Describing how tense the situation became, he said, "You have no idea how close we came to killing somebody." Charles Kaiser, *The Gay Metropolis* (Boston, MA: Houghton Mifflin, 1996), 197.
44. Because he still lives in the apartment, I have omitted Lawrence's address.
45. Probable Cause Affidavit (Lawrence).
46. Probable Cause Affidavit (Garner).
47. Complaint Affidavit (Garner), September 17, 1998.
48. Offense report, 5–6.
49. ADA is a reference to assistant district attorney.
50. The following is a narrative based on my interview with William Lilly.
51. The following is a narrative based on my interview with Donald Tipps.
52. In an e-mail to me (August 28, 2003), Tipps annotated this portion of the interview summary as follows, "As far as both of the men going to jail they went to jail because they were breaking the law not because of them being uncooperative."
53. I should mention that I have personally known Lewis since about 1994. We are acquaintances but not close friends.
54. None of these details about the incident appear in Quinn's investigative narrative.
55. Interview with person in Harris County judicial system, August 11, 2003. The person requested not to be identified.
56. Delmore interview; *Los Angeles Times*, July 1, 2003.
57. Tipps offers this as a possibility. (Tipps interview.)
58. Detail report for Harris County Law Enforcement, Sept. 18, 1998 (on file with author).
59. Tipps also offers this as a possibility. (Tipps interview.)
60. Interview with Bill Delmore, August 27, 2003.
61. According to the officers, they did not knock on Lawrence's door, but verbally announced their presence once inside. (Quinn interview; Tipps interview.)
62. *Los Angeles Times*, July 1, 2003.
63. Delmore interview.
64. Delmore interview.
65. Ibid.
66. Quinn interview.
67. Katine interview.
68. Lewis interview; Hill interview.
69. "Taking Credit for Lawrence vs. Garner Decision," *Washington Blade*, July 18, 2003 (printout from Internet on file with author). (Lewis interview; Hill interview.)
70. 381 U. S. 979 (1965).
71. David Garrow, *Sex & Liberty* (1994).
72. Eubanks has also been identified as "Roger David Nance" in one media account. "Texas Sex Bust Sparks Challenge," NewsPlanet, November 7, 1998 (on file with author).
73. Quinn interview.
74. "Texas Sex Bust Sparks Challenge," NewsPlanet, November 7, 1998. According to one account, Eubanks spent thirty days in jail. "Houston Case May Test Sodomy Law," *Dallas Morning News*, November 7, 1998 (on file with author).
75. Lewis interview.
76. Delmore agrees that this undercuts the test-case theory. (Delmore interview.)
77. Interviews with Lewis, Hill, Quinn, Parrott, Tipps, and Lilly. See also "Taking Credit for Lawrence vs. Garner Decision," *Washington Blade*, July 18, 2003. The story credits unnamed sources for the claim. A lawyer for Lawrence and Garner claimed that the motive for the false report was a "personality conflict between the caller and the people in the apartment." "Texas Sex Bust Sparks Challenge," November 7, 1998 (on file with author). The jealousy motive for the false report is supported by the fact that Garner was later arrested for a Class C misdemeanor assault on Eubanks. (Delmore interview.)
78. Delmore interview.
79. Roger Roots, *Are Cops Constitutional?*, 11 Seton Hall Const, L. J. 685, 718 (2001) (footnotes omitted).

80. See also Don Dripps, "Police, Plus Perjury, Equals Polygraphy," 86 J. *Crim. L. and Criminology* 693 (1996); Morgan Cloud, "The Dirty Little Secret," *Emory Law Journal* 43 (1994): 1311, 1311 (1994) ("Police perjury is the dirty little secret of our criminal justice system."); Myron Orfield, "Deterrence, Perjury, and the Heater Factor: An Exclusionary Rule in the Chicago Criminal Courts," *University of Colorado Law Review* 63 (1992) 75.

81. See, for example, William N. Eskridge, Jr., *Gaylaw,* 87 (1999). Especially in the context of law-enforcement operations to entrap homosexuals for violating public lewdness laws, "police officers often misrepresent the facts of their enticement rackets, in which they frequently invite propositions, then fabricate critical details, including offers of compensation." Evan Wolfson and Robert S. Mower, "When the Police Are in Our Bedrooms, Shouldn't the Courts Go in after Them?: An Update on the Fight against 'Sodomy' Laws," *Fordham Urban Law Journal* 997, 1006 (1994).

82. Delmore interview. There is, in fact, no evidence that whatever Lawrence and Garner were doing was non-consensual, commercial, or in public view.

83. Quinn interview.

84. James D. Woods, *The Corporate Closet* (Free Press, 1993), 65.

85. Quinn interview.

86. This distinction between homosexual acts and gays as people—captured by the phrase, "love the sinner, hate the sin"—is a classic formulation of the opposition to gay equality.

87. Tipps interview.

88. Lewis interview.

89. Hill interview.

90. Katine interview.

91. Hill interview.

92. I was unable to probe this possibility with Lilly, who refused an extended interview.

93. Lewis interview.

94. Katine interview.

95. *Alford v. North Carolina*, 400 U.S. 25 (1970) ("An individual accused of crime may voluntarily, knowingly, and understandingly consent to the imposition of a prison sentence even if he is unwilling or unable to admit his participation in the acts constituting a crime.").

96. I thank Don Dripps for these insights.

97. Katine interview.

98. Ibid.

99. Interview with Richard Carper, August 25, 2003. Carper is the supervisor of Justice of the Peace clerks for Harris County. He was present at Lawrence and Garner's arraignment.

100. Lawrence Hearing form (September 18, 1998; on file with author).

101. Garner Hearing form (September 19, 1998; on file with author). The different date on Garner's form may be a clerical error. Richard Carper, supervisor of the JP clerks for Harris County, recalls them appearing at the same time. (Carper interview.)

102. Lawrence Hearing form; Garner Hearing form.

103. Lawrence JP Judgment, November 20, 1998 (on file with author); Garner JP Judgment, November 20, 1998 (on file with author).

104. Hill interview.

105. Katine interview.

106. Lawrence Hearing form; Garner Hearing form.

107. Hill interview. A source inside the Harris County judicial system confirms this very easily could have been the outcome.

108. Except where noted, the narrative in this section is based on my interview with Lane Lewis.

109. I arrive at this date because Katine indicates the arrest became known to him within a day after the men were released from jail. (Katine interview.) This means he must have heard about the arrests on Saturday, September 19.

110. I have since learned the identity of both Tom and Harry. When I asked him for an interview, Harry refused to discuss the case. To protect their employment, I have decided not to reveal their names or their positions within the Harris County judicial system.

111. Katine concurs that Lawrence and Garner were very angry about being cited and about the way they were treated. "Had they simply been given a ticket it wouldn't have generated the same feelings of anger," says Katine. This anger may explain their ultimate decision to challenge the law, says Katine. (Katine interview.)

112. At the time, Parker was an at-large member of the Houston city council, the first openly gay person elected to office in the city. She has been involved in gay civil rights causes for more than two decades.

113. Among other things, Martin raises money for Democratic candidates and gay rights causes.

114. Katine interview.

115. The meeting must have occurred between the time Lawrence and Garner were initially arraigned (September 18) and the date of the first letter from the defendants' lawyers to the JP court indicating their representation and asking for a continuance in the arraignment date (October 13). Letter to Judge Parrott from David A. Jones, October 13, 1998 (on file with author).

116. Interview with Justice of the Peace Mike Parrott, August 6, 2003.

117. Judgment, Case Number CR31C1000002, Lawrence, John Geddes, November 20, 1998; Judgment, Case Number CR31C1000003, Garner, Tyron, November 20, 1998.

118. Parrott interview; Katine interview.

119. Judgment, Case Number CR31C1000002, Lawrence, John Geddes, November 20, 1998; Judgment, Case Number CR31C1000003, Garner, Tyron, November 20, 1998.

120. Parrott interview. Based on his discussion with Quinn, Parrott describes the relationship among Lawrence, Garner, and the third man who called the police as a "love triangle." Id. As for his opinion of gays, Parrott says, "That's the life they choose. As long as they do it in their homes, and not in front of me or my family or on TV, I don't care. I feel the same way about Republicans." Id. On the morality of homosexual acts, Parrott says: "They'll deal with that at another time, when they die." Id. Parrott was asked to be a grand marshal in the Houston Gay Pride Parade in 2003. He declined. "That's not a plus for me," he explained, noting that he is elected from a blue-collar, heavily union, socially conservative area, not from the heavily gay Houston district of Montrose. Id.

121. Katine interview.

122. *Lawrence*, 123 S. Ct. 2475.

123. Id., 2481.

124. Id.

125. Id., 2484.

126. Id., 2475

127. *Bowers v. Hardwick*, 478 U.S. 186 (1986).

128. Lewis interview.

CHAPTER 8

The Rule of *Lawrence*[1]

ANDREW KOPPELMAN

A basic question that law students are taught to ask whenever they read a case is: What rule of law has the court relied on here? The question is a basic one because the answer describes the rule that is going to govern future decisions. This chapter will try to address that problem with respect to *Lawrence v. Texas.*[2]

This is not a small task. It isn't easy to tell what rule the Court is laying down in that case. The statute challenged in *Lawrence* criminalized all homosexual sex. The Court struck it down as an improper infringement on personal liberty. The Court held that the statute "furthers no legitimate state interest which can justify its intrusion into the personal and private life of the individual,"[3] but it did not say whether the basis of its holding was the weakness of the state's interest, the degree of intrusion, or some combination of these. It was not clear whether the Court was applying strict scrutiny, minimal scrutiny, or something in between. It is most obscure which future cases will be affected by the holding of *Lawrence.*[4]

The *Lawrence* Court quotes with approval Justice Stevens's claim in his *Bowers v. Hardwick* dissent that "the fact that the governing majority in a State has traditionally viewed a particular practice as immoral is not a sufficient reason for upholding a law prohibiting the practice."[5] But the only evidence Stevens cited was the miscegenation laws, which were condemned by an entirely different constitutional principle. Neither he nor any other Justice intends, as Justice Scalia protests in dissent, to invalidate "laws against bigamy, same-sex marriage, adult incest, prostitution, masturbation, adultery, fornication, bestiality, and obscenity."[6] The Court is not saying that morals laws are never permissible.

The *Lawrence* Court does not say that the state interest has no weight but only that it lacks sufficient weight to justify the burden it places on individual liberty. But the Court surely isn't saying that private conduct between consenting adults is always permissible; otherwise most of the laws on Scalia's list really would be invalid. Prohibitions of adultery and fornication intrude on the personal and private life of individuals as much as sodomy laws do.[7]

More helpful is the Court's reliance on *Romer v. Evans*[8] to hold that the precedent of *Bowers v. Hardwick*,[9] which held sodomy unprotected by the right to privacy, had "sustained serious erosion."[10] Just how had *Romer* eroded *Hardwick*? The Court explained that *Romer* had

> invalidated an amendment to Colorado's constitution which named as a solitary class persons who were homosexuals, lesbians, or bisexual either by "orientation, conduct, practices or relationships," and deprived them of protection under state antidiscrimination laws. We concluded that the provision was "born of animosity toward the class of persons affected" and further that it had no rational relation to a legitimate governmental purpose.[11]

There is no logical inconsistency between the two cases: The burden on gays in *Romer* was extraordinary, while *Hardwick* involved a prohibition of conduct that imposed no punishment on persons who refrained from that conduct.[12] *Romer* nonetheless was pertinent to *Lawrence*, the Court held, because "[w]hen homosexual conduct is made criminal by the law of the State, that declaration in and of itself is an invitation to subject homosexual persons to discrimination both in the public and in the private spheres."[13]

The *Lawrence* Court thus suggested that if a law has the *effect* of encouraging prejudice against gay people, this will diminish the weight that is given to the state's purposes when the Court balances those purposes against the burden the law imposes. This gives rise to a new question: Why should that effect matter in this way?

Even for African Americans, the group that receives the highest level of constitutional protection against discrimination, disparate impact without more does not state a constitutional claim.[14] The Court, of course, did not hold that laws that discriminate against gays are subject to heightened scrutiny. All criminal laws encourage discrimination against those who violate them; discrimination against those who violate drug laws, for example in the granting of student loans, is increasingly common.

On the other hand, the Court has said that under certain circumstances, disparate impact can reveal an illicit motive. "Sometimes a clear pattern, unexplainable on grounds other than race, emerges from the effect of the state action even when the governing legislation appears neutral on its face."[15] Moreover, the social meaning of laws can sometimes be relevant to their constitutionality. The Texas statute's impact reveals something about its purpose. The fact that its audience will understand it as an invitation to discriminate is evidence that it was so intended.[16] And while it is logically possible for persons to discriminate against gays on moral grounds without any animosity toward them, this is a poor description of how antigay prejudice actually operates in the contemporary United States.[17]

Lawrence is full of language that indicates that the Court is concerned with the subordination of gays as a group, rather than just the liberty of individuals. At issue is the ability of gays to "retain their dignity as free persons."[18] *Hardwick* must be overruled because "[i]ts continuance as precedent demeans the lives of homosexual persons."[19] If any sodomy law remains on the books, "its stigma might remain"[20] even if it is unenforceable. Gay people are entitled to "respect for their private lives."[21] The state must not "demean their existence or control their destiny."[22]

The Court does not say that *Lawrence* is like *Romer* in that it involves "a bare ... desire to harm a politically unpopular group,"[23] but that is the most coherent implication of what the *Lawrence* opinion does say. Moreover, that language does appear in Justice O'Connor's concurrence.

O'Connor would have invalidated the Texas law under the equal protection clause of the Fourteenth Amendment. She observes that "[w]hen a law exhibits such a desire to harm a politically unpopular group, we have applied a more searching form of rational basis review to strike down such laws under the Equal Protection Clause."[24] Quoting *Romer*, she concludes that the Texas statute "raise[s] the inevitable inference that the disadvantage imposed is born of animosity toward the class of persons affected."[25] The majority does not expressly embrace O'Connor's equal protection theory, but it does declare it to be "a tenable argument."[26]

O'Connor's reasoning explains what is left mysterious by the majority opinion: Why the state interest is deemed insufficient to justify the burden on liberty here, though it would be sufficient in other cases where the law bans consensual conduct between adults. In those cases, there is no reason to think that there is animosity toward the persons affected, or a bare desire to harm a politically unpopular group. The prejudice against gay people evidently is what changes the equation in *Lawrence*.

This is not much of a principle to decide future cases with, though. The "bare desire to harm" criterion seems even more malleable than the liberty that the majority opinion purports to rely on. Just how does one decide which unequal treatment is the result of hostility and which has a rational basis?

The trouble is that laws that discriminate against gays often express moral disapproval *and* reflect a desire to harm an unpopular group.[27] If the analysis of *Lawrence* I have just offered is correct, the rule now seems to be that courts must determine, on a case-by-case basis, which is the primary purpose of any such law. This leaves plenty of room to cook the books when this is felt to be necessary to accommodate irresistible political forces. The exclusion of gay people from marriage and the army, both of which the Court seems disinclined to disturb, largely rests on primitive revulsion, and the refusal to recognize same-sex marriage rests on similarly dubious motives, but the Court doesn't need to admit any of this in order to uphold these exclusions (or, more likely, to refuse even to examine them).[28]

This is not to say that *Lawrence* produces no rule of law at all. Part of what troubled the Court in *Lawrence* was the fact that sodomy laws singling out gays are a fairly recent development in the law, only arising in the 1970s.[29] Similarly in *Romer*, the Court was troubled that the challenged disqualification "is unprecedented in our jurisprudence," and it declared that "[i]t is not within our constitutional tradition to enact laws of this sort."[30] Extraordinary burdens, it appears, arouse suspicion.

This suggests that one clear rule that emerges from (but probably does not exhaust) the fog of *Lawrence* is the following: *If a state singles out gays for unprecedentedly harsh treatment, the Court will presume that what is going on is a bare desire to harm, rather than mere moral disapproval.*

Traditional moralists will object that this presumption is unfair. If one thinks one's moral views correct, changing circumstances may require that one pursue those moral views through novel means. The novelty of the means, one might reasonably argue, should not automatically entail a presumption of bad motive. Some contemporary antigay rules are unprecedented, but the emergence of an active, widespread gay rights movement is also unprecedented. A prohibition such as the Texas law that singles out homosexual sex is one possible response to that movement. The Texas law could be, and was, supported by people of good will who do not question the equal dignity of gay people.[31]

The answer is that every legal presumption that protects some interest against the state has costs. It will surely impair some legitimate government interest. A rule that the state may not discriminate on the basis of race will sometimes prevent the state from pursuing legitimate ends.[32] A strong First Amendment will protect some worthless and harmful speech.[33]

What does this rule amount to in practice? I will try to clarify its meaning by taking up two live questions and show how Lawrence resolves them. The first is the question of whether the states can punish underage homosexual sex more severely than underage heterosexual sex. The second is whether states can decline to recognize same-sex marriages from other states.

The Underage Sex Case

Matthew Limon, a developmentally disabled man, had just turned eighteen when he had oral sex with a developmentally disabled boy who was a few weeks short of fifteen years of age. Kansas's general criminal sodomy law prohibits "sodomy with a child who is 14 or more years of age but less than 16 years of age," without regard to consent, the age of the offender, or the sex of the parties.[34] Had the encounter been heterosexual, however, the penalty for this statutory rape would have been fairly mild. Kansas's "Romeo and Juliet" law greatly reduces the penalties for young people under the age of nineteen who engage in consensual sexual activity with teenagers between the ages of fourteen and sixteen.[35] If that law had applied, Limon would have received, at most, a sentence of fifteen months. However, because the "Romeo and Juliet" law expressly excludes homosexual activity, Limon was sentenced to more than seventeen years in jail,[36] five years of court supervision after his release, and to be classified as a "sexual offender" for the rest of his life.[37]

The U.S. Supreme Court vacated Limon's conviction and remanded the case for reconsideration, one day after it decided *Lawrence v. Texas*,[38] in which it invalidated Texas's sodomy law. The Court indicated that the *Limon* case should be given "further consideration in light of *Lawrence*"[39] but did not explain further.

The appellate decision upholding Limon's conviction makes it clear that a remand was necessary. When presented with a claim that Limon's treatment violated equal protection, the Kansas Court of Appeals thought that the claim was foreclosed by *Bowers v. Hardwick*,[40] which had rejected a privacy-based challenge to a law prohibiting sodomy.

> The impact of *Bowers* on our case is obvious. The United States Supreme Court does not recognize homosexual behavior to be in a protected class requiring strict scrutiny of any statutes restricting it. Therefore, there is no denial of equal protection when that behavior is criminalized or treated differently, at least under an equal protection analysis.[41]

Whatever the merits of this interpretation of *Bowers v. Hardwick*, that interpretation was indispensable to the court's disposal of Limon's equal protection claim. *Hardwick* was overruled by *Lawrence.* The reasoning of the court of appeals was thus deprived of a key underpinning, and so remand was necessary.

Beyond this, however, it is not clear that Limon should get any comfort from *Lawrence.* There are plenty of reasons why the state could rationally treat homosexual sex differently from heterosexual sex. It could think that there is a moral difference between the two activities. It could think that the stigma attached to one activity is greater than that attached to the other, so that it is a graver thing to induce a teenager to have homosexual sex than to have heterosexual sex. There are plenty of bases on which the court could affirm Limon's conviction on remand.

Justice Kennedy's majority opinion was careful to limit the reach of its holding, and some of the opinion's language suggests that it has no relevance whatever to Limon's case. *Lawrence* was to be resolved "by determining whether the petitioners were free as adults to engage in the private conduct in the exercise of their liberty under the Due Process Clause of the Fourteenth Amendment to the Constitution."[42] Certain sexual privacies were protected, but the Court emphasized that "[t]he petitioners were adults at the time of the alleged offense,"[43] and it later emphasized that "[t]he present case does not involve minors."[44] The Court obviously did not intend to call into question the constitutionality of statutory rape laws.

The Court also limited its holding in other ways, by conspicuously ignoring legal arguments that were stronger and more persuasive than the mushy right to liberty (and which would have been very helpful to Limon) but which would have proven too much.

The Court did not hold that there was anything per se wrong with classifications on the basis of sexual orientation, much less that discrimination against gays was constitutionally suspect under the equal protection clause of the Fourteenth Amendment because the group is the object of pervasive prejudice.[45] That would probably have invalidated the U.S. military's exclusion of gays. President Bill Clinton ran into political disaster when he tried to take on the military's policy, and the Supreme Court evidently has no desire to start down that road.

Nor did the Court hold that discrimination against gay people was an impermissible form of sex discrimination.[46] That is the most powerful argument of all. If the state prosecutes Ricky because of his sexual activities with Fred, while these actions would not be taken against Lucy if she did exactly the same things with Fred, then Ricky is suffering legal disadvantage because of his sex.[47] In any prosecution under the Texas statute, the sex of the participants is an element of the crime that the prosecutor must prove.[48] But this argument goes too far for the present Supreme Court.

It implies the legality of same-sex marriage,[49] an issue that the Court made clear its intention to avoid.[50]

Nonetheless, *Lawrence* should be enough to get Limon out of jail. The singling out of gay youth for such remarkably harsh treatment would seem to pose a severe equal protection problem. Kansas must treat same-sex and opposite-sex statutory rape in equal terms.[51]

The Interstate Recognition Case

Same-sex marriage has come to the United States. Massachusetts now recognizes such marriages,[52] and increasing numbers of same-sex couples have married. Other states have virtually the same status: Vermont and Connecticut recognize "civil unions" and California recognizes "domestic partnerships" that have virtually all of the rights of marriage.[53] Are these statuses exportable? Will same-sex unions be recognized in other states?

Before *Lawrence*, this question was almost entirely unconstrained by constitutional law. After *Lawrence*, all states are constitutionally required to recognize such marriages under some circumstances.

Many people have confusedly thought, and some still think, that the full faith and credit clause of the Constitution[54] requires states to recognize marriages from other states. But this has never been the law. The clause requires states only to recognize other states' judgments, rendered after adversarial proceedings.[55] There is almost no authority for the proposition that full faith and credit applies to marriage,[56] and there is a great deal of authority to the contrary, indicating that states may decline to recognize foreign marriages when those marriages are contrary to the strong public policy of the forum state.[57]

American choice of law doctrine with respect to marriage recognition has depended on a heavily fact-specific weighing of incommensurable considerations. Courts have balanced the forum's public policy interest against the interests of other states in effectuating their own marriage laws and the interests of the parties in having their marriages recognized. The outcome has usually been recognition. There is, however, a notable body of law in which recognition has often been denied. These cases have involved differences in state laws concerning incest (for example, marriages of first cousins), marriageable age, remarriage after divorce, and above all, interracial marriage (until the Supreme Court struck down all restrictions on those marriages).

These older cases weigh against a *blanket* rule of nonrecognition for same-sex marriage, even where states have a public policy against recognizing such marriages, and even where that public policy is codified by statute. Such a blanket rule was not adopted even in the interracial marriage cases, in which the Southern states had an exceedingly strong policy against recognition. In every such case that did not involve cohabitation within the forum, and in some that did, the Southern courts recognized interracial marriages.

There is no legal basis for treating same-sex marriages in an unprecedentedly harsh fashion. The solution that is most consistent with existing choice of law rules is one in which states can control the marriages of their own domiciliaries: Citizens of Massachusetts are controlled by Massachusetts law and those of Alabama by Alabama law, regardless, in both cases, of whether they temporarily travel into a different jurisdiction with different marriage rules.

I have made this argument in the past as an interpretation of common law conflicts doctrine.[58] I emphasized that I was not making a constitutional argument.[59] I wasn't then, but I am now.

After *Lawrence v. Texas*, states are barred from treating gay people in an unprecedentedly harsh way. There is no precedent for a blanket rule of non-recognition of same-sex relationships. All states are thus constitutionally required to recognize at least some such relationships. Most prominently, the marriages of same-sex couples domiciled in Massachusetts and the civil unions of same-sex couples domiciled in Vermont, Connecticut, and California have a powerful claim to recognition, under some circumstances, everywhere in the United States.

Because different states have different rules concerning who may marry, the question of a marriage's validity may raise an issue of conflict of laws—that is to say, an issue in which a court must decide "whether or not and, if so, in what way, the answer to a legal question will be affected because the elements of the problem have contacts with more than one jurisdiction."[60] In conflicts cases, the "overwhelming tendency"[61] is to validate marriages, but the courts have frequently recited an exception in cases where recognition would violate the strong public policy of the forum state.

This area of the law has become somewhat archaic, because the public policy exception to marriage recognition has been invoked primarily in three contexts:[62] polygamy, incest, and miscegenation.[63] The first two were always misnomers to some extent. No state ever recognized polygamy.[64] Nor did any state ever violate the core instances of the incest taboo by legalizing parent-child or sibling marriages. The incest cases involved marriages between first cousins, aunts and nephews, uncles and nieces, or even more remote relations.[65]

Interracial marriage aroused the strongest passions in the courts, whose "opinions can be arranged along a discomfort continuum, with polygamy being the least offensive, incest falling in the middle and miscegenation giving courts the greatest amount of consternation."[66] In 1967, the Supreme

Court declared unconstitutional every miscegenation prohibition in the country, thereby eliminating any conflict of laws with respect to that issue.[67] Since that time, there has not been any comparably severe moral conflict among the states with respect to marriage. Until now.

Forty-three states have laws on the books declaring that they will not recognize same-sex marriages, and that such marriages are contrary to their public policy. They present a significant obstacle to the recognition of same-sex marriages from Massachusetts. It is less clear whether most are even relevant to the recognition of civil unions from other states, since almost all of them use the word "marriage" to describe what they are denying to same-sex couples.[68] Nonetheless, some of them have very strong language, describing same-sex marriages as "void" or "prohibited."[69] These provisions are widely understood as enacting a blanket rule of nonrecognition, under which states would "ignore marriage licenses granted to same-sex couples in other states."[70] That rule might be held by implication to reach civil unions as well. Under the blanket nonrecognition rule, a state's courts would never recognize any same-sex marriage for any purpose whatsoever. Those who have proposed this rule do not seem to have understood just how unprecedented a measure they are proposing.

The closest historical analogue to the radical moral disagreement over same-sex relationships is the divide between states that permitted and those that forbade marriage between whites and blacks. For this reason, the miscegenation cases deserve particularly close examination. Miscegenation prohibitions were in force as early as the 1660s, but only after the Civil War did they begin to function as a central sanction in the system of white supremacy. At one time or another, forty-one American colonies and states enacted them.[71]

The miscegenation taboo was held in the Southern states with great tenacity; it was close to the psychological core of racism.[72] "Although such marriages were infrequent throughout most of U.S. history, an enormous amount of time and energy was nonetheless spent in trying to prevent them from taking place."[73] When they defended the prohibition, Southern courts were at least as passionate in their denunciations as modern opponents of same-sex marriage.

> The purity of public morals, the moral and physical development of both races, and the highest advancement of our cherished southern civilization, under which two distinct races are to work out and accomplish the destiny to which the Almighty has assigned them on this continent—all require that they should be kept distinct and separate, and that connections and alliances so unnatural that God and nature seem to forbid them, should be prohibited by positive law, and be subject to no evasion.[74]

The Southern states typically went far beyond the recent legislation prohibiting same-sex marriage by making interracial marriage a felony; often it was specifically *marriage*, and not merely interracial sex, that was criminalized. In some states, it was necessary to prove cohabitation in order to convict for miscegenation; in others, the prosecutor was required to prove an actual marriage.[75] One conviction was reversed because, although the ceremony had taken place, the officiating notary's commission had expired.[76]

Today, on the other hand, even the states most strongly opposed to same-sex marriage have never attempted to make it a crime to enter into such marriages. Moreover, even before laws against consensual sodomy were invalidated by the U.S. Supreme Court, they were almost never enforced. It would be hard to argue that the Southern states' public policy against miscegenation was *less* strong than modern public policies against same-sex marriage.

Yet even in this charged context, the Southern states did not make a blunderbuss of their own public policy. Their decisions concerning the validity of interracial marriages were surprisingly fact-dependent. They did not utterly disregard the interests of the parties to the forbidden marriages or of the states that had recognized their marriages, but weighed these against the countervailing interests of the forum. Where those forum interests were attenuated, Southern courts sometimes upheld marriages between blacks and whites.

Three classes of choice-of-law problems arose involving interracial marriages. The first, "evasive" marriages,[77] were cases in which parties had traveled out of their home state for the express purpose of evading that state's prohibition of their marriages, and thereafter immediately returned home. Southern courts always invalidated these marriages. These are the types of cases that are most prominent in debates about recognition of same-sex marriage, but there are two other kinds of cases that have arisen. Second were "migratory" marriages: cases in which the parties had not intended to evade the law, but had contracted a marriage valid where they lived, and subsequently moved to a state where interracial marriages were prohibited. These were the most difficult cases, and the Southern authorities were evenly divided on how to deal with them. Finally, there were "extraterritorial" cases in which the parties had never lived within the state, but in which the marriage was relevant to litigation conducted there. Typically, after the death of one spouse, the other sought to inherit property that was located within the forum state. In these cases, the courts invariably recognized the marriages.[78]

The law with respect to the "evasive" marriages is quite clear. The rule is that states have the right to govern their own residents. In the interracial marriage cases, these marriages were almost never recognized.[79]

This anti-evasion principle was applied, however, only in cases where the parties were domiciliaries of the forum.[80] In "migratory" cases where the couple had been domiciled elsewhere at the time of the marriage, the authorities were divided.[81]

Finally, when the couple remained in another state, and the validity of their marriage happened to come into issue in litigation in the forum, the case was equally easy. In these "extraterritorial" cases, the marriages were routinely upheld, on the reasoning that, the purpose of the law being the prevention of such cohabitation, no harm would be done by recognizing the marriage after its dissolution by death for purposes of allowing the survivor to inherit the decedent's property in the state, or allowing the children to inherit as legitimate offspring. All deemed it dispositive that their states' laws were not intended to have any extraterritorial application. Typical was the pronouncement of the Mississippi Supreme Court in 1948:

> The manifest and recognized purpose of this statute was to prevent persons of Negro and white blood from living together in this state in the relationship of husband and wife. Where, as here, this did not occur, to permit one of the parties to such a marriage to inherit property in this state from the other does no violence to the purpose of [the miscegenation laws]. What we are requested to do is simply to recognize this marriage to the extent only of permitting one of the parties thereto to inherit from the other property in Mississippi, and to that extent it must and will be recognized.[82]

The blanket rule of nonrecognition, then, is very nearly unheard of in the United States. (It is nearly unheard of anywhere.[83]) Applying it here would violate the rule of *Lawrence*.

A blanket rule of nonrecognition for same-sex marriage would have extraordinary implications. Consider the position of the same-sex couple who make their home in Massachusetts, Vermont, Connecticut, or California. They do not seek to evade any other state's laws. They simply have done what their own state's laws authorize them to do. What is their status to be within the federal system?

The blanket nonrecognition rule would place such a couple in a difficult position. They would lose all the rights arising out of their marriage as soon as they crossed the border into any state that had such a rule. Moreover, even if they never left home, they would be treated as unmarried if their status should become relevant to litigation that takes place in another state.

The consequences would be harsher than any proponent of nonrecognition probably contemplated. To begin with the most extreme case: Suppose a lesbian couple is married and raising a child together in Massachusetts, and that the child's biological mother takes the child on a weekend trip to another state.[84] While there, the mother and child are both seriously injured in an automobile accident. As soon as she learns the news, the other spouse gets onto an airplane and soon arrives at the hospital. Under the blanket nonrecognition rule, this is what she would be told: "You may not visit either of these patients, because only family members may visit patients here, and you are not a family member of either of these people in any respect which our state recognizes. You may not participate in medical decisions for either of them. If the mother dies, you will not have any parental rights in the child. If there is no surviving biological relative, we will regard the child as an orphan, and place him in foster care."

This would be a bizarre rule. None of the various approaches to conflict of laws followed in the United States requires this result, although each is uncertain enough that it cannot be foreclosed.[85] All one can say is that no other type of marriage in American history has been treated so badly.

One might respond that this treatment is appropriate because of the novelty of same-sex marriage. "[I]f one is uncomfortable with affording same-sex marriages the same status as traditional marriages, one will likely reject the suggestion that same-sex marriage should be governed by the same principles. Instead, one will view them as a fundamentally new arrangement to which the marriage precedents do not apply."[86] But the same claim might have been made on behalf of the laws the Court invalidated in *Romer* and *Lawrence*. Antidiscrimination protection for gays, which the law invalidated in *Romer* sought to nullify, is also a novelty. Sodomy laws targeting gays arose in response to another historical novelty, an active gay rights movement. If the novelty of the situation to which the legislature was responding was not enough to save the law in those cases, it should not suffice here, either.

If my interpretation of *Lawrence* is correct, then the unprecedented character of a blanket rule of nonrecognition has constitutional implications. Such a rule would manifest unconstitutional animus toward gay people. However much states may dislike same-sex marriages, they must treat them less harshly than this.

Thus far there is little case law on recognition of foreign same-sex unions, and what there is involves the consequences of evasion. A New York court found that the surviving spouse in a Vermont civil union could bring a wrongful death action.[87] A Georgia Court declined to recognize a Vermont civil union in a case in which both parties were Georgia domiciliaries, though the court did not notice the significance of domicile.[88] A Connecticut court (before that state's legislature adopted civil unions) construed Connecticut law to deny it subject matter jurisdiction to dissolve a Vermont civil union entered into by a Connecticut domiciliary.[89] The last two of these cases included language that suggested a blanket rule of recognition, but they did so unreflectively, without noticing the practical or constitutional difficulties that such a rule would entail. Two judges, in Massachusetts and Iowa, each approved uncontested dissolutions of Vermont civil unions.[90] The question of migratory or extraterritorial civil unions has not yet arisen.

The domicile-based approach to marriage recognition is obviously unsatisfying to both sides of the debate. Those who object to same-sex marriage don't want it ever to be recognized in any context. Gay rights supporters have reasons of their own to be discontented. Most gay Americans who are in enduring, committed relationships, and who wish to marry do not live in Massachusetts, Vermont, Connecticut, or California and will not move to either of those states. But this underestimates the value for gays of having same-sex marriages legally recognized, at least for certain purposes, in every state. An important message is sent when courts nullify *all* same-sex marriages, even those in which their states have no legitimate interest. An equally important message is sent when they refrain from doing that.[91] This is not as much recognition as some hope for, but it is what the law now calls for. If you don't like it (I don't like it either), you had better try to change the law.

Conclusion

Lawrence, it appears, has a penumbra: There is a rule contained therein that is not stated in the opinion but that will govern future cases. There are precedents for this kind of signal from the Court. A week after it decided *Brown v. Board of Education*,[92] a case where the Court also faced considerable political resistance, it similarly remanded a case involving the exclusion of black people from opera performances in an amphitheater leased from the state.[93] That case did not involve any issue that was discussed in the *Brown* opinion, but it soon became clear that the *Brown* Court meant more than it was saying.

The broader upshot is that all anti-gay laws are now under suspicion. The severest ones are unconstitutional. The courts will not smash the great edifice of anti-gay law in the United States with a single judicial blow, and it would be foolish for them to try. But the edifice is crumbling.

Notes

1. This chapter is adapted from two earlier essays, Lawrence's Penumbra, Minn. L. Rev. 88 (2004): 1171–83, and Interstate recognition of same-sex civil unions after *Lawrence v. Texas*, Ohio St. L. J. 65 (2004): 1265–82.
2. 123 S.Ct. 2472 (2003).
3. Ibid., 2484.
4. When the reasoning of Lawrence is scrutinized by a trained logician, the consequences are not pretty. See Richard D. Mohr, "The Shag-a-delic Supreme Court: 'Anal Sex,' 'Mystery,'

'Destiny,' and the 'Transcendent' in *Lawrence v. Texas*," *Cardozo Women's Law Journal* 10 (2004): 365–395.

5. *Lawrence*, 123 S.Ct. at 2483, quoting *Bowers v. Hardwick*, 478 U.S. 186, 216 (1986) (Justice Stevens, dissenting).

6. *Lawrence*, 123 S.Ct 2490 (Justice Scalia, dissenting).

7. And such laws are occasionally enforced. See Richard A. Posner and Katharine B. Silbaugh, *A Guide to America's Sex Laws* (Chicago: University of Chicago Press, 1996), 98, 103.

8. 517 U.S. 620 (1996).

9. 478 U.S. 186 (1986).

10. *Lawrence*, 123 S.Ct., 2482.

11. Ibid., quoting Romer, 517 U.S., 624, 634 (citations omitted).

12. The consistency of the two cases is argued further in Andrew Koppelman, *The Gay Rights Question in Contemporary American Law* (Chicago and London: University of Chicago Press, 2002), 6–34.

13. *Lawrence*, 123 S.Ct., 2482.

14. *Washington v. Davis*, 426 U.S. 229 (1976).

15. *Village of Arlington Heights v. Metropolitan Dev. Housing Corp.*, 429 U.S. 252, 266 (1977).

16. See Andrew Koppelman, "On the Moral Foundations of Legal Expressivism," *Maryland Law Review* 60 (2001): 779, n.12.

17. See Koppelman, *The Gay Rights Question*, 21–25.

18. *Lawrence*, 123 S.Ct., 2478.

19. Ibid., 2482.

20. Ibid.

21. Ibid., 2484.

22. Ibid.

23. *Dept. of Agriculture v. Moreno*, 413 U.S. 528, 534 (1973), quoted in *Lawrence*, 123 S.Ct., 2485 (Justice O'Connor, concurring in the judgment).

24. *Lawrence*, 123 S.Ct., 2485 (Justice O'Connor, concurring in the judgment).

25. Ibid., p. 2486, quoting *Romer*, 116 S.Ct., 634.

26. *Lawrence*, 123 S.Ct., 2482.

27. See Andrew Koppelman, "*Romer v. Evans* and Invidious Intent," *William & Mary Bill of Rights Journal* 6 (1997): 89–146, reprinted in Koppelman, *The Gay Rights Question*.

28. Better to refuse to hear a case than to decide it wrongly. See Andrew Koppelman, "The Miscegenation Analogy: Sodomy Law as Sex Discrimination," *Yale Law Journal* 98 (1988): 162–64.

29. See *Lawrence*, 123 S.Ct., 2479–80.

30. *Romer*, 517 U.S., 633.

31. See, e.g., Patrick Lee and Robert P. George, "What Sex Can Be: Self-Alienation, Illusion, or One-Flesh Union," *American Journal of Jurisprudence*, 42 (1997): 135–157.

32. David A. Strauss, "The Myth of Colorblindness," *Sup. Ct. Rev. 1986*: 99–134.

33. Frederick Schauer, *Free Speech: A Philosophical Enquiry* (Cambridge: Cambridge University Press, 1982), 8; George Kateb, "The Freedom of Worthless and Harmful Speech," in Bernard Yack, ed., *Liberalism without Illusions* (Chicago: University of Chicago Press, 1996).

34. Kan. Stat. Ann. § 21-3505.

35. The law also requires that the age difference be less than four years. Kan. Stat. Ann. § 21-3522. The more specific "Romeo and Juliet" statute controls whenever an activity is covered by both this law and the general sodomy law. See *State v. Williams*, 829 P.2d 892, 897 (Kan. 1992).

36. To be precise, 206 months.

37. These facts are drawn from petition for writ of certiorari, *Limon v. Kansas* (S.Ct. No. 02-583). The consequences of being classified as a sexual offender are potentially severe. Under the Kansas Offender Registration Act (Kan. Stat. Ann. § 22-4901 et seq.), *Limon* would have to register with the sheriff of any county in which he resides or is temporarily domiciled. The information required under the registration in effect becomes public information open to inspection at the Sheriff's office and on any internet website sponsored by a Sheriff's department or the Kansas Bureau of Investigation. This registration provision is in effect for ten years from conviction or, if confined, for ten years after parole or release if this is a first conviction. Upon a second or subsequent conviction, registration would be required for the rest of the offender's lifetime. Kan. Stat. Ann. § 22-4906.

38. 123 S.Ct. 2472 (2003).
39. *Limon v. Kansas*, 123 S.Ct. 2638 (2003).
40. 478 U.S. 186 (1986).
41. *Kansas v. Limon*, No. 85,898 (Kan. App. 2002), in Appendix to Petition for Writ of Certiorari, *Limon v. Kansas*, 12a.
42. *Lawrence*, 123 S.Ct., 2476.
43. Ibid.
44. Ibid., 2484.
45. See *Rowland v. Mad River Local School Dist.*, 470 U.S. 1009 (1985) (Brennan, J., joined by Marshall, J., dissenting from denial of cert.); *Watkins v. United States Army*, 847 F.2d 1329 (9th Cir. 1988), aff'd on other grounds, 875 F.2d 699 (9th Cir. 1989) (en banc), cert. denied, 498 U.S. 957 (1990); see also "The Constitutional Status of Sexual Orientation: Homosexuality as a Suspect Classification," *Harvard Law Review* 98 (1985): 1285–1309; "An Argument for the Application of Equal Protection Heightened Scrutiny to Classifications Based on Homosexuality," *S. Cal. L. Rev.* 57 (1984): 797–836.
46. See Koppelman, *The Gay Rights Question*, 53–71.
47. *Lawrence*, 123 S.Ct. at 2495 (Scalia, J., dissenting) (citations omitted). This misstates what the Court did in the miscegenation cases. In both *Loving*, which discussed White Supremacy, and its precursor *McLaughlin v. Florida*, 379 U.S. 184 (1964), which did not, the Court held that the statutes classified on the basis of race and so were subject to strict scrutiny. If a law classifies by race on its face, then the challenger has no burden of proving a discriminatory purpose. The same is true of sex-based classifications. See generally Koppelman, *The Gay Rights Question*, 55–63.
48. Justice O'Connor writes that "Texas treats the same conduct differently based solely on the participants," 123 S.Ct., 2485 (Justice O'Connor, concurring in the judgment), but this is not accurate. She should have written that Texas treats the same conduct differently based solely on the *sex* of the participants.
49. See Koppelman, *The Gay Rights Question*, 71.
50. "The present case ... does not involve whether the government must give formal recognition to any relationship that homosexual persons seek to enter." *Lawrence*, 123 S.Ct., p. 2484. For a similar reservation, see ibid., 2487–88 (Justice O'Connor, concurring in the judgment).
51. The Court of Appeals of Kansas, on remand, upheld Limon's sentence. *State v. Limon*, 83 P.3d 229 (2004). The tortured character of its reasoning however confirms the claim I have made, that the statute bespeaks animus toward gays. For example, the court argues that the state can treat homosexual sex more harshly because "[t]he survival of society requires a continuous replenishment of its members," and "sexual acts between same-sex couples do not lead to procreation on their own." Ibid., 237. It is hard to imagine any other context in which a judge would attribute to the legislature the claim that statutory rape is *less* harmful if it results in pregnancy, or the hope that fourteen-year-old girls who have sex will become pregnant. The fact that otherwise sane people are willing to pretend to credit these rationalizations is itself powerful evidence of unconstitutional animus. See ibid., 243–49 (Justice Pierron, dissenting). The Kansas Supreme Court has agreed to review the decision.
52. See in re Opinions of the Justices to the Senate, 802 N.E. 2d 565, 570 (Mass. 2004); *Goodridge v. Department of Public Health*, 798 N.E. 2d 941 (Mass. 2003).
53. See 15 V.S.A. § 1204; Conn. Pub. Act No. 05-10 (2005); 2003 Ca. A.B. 205, § 297.5(a). For economy, I will refer to both statuses hereinafter as civil unions.
54. The full faith and credit clause of the Constitution provides:

> Full Faith and Credit shall be given in each State to the public Acts, Records, and judicial Proceedings of every other State. And Congress may by General Laws prescribe the Manner in which such Acts, Records and Proceedings shall be proved, and the Effect thereof.

U.S. Constitution, Art. IV, sec. 1.
55. See Andrew Koppelman, "Dumb and DOMA: Why the Defense of Marriage Act is Unconstitutional," *Iowa L. Rev.* 83 (1997): 17; Ralph U. Whitten, "Exporting and Importing Domestic Partnerships: Some Conflict-of-Laws Questions and Concerns," *B.Y.U. L. Rev.* 2001: 1246–49.

56. Koppelman, "Dumb and DOMA: Why the Defense of Marriage Act Is Unconstitutional," 10–15, Andrew Koppelman, "Same-Sex Marriage, Choice of Law, and Public Policy," *Tex. L. Rev.* 76 (1998): 971 n. 183. Both of these articles are reprinted in abridged and slightly revised form in Koppelman, *The Gay Rights Question.*
57. Koppelman, "Same-Sex Marriage, Choice of Law, and Public Policy," 946–62; see also "Developments in the Law—The Law of Marriage and Family: Constitutional Constraints on Interstate Same-Sex Marriage Recognition," *Harvard Law Review* 116 (2003): 2028–2051.
58. See Koppelman, "Dumb and DOMA: Why the Defense of Marriage Act Is Unconstitutional."
59. See Koppelman, "Same-Sex Marriage, Choice of Law, and Public Policy," 933. DOMA is unconstitutional, but that conclusion has little effect on states' freedom to craft their own laws. The only effect that DOMA has on choice of law rules is to authorize states to deny recognition to same-sex marriage when such denial would violate due process, or when it would nullify final judgments from other states. Congress surely did not intend this result, but DOMA is a poorly conceived and drafted statute. See generally Koppelman, "Dumb and DOMA: Why the Defense of Marriage Act Is Unconstitutional."
60. Russell J. Weintraub, *Commentary on the Conflict of Laws*, 3rd ed. (Mineola, NY: Foundation Press, 1986), 1.
61. William M. Richman and William L. Reynolds, *Understanding Conflict of Laws*, 2nd ed. (New York: Matthew Bender, 1993), 362.
62. There have also been cases involving differences in age restrictions and rules concerning remarriage after divorce.
63. I will not put scare quotes around this word, but use it with the same caveats set forth by Peggy Pascoe:

    Many scholars avoid using the word *miscegenation*, which dates to the 1860s, means race mixing, and has, to twentieth-century minds, embarrassingly biological connotations; they speak of laws against "interracial" or "cross-cultural" relationships. Contemporaries usually referred to "anti-miscegenation" laws. Neither alternative seems satisfactory, since the first avoids naming the ugliness that was so much a part of the laws and the second implies that "miscegenation" was a distinct racial phenomenon rather than a categorization imposed on certain relationships. I retain the term *miscegenation* when speaking of the laws and court cases that relied on the concept, but not when speaking of people or particular relationships.

    Peggy Pascoe, "Miscegenation Law, Court Cases, and Ideologies of 'Race' in Twentieth-Century America," *J. Am. Hist.* 83 (1996): 48 n.11.
64. See Koppelman, "Same-Sex Marriage, Choice of Law, and Public Policy," 946–48.
65. Ibid., 948.
66. Deborah M. Henson, "Will Same-Sex Marriages Be Recognized in Sister States? Full Faith and Credit and Due Process Limitations on States' Choice of Law Regarding the Status and Incidents of Homosexual Marriages Following Hawaii's *Baehr v. Lewin*," *U. Louisville J. Fam. L.* 32 (1993–94): 573.
67. *Loving v. Virginia*, 388 U.S. 1 (1967).
68. However, the laws of Arkansas, Georgia, Kentucky, Louisiana, Michigan, Nebraska, North Dakota, Ohio, Utah, and Virginia bar recognition of relationships similar to marriage as well.
69. Koppelman, "Same-Sex Marriage, Choice of Law, and Public Policy," 965–70; see also my compilation of the statutes in Andrew Koppelman, "Interstate recognition of same-sex marriages and civil unions: a handbook for judges," *U. Pa. L. Rev.* 153 (2005): 2165–94.
70. This formulation appears in two executive orders issued a few days apart by Governors Kirk Fordice of Mississippi and Fob James, Jr. of Alabama, declaring that they would not recognize same-sex marriages. See State of Mississippi, Office of the Governor, Executive Order No. 770 (Aug. 22, 1996) (same-sex marriage in another state "shall not be recognized as a valid marriage, shall produce no civil effects nor confer any of the benefits, burdens or obligations of marriage"); State of Alabama, Office of the Governor, Executive Order No. 24 (Aug. 29, 1996) (same).
71. See Pascoe, "Miscegenation Law," 49.
72. See generally Andrew Koppelman, "Why Discrimination against Lesbians and Gay Men Is Sex Discrimination," *New York University Law Review* 69 (1994): 220–234.

73. Peggy Pascoe, "Race, Gender, and Intercultural Relations: The Case of Interracial Marriage," *Frontiers* 12 (1991): 6.
74. *Kinney v. Commonwealth*, 71 Va. (30 Gratt.) 858, 869, 32 Am. Rep. 690, 699 (1878); for similar language in other decisions, see Koppelman, "Same-Sex Marriage, Choice of Law, and Public Policy," 950 n. 98.
75. See Koppelman, "Same-Sex Marriage, Choice of Law, and Public Policy," 950 nn. 99–100.
76. *Williams v. State*, 125 So. 690 (Ala. App. 1930).
77. I borrow this useful nomenclature from *Harvard Law Review*, 2038.
78. A fourth category of case did not arise with interracial marriages, but is quite important in the same-sex marriage context: "visitor" marriages, in which the state must ascertain the marital status of a person who is merely passing through the state. In such cases, I argue elsewhere, the marriages ought always to be recognized. See Andrew Koppelman, "Interstate recognition of same-sex marriages and civil unions: a handbook for judges," *U. Pa. L. Rev.* 153 (2005): 2143–94.
79. Koppelman, "Same-Sex Marriage, Choice of Law, and Public Policy," 952–54.
80. Where the parties had different domiciles with different policies at the time of celebration, authority was sparse and the commentators were divided. See Rebecca Bailey-Harris, "Madame Butterfly and the Conflict of Laws," *Am. J. Comp. L.* 39 (1991): 175.
81. See Koppelman, "Same-Sex Marriage, Choice of Law, and Public Policy," 954–61.
82. *Miller v. Lucks*, 203 Miss. 824, 832, 36 So. 2d 140, 3 A.L.R. 2d 236 (1948).
83. See Koppelman, "Same-Sex Marriage, Choice of Law, and Public Policy," 992–1001 (surveying marriage recognition rules in jurisdictions outside the United States).
84. Vermont and California both provide that the child of either party to a civil union shall be regarded as the child of both. See 23 Vt. Stat. § 1204(f); 2003 Ca. A.B. 205, § 297.5(d). An obvious consequence is that, in order for the spouse of the biological mother to assert parental rights in a legal proceeding, he or she must plead the existence of the civil union.
85. See generally Whitten. Unfortunately, one court has already managed to reach this result, holding that, because Virginia does not recognize same-sex relationships, a parental tie recognized in Vermont can be severed by the other parent unilaterally transporting the child to Virginia. The case is on appeal. See Christina Nuckols, "Two Women, Two States, One Child," *Virginian Pilot*, Dec. 13, 2004.
86. *Harvard Law Review*, 2050–51.
87. *Langan v. St. Vincent's*, 765 N.Y.S. 2d 411 (N.Y. Sup. 2003).
88. *Burns v. Burns*, 560 S.E. 2d 47 (Ga. App. 2002).
89. *Rosengarten v. Downes*, 802 A.2d 170 (Conn. App. 2002).
90. *Salucco v. Alldredge*, 17 Mass. L. Rptr. 498 (2002); Frank Santiago, "Iowa Judge OK's Lesbian Divorce," *Des Moines Register*, Dec. 12, 2003, 1A.
91. On the value of state action that seeks to alter the social status of unfairly stigmatized groups, see generally Andrew Koppelman, *Antidiscrimination Law and Social Equality* (New Haven: Yale University Press, 1996).
92. 347 U.S. 483 (1954).
93. *Muir v. Louisville Park Theatrical Association*, 347 U.S. 971 (1954).
94. The Court remained cryptic for some time, however. In a series of *per curiam* opinions after *Brown*, the Court affirmed lower court decisions invalidating laws segregating public beaches and bathhouses, municipal golf courses, a municipal bus system, courtroom seating, and public restaurants. See Erwin Chemerinsky, *Constitutional Law: Principles and Policies*, 2nd. ed. (New York and Gaithersburg: Aspen, 2002), 681–82. The first of these courts reasoned that after *Brown*,

> it is obvious that racial segregation in recreational activities can no longer be sustained as a proper exercise of the police power of the State; for if that power cannot be invoked to sustain racial segregation in the schools, where attendance is compulsory and racial friction may be apprehended from the enforced commingling of the races, it cannot be sustained with respect to public beach and bathhouse facilities, the use of which is entirely optional.

Mayor and City Council of Baltimore City v. Dawson, 220 F.2d 386, 387 (4th Cir.), aff'd, 350 U.S. 877 (1955). This is a pretty tortured reading of *Brown*, which focused solely on the unequal educational results of segregation. Presumably the patrons of the black beaches got just as wet as the patrons of the white ones. *See Lonesome v. Maxwell*, 123 F.Supp. 193 (D.C.Md. 1954) (noting earlier court finding and parties' stipulation that Baltimore beach facilities were physically equal for both races). Nonetheless, the Supreme Court upheld this and the following cases without comment, until at last it cited the whole string of cases for the proposition that "it is no longer open to question that a State may not constitutionally require segregation of public facilities." *Johnson v. Virginia*, 373 U.S. 61 (1963).

Neither the majority opinion nor O'Connor's concurrence mentioned this argument, but Scalia thought he discerned it in O'Connor's reasoning. He sought to rebut the claim that *Loving v. Virginia*, 388 U.S. 1 (1967), which held that laws against interracial marriage were racially discriminatory, was relevant to gays' claims.

> In Loving, however, we correctly applied heightened scrutiny, rather than the usual rational-basis review, because the Virginia statute was "designed to maintain White Supremacy." A racially discriminatory purpose is always sufficient to subject a law to strict scrutiny, even a facially neutral law that makes no mention of race. No purpose to discriminate against men or women as a class can be gleaned from the Texas law, so rational-basis review applies.

CHAPTER 9

Lawrence, Privacy, and the Marital Bedroom

A Few Telltale Signs of Ironic Worry

JOE ROLLINS

Introduction

Queer Americans have much to be happy about since the Supreme Court's decision in *Lawrence v. Texas* (2003). The demise of *Bowers v. Hardwick* (1986) has decriminalized gay and lesbian identities and is good reason for celebration in itself. From a practical, legal standpoint, the most important change is the removal of a key mechanism with which to deny the rights claims of sexual minorities. Same-sex families will perhaps gain the most, as the default criminal status of gay and lesbian parents no longer stands as an obstacle in custody and adoption proceedings. But as a growing body of case law already indicates, *Lawrence* may not be the political solution many of us had hoped.[1] The opinion relies on a complex interplay of ironies, epistemological gaps, and silences, and thus it is narratively unstable and leaves queer citizens in a precarious social, cultural, and political position.

All legal contests superimpose narrative order on a material world, rendering coherent, meaningful, and predictable stories from events that are often random, meaningless, chaotic, and unintentional. Frequently, the strategies used to impose order and systematize this messiness are drawn from discourses that inspire belief not because of substance, but because they are produced at sites that occupy an elevated position atop the hierarchy of credibility: usually science.[2] With increasing frequency, legal narratives turn to the products of scientific study to simplify, justify, explain, and determine legal solutions to sticky problems.[3] The achievements of scientists are conscripted to legal ends: settling disputes and reinforcing the power of the state. Legal disputes involving sexuality upset this balance, in part, because the relationship between science and sexuality is highly dysfunctional. Despite enthusiastic study, very little about sexual identity is known with scientific certainty and, as a result, legal scripts must instead rely on the more obviously political discourses of religion, tradition, morality, and history. Making meaning in these situations and with these components often takes on the appearance of moving heavy, cumbersome objects in a zero-gravity environment.[4]

After the Supreme Court decided *Bowers v. Hardwick* (1986), a sizeable industry of legal analysis grew up in this unpredictable milieu. Importantly, legal scholars produced a formidable set of critiques calling into view the Court's schematic strategies—its shortcomings and flaws.[5] This body of literature spotlights the Court's inability to comprehend the nature of the subject at hand and to properly situate it within a workable framework; act, identity, behavior, the Constitution, and the Bible were schematically sampled and woven into a web of heteronormative and homophobic possibilities.[6] The schematic confusions that grounded the *Bowers* opinion were not, however, limited to that text and reappear in *Lawrence*. If a binary construction of sexuality could be determined with scientific clarity, we could know for certain that there are two kinds of people in the world—gay and straight—and the legal construction of social institutions could proceed from that simple, dualistic truth. But we do not know any such thing; sexuality exists in our culture as both real and material at the same time that it is thought to be a social construct relevant only in the domain of symbols and epistemology. Because these two sets of truths operate simultaneously, both appear in legal discourse. Inasmuch as *Lawrence* draws from gay-affirmative research, acknowledges the constructedness of the homosexual subject, and tears down one important boundary between gay and straight citizens, it also accepts the distinction between gay and straight as real and material, privileges the status quo, and reifies extant hierarchies of sexual value and gender difference.[7] In this chapter, I want to consider not only the rhetorical strategies at work in *Lawrence* but also to place those practices in a larger political and social context. At the same time that the opinion removes one legal tactic for distinguishing between homo- and heterosexuality, it relies upon and reinforces that same distinction and maintains a qualitative hierarchy that re-establishes heterosexuality as culturally and politically superior. These schematic strategies reveal a gap between the literal text of *Lawrence* and the figurative meanings we must use to make sense of it. Because of the literal and the figurative conflict, it is productive to read the decision through the interpretive lens of irony.

Ironic communication has at least three components. The first is semantic, whereby there is an apparent conflict between a statement and its intended meaning. Second, there is a subjective dimension whereby the sender (the ironist) and receiver (the interpreter) might or might not work together to "get" the irony; this interaction between speaker and audience defines a discursive community that either includes (those who get the irony) or excludes participants (those who do not). Third, irony embodies an evaluative dimension that allows for the expression of a judgment.[8] Attending to these three communicative elements in the text of *Lawrence v. Texas* reveals the gaps between the language and epistemology of that script and shows more clearly its political limitations. Attending to the semantic dimension of a judicial script allows us to see what rhetorical choices the Justices have made as they position a case within existing chains of precedent. A subjective analysis helps us to see how the Justices know the juridical subjects interpolated by their opinions. Paying attention to these elements then allows us to see the hierarchy of values and the unwritten premises upon which a decision is founded, and to predict their future utility.

The following analysis proceeds in three phases. Part I explores the semantic dimension of the *Lawrence* text, evaluating in particular the effect of anchoring that text to the Court's privacy precedents. Part II considers the subjective dimension of the script, detailing what Janet Halley has called the "practices of categorization" through which legal subjects are rendered visible and given meaning.[9] Finally, Part III returns the discussion to the evaluative political thread that runs through the *Lawrence* opinions. When viewed from these three angles, *Lawrence* may not appear to be the cause for celebration that it seems to have been at first glance.

Part I: Semantics

A constitutional right of privacy has been debated throughout the course of the twentieth century. Not only are we unsure about what parts of the Constitution may contain a right to privacy, we are uncertain as to exactly what aspects of our lives might be protected by such a right. It seems clear, however, that what privacy rights do exist orbit the nucleus of the male-female reproductive sexual dyad.[10] When the Supreme Court first articulated a constitutional right of privacy in *Griswold*, it drew a boundary around the marital bedroom and worried about police searching that private sanctuary for telltale signs of contraceptive use. Since 1965, that spatial boundary has not expanded but contracted. Instead of growing spatially outward to operate at the boundary of public and private space—the boundary between home, hearth, family, and the state outside—this constriction has refined the concept of privacy such that it is genitally focused and reproductively specific, placing particular emphasis on the reproductive possibilities that may occur from genital contact. *Bowers* placed gays and lesbians outside this configuration in part because, ostensibly, the reproductive component of this configuration was missing. In the forgetful words of Justice White: "No connection between family, marriage, or procreation on the one hand and homosexual activity on the other has been demonstrated, either by the Court of Appeals or by respondent."[11]

Judith Butler accurately describes the relationship between sexuality, marriage, and legitimacy: "Sexuality is already thought in terms of marriage and marriage is already thought as the purchase on legitimacy."[12] Running through each of these terms is a conception of privacy that is partially legal, social, spatial, and reproductive, resulting in a closed, circular system, understood as natural, from which any alternative possibilities can be excluded.[13] Marriage is the contract through which the state publicly confers legitimacy on the marital dyad, and the private nature of sexuality has long been imagined as the interior reason that requires the state to exclude itself, but that sexuality is linked to reproduction or reproductive possibilities. Sexual and reproductive choices made outside the marital contract receive some measure of privacy, but they frequently lack the legitimacy of those made by married couples and, if American welfare politics or fights over abortion funding are taken as indicators, the right to privacy becomes even more flimsy when coupled with questions of economic privilege.

After reciting the facts of the case and summarizing the Texas statutory scheme, Justice Kennedy's majority opinion frames the three questions addressed by the Court: (1) whether the Equal Protection Clause of the Fourteenth Amendment allows the criminalization of sodomy between same-sex couples but not heterosexual ones, (2) whether such criminalization violates vital interests in liberty and privacy protected by the Due Process Clause of the Fourteenth Amendment, and (3) whether *Bowers v. Hardwick* should be overruled.[14] Five members of the Court joined Justice Kennedy's opinion, agreeing that the Texas statute violated a liberty interest protected by the Due Process Clause and overruling *Bowers v. Hardwick*. In a concurring opinion, Justice O'Connor agreed that the Texas statute was unconstitutional but argued that it should be stricken for equal protection deficiencies. Tellingly, she would have left *Bowers* in place as precedent and left open the question of whether she would have supported the continued criminalization of sodomy provided the prohibition applied to both gay and straight people.

Not surprisingly, Justice Kennedy anchors his due process argument in a chain of precedents that features *Griswold v. Connecticut*.[15] He then draws the privacy right articulated through the due process- and privacy-related cases the Court decided prior to *Bowers: Eisenstadt v. Baird, Roe v. Wade,* and *Carey v. Population Services Int'l*.[16] When he turns his attention to *Bowers*, he shifts his attention to the schematic resources by which sexual expression is given meaning in our culture:

> Were we to hold the statute invalid under the Equal Protection Clause some might question whether a prohibition would be valid if drawn differently, say, to prohibit the conduct both between same-sex and different-sex participants. Equality of treatment and the due process right to demand respect for conduct protected by the substantive guarantee of liberty are linked in important respects, and a decision on the latter point advances both interests. If protected conduct is made criminal and the law which does so remains unexamined for its substantive validity, its stigma might remain even if it were not enforceable as drawn for equal protection reasons. When homosexual conduct is made criminal by the law of the State, that declaration in and of itself is an invitation to subject homosexual persons to discrimination both in the public and in the private spheres. The central holding of Bowers has been brought in question by this case, and it should be addressed. Its continuance as precedent demeans the lives of homosexual persons.[17]

Here, the definitional potency of sodomy is redrawn to include any non-procreative sexual acts and includes heterosexuals as well as homosexuals. Crucially, Justice Kennedy recognizes that if the acts specified in the Texas statute remain criminal, it will be homosexuals who bear the burden of enforcement. Moreover, although he does not state it explicitly here, he later recognizes that the marital contract that establishes a boundary between the public and private spheres is unavailable to gays and lesbians.

Justice Kennedy then moves forward from *Bowers* to build a newly forged chain of precedent. Here he considers which of two post-*Bowers* decisions provides the more appropriate point at which to readjust the relationship between *Bowers* and *Lawrence*: *Planned Parenthood of Southeastern Pa. v. Casey* or *Romer v. Evans*. Rather than tethering *Lawrence* to the class-based distinction already recognized in *Romer*, Justice Kennedy reaches to *Casey*: "At the heart of liberty is the right to define one's own concept of existence, of meaning, of the universe, and the mystery of human life."[18] Justice Kennedy's concerns are undoubtedly on point—tethering *Lawrence* to *Romer* and adopting Justice O'Connor's position would leave open the possibility for criminalizing sodomy regardless of the sexual orientation of the participants—yet there remains a flaw in the Court's preferred analogy. *Casey* stands as confirmation that the Constitution protects "personal decisions relating to marriage, procreation, contraception, family relationships, child rearing and education."[19] Meanwhile, resisting the inclusion of same-sex relationships within this framework has become a national obsession. Indeed, it is the determined *exclusion* of gays and lesbians from this framework that presently grounds debate about same-sex marriage, a point addressed in more detail in Part III. Situating the *Lawrence* decision in this constitutional framework has potential but may well become a double-edged sword. In the Court's admirable attempt to remove the stigma associated with homosexuality, there lie the seeds for future exclusion from the legal, social, political, and cultural privileges institutionally conferred on heterosexuals. A constitutional right of privacy is closely linked to our notion of the marital, familial bedroom. Expanding the private sanctuary of marital bedrooms to include homosexuals may invite the homosexual into the private space of family life and may therefore generate substantial legal and political backlash. As Butler writes, "Over and against this life-giving heterosexuality at the foundation of culture is the specter of homosexual parenting, a practice that not only departs from nature and from culture, but centers on the dangerous and artificial fabrication of the human and is figured as a kind of violence or destruction."[20] The long-term value of *Lawrence* will depend not only on the decriminalization of sodomy, but on the degree to which gay and lesbian households are seen as private spaces outside the gaze of the state, occupied by families comprised of citizens and not subversives.

Part II: Subjectivity

In addition to the semantics of the opinion, there is also a subjective dimension whereby discursive communities are established. Justice Kennedy understands that homosexuals are a segment of society, one that is defined by an identity claim, and his opinion is grounded in that premise. His words depict gays and lesbians as a group of people who regularly face irrational fear, hostility, and discrimination. Justice O'Connor's opinion also depicts homosexuals as a segment of society, but in her case, the community is one defined by acts that might be made criminal by the state. Justice Scalia's dissenting opinion relies on both strategies: Homosexuals are a group of properly despised people, one defined by their criminal activities. Despite these variations, each opinion ultimately reaffirms a binary construction of sexuality and reproduces the existing sexual hierarchy.

In her analysis of *Bowers*, Nan Hunter observed that both pro- and anti-homosexual political interests "require a reliable definitional structure on which to ground their arguments and a coherent system for identifying homosexuality."[21] Sodomy, as she noted then, remains an utterly confused category, one that might be linked to desires, identities, or behaviors.[22] The epistemological choices we make regarding sexuality are fraught with political potential, and as Steven Epstein has argued, there are limits to social constructionism.[23] For the *Lawrence* Court, static identity categories are both necessary and useful. The *Bowers* Court elided acts with identities and defined homosexuality as analogous to sodomy at the same time that it excluded heterosexuals from that definitional possibility. In other words, sodomy defined the class of homosexuals whether they committed the act or not; heterosexual sodomites were excused their transgressions. The gender/sexuality nexus at work in *Bowers* was somewhat trickier for the Court because the Georgia statute criminalized sodomy whether committed by homosexual or heterosexual persons. Ultimately, the heterosexual plaintiffs involved in that case were dropped from the litigation. In *Lawrence*, the intersection of gender and sexuality plays differently because the Texas statute at issue applied only to same-sex couplings. Here, the conceptual link between sodomy and homosexuality remains intact at the same time that a new link between sodomy and heterosexuality is being forged.

Justice Kennedy's opinion in *Lawrence* directly refutes the central misapprehension of *Bowers*: "The issue presented is whether the Federal Constitution confers a fundamental right upon homosexuals to engage in sodomy and hence invalidates the laws of the many States that still make such conduct illegal and have done so for a very long time."[24] Justice Kennedy's opinion acknowledges the flawed construction at work beneath this formulation, and draws the analogy differently: "To say that the issue in *Bowers* was simply the right to engage in certain sexual conduct demeans the claim the individual put forward, just as it would demean a married couple were it to be said marriage is simply about the right to have sexual intercourse."[25] In this moment, Justice Kennedy's opinion draws down the boundary between homo- and heterosexuality, uncouples the conceptual link that was central to *Bowers* by removing sodomy from the equation, and sets the two identity categories in an analogous relationship. Once sexual identity categories are freed from the act of sodomy, he realigns the necessary schematic elements to characterize identity as expressive, a symbol emanating from choices we make when we form enduring personal bonds; the homosexual subject remains intact, but is ontologically redefined.

Justice Kennedy then addresses the *Bowers* Court's conception of sodomy, citing the work of scholars Jonathan N. Katz, John D'Emilio, and Estelle Freedman: "Thus early American sodomy laws were not directed at homosexuals as such but instead sought to prohibit nonprocreative sexual activity more generally. This does not suggest approval of homosexual conduct. It does tend to show that this particular form of conduct was not thought of as a separate category from like conduct between heterosexual persons."[26] Here, sodomy appears to have been removed from the categorization practices that define sexual identity—anyone can commit it; homo- and heterosexual persons might engage in nonprocreative sexual acts. Nonetheless, in other passages it remains apparent that, as Rubin describes, homo- and heterosexuality remain hierarchically organized and that procreative, marital, private heterosexuality is still unquestioned atop a system of sexual value allocation. Justice Kennedy's reconfiguration requires quoting at length:

> The statutes do seek to control a personal relationship that, whether or not entitled to formal recognition in the law, is within the liberty of persons to choose without being punished as criminals. This, as a general rule, should counsel against attempts by the State, or a court, to define the meaning of the relationship or to set its boundaries absent injury to a person or abuse of an institution the law protects. It suffices for us to acknowledge that adults may choose to enter upon this relationship in the confines of their homes and their own private lives and still retain their dignity as free persons. When sexuality finds overt expression in intimate conduct with another person, the conduct can be but one element in a personal bond that is more enduring. The liberty protected by the Constitution allows homosexual persons the right to make this choice.[27]

Several moments from this passage merit closer inspection. First, the acts for which Lawrence and Garner were arrested are here depicted as a "personal relationship" that individuals are entitled to enter without being branded as criminals. This depiction presents Justice Kennedy with a difficult choice: turn what may have been a casual tryst into a relationship and risk letting sexual deviants into the sanctified marital bedroom, or extend the mantle of constitutional protection around a casual tryst. Avoiding the danger of the latter approach, Justice Kennedy instead elevates the coupling to the status of a relationship, one that is "one element in a personal bond that is more enduring." This rhetorical choice raises the specter of requiring that the relationships entered by gays and lesbians are entitled recognition in the law, and in fact, may ultimately become a threat to an institution the law protects. In the final sentence, we see that entering into such a relationship is a "choice" that "homosexual persons" have a right to make. Justice Kennedy's artful equivocation brings gay and lesbian subjects into the schemas of constitutional law, but he is only willing to advance a short distance.

While sexual identity categories are primary and determinative in this case, the State of Texas was unwilling to risk the possibility that other damaging practices of categorization might have also been useful. One of the briefs for the State of Texas begins by asserting the following: "There is no evidence that Lawrence and Garner were adults, that their acts were performed by mutual consent, that there was no money exchanged, or that the two men were unrelated."[28] Emphasizing these points is almost comical because there was no evidence that Lawrence and Garner were not adults, and anyone who had seen the two in person or photographs would have been unlikely to mistake them for minors. There was never any allegation by the state that theirs was an act of prostitution, and considering that Lawrence is white and Garner African American, as noted a few sentences later in the same brief, the suggestion that they might be related (biologically, if not legally) seems especially disingenuous.

Part III: Evaluation

The semantic and subjective contests taking place in the *Lawrence* opinions vary slightly, but ultimately operate in similar domains. Justice Kennedy's script shows a determined effort to reallocate the schematic resources through which we understand sexuality, to cloak same-sex relationships with the protections of a right to privacy, and depicts gays and lesbians as a disadvantaged political minority. Justice Scalia's opinion is equally focused on contesting that schematic reallocation. On his reading, gays and lesbians are a group of deviants defined by behavior, one that is properly criminalized and not entitled to state protection. The discursive instability these two scripts make apparent is not, however, unexpected, and as Umphrey shows us, is constitutive; silences and the unstable relationship between power and knowledge are key components in our system of sexual identity.[29] Justices Kennedy, O'Connor, and Scalia have all produced opinions that rely on a binary construction of sexuality and although the Court majority overturned *Bowers* and struck the Texas sodomy statute, the homosexual subject remains intact. Despite the fact that Justice Kennedy's opinion works to remove the stigma associated with homosexuality, he joins O'Connor and Scalia in his worry about same-sex marriage. In the end, refusing to require that same-sex couples might be entitled to the same rights and responsibilities as heterosexual ones casts an evaluative badge of inferiority on the former while maintaining the superiority of the latter.

Justice Kennedy's opinion raises the specter of same-sex marriage in two passages. As noted, the definitional centrality of sodomy, its association with homosexuality and its removal from heterosexuality, is here displaced by a construction of sexuality as contingent upon relationships bonded through intimate conduct. The meaning of such conduct, he asserts, should not be determined by the state, "absent injury to a person or abuse of an institution the law protects."[30] The reference in this passage is oddly unclear; which institutions are open to abuse, and how same-sex couples might abuse them, are difficult questions to answer from the immediate context of the quotation. What might qualify as the abuse of a state-protected institution? The script becomes clearer later on:

> The present case does not involve minors. It does not involve persons who might be injured or coerced or who are situated in relationships where consent might not easily be refused. It does not involve public conduct or prostitution. *It does not involve whether the government must give formal recognition to any relationship that homosexual persons seek to enter.* The case does involve two adults who, with full and mutual consent from each other, engaged in sexual practices common to a homosexual lifestyle.[31]

It is instructive to juxtapose this passage with the thinking of Justices O'Connor and Scalia. From Justice O'Connor:

> That this law as applied to private, consensual conduct is unconstitutional under the Equal Protection Clause does not mean that other laws distinguishing between heterosexuals and homosexuals would fail under rational basis review. Texas cannot assert any legitimate state interest here, such as national security or preserving the traditional institution of marriage. Unlike the moral disapproval of same-sex relations—the asserted state interest in this case—other reasons exist to promote the institution of marriage beyond the mere moral disapproval of an excluded group.[32]

And from Justice Scalia's dissent, several noteworthy moments:

> State laws against bigamy, same-sex marriage, adult incest, prostitution, masturbation, adultery, fornication, bestiality, and obscenity are likewise sustainable only in light of *Bowers'* validation of laws based on moral choices. Every single one of these laws is called into question by today's decision; the Court makes no effort to cabin the scope of its decision to exclude them from its holding ... What a massive disruption of the current social order, therefore, the overruling of *Bowers* entails.[33]

Sitting next to one another, these three passages represent a continuum of possibilities for understanding the relationships between gender, sexuality, marriage, and privacy. Several schematic strategies are immediately apparent and despite their disagreements, all three display the same evaluative tendency: Same-sex unions are not as valuable as marriages. Justice Scalia's list of sexual horrors echoes his standard worries and, as usual, his schematic strategy relies on hyperbole and a highly creative rhetorical move toward the absurd.[34] On his reasoning, homosexuality is analogous to any number of deviant behaviors—but tellingly, the one apt analogy that he cannot make is the one between homo- and heterosexuality. Maintaining the superiority of heterosexuality requires overlooking the fact that his list of horrors might well be associated with heterosexual encounters. Each of the other items quoted in the passage above is more closely aligned with heterosexual behavior, and more frequently practiced by heterosexuals (if only because there are more of them), but recognizing this possibility would undermine the ironic evaluation of his rhetorical strategy: assign sexual excesses to the appropriately regulated perverts so that heterosexuality may appear to remain pure and unencumbered by state intrusion. Interpreting his worries as a concern for gender oppression is premature since rape, unintentional pregnancy, child abuse, and domestic violence have escaped his attention. Looking too closely at the very real problems associated with heterosexuality, and ignoring the very real similarities between homo- and heterosexuality, would indeed disrupt the social order in ways that Justice Scalia could not possibly support. Nonetheless, his evaluation of same-sex relationships is made strikingly, if inaccurately, clear by analogy and placement within the schematic strategy of his script.

Justice O'Connor is more gentle, but equally evaluative. Whereas Justice Scalia presents moral disapproval of same-sex relations as sufficient justification for the Texas statute, Justice O'Connor would have required Texas to demonstrate that the statute in question furthered some more pressing state interest. Seemingly, if the state had persuaded her that criminalizing same-sex couplings was necessary to preserving the institution of marriage—a position she suggests is possible—the statute may have passed muster in her view. At oral argument, counsel for Lawrence and Garner was cautious in his treatment of the relationship between sexual identity, acts of sodomy, and marriage, never stretching the possibilities for striking down the Texas statute to include state recognition of same-sex marriage. Indeed, he distinguished between the statute at issue and the prohibition against bigamy by relying on the need to protect the institution of marriage, a point Justice O'Connor re-emphasized in the passage cited above without any insight into how or why same-sex marriage would undermine that institution. (This is one piece of argument and evidence that opponents of same-sex marriage cannot present. Indeed, as the lawyer defending the statute admitted during oral argument, Texas does not criminalize pre- or extramarital sex among heterosexuals, both of which would seem to threaten marriage in far more proximal ways. Admitting as much, however, would require regulating heterosexuality far more than many straight people are inclined to allow, and would force the admission that the real damage to the institution is already being done by those who have access to it.) In the silences of Justice O'Connor's opinion, we can see her worries about taking gender out of the marital union.

In his opinion, Justice Scalia makes one of the potentially queerest arguments to emerge from the lot. In his consideration of the equal protection argument, he observes that the Texas statute applies equally to all persons regardless of gender or sexual orientation:

> Men and women, heterosexuals and homosexuals, are all subject to its prohibition of deviate sexual intercourse with someone of the same sex. To be sure [the Texas statute] does distinguish between the sexes insofar as concerns the partner with whom the sexual acts are performed: men can violate the law only with other men and women only with other women. But this cannot itself be a denial of equal protection, since it is precisely the same distinction regarding partner that is drawn in state laws prohibiting marriage with someone of the same sex while permitting marriage with someone of the opposite sex.[35]

Ironically, Scalia here implicitly recognizes that the distinctions between gender, sexual orientation, and sexual behavior are not in themselves dispositive. It is possible to read this passage as an acknowledgment that heterosexual men may commit acts of sodomy with other heterosexual men. It seems that this is unlikely to have been his interpretation, however, and it is more plausible that he is simply insisting that homosexuals should remain celibate, become heterosexual, and that heterosexuals should only have procreative sex.

On his final point, however, his logic is flawless and a cause for optimism among those who champion same-sex marriage. If the Texas statute in question here falls, there is little reason to believe that laws restricting same-sex marriages can continue to withstand constitutional scrutiny. Justice Scalia emphasizes the point twice later in his dissent: "This reasoning leaves on pretty shaky grounds state laws limiting marriage to opposite-sex couples."[36] In his final hyperbolic paragraphs, Justice Scalia drives home his worries:

> At the end of its opinion—after having laid waste the foundations of our rational-basis jurisprudence—the Court says that the present case "does not involve whether the government must give formal recognition to any relationship that homosexual persons seek to enter." Do not believe it. More illuminating than this bald, unreasoned

disclaimer is the progression of thought displayed by an earlier passage in the Court's opinion, which notes the constitutional protections afforded to "personal decisions relating to *marriage*, procreation, contraception, family relationships, child rearing, and education," and then declares that "persons in a homosexual relationship may seek autonomy for these purposes, just as heterosexual persons do."[37]

The worry here is semantic, subjective, and evaluative, and shows how the Court's decision is a double-edged sword. *Lawrence* is rhetorically situated among the Court's privacy jurisprudence and thus the analogy between homo- and heterosexuality is drawn more closely than any of the Justices can comfortably accept. Although the subjective distinction between homo- and heterosexual identity categories remains intact, the majority's vague reference to same-sex *relationships* seems to be of particular concern for Justice Scalia. Justice Kennedy's opinion tries to silence the possibility of same-sex marriage and the interpretive possibilities of that silence are multiple.

Nan Hunter writes in her discussion of *Bowers*: "It is not acts alone, but those acts in conjunction with same-gender desire that marks homosexuality. Gender is central to sexual orientation, and much of the positive social value of homosexuality lies in its creation of a zone of antiorthodoxy for men and women, of whatever sexual orientation."[38] The problem *Lawrence* presents for the Court, then, is not that it knocks down sodomy laws, but that it does so while trying to achieve a precarious ironic balance: If marriage requires gender and is semantically bounded by a legal right of privacy, the value and meaning of gender difference is left stranded on an evaluative razor's edge between magnified constitutive significance in the case of marriage on one side, and irrelevance to sexual expression, identity, and privacy on the other. Justice Scalia's nescient opinion avoids drawing any fixed meaning from sexual acts and worries that same-sex relationships may be elevated to the same position as marriage. Ironically, each of these opinions glosses over the fact that marriage is not necessarily about any of the sanctified holiness that its proponents make it out to be. Marriage need not be anything romantic, enduring, bonded, or even sexual—it may be purely economic, convenient, or endured out of boredom. In *Lawrence*, sodomy has been removed as the legal and behavioral badge of stigma with which *Bowers* branded homosexuals. At the same time, marriage is further elevated and venerated, granted to heterosexuals; homosexuals are left branded with the stigma of exclusion. This new pastiche of schematic resources ironically reallocates new silences and unknowable elements within our sexual/gender system but maintains the legal, social, and political inferiority of same-sex unions.

Notes

1. See, e.g., *State of Kansas v. Limon* 32 Kan. App. 2d 369 (2004); *Lofton v. Sec'y of the Dept. of Children and Family Services* 358 F.3d 804 (2004).
2. As Paul Gewirtz observes, the move toward narrative and rhetoric in legal analysis is partly a reaction against both the "scientistic" approach of the "law and economics" movement but also resists the abstractions of critical legal scholarship. See "Narrative and Rhetoric in the Law," in *Law's Stories: Narrative and Rhetoric in the Law*, eds. Peter Brooks and Paul Gewirtz (New Haven, CT: Yale University Press, 1996): 2–13, 13.
3. See Heidi Li Feldman, "Science and Uncertainty in Mass Exposure Litigation," *Texas Law Review* 74 (1995): 1–48; Edward J. Imwinkelried, "Evaluating the Reliability of Nonscientific Expert Testimony: A Partial Answer to the Questions Left Unresolved by *Kumho Tire Co. v. Carmichael*," *Maine Law Review* 52 (2000): 19–41; Joseph Sanders, "Complex Litigation at the Millennium: *Kumho* and How We Know," *Law and Contemporary Problems* 64 (2001): 373–415.
4. Or, to return to Eve Kosofsky Sedgwick's potent metaphor, sexuality has the extreme propulsive effect of wearing flippers in a swimming pool; movements and outcomes are hard to calibrate. See *Epistemology of the Closet* (Berkeley: University of California Press, 1990): 3.
5. Following Ewick and Silbey, schemas may be defined to include cultural codes, hierarchies of value, logics, conventions and vocabularies of motive—the linguistic and symbolic materials through which we can know the world and make sense of it. See Patricia Ewick and Susan S. Silbey, *The Common Place of Law: Stories from Everyday Life* (Chicago: University of Chicago Press, 1998): 40.
6. See, e.g., Janet Halley, "Reasoning about Sodomy: Act and Identity in and after *Bowers v. Hardwick*," *Virginia Law Review* 79 (1993) 1721; "The Construction of Heterosexuality," in *Fear of a Queer Planet: Queer Politics and Social Theory*, ed. Michael Warner (Minneapolis: University of Minnesota Press, 1993) 82–102; Nan D. Hunter, "Life after Hardwick," in *Sex Wars*, eds. Lisa Duggan and Nan D. Hunter (New York: Routledge, 1995) 85–100; Kendall Thomas, "Beyond the Privacy Principle," *Columbia Law Review* 92 (1992): 1431–1516.
7. See Gayle Rubin, "Thinking Sex: Notes for a Radical Theory of the Politics of Sexuality," in *The Lesbian and Gay Studies Reader*, ed. Henry Abelove et al., (New York: Routledge, 1993): 3–44.
8. I borrow this framework from Linda Hutcheon, *Irony's Edge: The Theory and Politics of Irony* (New York: Routledge, 1995).
9. See Halley, "Reasoning about Sodomy," 83.
10. For a useful treatment of this construction, see Martha Fineman, *The Neutered Mother, The Sexual Family, and Other Twentieth Century Tragedies* (New York: Routledge, 1995).
11. 478 U.S. 186, 191.
12. Judith Butler, "Is Kinship Always Already Heterosexual," in *Left Liberalism/Left Critique*, eds. Wendy Brown and Janet Halley (Durham: Duke University Press, 2002): 229–258, 232.
13. Circularity is not uncommon in these debates, and has surfaced in both the arguments of litigants and the rulings of judges, see William N. Eskridge, *Equality Practice: Civil Unions and the Future of Gay Rights* (New York: Routledge, 2002): 19.
14. See *Lawrence v. Texas* 529 U.S. 558, 564.
15. 381 U.S. 479 (1965).
16. 405 U.S. 438 (1972); 410 U.S. 113 (1973); 431 U.S. 678 (1977).
17. *Lawrence*, 575.
18. 505 U.S. 833 (1992), 851.
19. See *Lawrence* at 573–573, citing *Casey*, 851.
20. See Butler, "Is Kinship Always Already Heterosexual," 244.
21. See Hunter, "Life after *Hardwick*," 86.
22. For further discussion of the difficulties of sexual definition, see Donald P. Green et al., "Measuring Gay Populations and Antigay Hate Crime," *Social Science Quarterly* 82 (2001): 281–296.
23. Steven Epstein, "Gay Politics, Ethnic Identity: The Limits of Social Constructionism," *Socialist Review* 93/94 (1987): 9–54.
24. *Bowers v. Hardwick* 478 U.S. 186 (1986), 190.
25. *Lawrence*, 567.
26. Ibid., 568–569.

27. *Lawrence*, 567.
28. See Brief of *Amici Curiae* Texas Legislators, Representative Warren Chisum et al. in Support of Respondent, 2002 U.S. Briefs 102, February 18, 2003.
29. Martha Merrill Umphrey, "The Dialogics of Legal Meaning: Spectacular Trials, the Unwritten Law, and Narratives of Criminal Responsibility," *Law & Society Review* 22 (1999): 393–420.
30. *Lawrence*, 567.
31. Ibid., 578, emphasis added.
32. Ibid., 585.
33. Ibid., 591.
34. See, e.g., *Barnes v. Glen Theater, Inc.* 501 U.S. 560. In his opinion there, Scalia's list of immoral behaviors includes the following: sadomasochism, cockfighting, bestiality, suicide, drug use, prostitution, and sodomy. Even more imaginatively, he posits that a state law prohibiting public nudity would be violated even if "60,000 fully consenting adults crowded into the Hoosier Dome to display their genitals to one another, even if there were not an offended innocent in the crowd."
35. *Lawrence*, 600.
36. Ibid., 601.
37. Ibid., 604.
38. See Hunter, "Life after Hardwick," 99.

CHAPTER 10

The Continuing Triumph of Neo-Conservatism in American Constitutional Law

ANNA MARIE SMITH

Lawrence[1] attempts to depict social relations such that there are only two significant types of actors: the individual and the State. The very first paragraph performs the necessary distillation work:

> Liberty protects the person from unwarranted government intrusions into a dwelling or other private places. In our tradition the State is not omnipresent in the home. And there are other spheres of our lives and existence, outside the home, where the State should not be a dominant presence. Freedom extends beyond spatial bounds. Liberty presumes an autonomy of self that includes freedom of thought, belief, expression, and certain intimate conduct. The instant case involves liberty of the person both in its spatial and more transcendent dimensions. (*Lawrence*, 562)

It is the liberty of the "person" against the State that is invoked here. That liberty is spatial, referring to the sanctity of the physical household itself, and conceptual, entailing the sorts of conduct that we associate with the person's private life. To be sure, the Court refers in passing to "other spheres" in society, and it indicates, by using the term "includes," that its list of features belonging to the autonomous self is not meant to be exhaustive. No mention is made here, for example, of the right to bear arms—and whether that right is possessed by the individual or by the states. Nor is there any mention of the individual's right to vote, right to own property, or right to enter into contracts. But the list is nevertheless a telling one. The Court explains, in the body of the *Lawrence* decision, that it is extending the right to privacy by striking down sodomy law as an unconstitutional infringement upon the individual's civil liberty right to due process, and that it is overturning *Bowers.* But the Court also implicitly attempts to foreclose another possibility at the same time, namely the recognition of sexual orientation as a suspect form of classification under the equal protection doctrine. The Court gives with one hand as it takes away with the other.

The Individual in *Lawrence* and the Erasure of Social Justice

Although the Court carefully indicates that its list of freedoms necessary for the preservation and development of individual autonomy is not meant to be exhaustive, it is nevertheless striking that it does not include the First Amendment "right of the people peaceably to assemble." By leaving out the right to assemble, the decision symbolically suppresses the argument that a person cannot be said to have individual autonomy unless he or she has the right, in the event that he or she belongs to a historically disadvantaged group, to engage in a special type of collective struggle. That struggle will have, as one of its primary goals, the passage of civil rights law to protect the group from further discrimination, and, in cases in which discrimination has been especially severe, the attainment of redistributive group rights designed to repair the damage that has been done to the group over time through its structural disempowerment. A good example of the former is, of course, the Civil Rights Acts of 1964 and 1965, which were passed only after blacks engaged in collective struggle against racial discrimination for years. Indigenous people's land claims, by contrast, exemplify the latter; they constitute one of the processes through which traditional groups who have suffered impoverishment, displacement, and genocide as a result of racist policies have won some small degree of reparation.[2]

The social justice issues at stake are extraordinarily high. The individual's right to be free from discrimination based on his or her membership in a traditionally disadvantaged group, and the group right to reparations for the collective membership of severely disadvantaged groups, cannot be understood as the mere sum of the personal liberties enjoyed by each individual member in the group. Civil rights and the group right to reparation exist in classes of their own. There is, nevertheless, a logical connection between individual liberty, properly construed, and civil rights and redistributive group rights. On the one hand, the individual can only realize the potential that exists in embryonic form in his or her privacy rights insofar as he or she is endowed with adequate material resources. If he or she belongs to a traditionally disadvantaged group, he or she will typically suffer from the unequal distribution of life chances, and will, in all likelihood, have to wage an uphill battle to gain the level of material adequacy in question. If his or her group obtains some type of protection from discrimination, and remains politically active enough to ensure that such civil rights measures are vigorously and equitably applied, then he or she will have a much greater opportunity to breathe life into his or her otherwise dormant liberties and to make the most of them. If the group has suffered from severe forms of deprivation, the members of the group will typically require a great deal more than mere anti-discrimination legislation to level out the playing field. The delivery of reparations to this group will enhance its collective resource base and go some distance toward placing its individual members in a more egalitarian position.

On the other hand, an effective collective struggle for civil rights and group rights can only take place if individuals have the right to gather in public places, unmolested by lone bigots, vigilante groups, arbitrary police officers, censorious teachers, and intrusive social workers. Isolated individuals might share the same structural positioning vis-à-vis discrimination, exclusion, and exploitation, and yet, because they lack the opportunity to come together, learn from one another's experiences, establish a collective plan of action, and organize effectively for social change, they might never be able to make their voices heard in an effective manner.[3] The Jim Crow legal regime, combined with the terrorism of lynching and race riots, were highly successful in delaying the emergence of a powerful civil rights movement. Anti-union legislation can, in the same way, frustrate organizing efforts on the part of wage laborers. When high schools ban queer organizing and censor Internet material on homosexuality, they are not only violating the individual rights of their students; by extension, their actions are interfering with the students' right to engage in collective struggle against oppression.

But we have to move far afield—into the terrain occupied by Justice Marshall's dissent on *Bakke*,[4] among other texts—to begin this discussion. As we will see, our ideal *Lawrence* individual is a quintessential loner who does not belong to any legally significant group. In particular, the Court portrays him or her as if he or she does not belong to a traditionally disadvantaged group. By all appearances, the imaginary *Lawrence* individual has no stake whatsoever in any collective struggle. He or she may inhabit several spheres, in addition to the home, but he or she does so as an anonymous person whose identity lacks any significant traces of intersubjectivity and collective practice. And, for all its multi-spherical nature, the society that the Court conjures up as his or her imaginary milieu is perfectly unscathed by institutionalized inequality and historical patterns of discrimination and exclusion.

Abstract Individualism in Privacy Doctrine and the *Casey* "Exception"

Reciting the doctrine of the penumbral right to privacy entailed in the right to due process, and reviewing *Bowers v. Hardwick*,[5] for example, the *Lawrence* Court steps gingerly around several passages in *Casey*.[6] The right to privacy recognized by the Court in *Griswold*,[7] *Eisenstadt*,[8] and *Roe v. Wade*[9] belonged to individuals who were not socially positioned in any particularly significant manner. Individuals had the right to choose contraception and abortion simply because they possessed the right "to be free from unwarranted governmental intrusion in intimate matters such as the decision to bear a child" (*Lawrence*, citing *Eisenstadt*, 562). Any individual, regardless of the lot in life that he or she happened to bear as a result of historically institutionalized patterns of discrimination, possessed this right. One gets the sense that if a new reproductive technology were suddenly invented that allowed men to get pregnant, then pregnant men would immediately enjoy the protection of *Roe*. For the *Roe* Court, there was nothing special about the subject who qualified for a privacy right. Women did not have a right to choose an abortion in consultation with their doctors because they belonged to a group that had suffered from generations of discrimination. The archetypal bearer of the right to privacy was recognized by the Court only as an isolated and anonymous individual. He or she did not possess any specific type of disadvantage as a result of his or her location in the historically sedimented and hierarchically organized social field of power relations. As such, the Court was able to build up the privacy doctrine without setting the stage for the advancement of equal protection claims or group rights; throughout, the Court attempted to maintain a solid wall between civil liberties individualism and the social situatedness of civil rights.

Privacy doctrine also evolved such that the State was only required to refrain from placing an "undue burden" upon the individual seeking to exercise his or her liberties. At its most pernicious, the Court's refusal to examine the structural positioning of special types of individuals attempting to exercise their right to privacy gave rise to the decisions that allowed states to withhold Medicaid funds from poor women seeking an abortion,[10] allowed Congress to ban the use of federal Medicaid funds for abortion,[11] allowed states to prohibit the use of public employees and facilities to perform or assist abortions,[12] and allowed the federal Department of Health and Human Services to prohibit the recipients of federal public health service funds from engaging in abortion-related activities.[13] For the Court, it was the market, not the State, that had created the conditions that had led to poor women's neediness and their inability to pay for private abortion facilities; since the market was effectively responsible for placing private abortion beyond the reach of needy women, the State was innocent. The State may wish to ameliorate the situation, but it was not obliged to do so. The Court therefore concluded that the prohibition of public subsidies to poor women for abortion was constitutional. The Court's neo-conservative tradition of stripping all social features from the archetypal bearer of the right to privacy allowed it to ignore the fact that unless poor women received governmental subsidies, their right to privacy was nothing more than a hollow sham.

Casey threatens to complicate privacy doctrine by introducing a new type of actor, namely the historically situated bearer of the right to due process. On the one hand, *Casey* simply rehearses the familiar doctrine: "Our law affords constitutional protection to personal decisions relating to marriage, procreation, contraception, family relationships, child rearing and education" (*Casey*, 851). It does not matter to the Court whether these personal decisions are being made by women or men, wealthy persons or the indigent, blacks or whites, Christians, Jews, or atheists. To be sure, *Griswold* originally referred solely to the rights of the marital couple to choose contraception, but Eisenstadt quickly erased the marital distinction by recognizing the "right of the *individual,* married or single, to be free from unwarranted governmental intrusion into matters so fundamentally affecting a person as the decision whether or not to bear a child" (*Griswold*, 453, emphasis in the original). What matters is the social sphere in which the individual is making the choice in question, namely the intimate sphere. Once the Court is assured that the decision-maker meets the bare-bones qualification of competent adulthood, it does not inquire further about his or her social situatedness.

But *Casey* then veers off into unfamiliar territory:

> Though abortion is conduct, it does not follow that the State is entitled to proscribe it in all instances. That is because the liberty of the woman is at stake in a sense unique to the human condition and so unique to the law. The mother who carries a child to full term is subject to anxieties, to physical constraints, to pain that only she

must bear. ... Her suffering is too intimate and personal for the State to insist, without more, upon its own vision of the woman's role, however dominant that vision has been in the course of our history and our culture. The destiny of the woman must be shaped to a large extent on her own conception of her spiritual imperatives and her place in society. (*Casey*, 852)

There is something "unique" about the suffering of the pregnant woman; suddenly, she is not just any featureless individual. She has a special physiological makeup that allows her to conceive and bear a child, but that also causes her, and her alone, to endure the anxieties, limitations to her physical freedom, and pain relating to these activities. However, we could imagine that one day, that physiological difference will no longer be significant; perhaps a technological innovation will allow men to bear a child as well. It is conceivable that the pregnant woman's physiological uniqueness is merely a temporary condition.

But *Casey* goes even further. In a subsequent passage, it refers to the social situation occupied by women since *Roe* was handed down, and, by implication, the history of discrimination that they faced beforehand. In the passage in question (*Casey*, 855–7), the *Casey* Court is dealing with an argument that had been made in favor of overturning *Roe*. Referring analogically to commercial law, the anti-*Roe* side had made the point that no one would really face a heavy burden if *Roe* were overturned; sexually active heterosexual couples could simply avail themselves of contraceptive services. In this sense, the anti-*Roe* side argued, no one is conducting their lives in a particular manner on the basis of a reasonable expectation that *Roe* would remain the law of the land. The Court objects that the anti-*Roe* side has a much too narrow view of the way in which the establishment of the right to choose an abortion has transformed American society. For the Court, *Roe* has made a huge difference in terms of personal relationships and socioeconomic trends; its impact cannot be limited to "specific instances of sexual activity" alone (*Roe*, 856). To maintain such a narrow view, the Court argues,

would be simply to refuse to face the fact that for two decades of economic and social developments, people have organized intimate relationships and made choices that define their views of themselves and their places in society, in reliance on the availability of abortion in the event that contraception should fail. (*Roe*, 856)

To be sure, we have the reappearance of our anonymous, de-gendered bearer of the right to privacy, namely the "people." But the passage appears to mark a bold departure, for it ostensibly links the individualistic right to privacy to an extraordinarily broad range of intersubjective relationships that spans the boundaries among the intimate sphere, the market, and society as a whole. Even more surprising, the Court dwells momentarily on the specific character of women's reliance upon *Roe*:

> The ability of women to participate equally in the economic and social life of the Nation has been facilitated by their ability to control their reproductive lives. The Constitution serves human values, and while the effect of reliance on *Roe* cannot be exactly measured, neither can the certain cost of overruling *Roe* for people who have ordered their thinking and living around that case be dismissed. (*Roe*, 856)

Here the social situatedness of women matters to the Court a great deal. The Court is essentially arguing that since *Roe* was decided, women in the United States have quite reasonably taken for granted that they have the right to have an abortion. As such, they have adopted a new perspective on their life course. They are much more likely to pursue work in the paid wage labor market during their childbearing years, and they are much more likely to participate equally in social affairs outside the home. This enhancement in women's equality is a remarkable development precisely because of the fact that women had faced such profoundly unequal treatment before the period in which *Roe* was decided. The Court's argument is not entirely without merit. The choice to work outside the home for wages had been closed to many women—especially for white middle-class married women— before the 1970s. In addition, all women had been excluded from leadership in significant social organizations and from equal participation in the political process. Women, as a group, had faced discrimination and exclusion for generations.

Casey overstates the case for *Roe*'s impact somewhat for white middle-class married women, however. It was not only the invention of better birth control technologies and access to safe and legal abortions that caused the advancement of these women's socio-political equality and the increase in labor force participation among white middle-class married women. Mainstream feminist activism and the decline in male earnings certainly had an impact as well. As for *Roe*'s impact upon poor women—especially poor women of color—*Casey* is silent. These women had always worked for wages outside the home; abortion rights did nothing to change that trend. Before *Roe*, women from all class backgrounds practiced birth control and sought abortions. It was only the women who could afford to pay the relatively high cost of private specialist doctors who could obtain a safe medical abortion procedure. All others had to resort to dangerous folk methods or back-alley charlatans. *Roe*'s greatest impact was to level out the class differences among women; now women of limited means did not have to risk their future fertility, or even their lives, when they underwent an abortion. The availability of safe and legal abortion for poor women is particularly important given the fact that they are typically underserved where the provision of adequate primary care, gynecological, and contraceptive medicine are concerned.[14]

Casey is not, therefore, placing the woman seeking an abortion in a fully elaborated historical setting. It is suppressing the Court's own callous disregard of poor women's special need for governmental subsidies in its previous decisions, and it is ignoring the class-leveling effect of *Roe*. *Casey* provides an extremely biased narrative about abortion rights; the *Roe* decision is depicted as a watershed moment that ushered all women into a new era of substantial empowerment, when the Court itself had worked steadily since *Roe* to diminish the right to privacy for poor women. It is nevertheless important to note that the Court could not have even opened up this line of argumentation on the significance of *Roe* at all if it had persisted in its tendency to strip away from the bearer of privacy rights all traces of social situatedness. One of the reasons the *Casey* Court gives for upholding *Roe* is that because women had faced discrimination as a group for generations before *Roe*, they are currently relying upon *Roe* in a special way such that they have obtained an unprecedented degree of equality. Given the fact that women as a group have been traditionally positioned unequally in our social structures, the overturning of *Roe* would in fact cause women an especially profound type of hardship.

These passages, however, could be technically dismissed as dicta on the grounds that they do not go to the heart of the matter in question. In essence, *Casey* determined that although *Roe* would still be allowed to stand, Pennsylvania's restrictions on abortion were constitutional (except for the spousal-notification rule). It could be argued that the passage on the social positioning of women seeking an abortion could be deleted from *Casey* without destroying the fundamental logic of the decision itself. Abortion rights advocates may very well have a difficult time in mobilizing these passages to good effect in future cases. But even in the midst of this striking departure from its own individualistic approach to due process rights, the Court remains consistent insofar as it ignores the structural positioning of poor women in particular. Before *Casey*, the greatest inroads against *Roe* had been made by the Court in the area of allowing the State to withhold public subsidies for abortion. Because *Casey* upholds *Roe* while implicitly suppressing an analysis of abortion rights that is sensitive to economic class differences among women, *Casey* actually perpetuates the Court's neo-conservative work where it counts the most. Its invocations of women's historical experience ultimately become a superficial gesture.

The Oxymoronic Character of the "Homosexual Community" in *Lawrence*

The *Lawrence* decision resembles *Casey* in the following sense: It appears, on the surface, to be boldly enhancing rights and freedoms, but in effect, it implicitly advances the neo-conservative agenda. The Court consistently renders the petitioners in *Lawrence* into anonymous "everymen" as the decision seizes upon countless opportunities to evacuate their specific identities, conduct, and historical positioning such that they become bland and empty shells. It criticizes the *Bowers* Court for the way that it framed the case with reference to social and historical codes. *Bowers* states, "The issue presented is whether the federal Constitution confers a fundamental right upon homosexuals to engage in sodomy." *Lawrence* chastises the *Bowers's* decision for its narrow perspective, arguing that it "demeans the claim the individual brought forward" by refusing to acknowledge the way in which the prohibition of sodomy has

> far-reaching consequences, touching upon the most private human conduct, sexual behavior, and in the most private of places, the home. The statutes do seek to control a personal relationship that, whether or not entitled to formal recognition in the law, is within the liberty of persons to choose without being punished as criminals. (*Lawrence*, 567)

We could dwell on the *Lawrence* Court's obvious queasiness about oral and anal sex, but, for my purposes, it is more interesting to note the neo-conservative Court's individualizing abstraction work here. We have the neurotic deployment of the exemplary; the phrase, "the most private," gets quite a work-out. Any historical or phenomenological specificity of the practice—who these men are, what they think they are doing, how they met each other, how their sex act contributes further to their sense of self, the socio-historical context of their interaction, and so on—is suppressed. We are invited instead to move immediately to the general class of practices to which the Court assigns this sex act: the sanitized category of "sexual behavior" that takes place in the home between two hollowed out entities, the consenting adults. While it is true that the Court mentions the phrase "homosexual persons" only a few sentences later (*Lawrence*, 567), it does so only after it has deployed many other sanitizing abstractions, such as its reference to "adults" and "free persons." This anonymous subject, the Court says, should be able to engage in "intimate conduct" in the "confines of their homes and their own private lives." Such intimate conduct may lead in turn to the formation of an enduring "personal bond" between the two parties; they should be able to pursue this utterly universal human interest without sacrificing their "dignity" (*Lawrence*, 567).

It is certainly true that some degree of abstraction is required in any Supreme Court decision such that the Court is able to argue, by analogy, that precedents ostensibly dealing with completely different empirical situations actually have authority. The *Lawrence* decision returns to privacy doctrine as it addresses the question of whether the State may be used by the majority to enforce its moral views. Referring to *Casey*, a decision that, as we have seen, dealt with a constitutional challenge to state abortion law, the Court states in *Lawrence*, "our obligation is to define the liberty of all, not to mandate our own moral code" (*Lawrence*, 571). Given the rhetorical constraints of Supreme Court rulings, then, some level of abstraction is necessary; without this device, the Court could not make sweeping generalizations about the trend in laws and traditions "in the past half century" (*Lawrence*, 571): "these references show an emerging awareness that liberty gives substantial protection to adult persons in deciding how to conduct their private lives in matters pertaining to sex" (*Lawrence*, 572).

It is also entirely possible that the Court could have embraced the homosexual identity of the petitioners, placed them in a historical context, and yet arrived at a thoroughly reactionary conclusion. *Bowers* is a case in point; that decision performed very little sanitization and abstraction work. On the contrary, it dwelled on the substance of the petitioners' identity and referred, with a bigoted sneer, to the "facetious" (*Bowers*, 194) nature of any claim to a constitutional right to engage in "homosexual sodomy" (*Bowers*, 191). It mobilized several historical references, but only in an attempt to portray homophobia as a fundamental principle of Western civilization, and to distinguish "between family, marriage, or procreation on the one hand and homosexual activity on the other" (*Bowers*, 190–91). Indeed, the Court refused to grant standing to the heterosexual couple who came forward and said that the Georgia's facially neutral sodomy law "chilled and deterred" them from engaging in sodomy (*Bowers*, 188, note 2).

The abstraction work that *Lawrence* performs with respect to the identities of the petitioners, however, is multifaceted and strategic in nature. It certainly does create an avenue for the Court to attack the bigotry of *Bowers*, and to harness some of the best parts of privacy doctrine. But even as the Court repudiates *Bowers*, it attempts to circumscribe the legal implications. Taking the state law as our only indication, we might have expected rather more generalization in *Bowers* and a little less abstraction in *Lawrence*, given the fact that the Texas law under examination in *Lawrence* prohibited "deviate sexual intercourse" but only when it is practiced with "another individual of the same sex." And yet *Lawrence* ascends to the abstract wherever possible.

Citing *Casey*, for example, *Lawrence* invokes the constitutional right of the individual to make "personal decisions" in an autonomous manner, and draws an equivalence between homosexuals and heterosexuals: "persons in a homosexual relationship may seek autonomy for these purposes, just as heterosexual persons do" (*Lawrence*, 574). The equivalence is not a perfect one, however; "homosexual" is a modifier for "relationships" while "heterosexual" refers to a specific group of "persons." *Lawrence* constructs a society in which we have, first, some very plain unmodified "persons"—individuals who lack any connection whatsoever to any specific group that shares a common cultural milieu and a tradition of discrimination—engaging in a special type of intimate practice, namely the "homosexual relationship." Given the fact that they have no special kind of affinity with any particular group, we can presume that the urge to engage in "homosexual conduct" will be experienced within the generic groups of individuals on a random basis. Suddenly, with no exposure to any particular community or culture, a few of them just up and choose same-sex erotic practices. The "homosexual relationship," then, has no social context; not only is there no "homosexual community," the very term becomes an oxymoron. The "homosexual relationship" is a purely random phenomenon that springs up in isolated contexts as the result of spontaneous individualistic choices. As such, "homosexual" is shorn of any socio-political meaning. Being "homosexual" is like preferring spicy food or choosing, when offered a well-equipped hotel room, to take a bath instead of a shower. From this perspective, being "homosexual" has very little in common with being Catholic—that is to say, with being a member of a social group that is protected from discriminatory law by an elevated level of judicial scrutiny.[15]

Lawrence Holds the Line on Suspect Class Status for Queers

By the time we arrive at the passage that deals with equal protection, *Lawrence* has carefully stacked the deck. If homosexuals do not constitute a special class of persons who share a unique history of socio-political exclusion, then the Court does not have to apply a strict level of scrutiny to any cases involving anti-homosexual law. The Texas sodomy law does single out only those individuals who engage in "deviant sexual intercourse" with partners of the same sex for prohibition. However, the Court, having evacuated all historical substance out of the group of persons affected by the law, can view the equal protection question in a narrow and superficial manner. It acknowledges that the law is not facially neutral, but then merely states that if it decided to hold the statute invalid on equal protection grounds, "some might question whether a prohibition would be valid if drawn differently, say, to prohibit the conduct both between same-sex and different-sex participants" (*Lawrence*, 575). To be sure, by proceeding on due process grounds, the Court is invoking the stronger argument, since due process rights rest upon a fundamental liberty interest and the equal protection claim is relatively weaker.[16]

In any event, the Court wants to steer a careful course between leaving the bigotry of *Bowers* completely intact and granting homosexuals the status of a protected class. First, it dismisses the possibility of finding the law unconstitutional on both grounds without explanation; the choice before the Court, it tells us, is either/or—either a due process decision or an equal protection decision. Second, it misrecognizes the equal protection issue as a relatively unimportant legal technicality. Since there is no homosexual community, and all we have are generic persons who spontaneously chose to enter into a "homosexual relationship," then the problem with the Texas law is threefold: (1) it allows the state to interfere with intimate conduct between consenting adults; (2) it assigns a mark, the brand of "stigma," to an otherwise random collection of individuals; and (3) it does so on the basis of animus. Third, *Lawrence* solves its own either/or puzzle in favor of due process; it claims that a due process ruling satisfies both the equal protection claim for equal treatment and the privacy claim for noninterference by the State in the area of intimate conduct (*Lawrence*, 574–75).

To be sure, *Lawrence* once again refers to "homosexual persons" in this passage. Up until this point, the term "homosexual" was used most often to modify the term "conduct." Further, the passages in which "homosexual" is deployed to carve out a special type of person from the general population are almost all framed in either tentative or critical terms. We have Hardwick "alleging" that he was a practicing homosexual (*Lawrence*, 566); the citations of *Bowers* that are later criticized (*Lawrence*, 566); the scholarly claim that homosexuality emerges as a special category of person in the late nineteenth century—a claim that is introduced with a skeptical phrase, "according to some scholars" (*Lawrence*, 568); a negative empirical claim: "thus early American sodomy laws were not directed at homosexuals as such but instead sought to prohibit nonprocreative sexual activity more generally"(*Lawrence*, 568); a highly qualified remark on the history of homophobia: "despite the absence of prosecutions, there may have been periods in which there was public criticism of homosexuals as such and an insistence that the criminal laws be enforced to discourage their practices" (*Lawrence*, 570); yet another petitioner "alleging" that he was a practicing homosexual, this time before the European Court of Human Rights (*Lawrence*, 573); and two references to homosexuals in the *Romer v. Evans*[17] case (*Lawrence*, 574). We have, by contrast, sixteen instances in which the term homosexual is used, without tentative or skeptical prefatory remarks (such as "so-called," "alleged," and so on), to modify nouns such as conduct, sodomy, acts, or relationships, and only three of those references were imposed upon the Court insofar as they were already contained in texts that it was citing. As we have already seen, *Lawrence* does refer to the liberty interest of the "homosexual person" at one instance, but only after it performs tremendous abstraction and sanitization work upon that subject (*Lawrence*, 567).

In the equal protection passage, however, the Court moves back and forth between references to "homosexual conduct" and "homosexual persons." The meaning of the latter phrase, however, is not entirely clear:

> When homosexual conduct is made criminal by the law of the State, that declaration in and of itself is an invitation to subject homosexual persons to discrimination both in the public and in the private spheres. ... [*Bowers's*] continuance as precedent demeans the lives of homosexual persons (*Lawrence*, 575).

The love that dare not speak its name now becomes heterosexual sodomy, in a sense, as the Court irrationally persists in misinterpreting the range of practices in question. Even though the Texas law was not facially neutral, the *Lawrence* Court is overturning *Bowers,* and *Bowers* had left a key question open, namely whether the state could regulate oral and anal sex when it is performed by an opposite-sex couple. As Janet Halley has so effectively argued, official homophobia augments its rhetorical force by constantly flickering back and forth between prohibiting sexual conduct that is popularly—albeit erroneously—associated exclusively with homosexuals and discriminating against homosexuals as a class of persons, according to the strategic demands of the day.[18] When the focus is placed on sodomy law only insofar as it exclusively targets anal and oral sex acts that are practiced by same-sex couples, queers lose the possibility of forming alliances with sexual liberationist heterosexuals to protest puritanical sexual regulation of all kinds. When the military bans homosexual persons from performing military service unless they can prove that they do not have a proclivity to engage in sodomy, it gives rise to defense strategies in which the individuals who are deemed homosexual attempt to embrace a wholesome morality and to distance themselves from same-sex erotic desire altogether.

If Halley is right, we should be on guard whenever we see a conservative official institution such as the Supreme Court shifting back and forth between references to homosexual conduct and homosexual identity. Further, it is not clear exactly what this elusive phrase, the "homosexual person," means in the equal protection passage in *Lawrence*. The weight of the repeated associations of the term "homosexual" with "conduct" create the impression that homosexuality does not really qualify as a legally significant state of being for the Court. To be sure, we have the references to "homosexuals" and to a "solitary class of persons who were homosexual, lesbian, or bisexual" in the previous passage dealing with *Romer* (*Lawrence*, 574). But we should recall the way in which *Romer* unfolded.

In *Romer*, the Court had to refer to "homosexuals" as a class because the Colorado legislators and voters had created this category in the state's constitutional amendment. The *Romer* Court accepted the coherence of the term "homosexual class," but only with reference to a single measure, namely a law that was determined by the Court to be motivated solely by animus toward the class itself. The law that apparently gave birth to the legally recognizable class ultimately failed the rational basis test. For the purposes of the specific constitutional challenge in *Romer*, then, the Court had to acknowledge the existence of homosexual persons as a legally significant category, but only insofar as it was applying the rational basis test to this particular piece of legislation. The phrase, "homosexual class," that is cited twice in *Lawrence* with reference to *Romer*, could be construed as an entity that only gained constitutional significance when this specific state law had begun to fence the members of this group out of the political process. Overturn the law, as *Romer* quite properly did, and the concept of the "homosexual class" could very well lose any constitutionally relevant meaning for the Court. If Colorado had barred left-handed hairdressers from participating fully in the political process, the term the "left-handed hairdresser class" would have briefly gained a legally significant meaning in constitutional law, and it would have lost all legal significance as soon as the Court found that that particular exclusion failed the rational basis test as well.[19]

On one possible reading of the *Lawrence* passage on equal protection, the term "homosexual class" has a constitutional law career that begins and ends with a single body of legislation. It is when the state makes "homosexual conduct" criminal—and the Supreme Court upholds that state law in *Bowers*—that the "stigma" of homosexuality is attached to an otherwise unremarkable group of generic individuals such that they become "homosexual persons," and as such are singled out for discrimination (*Lawrence*, 575). Strike down the law, overturn *Bowers*, and the stigma dissipates. The collective term "homosexual class" then loses its significance for the Court. Both the signifier and its signified fade away. In this reading, then, we are left once again with the sense that as far as constitutional law is concerned, the concept of the "homosexual community" has no legal significance. "Homosexual conduct" emerges on a random basis, as choices regarding intimate conduct are spontaneously made by isolated individuals.

The purpose of the equal protection clause in the Fourteenth Amendment is to prohibit laws that classify individuals into groups in an unjust manner. Given our history of slavery, Jim Crow discrimination, and racism, race has been rightly deemed a suspect type of classification. Any law that classifies individuals on the basis of race will receive the highest form of equal protection scrutiny by the Court. Since the late 1970s, however, the Court has consistently ignored the fact that blacks make up a group that has been subject to severe racial discrimination for centuries. It has instead applied the equal protection clause in a highly de-historicized formalistic manner. It has overturned and weakened affirmative action programs for blacks on the grounds that such reparative measures impose unfair burdens on whites, and that whites also have an equal protection right to be free from racial classification. For this Court, an argument that merely showed that blacks have long endured gross under-representation within a student body, a given profession, or an area of business opportunity falls far short of the mark. It has held that it is only when specific black individuals have suffered from documented acts of racial discrimination that has been directed against them on a personal basis that they can seek a remedy in the form of affirmative action, and that that remedy has be narrowly tailored to address these specific discriminatory acts.[20]

There are no affirmative action programs at stake in *Lawrence,* but *Lawrence* nevertheless is used by the Court to weaken the protection offered by the equal protection clause yet again. We ought to applaud the Court for striking down *Bowers* and yet criticize it for the way it which it achieves that goal by perpetuating its neo-conservative individualism. If equal protection status is extended to a group when it has taken the form of a "discrete and insular minority"[21] that has been subject to a "history of purposeful unequal treatment"[22] and "subjected to unique disabilities on the basis of stereotyped characteristics not truly indicative of their abilities,"[23] then there is no good reason for the Court not to determine that laws singling out lesbians, gay men, bisexuals, and transgendered (LGBT) individuals for exclusion deserve strict scrutiny. Because *Lawrence* not only overturns *Bowers,* but also frames its references to homosexuality in such individualistic terms, *Lawrence* attempts to hold the neo-conservative line by effectively foreclosing the extension of "suspect" class status to queers as well. We have recently witnessed a whole new movement at the state and federal level to introduce sexual orientation classifications in law that will have a discriminatory effect upon queers. Thanks to the Court's neo-conservative stance on equal protection, it will be extremely difficult to win suspect class status for homosexuals. As such, Congress and the states will not have to pass the strict scrutiny test; they will not have to show that they are pursuing a compelling governmental interest and applying precisely designed measures to do so, when they enact laws that impose special burdens or exclusions upon homosexuals. The legislative bodies establishing anti-homosexual law will enjoy the Court's most deferential treatment.

To be sure, queer advocates could still invoke *Romer,* but because *Romer* did not determine that sexual orientation was a suspect classification, it only deployed the weakest type of scrutiny, namely the rational basis test. The Colorado amendment was struck down only because the Court could not find any possible legitimate governmental purpose that would be served, in any possible scenario, by prohibiting anti-discrimination law protecting homosexuals. Being unable to find that the law bore a rational relationship to any legitimate state interest, the Court was obliged to conclude that the Colorado amendment was the product of animus alone, and therefore struck it down as unconstitutional.

The bitter irony is that the Court insists upon treating homosexuality like a phenomenon that can spring up spontaneously among absolutely isolated generic individuals without any support whatsoever from a progressive social movement. True, individuals have experienced a fleeting desire to engage in same-sex erotic behavior in all sorts of cultural conditions and social formations; we would have to concede that men have had sex with men, and women have had sex with women, in theocracies and fascist dictatorships. From the perspective of the sexual liberation movement, however, the socio-political context of same-sex erotic practices matters a great deal. What we sexual liberationists want is not simply more homosexual desire; we want to transform the basic institutions of society, including the family, the schools, the labor market, the law, and the State, that have traditionally privileged racialized marital heterosexuality and patriarchal family values, and exacted a tremendous cost upon those who have deviated from the norm. Without sexual liberation, we would have "homosexuality" in the most minimal and least transgressive sense: usually furtive, sometimes guilt-ridden, but always private acts between anonymous individuals that do not give rise to a collective struggle to overthrow homophobia and the racialized patriarchy. It would appear that that sort of "homosexual conduct" would suit this Court just fine.

Whither Same-Sex Marriage?

There is, of course, a second route to strict scrutiny. The Court has applied the highest level of judicial review where it has found that a law has had an unequal impact upon different groups of individuals such that a fundamental right has been violated, even if the classification in question does not correspond to a recognized suspect class.[24] It has applied strict scrutiny on these grounds in cases involving the right to procreation,[25] the right to vote,[26] the right of equal access to the courts,[27] and the right of interstate migration.[28] For example, an Alabama electoral apportionment scheme was struck down by the Court on the grounds that it violated the right to vote.[29] It decided that the state's scheme had diluted some citizens' votes and therefore violated the democratic principle of "one person, one vote." The citizens who suffered from this arrangement did not all belong to a suspect class; they came from different racial backgrounds, for example. Their identities, however, were not relevant to the Court's deliberations. They were being subjected to unequal treatment such that their right to vote was being infringed upon. The Court had to take an additional step; it had to find that the right in question was "fundamental." In this case, it did so; the Court decided that the right to vote is "fundamental" since it is the "essence of a democratic society."[30]

Would a case brought by queers against the federal Defense of Marriage Act (DOMA) of 1996[31] and similar state measures be treated in same way? After all, these laws exclude homosexuals from the marriage-eligible class, and therefore infringe upon a right that is arguably fundamental, namely the right to marry. This second route to strict scrutiny does not necessarily require a finding on the part of the Court that the group that is suffering from unequal treatment by the law qualifies as a suspect class. The trend in constitutional law, however, has moved sharply in the opposite direction. The Court has made it quite clear that it would not keep expanding the list of fundamental rights that would receive strict scrutiny under the equal protection clause.[32] In *San Antonio Independent School Board District v. Rodriguez*,[33] the Court refused to apply the strict scrutiny test. The petitioners argued that Texas's public school funding system was inequitable, since it condemned those who lived in districts with a preponderance of poor households to insufficiently funded schools. It is difficult to imagine a right that is more basic to a democratic society than the right to education. The Court nevertheless decided that it was not enough merely to weigh the relative social significance of the right in question; a right could only be deemed "fundamental" if it was "explicitly or implicitly guaranteed by the Constitution."[34] Since *Rodriguez* was handed down, the Court has maintained this extremely narrow interpretation, one that is perfectly consistent with the neo-conservative individualistic ideology of the majority on the Court.

In all likelihood, then, the question will be whether a state or federal measure that excluded homosexuals from the marriage-eligible class fails the rational basis test. Given the extremely deferential posture toward the legislature that the Court takes when applying this test, and the profoundly institutionalized governmental interest in regulating marriage in order to promote a conservative form of social order and in bolstering the patriarchal, heterosexual, marital nuclear family, such a challenge would probably fail. Indeed, the Court signals its position on the matter in *Lawrence* itself.

> [The present] case does not involve whether the government must give formal recognition to any relationship that homosexual persons seek to enter. The case does involve two adults who, with full and mutual consent from each other, engaged in sexual practices common to a homosexual lifestyle. (*Lawrence*, 578)

Again, there is, in this concluding passage of *Lawrence*, the attempt to disassociate homosexuality from a community that has a shared historical experience of discrimination and exclusion; here the term "homosexual" modifies an entity that has no significance whatsoever in equal protection doctrine, namely a mere "lifestyle." Moreover, the Court confidently asserts that overturning *Bowers* will do absolutely nothing to assist the campaign to gain recognition for same-sex marriage.

This is not to say that the campaign to promote same-sex marriage necessarily ought to be the queer community's top priority at present. Marriage is an extremely conservative institution that imposes a one-size-fits-all regulatory form of monogamous domesticity upon each and every couple. The same-sex marriage campaign, by the very nature of marriage law itself, presses queer advocates to abandon the sexual liberation movement and to champion anti-feminist ideas. At a time when single-parenting is under attack, especially among the poor and people of color, our spokespersons and advocates are eagerly repeating dangerous and fallacious claims, such as "children are better off if they are reared by a stable, monogamous couple," or "marriage is the foundation of the social order."[35] If we queers could mobilize to bring homophobia and the racialized patriarchy[36] to an end, and to open up the space for everyone—gay and straight alike—to experiment freely with alternatives to conservative "family values," we would be much better off. And if individual Americans had access to a much more complete set of welfare state entitlements, then it is entirely possible that the same-sex marriage campaign would quickly fade away. To be sure, some folks would choose to enter enduring monogamous relationships and many couples would want to pronounce their vows before their communities. We would still have plenty of private commitment ceremonies, but we would not assist a reactionary State to extend its social control grip on our lives by seeking legal recognition for our domestic arrangements. For their part, heterosexuals would continue to vote on the marriage question with their feet, as it were, by either exiting marriage through divorce or avoiding it altogether in favor of nonmarital cohabitation. If no one had to get married to gain access to health care or a decent pension plan, then perhaps the religious zealots who want to prop this failing institution up for a few more decades would have a tougher time of it.

Coda: The Possible Family Law Articulations of *Lawrence* beyond Same-Sex Marriage

American sodomy law is unique in several respects; for our purposes, its gendered effects are particularly noteworthy. Sodomy law in the United States was actively applied not only to gay men—that is, to their conduct and identity by turns—but to lesbians as well. This was not the case, however, in Britain. As Jeffrey Weeks remarks, "There is a long tradition in the Christian West of hostility toward homosexuality, although this usually took the form of the formal regulation of male homosexual activity rather than lesbian."[37] Henry VIII proclaimed the infamous law against buggery in 1533, thereby prohibiting all "crimes against nature." The law was largely used, in practice, to prosecute the men who had sex with other men. Women emerged in a few sodomy cases in the eighteenth century, but they were typically situated as the alleged victims of anal intercourse with a man. Although the purpose behind Britain's sodomy law was to perpetuate the Christian Church's campaign against all non-procreative sex, it was directed exclusively at men: "though lesbian behavior was variously condemned, its threat was less explicitly recognized in legal regulation, in Anglo-Saxon cultures at least."[38]

Lesbians in the United States, by contrast, have in fact been subjected to extensive discrimination and criminal prosecution on the grounds that we have performed, or have the proclivity to perform, sodomy. Sodomy law was most commonly used not to prosecute individuals who were actually charged with breaking the law itself, but to "impose legal disabilities on persons who [could] be identified as 'homosexual' without regard to any proof that they have engaged in the proscribed conduct."[39] In one particularly devastating effect of sodomy law and *Bowers*, lesbians have been routinely denied custody in family court by judges who claimed that their sexual orientation made them unfit to be parents since they either engaged regularly in criminal activity or had the inclination to do so.[40]

The infringement of the parenting rights of lesbians and gay men by the State constitutes an arbitrary use of power that should be considered repugnant in any democracy. The Court has in fact recognized the privacy of the parent-child dyad,[41] and Congress has passed legislation that makes it clear that unless the state is able to demonstrate that a parent has neglected or abused his or her child, the state cannot impose remedial training upon the parent or remove the child from the parent's care.[42] To be sure, the State ought to intervene in the domestic life of its citizens but in only two ways. It ought to ensure that neglect and abuse are not taking place within the household, and it ought to provide a nontaxable caregivers' entitlement to parents with custody of dependent children and to those adults who are caring for the chronically ill, the severely disabled, and the elderly. Much of American family law and social policy is discriminatory and exclusionary, excessively interventionary with respect to the policing of morals, and grossly inadequate with respect to the right of the poor in a democratic society to redistributive justice. The federal and state governments should scrap American family law and welfare law, and pursue instead these two goals—the protection of dependents from neglect and above, and the subsidization of caregiving—in an even-handed manner in accordance with secular and inclusionary democratic principles.

By striking down sodomy law, *Lawrence* removes one of the weapons that has been wielded by homophobic family court judges against perfectly suitable lesbian and gay parents. Given the enormous latitude of the courts to determine the "child's best interests," we cannot guarantee that *Lawrence*, in and of itself, will usher in a radical transformation in child custody law. However, the dependence of homophobic family courts upon state sodomy law, and, by extension, *Bowers,* was so deeply institutionalized that at least one new possibility may open before us. Paradoxically enough, the individualistic liberty interest championed in *Lawrence* may very well contribute to the expansion of queer parenting rights, a type of freedom that, by its very nature, carves out a privacy right not for a lone individual pursuing his or her own self-regarding interest, but for an adult insofar as he or she is participating in a relation with a dependent, and insofar as he or she is engaging in altruistic, other-regarding, caregiving activity toward that dependent. In the end, *Lawrence,* for all its neo-conservative individualism, might pave the way for more decisions in family court that favor queer parenting.

Notes

1. *Lawrence v. Texas*, 539 U.S. 558 (2003). Henceforth cited in the text as *Lawrence.*
2. For a liberal democratic argument in favor of reparation for indigenous peoples, see William Kymlicka, *Multicultural Citizenship: A Liberal Theory of Minority Rights* (New York: Oxford University Press, 1995).
3. For a similar argument, see Iris Marion Young, *Inclusion and Democracy* (New York: Oxford University Press, 2000).
4. *Regents of the University of California v. Bakke* 438 U.S. 265 (1978) (Justice Marshall, dissenting).
5. *Bowers v. Harwick* 478 U.S. 186 (1986). Henceforth cited in the text as *Bowers.*
6. *Planned Parenthood of Southeastern Pa. v. Casey* 505 U.S. 833 (1992). Henceforth cited in the text as *Casey.*
7. *Griswold v. Connecticut*, 381 U.S. 479 (1965).

8. *Eisenstadt v. Baird,* 405 U.S. 438 (1972).
9. *Roe v. Wade,* 410 U.S. 113 (1973). Henceforth cited in the text as *Roe.*
10. *Maher v. Roe,* 432 U.S. 464 (1977).
11. *Harris v. McRae,* 448 U.S. 297 (1980).
12. *Webster v. Reproductive Health Services et al.,* 492 U.S. 490 (1989).
13. *Rust v. Sullivan,* 500 U.S. 173 (1991). The Court has typically refused to accept the argument that indigency ought to provide a basis for stricter scrutiny of legislative measures. See, for example, *Dandridge v. Williams,* 397 U.S. 471 (1970). It has generally struck down welfare laws only insofar as they infringe upon a "fundamental right" such as the right to travel freely from one state to another (*Shapiro v. Thompson,* 394 U.S. 618 (1969)). While *King v. Smith,* 392 U.S. 309 (1968) established a limited statutory entitlement to poverty assistance, that entitlement was effectively eliminated when the Social Security Act was radically changed in 1996 with the passage of the Personal Responsibility and Work Opportunity Reconciliation Act (Pub. L. No. 104–193 110 Stat. 2105 (1996)). The Court has struck down voting legislation that conditioned the right to vote on the paying of a tax or the ownership of property on equal protection grounds (*Harper v. Virginia State Board of Education,* 383 U.S. 663 (1966) and *Kramer v. Unions Free School District,* 395 U.S. 621 (1969)). But the Court has, on the whole, tended to rule that governmental agencies must make special publicly funded provisions for indigents to enable them to exercise a constitutional right only where their right to a fair trial is at stake. It has ruled, for example, that governmental fees for trial transcripts must be waived for indigent defendants such that they can appeal their convictions (*Griffin v. Illinois,* 351 U.S. 12 (1963)) and that the states must incur the cost of attorneys' fees if a defendant in a criminal prosecution cannot afford one (*Gideon v. Wainwright,* 372 U.S. 335 (1963)). For the Court, the life and liberty interests at stake where equal treatment by the criminal justice system is concerned are unusually substantial. Beyond this exceptional area, the Court tends to treat the economic disparities that make constitutional rights and liberties difficult or impossible to exercise for indigent individuals as if they were constitutionally insignificant. Donald Lively, *Landmark Supreme Court Cases: A Reference Guide* (Westport, CT: Greenwood Press, 1999), 298.
14. Rep. Shirley Chisholm, "Facing the Abortion Question," in *Black Women in White America: A Documentary History,* ed. Gerda Lerner (New York: Vintage, 1972), 602–7; and Rosalind Petchesky, *Abortion and Woman's Choice: The State, Sexuality, and Reproductive Freedom* (Boston: Northeastern University Press, 1990).
15. Where the extremely constrained language game of constitutional law is concerned, it is important to note the pitfalls that queer advocacy encounters when it attempts to contend with the entire issue of "immutability." In the past, the Court has deemed inherently suspect any classification used to exclude a group if that group has been: (a) socially recognized, over a significant length of time, as a coherent, discrete, and insular entity; (b) subjected to discriminatory discourse, including stigmatization and derogatory stereotyping; and (c) chronically vulnerable to exclusion, *en masse,* from participating in the political process. In one of its many neo-conservative moves, the Court is becoming much more reluctant to expand the list of groups to whom it bestows protected class status. Queer advocates have therefore often turned to the argument that homosexuality is just "like race" and that since African Americans are still recognized as a "suspect" class, homosexuals should receive the same treatment. One of the many weaknesses of the strategy to render homosexuality and blackness equivalent consists in the fact that it tends to lead to attempts by queer advocates to shore up the idea that homosexuality is immutable. Race is, after all, widely misconstrued as being grounded in objectively measurable physiological difference, and racial difference appears to visibly mark the individual for life in an immutable fashion. Homosexuality, by contrast, is generally regarded, first, as a collective phenomenon that is much more vulnerable to social influences and second, as an individual experience that can be relatively easily induced or discouraged by others. Thus many queer advocates have either attempted to show that homosexuality is actually grounded in physiological difference, or is present at birth in the form of an irrepressible psychological condition. We tend to ignore, by contrast, the fact that religious groups have achieved some degree of protection from discrimination even though religious organizations openly practice proselytization. The law knows no difference between a recent convert and a life-long practitioner for whom a given religious faith has been shared by his or her forebears for generations. The problem of the notion that "we are just born

that way" is that queers might underestimate the importance of promoting homosexuality, that is, of doing the extremely valuable work of creating the most conducive conditions imaginable for all adults to explore their sexuality freely. For more discussion of the principle of immutability and constitutional law doctrine, see Janet Halley, "'Like Race' Arguments," in *What's Left of Theory? New Work on the Politics of Literary Theory*, eds. Judith Butler, John Guillory, and Kendall Thomas (New York: Routledge, 2000), 40–74. For the argument that all women are trapped within the institution of "compulsory heterosexuality" unless every single one of them is truly free to practice lesbianism, see Adrienne Rich, "Compulsory Heterosexuality and Lesbian Existence," in *The Lesbian and Gay Studies Reader*, eds. Henry Abelove et al. (New York: Routledge, 1993), 227–54.

16. Jeffrey Shaman, *Constitutional Interpretation: Illusion and Reality* (Westport, CT: Greenwood Press, 2001), 234, 237. My thanks to Matt Faiella, a law student in the Cornell Law School, for discussing this point with me.

17. *Romer v. Evans*, 517 U.S. 620 (1996). Henceforth cited in the text as *Romer*.

18. See the stimulating and provocative discussion by Janet Halley, "Reasoning about Sodomy: Act and Identity in and after *Bowers v. Hardwick*," *Virginia Law Review* 79 (1993): 1721–79 and *Don't: A Reader's Guide to the Military's Anti-Gay Policy* (Durham, NC: Duke University Press, 1999).

19. See, for example, the cameo role played in constitutional law by the butchers in Louisiana who did not belong to the monopoly favored by the state. *Slaughter-House Cases*, 83 U.S. (16 Wall.) 36 (1973). If the Supreme Court had interpreted the Fourteenth Amendment properly, it would have found that there was no rational basis for Louisiana's exclusion of the non-monopoly butchers from the slaughterhouse business (Shaman, *Constitutional Interpretation*, 227–30). But if the case were decided today, under the fully developed multiple-tier equal protection doctrine, the Court would make such a rational basis determination without finding that all butchers who did not belong to state-protected monopolies constituted a "suspect class."

20. See, for example, *Bakke, City of Richmond v. Croson*, 488 U.S. 469 (1989), *Adarand Constructors v. Pena*, 515 U.S. 200 (1995), *Gratz v. Bollinger*, 539 U.S. 244 (2003), and *Grutter v. Bollinger*, 539 U.S. 306 (2003).

21. *United States v. Carolene Prods. Co.*, 304 U.S. 144, 152–3, (1938), n. 4.

22. *San Antonio Independent School District v. Rodriguez*, 411 U.S. 1, 28 (1973).

23. *Massachusetts Bd. of Retirement v. Murgia*, 427 U.S. 307 (1976).

24. Shaman, *Constitutional Interpretation*, 240–41.

25. *Skinner v. Oklahoma*, 316 U.S. 535 (1942).

26. *Reynolds v. Sims*, 377 U.S. 533 (1964).

27. *Griffin v. Illinois*, 351 U.S. 12 (1956).

28. *Shapiro v. Thompson*, 394 U.S. 618 (1969).

29. *Reynolds.*

30. *Reynolds*, 555.

31. 28 U.S.C. 1738C(a).

32. Shaman, *Constitutional Interpretation*, 241–4.

33. 411 U.S. 1 (1973).

34. *Rodriguez*, 33.

35. For an example of the way in which such anti-feminist arguments have been integrated into legal rhetoric that upholds the right of homosexuals to marry, see *Goodridge v. Dep't of Public Health*, 440 Mass. 309 (2003). On the feminist critique of legal marriage, see Martha Fineman, *The Neutered Mother, The Sexual Family and Other 20th Century Tragedies* (New York: Routledge, 1995). On the queer critique of legal marriage for same-sex couples, see Janet Halley in Robert Wintemute and Mads Andenas, eds., *The Legal Recognition of Same-Sex Partnerships* (New York: Hart Publishing, 2001) and Lisa Duggan, "Holy Matrimony!" *The Nation* (March 15, 2004), (available at: http://www.thenation.com). For a general discussion of the denigration of single mothers in welfare policy, see Linda Gordon, *Pitied but Not Entitled: Single Mothers and the History of Welfare* (Cambridge: Harvard University Press, 1995) and Gwendolyn Mink, *Welfare's End* (Ithaca: Cornell University Press, 1998). For detail on the integration of sexual regulation measures in contemporary welfare law in the United States, see Anna Marie Smith, "The Sexual Regulation Dimension of Contemporary Welfare Reform: A Fifty State Overview," *Michigan Journal of Gender and Law*, vol. 8, no. 2

(2002), 121–218. For a feminist critique of the promotion of marriage as a solution to poverty, see the manifesto, "No Promotion of Marriage in Welfare Reform!", written by Martha Fineman, Gwendolyn Mink, and Anna Marie Smith, posted on http://.falcon.arts.cornell.edu/ams3.

36. On the juxtaposition of racism and sexism in American society see Zillah Eisenstein, *The Color of Gender: Reimaging Democracy* (Berkeley: University of California Press, 1994) and Kimberlé Crenshaw. "Whose Story is it Anyway? Feminist and Antiracist Appropriations of Anita Hill," *Race-ing Justice, Engendering Power*, ed. Toni Morrison (New York: Pantheon, 1992), 402–40.

37. Jeffrey Weeks, *Sex, Politics and Society: The Regulation of Sexuality since 1800* (London: Longman, 1981), 99.

38. Ibid. I have discussed this theme in greater detail in "The Regulation of Lesbian Sexuality Through Erasure: The Case of Jennifer Saunders," in *Resisting the Political: Feminism and the New Democracy*, ed. Jodi Dean (London: Sage Press, 1997), 181–97.

39. Brief of *Amici Curiae* Human Rights Campaign et al., *Lawrence* (No. 02–102), 10.

40. National Center for Lesbian Rights, "National Center for Lesbian Rights Hails Supreme Court Decision Striking Texas Sodomy Statute," press release, June 26, 2003. Available at: http://www.nclrights.org (accessed November 23, 2004).

41. See, for example, *Moore v. East Cleveland*, 431 U.S. 494, 494 (1977) (deciding that a local ordinance that imposes a fixed definition of the family by limiting occupancy of a dwelling unit to members of a single family, and by recognizing as a "family" only parents and their children, violates due process); *Moore v. East Cleveland*, 503 ("Our decisions establish that the Constitution protects the sanctity of the family precisely because the institution of the family is deeply rooted in this Nation's history and tradition."); *Wisconsin v. Yoder*, 406 U.S. 205 (1972) (deciding that Amish children should be exempted from state compulsory school attendance law to protect the free exercise rights of Amish families, and that the State may not unreasonably interfere with parents' traditional interest in directing the religious upbringing and education of their children); *Stanley v. Illinois*, 405 U.S. 645 (1972) (deciding that an Illinois statute that excluded unwed fathers from the category of parents, and therefore allowed the state to presume that unwed fathers are unfit parents, violates the due process and equal protection clauses of the Constitution); *Stanley v. Illinois*, 652 (deciding that the interest of a biological father who has taken an active part in the rearing of his children in retaining custody of his children is "cognizable and substantial"); *Ginsberg v. New York*, 390 U.S. 629, 639 (1968) ("Constitutional interpretation has consistently recognized that the parents' claim to authority in their own household to direct the rearing of their children is basic in the structure of our society."); *Griswold*, 512 ("Specific guarantees in the Bill of Rights have penumbras, formed by emanations from those guarantees that help give them life and substance … Various guarantees create zones of privacy."); *Poe v. Ullman*, 367 U.S. 497, 551–2 (1961) (Justice Harlan, dissenting) ("The home derives its preeminence as the seat of family life. And the integrity of that life is something so fundamental that it has been found to draw to its protection the principles of more than one explicitly granted Constitutional right."); *Pierce v. Society of Sisters*, 268 U.S. 510 (1925) (striking down state law prohibiting children from attending parochial schools); and *Meyer v. Nebraska*, 262 U.S. 390 (1923) (striking down state law prohibiting the teaching of foreign languages to children).

42. The Adoption and Safe Families Act of 1997 (Pub. L. No. 105–89, 111 Stat. 2115 (1997)). Even where the state has proven that a parent has neglected or abused his or her child, this law orders state child welfare agencies to make a "reasonable effort" to preserve and to reunify families, unless that effort contradicts the best interest of the child.

CHAPTER 11

Sexuality, Marriage, and Relationships
The Radical Potential of Lawrence

JO ANN CITRON AND MARY LYNDON SHANLEY

On May 1, 2003, six weeks after the U.S. Supreme Court had heard oral arguments and eight weeks before it handed down its decision in *Lawrence v. Texas*,[1] Justice Sandra Day O'Connor addressed the students at Gonzaga College High School in Washington, D.C.[2] Following her prepared remarks, O'Connor was asked this question:

> [For] much of the twentieth century, race was a burning issue facing the courts. Could you conjecture what the burning issue might be for the twenty-first century?

Her reply went largely unnoticed by the press, but it was stunning:

> Yes, I think we see issues cropping up around the country relating to how [pause] homosexuals are treated, for example, legally, and we see a number of cases in that area.

Justice O'Connor was surely thinking not only about the pending decision in *Lawrence*, but also about the Supreme Court's earlier decisions in *Romer v. Evans* (1996)[3] and *Bowers v. Hardwick* (1986),[4] cases that profoundly influenced how she and the other Justices would ground their opinions in *Lawrence*.

At issue in the Texas case was the constitutionality of that state's Homosexual Conduct Law, which made it a crime to commit sodomy with a person of the same sex. *Lawrence* began when the Houston police received a report that someone with a gun was acting crazy inside a residence and entered the apartment of John Lawrence where they observed Lawrence and Tyron Garner engaging in anal intercourse. Both men were arrested, held in jail overnight, charged, and convicted before a Justice of the Peace of violating the state anti-sodomy law. Their challenge to the sodomy statute was unsuccessful at trial and the state appeals court, invoking *Bowers v. Hardwick*, rejected their appeal on both equal protection and due process grounds. Appeal to the U.S. Supreme Court followed and in a 6–3 decision the Court struck down the Texas statute: Justices Stevens, Souter, Ginsburg, and Breyer joined Justice Kennedy's opinion applying a due process analysis and explicitly overturning *Bowers v. Hardwick*; Justice O'Connor filed an opinion concurring in the judgment but analyzing the case under the Equal Protection Clause, an analysis that would have left *Bowers* intact; Justices Rehnquist and Thomas joined Justice Scalia's dissenting opinion taking the court to task for overruling *Bowers*, for finding a right to liberty under the Due Process Clause, for decreeing the end of all morals legislation, and for opening the door to gay marriage; and Justice Thomas wrote separately in dissent to opine that while the Texas law was "uncommonly silly,"[5] the Constitution does not contain a general right to privacy or to liberty that would allow the court to grant petitioners relief.

Lawrence v. Texas was first and foremost a successful challenge to the state's authority to regulate sexual activity between consenting adults. Sodomy is now legal throughout the United States, regardless of the sex of the participants. But the significance of *Lawrence* goes far beyond a narrow holding that struck down the few sodomy statutes that had survived, largely unenforced, into the twenty-first century. The substantive due process analysis that eliminated the remaining sodomy statutes also eliminated from the law the misguided pronouncements of *Bowers v. Hardwick*. The *Lawrence* court rejected *Bowers's* moralistic and cramped approach to homosexual sex and instead characterized the issue as whether gay men and lesbians have "the right to choose to enter upon relationships in the confines of their homes and their own private lives and still retain their *dignity as free persons*."[6] In establishing that this is a right the Constitution will protect, the majority decision spoke eloquently of the importance of relationships, of the place of sex within those relationships, and of the significance of sexual conduct to individual autonomy and identity. And by analyzing the sodomy statute under substantive due process, the majority moved this case about homosexual sex into a line of cases that address the core social values of marriage and family, procreation and contraception, and the rearing and education of children. Where *Bowers* spoke disparagingly of homosexuals as moral pariahs and social outsiders, *Lawrence* spoke respectfully of homosexuals as individuals whose intimate and family relationships are no less worthy of respect and constitutional protection than are those of their heterosexual counterparts. The emphasis on sex as worthy of constitutional protection because it is an important aspect of relationship not only marked a significant change in the posture of the Court toward a class of citizens who have, until now, enjoyed limited constitutional protection, but also created the potential to expand and deepen legal thinking about sexuality, marriage, and intimate relationship.

Framing the Issue

Romer v. Evans and Bowers v. Hardwick
Two prior cases form an indispensable background to *Lawrence*: *Romer v. Evans* and *Bowers v. Hardwick*. *Romer* was a 1996 case that struck down a popular referendum amending the Colorado state constitution to prohibit any branch of government from conferring legal protections upon homosexuals. The amendment opened the door to state-sanctioned discrimination against gays both publicly and privately. Justice Kennedy, writing for the majority in *Romer*, held that Amendment 2 violated the Equal Protection Clause, which says simply that no state shall deny to any person within its jurisdiction the equal protection of the laws. The civil rights movement is the history of how equal protection has been invoked to protect disfavored minorities from the political tyranny of the majority. Justice Kennedy reasoned that for Colorado to impose such wide-ranging legal disabilities upon a single named group was inexplicable by anything but animus toward the affected class. And because animus, without more, lacks any rational relationship to a legitimate state interest, Amendment 2 must fail. In holding that Amendment 2 did not meet even the rational relation test, the court spared itself the agony of having to debate whether homosexuality was to become a new suspect class in America, which would require that any law affecting homosexuals be subjected to strict scrutiny.[7] Justice O'Connor had joined Justice Kennedy's opinion in *Romer*, and she would have decided the Texas sodomy case the same way. In analyzing *Romer* under equal protection, the Court made it clear that what was at stake in the referendum fight was the civil rights of a despised minority; this would be Justice O'Connor's approach in *Lawrence* as well.

Against the majority's understanding in *Romer* that animus toward homosexuals is a civil rights issue was Justice Scalia's insistence that animus toward homosexuals is but a feature of the culture wars and that courts have no business standing on one side or the other of a cultural

212 • Jo Ann Citron and Mary Lyndon Shanley

divide.[8] Coloradoans, Scalia argued, are politically *"entitled* to be hostile toward homosexual conduct."[9] In analyzing the issues *Romer* raised, Scalia notably looked not to civil rights jurisprudence but to *Bowers v. Hardwick.* If it is constitutionally permissible for a state to criminalize sodomy, Scalia reasoned, "surely it is constitutionally permissible for a State to enact other laws merely *disfavoring* homosexual conduct."[10]

It is worth pausing to recall the details of *Bowers*, for it would loom over every aspect of the opinions in *Lawrence v. Texas.* Michael Hardwick was arrested by an Atlanta police officer who visited his home one morning carrying an arrest warrant in connection with a minor offense for which Hardwick had already paid the fine. The officer entered the house, found his way to a bedroom, pushed open the door, and came upon Hardwick and another man having oral sex. The police officer placed both men under arrest, watched as they dressed, handcuffed them, and drove them to the station where they were charged with violating Georgia's sodomy law, a crime punishable by up to twenty years in prison.[11] The criminal statute at issue in *Bowers* applied to both heterosexuals and homosexuals and was initially challenged by John and Mary Doe, a married couple, along with Michael Hardwick. The Does claimed that the statute and Hardwick's arrest under it had "chilled and deterred" them from sexual activity. However, the Federal District Court dismissed them from the case for lack of standing because they had neither sustained, nor were in immediate danger of sustaining, any direct injury from the law since it was rarely enforced and they had not been arrested.[12]

Had the Georgia law targeted homosexuals specifically, Hardwick could have challenged it on equal protection grounds. But because the statute— at least on its face—applied to all persons equally, Hardwick's challenge looked to privacy and due process. Hardwick's brief presented the Supreme Court with the following question: May the state send its police into private bedrooms to arrest adults for engaging in consensual, noncommercial sexual acts, with no justification beyond the assertion that those acts are immoral?[13] With the heterosexual petitioners conveniently dismissed from the case, the U.S. Supreme Court disregarded the statute's plain language and defined the question before it not as whether state prohibitions on sodomy were justifiable restrictions on sexual freedom for everyone, but rather "whether the Federal Constitution confers a fundamental right upon homosexuals to engage in sodomy."[14] To such a question the Court, not surprisingly, responded "no," and for the next seventeen years *Bowers v. Hardwick* was invoked to permit discrimination against homosexuals on the grounds that the activity that defines them enjoys no constitutional protections. This was the legal landscape that John Lawrence and Tyron Garner sought to rearrange.[15]

The facts in *Lawrence* were strikingly similar to the facts in *Bowers*. In both cases, police entered the home and found two men engaging in sexual conduct proscribed by a state statute. In both cases, the men were arrested. Whereas the state declined to seek an indictment against Michael Hardwick, the defendants in *Lawrence* were convicted and the convictions were affirmed. On appeal to the U. S. Supreme Court, both Texas and Lawrence and Garner agreed that the questions to be decided were (1) whether the Texas statute violated the Equal Protection Clause, (2) whether the Texas statute violated the Due Process Clause, and (3) whether *Bowers v. Hardwick* should be overruled.[16] Because the Texas law proscribed only homosexual sodomy, the Court could have struck down the statute on equal protection grounds using the same theory enunciated in *Romer*, namely that there was no reason apart from animus to criminalize sodomy among homosexuals while allowing heterosexuals to practice it with impunity. Using the Equal Protection Clause to strike down the Texas law would have eliminated only those statutes that applied exclusively to homosexuals and would have permitted criminalization of sexual acts as long as the prohibitions applied to everyone.[17] This was the approach Justice O'Connor advocated in her concurring opinion in *Lawrence*. She had joined Justice Kennedy's opinion in *Romer*, and she would have decided *Lawrence* in the same way, holding that the Texas statute impermissibly denied the disfavored homosexual minority the protection of laws that applied to everyone else. She argued that the Texas statute was unconstitutional because there was no reason, apart from moral disapproval, to criminalize homosexual sodomy while allowing heterosexual sodomy to go unpunished, and moral disapproval of a particular group can never be a legitimate basis for the enactment of laws.

However, O'Connor's was the lone voice on the *Lawrence* court to invoke equal protection. The other five justices who voted to strike down the Homosexual Conduct Law did so under the Fourteenth Amendment's Due Process Clause: No state shall deprive any person of life, liberty, or property without due process of law. The *Lawrence* holding was actually quite narrow: The Constitution protects private sexual conduct between consenting adults from being criminalized, and this protection applies to otherwise permissible conduct regardless of particular sexual practices or the lifestyle of the participants.[18] Writing for the majority, Justice Kennedy went out of his way to point out that the issue before the court did not involve "whether the government must give formal recognition to any relationship that homosexual persons seek to enter."[19] It involved only "whether the majority may use the power of the State to enforce [their moral] views on the whole society through operation of the criminal law."[20] The Court answered that they may not. The conclusion reached by the majority under a due process analysis was the same as the conclusion reached by Justice O'Connor under an equal protection analysis. What, then, was the significance of the Court's decision to analyze the facts in *Lawrence* under the Due Process rather than the Equal Protection Clause?

For one thing, deciding the case under substantive due process allowed the Court to accept the petitioners' invitation to overrule *Bowers v. Hardwick*, whose homophobia was a moral affront and a legal embarrassment. But the due process analysis had implications far beyond what happened to *Bowers*. Substantive due process is the doctrine that the Court has traditionally used to protect individual rights pertaining to marriage, procreation, contraception, family relationships, child rearing, and education. These rights are deemed "fundamental," a legal term of art for rights that, while not made explicit anywhere in the Constitution, are nevertheless thought to be "implicit in the concept of ordered liberty" such that "neither liberty nor justice would exist if [they] were sacrificed."[21] The majority's decision to analyze the statute under due process thereby moved a case about homosexual sodomy into a well-developed jurisprudence of privacy and fundamental rights involving the intimate associations of marriage and family from which *Bowers* had banished it. Central to that jurisprudence was the landmark case of *Griswold v. Connecticut* that established that the state's ban on contraception violates a married couple's right to privacy.

Griswold v. Connecticut

It could be said that modern privacy jurisprudence in this country was born at the moment that Justice Douglas, writing for the court in *Griswold v. Connecticut*, imagined the police entering the marital bedroom to search for "telltale signs of the use of contraceptives."[22] The very idea was "repulsive" to notions surrounding the sanctity of both the marital bedroom as a *place* and the marriage relationship as an *association*. At issue in *Griswold* were two Connecticut statutes that authorized the state to imprison anyone found guilty of using or promoting contraceptives. The criminal statutes reached both the persons seeking to avoid pregnancy and the doctors and clinic workers who provided, prescribed, or even described contraceptives. The plaintiffs were directors of Planned Parenthood who had been convicted of advising married persons about how to avoid conception. The court held that the statutes violated the right to privacy by interfering with the intimate association of marriage. Seven justices concurred with Justice Douglas's opinion for the Court that a right to privacy exists and that it protects the marital relationship and secures the marital bedroom. But the Justices could not agree about where to find it.

Justice Douglas invoked privacy guarantees that hover somewhere in the vicinity of the First Amendment. Though not mentioned in the Constitution, associational rights had long found protection there. The right of the people to assemble and to dissent has always been held critical to the operation of democracy. Protection of the political process has been augmented by protection of associations that yield social, legal, and economic benefits—all public matters. The move that *Griswold* made was to bring "intimate relationships" within the protection of "associations" that until then had a largely public meaning. "The present case," Justice Douglas wrote, "concerns a relationship lying within the zone of privacy":

> Marriage is a coming together for better or for worse, hopefully enduring, and intimate to the degree of being sacred. It is an association that promotes a way of life, not causes; a harmony in living, not political faiths; a bilateral loyalty, not commercial or social projects. Yet it is an association for as noble a purpose as any involved in our prior decisions.[23]

Marriage and the family occupy a "sacred" position in the panoply of human institutions and so deserve special protection. A law that "seeks to achieve its goals by means of having a maximum destructive impact upon that relationship"[24] cannot stand.

The right to privacy that Douglas invoked is part of what he termed the "penumbras" and "emanations" within the Bill of Rights—guarantees that find no explicit expression in the amendments but that figure in their implications. The associational rights that protect the marital relationship from government interference were for Douglas attached to the First Amendment. Justice Goldberg's concurring opinion found the right to privacy in the Ninth Amendment, which promises that the "enumeration in the Constitution of certain rights shall not be construed to deny or disparage others retained by the people." Justice White concurred but found the statute without any plausible justification; he could not see "how the ban on the use of contraceptives by married couples in any way reinforces the State's ban on illicit sexual relationship."[25] Justice Harlan concurred and reaffirmed the position he had taken in his dissenting opinion in *Poe v. Ullman* (a case that upheld the very statute that *Griswold* would strike down) that a ban on contraception "violates basic values 'implicit in the concept of ordered liberty'" guaranteed by the Due Process Clause.[26] Harlan's dissent in *Poe v. Ullman* and its encore in his *Griswold* concurrence are critical statements in the development of the Constitutional doctrine of substantive due process, the doctrine at the heart of the sodomy cases.

The Due Process Clause is understood to have a substantive as well as a procedural component.[27] In its procedural mode, it guarantees that the government cannot deprive an individual of life, liberty, or property without providing notice and an opportunity to be heard.[28] In its substantive mode, it guarantees that, absent a compelling state interest, the government cannot interfere with an individual's fundamental liberty interests, though considerable dispute circulates around identifying what those interests are. Strict constructionists resist identifying any right beyond those enumerated by the Bill of Rights or explicitly set forth elsewhere in the Constitution. However, over time the majority view has been that due process reaches beyond enumerated rights to embrace rights that are deemed "fundamental," that belong to the citizens of all free governments and the securing of which is the very reason that men and women enter into society. This is what Justice Cardozo meant by the phrase "implicit in the concept of ordered liberty" and what Harlan described in his dissent in *Poe v. Ullman*:

> Due process has not been reduced to any formula; its content cannot be determined by reference to any code. The best that can be said is that through the course of this Court's decisions it has represented the balance which our Nation, built upon postulates of respect for the liberty of the individual, has struck between that liberty and the demands of organized society. ... The balance of which I speak is the balance struck by this country, having regard to what history teaches are the traditions from which it developed as well as the traditions from which it broke.[29]

Much of Justice Harlan's dissent in *Poe* concerned the physical privacy of the home, but he rejected the notion that what is being protected is "home" as some kind of "place," as if an intrusion could be satisfactorily dealt with by the Fourth Amendment's guarantee of the right of the people to be secure in their houses. Fourteenth Amendment protections are needed because the presence of the contraception police in the marital bedroom represents

> not an intrusion into the home so much as on the life which characteristically has its place in the home. ... Certainly the safeguarding of the home does not follow merely from the sanctity of property rights. The home derives its pre-eminence as the seat of family life. And the integrity of that life is something so fundamental that it has been found to draw to its protection the principles of more than one explicitly granted Constitutional right.[30]

Two considerations permeated the support for family privacy. One was the sanctity of families and the privacy needed to conduct family life. The other was sex. What married couples in Connecticut were deprived of was engaging in sex free from any fear of conceiving a child or contracting a venereal disease if they didn't use contraceptives, and fear of prosecution by the state if they did. As long as any legally permissible act of sexual intercourse had to carry with it the possibility of pregnancy or sexually transmitted disease, Connecticut was interfering with sexual freedom. Whatever the *Griswold* decision might have *said* about the nobility of "family," what the case *did* was effectively to constitutionalize non-procreative sex for married people.

The unmarried had to wait to claim their sexual freedom until 1972, when Bill Baird gave a package of vaginal foam to a single woman attending one of his lectures. Massachusetts law prohibited single, but not married, persons from obtaining contraceptives for the purpose of preventing pregnancy. At issue in *Eisenstadt v. Baird* was whether the different treatment of married and unmarried persons violated the Equal Protection Clause.[31] The Supreme Court held that it did. *Eisenstadt* recognized that marriage is not some magical status that merges two persons into an undifferentiated unit but is rather a coming together of two separate, autonomous individuals:

> It is true that in *Griswold* the right of privacy in question inhered in the marital relationship. Yet the marital couple is not an independent entity with a mind and heart of its own, but an association of two individuals each with a separate intellect and emotional makeup. If the right of privacy means anything, it is the right of the *individual*, married or single, to be free from unwarranted governmental intrusion into matters so fundamentally affecting a person as the decision whether to bear or beget a child.[32]

Eisenstadt's vindication of an individual's right to sexual expression did not depend upon the sanctity of family, home or the marital union. Brennan resisted reifying marriage and rejected the view that the sexual union of two married individuals is somehow different from the sexual union of two unmarried individuals. In addition, by framing what was at stake not as an intimate association, as *Griswold* had done, but rather as "the decision whether to bear or beget a child," *Eisenstadt* imagined an unmarried, autonomous individual for whom sex and procreation are disjoined terms.

Griswold's Legacy: Marital Privacy or Sexual Freedom?

Once "sex" became divorced from "procreation" (*Griswold*) and the right to sexual privacy was extended to single persons (*Eisenstadt*), what legal principle operated to confine the protection of sexual freedom to heterosexuals? This is the question at the heart of the sodomy cases. *Bowers* answered it by focusing on sodomy and detailing a long history of moral disapproval of homosexuality. But after *Romer,* it was not at all clear that mere moral disapproval could ever be a rational or legitimate reason for laws disfavoring a particular group. *Lawrence* answered the question by talking about intimate associations and individual autonomy, and by referring to a long history of protecting fundamental rights such as marriage and family relationships.

Because the Texas law targeted homosexuals in particular, *Lawrence v. Texas* could easily have been decided on equal protection grounds and nothing need have been said about relationships, privacy, protected spaces, dignity, identity, autonomy, or personal rights, let alone marriage. Such an approach was preferred by Justice O'Connor, who had voted with the majority in *Bowers* and who would not vote to overturn it. O'Connor had also, of course, joined Kennedy's opinion in *Romer*, which held that expressing moral disapproval of homosexuality is not a legitimate State interest. The briefs had invited the justices to apply an equal protection analysis, and O'Connor was correct that equal protection was adequate to decide the relatively narrow question of the constitutionality of the Homosexual Conduct Law. Even Clarence Thomas thought the law "a waste of law enforcement resources" though he joined Scalia's dissent and voted to uphold it.[33] But Kennedy and the four justices who joined his opinion rejected the equal protection argument so readily at hand in favor of a due process analysis.

First of all, due process was the theory upon which the *Bowers* court relied and deciding *Lawrence* under equal protection would have left *Bowers* intact. *Bowers* had been relied upon for, among other things, the following: homosexuals are not permitted to serve in the armed forces; bisexuals may be discharged from the armed forces; the Defense Department may conduct expanded investigations of gay and lesbian applicants for secret security clearance; there is no right to commit adultery; a grandparent has no liberty interest in the adoption of her grandchildren; a prisoner has no right to HIV testing; a fireman does not have a fundamental interest in promotion; police departments may ask prospective employees about their homosexual activity; and the State may restrict surnames given to children at birth.[34] The *Lawrence* court bravely acknowledged that the shaky reasoning in *Bowers* had been the target of substantial and continuing disapproval and that its continuance as precedent "demeans the lives of homosexual persons."[35] Then, in considerable detail, Kennedy dismantled *Bowers* piece by shoddy piece. The *Bowers* court misapprehended the issue before it, which was not whether the Constitution confers a fundamental right to engage in sodomy but whether it protects "the most private human conduct, sexual behavior … in the most private of places, the home."[36] Kennedy explained how the *Bowers* court misused history: there is no longstanding history of American law directed at homosexual conduct; how Justice Burger's contention that condemnation of homosexual practices was rooted firmly in the Judeo-Christian tradition was dubious at best; and how

Burger's sweeping references to the history of Western civilization failed to account for pockets of civilization—Europe, for example—that had repealed or invalidated laws against homosexual conduct. Kennedy's criticism of Burger's cramped and self-serving view of history echoed Harlan's description of history's proper role in balancing the due process claims of the individual against the demands of society. History teaches "the traditions from which [the country] *developed as well as the traditions from which it broke.* ... [A]n apparently novel claim ... must take its place in relation to what went before and further [cut] a channel for what is to come."[37]

Kennedy also pointed out that laws targeting homosexuals developed only in the final third of the twentieth century, that laws prohibiting sodomy were not enforced against consenting adults acting in private, that the rules of evidence made sodomy prosecutions difficult, and that criminal prohibitions against sodomy were directed not at homosexuals but at non-procreative sex generally. And, most importantly, however much homosexuality may be condemned by however many people, the majority may not use the power of the State to enforce their views upon all of society through operation of the criminal laws. As Justice Stevens had argued in dissent in *Bowers*, neither history nor tradition could save anti-miscegenation laws and neither history nor tradition should have been able to save anti-sodomy laws, regardless of the category of persons engaging in the practice. Invoking his fellow jurist's dissent,[38] Justice Kennedy pronounced that "*Bowers* was not correct when it was decided, and it is not correct today. It ought not to remain binding precedent. *Bowers v. Hardwick* should be and now is overruled."[39] Rarely does the Supreme Court speak so boldly and emphatically when rejecting its own precedents.

Just as remarkable as the ringing tones in which Kennedy dispatched *Bowers* were the respectful ones in which he described the liberty interest at the heart of the petitioners' challenge. The constitutional doctrines of privacy and liberty, while implicated in one another, are not coterminous, as the concurrences in *Griswold* made clear. Even now, some forty years after *Griswold*, privacy protections are analytically distinct from due process.[40] *Lawrence* might have been resolved by holding simply, as Douglas had done, that the petitioners had a right to privacy that the Texas statute infringed upon: they were consenting adults, they were acting in private, and their association was protected by the emanations and penumbras of the First Amendment. But to describe what is at stake as mere sexual conduct

> demeans the claim the individual put forward, just as it would demean *a married couple* were it to be said *marriage* is simply about the right to have sexual intercourse. ... When sexuality finds overt

expression in intimate conduct with another person, the conduct can be but one element in *a personal bond that is more enduring*.[41]

As has been observed many times, there was no evidence that Lawrence and Garner were life partners or that they were having anything but a casual sexual encounter when the police entered the apartment. But Kennedy's opinion characterized the matter as involving an association not unlike the intimate association in *Griswold*, which "described the protected interest as a right to privacy and placed emphasis on the *marriage relation* and the protected space of the *marital bedroom*."[42]

A court's holding—the narrowest possible principle of law at the core of the decision—can usually be reduced to a single sentence. Everything else is dicta, words that surround but do not articulate, the legal principle that resolves the dispute. But judicial opinions are like any other piece of writing in containing subtext as well as text. The holding at the core of the *Lawrence* decision, that adults have a due process liberty interest in their private, consensual sexual conduct, is hardly an adequate expression of what the case *means*. This is precisely what Kennedy meant when he said that to characterize the stakes as "simply ... sexual conduct" demeans the claim.[43] It would be hard to overstate the significance of the language Kennedy used to describe what is at stake here. By using phrases such as "intimate sexual conduct" and by referring repeatedly to "marriage," "the marriage relationship," and "the marital bedroom," Kennedy normalized homosexual sex, the homosexual relationships that expand upon sex, and the homosexual persons who engage in sex as one part of those relationships. Justice Burger's sodomites are no different from Justice Douglas's married folks who are having sex in the house next door, the one with the picket fence, whose bedrooms are "sacred precincts" that the police may not invade.

Moreover, the majority in *Lawrence* went beyond privacy in its spatial dimension to invoke liberty in its broader aspects. The right at issue here is not only the right of privacy that restricts the State from telling a man, sitting alone in his house, what books he may read or what films he may watch.[44] The decision begins with the word "liberty" and the paragraph is worth quoting in full:

Liberty protects the person from unwarranted government intrusions into a dwelling or other private places. In our tradition the State is not omnipresent in the home. And there are other spheres of our lives and existence, outside the home, where the State should not be a dominant presence. Freedom extends beyond spatial bounds. Liberty presumes an autonomy of self that includes freedom of thought, belief, expression, and certain intimate conduct. The instant case involves liberty of the person both in its spatial and more transcendent dimensions.[45]

The Court both affirmed the importance of physical privacy, the sacred space of the home, and insisted that the freedom that protects it is not limited to particular places; adults must have the ability to define themselves, to assert and to discover who they are through "freedom of thought, belief, expression, and certain intimate conduct."[46] Having framed the case as one of personal liberty, the Court held that it "should be resolved by determining whether the petitioners were free as adults to engage in the private conduct in the exercise of their liberty under the Due Process Clause of the Fourteenth Amendment to the Constitution."[47]

The defense of individual liberty under substantive due process is the theory that the Supreme Court has historically invoked to protect marriage,[48] procreation,[49] contraception,[50] family relationships,[51] child rearing,[52] and education.[53] The Court described the liberty interest at stake in *Lawrence* as akin to these. The question, as the Court posed it, was whether Texas could make it a crime for two persons of the same sex to engage in "intimate sexual conduct"—not "sodomy."[54] The Court's phrase was more than a euphemism. It signaled that whatever the sex of the actors, the activity of the *Lawrence* couple was no different from the activity of the imagined *Griswold* spouses or of the pairs of individuals in *Eisenstadt*. The spectral figure of the policeman in the bedroom that had so repulsed Justice Douglas became real first in *Bowers* and again in *Lawrence*. In 1986, the *Bowers* Court could hardly peer into that space without seeing a public history of moral disapproval. In 2003, the *Lawrence* Court looked into the same space and saw, remarkably, something akin to a marital bedroom.

Lawrence's Legacy: Sexual Freedom or Heteronormativity?

As several commentators have pointed out, there is no indication in the record that Lawrence and Garner were involved in anything other than the most transient sexual encounter. Katherine Franke argues that the Court "domesticated" the sexual acts between John Lawrence and Tyron Garner by portraying gay men "as domesticated creatures, settling down into marital-like relationships in which they can both cultivate and nurture desires for exclusivity, fidelity, and longevity in place of other more explicitly erotic desires."[55] Other commentators argue that "segments of the *Lawrence* opinion embody the heteronormative impulses of a court struggling to position the gay men before it as comparable to married persons, even though neither the record nor their attorneys suggested that John

Lawrence and Tyron Garner had anything other than a mutually desired fleeting encounter."[56] To the Court's statement that "[sexual conduct] can be but one element in a personal bond that is more enduring," Franke asks, "More enduring than what? Than sex?"[57] To which one might respond, "Well, yes." A sexual encounter can occur anywhere along the continuum between a one-night stand and a committed long-term relationship, whether or not that relationship is sanctioned by the State. As Carlos Ball observes, "the Texas sodomy statute implicated liberty interests associated with personal relationships as much as liberty interests associated with sexual conduct." To the Court "it made no sense to discuss the freedom to engage in sexual conduct without bringing into the liberty analysis the ability of individual to form and maintain the kinds of personal relationships that often accompany that conduct."[58] Thus, *Lawrence v. Texas* is immediately about sexual freedom and also potentially about marriage and other intimate or nonconjugal relationships.

As a legal opinion, *Lawrence* stands for the proposition that the due process clause protects a person's liberty interest in exploring identity through sexual practices undertaken in private with other consenting adults, *no matter what those practices look like.* Yet the Court repeatedly reached beyond the sexual conduct that is its putative subject to position the sexual encounter within an array of intimacies. Both *Bowers* and *Lawrence* showed great respect for heterosexual marriage and deemed it worthy of constitutional protection. *Bowers* promoted heteronormativity by treating gay sexual practices with contempt and allowing them to be criminalized; *Lawrence* promoted it by normalizing homosexuality and making gay relationships look like marital ones. The *Lawrence* majority opinion embraced the population that *Bowers* spurned by eliding the differences between the "insiders" and the "outsiders."

The liberty of the person in its spatial dimension protects what a person may do in the privacy of his home; the liberty of the person in its more transcendent dimension protects not just what a person does, but who a person *is*; not just association, but *autonomy*; not just conduct, but *identity*. As Justice Kennedy explained, quoting *Planned Parenthood of Southeastern Pa. v. Casey*:

> At the heart of liberty is the right to define one's own concept of existence, of meaning, of the universe, and of the mystery of human life. Beliefs about these matters could not define the attributes of personhood were they formed under compulsion of the State.[59]

This last is what Scalia scorns as *Casey*'s "famed sweet-mystery-of-life passage."[60] The right to define one's concept of existence for oneself is part of what *Lawrence* defends, and this would suggest that the decision embraces far more than the "narrow version of liberty" that Franke attributes to it.[61] The core of Blackmun's dissent in *Bowers* was that the ability to define one's identity, which is central to any concept of liberty, depends to a significant degree upon intimate sexual relationships.[62] Certain sexual conduct, as Blackmun put it, "touches the heart of what makes [homosexuals] what they are."[63] As Jamie Weinstein and Tobyn DeMarco put it, "The right to make autonomous, free choices about private, consensual, adult sexual activity is a central feature of this project of identity construction."[64] *Lawrence* affirmed the right of individuals to make autonomous, free choices about acts that define their identities and constitute them as persons. One's sexuality is part of what it means to be a particular person.[65] *Lawrence* draws upon both privacy and substantive due process to protect the sexual conduct that establishes an intimate relationship and also defines a personal identity. The law will protect both the association and the individual autonomy that combine to yield identity. Kennedy's opinion transforms the sodomy cases into an exploration of the role of sexual conduct in forming a variety of intimate associations and personal relationships that privacy will protect.

The implications of the due process analysis that Kennedy applied did not stop with *Bowers* and the removal of proscriptions against sodomy. Although both Kennedy writing for the majority and O'Connor writing for herself were careful to distinguish laws that impose criminal penalties on the sexual conduct that defines homosexuals from laws that would grant legal recognition to homosexual relationships, Scalia complained in dissent that the reasoning in the *Lawrence* decision left no room for any principled denial of marriage to same-sex couples. He viewed the overruling of *Bowers* as a "massive disruption of the current social order"[66] and feared that O'Connor's equal protection analysis left laws limiting marriage to opposite-sex partners "on pretty shaky grounds" because logically "preserving the traditional institution of marriage is just a kinder way of describing the State's moral disapproval of same-sex couples."[67] And because he believes that the Due Process Clause grants no right to liberty in the first place, he described the majority as having signed onto the homosexual agenda and impermissibly taken sides in the culture war.[68] "The Court today pretends that ... we need not fear judicial imposition of homosexual marriage ... Do not believe it," he warned.[69] Scalia was, as we know, correct. Within five months of the issuance of the decision in the Texas sodomy case, the Massachusetts Supreme Judicial Court would construe civil marriage to mean "the voluntary union of two persons as spouses, to the exclusion of all others."[70] In Massachusetts the sexual outlaws now have in-laws.

Conclusion

Deciding *Lawrence v. Texas* on substantive due process grounds was a deliberate choice with far-reaching implications. Either privacy or equal protection would have been adequate to strike down Texas's sodomy statute, but a due process analysis was necessary to overturn *Bowers,* to affirm the dignity of homosexuals, and to extend the reach of the protections afforded sexual relationships. The liberty guaranteed by the Due Process Clause protects the freedom both to make choices, including choices about sexual activity, and to form intimate relationships. In ringing language, *Lawrence* affirmed both these freedoms. That is its radical potential. *Bowers* had said, "These homosexual sodomites are not decent people, and not like us," while *Lawrence* said, "These homosexual sodomites are decent people, and just like us." The change in moral judgment is of the utmost importance. Yet in both cases, the normative standard of a rights-bearing individual in a relationship is heterosexual. In *Griswold,* the case that articulated the nature of the right that has been extended to others, the subjects are a married heterosexual couple. In *Lawrence,* heterosexual relations remain the norm against which others are measured.

However, *Lawrence* contains language and concepts that would allow it to move beyond the marital paradigm to an affirmation of other kinds of relationships. The majority and dissenting opinions in the substantive due process cases that form the legacy on which *Lawrence* draws engage in an extended conversation over the importance of sexual freedom both to identity formation and individual happiness, and to the formation and sustaining of intimate associations. To charge that "sex gets figured, if at all, in *Lawrence* as instrumental to the formation of intimate relationships—it seems not to have a social or legal status in its own right"[71] follows only one strand of the intertwined skein that runs from *Griswold* through *Lawrence.* At the same time that *Lawrence* hearkened back to *Griswold* and the protections given to marital sex engaged in primarily in "the marital bedroom," it also suggested, in Laurence Tribe's words, that "regardless of whether we label it 'autonomy' or 'agency,' we are speaking of a capacity of individuals to construct for themselves a life (including a sexual life) that is not completely beholden to societal power relations."[72] The majority's declaration in *Lawrence* that "liberty presumes an autonomy of self that includes freedom of thought, belief, expression, and certain intimate conduct" has the potential to extend recognition and protection to a variety of relationships that enrich both individuals and society.

Notes

1. *Lawrence v. Texas,* 539 U.S. 558 (2003).
2. Her address was part of the Students and Leaders Program organized by Comcast and C-Span. Her complete remarks are available as a video clip at http://www.studentsandleaders.org/video/justice_oconnor.asp (accessed November 20, 2004).

3. *Romer v. Evans*, 517 U.S. 620 (1996).
4. *Bowers v. Hardwick*, 478 U.S. 186 (1986).
5. *Lawrence*, 606.
6. *Lawrence*, 567 (emphasis added).
7. "Strict scrutiny" is the Court's most rigorous form of review, reserved under equal protection analysis for what are known as "protected categories" or "suspect classes." Strict scrutiny looks at laws affecting the categories of race and national origin and asks if they are as narrowly tailored as possible to promote a compelling government interest. The fact that few laws survive under this analysis has led commentators to note that strict scrutiny is strict in theory but fatal in fact. See Gerald Gunther, *Harvard Law Review* 1 (1972), 86.
8. *Romer*, 636 (Justice Scalia, dissenting).
9. *Romer*, 644 (emphasis in original).
10. *Romer*, 641 (emphasis in original).
11. Hardwick appeared at a municipal court hearing on the sodomy charges. Although the district attorney declined to seek an indictment at that time, the possibility of future prosecution remained open. Hardwick then brought his constitutional challenge. For a full account of the arrest and its legal aftermath, see Joyce Murdoch and Deb Price, *Courting Justice: Gay Men and Lesbians vs. the Supreme Court* (New York: Basic Books, 2001).
12. The 11th Circuit affirmed the dismissal. *Hardwick v. Bowers*, 760 F.2d 1202 (1985), 188, n2.
13. Brief of Respondent at 1, *Bowers v. Hardwick*, 478 U.S. 186 (1986).
14. *Bowers*, 190 (1986).
15. *Romer* was decided on equal protection grounds and so had no effect upon *Bowers*, a substantive due process case.
16. Brief of Petitioners, Respondent's Brief in Opposition, *Lawrence v. Texas*, 559 U.S. 558 (2003).
17. The only other states with same-sex sodomy laws were Oklahoma, Missouri, and Kansas.
18. That is, sexual activity, such as erotic asphyxiation, resulting in death might be criminalized under other applicable law.
19. *Lawrence*, 578.
20. *Lawrence*, 571.
21. *Palko v. Connecticut*, 302 U.S 319, 325 and 326 (1937).
22. *Griswold*, 381 U.S. 479, 485 (1965).
23. *Griswold*, 486.
24. *Griswold*, 485.
25. *Griswold*, 505 (Justice White, concurring).
26. *Griswold*, 500 (Justice Harlan, concurring, quoting *Palko v. Connecticut*, 302 U.S 319, 325 (1937)). In Justice Harlan's view there was no need to enunciate a new right to privacy; the Due Process Clause "stands … on its own bottom."
27. Since at least 1887, courts have recognized that the Constitution bars certain governmental actions regardless of the fairness of the procedures used to implement them. *See Planned Parenthood of Southeastern Pa. v. Casey*, 505 U.S. 833, 847 (1992) and cases cited.
28. In some instances, the Due Process Clause is satisfied if the hearing occurs *after* the deprivation. The curiosity of a post-deprivation hearing is familiar to anyone who has heard the White Queen describe the plight of the King's Messenger: "He's in prison now, being punished: and the trial doesn't even begin till next Wednesday." Lewis Carroll, *Through the Looking-Glass*, 1872.
29. *Poe v. Ullman*, 367 U.S. 497, 542 (1961) (Justice Harlan, dissenting).
30. *Poe*, 551–552 (Justice Harlan, dissenting).
31. *Eisenstadt v. Baird*, 405 U.S. 438 (1972). Massachusetts defended the differential treatment by arguing that the law was intended to discourage premarital intercourse, to protect the health of the community, and to prohibit contraception. The Supreme Court thought it plainly unreasonable that Massachusetts would prescribe pregnancy and the birth of an unwanted child as punishment for fornication; moreover, the health needs of the unmarried are presumably just as great as the health needs of the married. The court ducked the question of whether the state may impose a general prohibition on contraception by opining that whatever the rights of access may be, they must be the same for all.
32. *Eisenstadt*, 453 (emphasis in original; citations omitted).
33. *Lawrence*, 605 (Justice Thomas, dissenting).
34. *Lawrence*, 590 (Justice Scalia, dissenting).
35. *Lawrence*, 575.

36. *Lawrence*, 575.
37. *Poe*, 542–543 (1961) (Justice Harlan, dissenting, emphasis added, internal quotation marks omitted).
38. Justice Blackmun's passionate and eloquent dissent in *Bowers* is far more often quoted than is Justice Stevens's. But Kennedy may have chosen to quote Stevens because he was a sitting member of the *Lawrence* court.
39. *Lawrence*, 578.
40. It could be argued that in the contraception and abortion cases after *Griswold*, the distinctions between privacy and due process became more blurred than they were in 1965. The point that *Lawrence* makes about the constitutional theories of equality of treatment and due process, that they "are linked in important respects, and a decision on [either] advances both interests" (575), is equally true of privacy and due process.
41. *Lawrence*, 567 (emphasis added).
42. *Lawrence*, 564–565 (emphasis added).
43. *Lawrence*, 568.
44. *Stanley v. Georgia*, 394 U.S. 557, 559 (1969) (private possession of obscene matter cannot be criminalized even if the matter itself is unprotected).
45. *Lawrence*, 562.
46. *Lawrence*, 562.
47. *Lawrence*, 564.
48. *Loving v. Virginia*, 388 U.S. 1 (1967).
49. *Skinner v. Oklahoma*, 316 U.S. 535 (1942).
50. *Griswold v. Connecticut*, 381 U.S. 479 (1965).
51. *Prince v. Massachusetts*, 321 U.S. 158 (1944).
52. *Pierce v. Society of Sisters*, 268 U.S. 510 (1925).
53. *Meyer v. Nebraska*, 262 U.S. 390 (1923).
54. *Lawrence*, 562.
55. Katherine M. Franke, "The Domesticated Liberty of *Lawrence v. Texas*," *Columbia Law Review* 104 (June 2004), 1408–09.
56. Nan D. Hunter, "Living with Lawrence," *Minnesota Law Review* 88 (May 2004), 1138, citing Kendall Thomas, "Our *Brown*? Reading *Lawrence v. Texas*" (January 4, 2004) (unpublished manuscript).
57. Franke, "The Domesticated Liberty of *Lawrence v. Texas*," 1408.
58. Carlos A. Ball, "The Positive in the Fundamental Right to Marry: Same-Sex Marriage in the Aftermath of *Lawrence v. Texas*," *Minnesota Law Review* 88 (May 2004), 1212.
59. *Lawrence*, 574, quoting *Planned Parenthood of Southeastern Pa. v. Casey*, 505 U.S. 833, 851 (1992).
60. *Lawrence*, 588 (Justice Scalia, dissenting).
61. The *Lawrence* Court's rejection of equal protection analysis was a strong affirmation of an individual's right to freedom of sexual expression, for it struck down *all* remaining sodomy laws, not just those targeting homosexuals. *Lawrence* thus places *all* non-procreative sexual intimacy beyond the reach of the state's penal code. This aspect of the decision affirms a right to sexuality and sexual expression.
62. *Bowers*, 205 (Justice Blackmun, dissenting).
63. *Bowers*, 211 (Justice Blackmun, dissenting).
64. Jamie Weinstein and Tobyn DeMarco, "Challenging Dissent: The Ontology and Logic of *Lawrence v. Texas*, *Cardozo Women's Law Journal* 10 (Winter 2004): 423–65, 423.
65. Laurence Tribe, "The 'Fundamental Right' that Dare Not Speak Its Name," *Harvard Law Review* 117 (April 2004), 1911. Also see Justice Blackmun in *Bowers*: "It is precisely because the issue raised by this case touches the heart of what makes individuals what they are that we should be especially sensitive to the rights of those whose choices upset the majority."
66. *Lawrence*, 591 (Justice Scalia, dissenting).
67. *Lawrence*, 601 (Justice Scalia, dissenting, internal quotes and emphasis omitted).
68. *Lawrence*, 602 (Justice Scalia, dissenting).
69. *Lawrence*, 604 (Justice Scalia, dissenting).
70. *Goodridge v. Department of Public Health*, 440 Mass. 309, 343 (2003). The Massachusetts decision was based upon its own state Constitution and did not rely upon U.S. Supreme Court jurisprudence, though both the majority and the dissenters cited *Lawrence* liberally.

71. Franke, "The Domesticated Liberty of *Lawrence v. Texas*," 1417. Franke's contention that the Court relied on "a narrow version of liberty that is both geographized and domesticated—not a robust conception of sexual freedom or liberty" (1400) similarly seems to ignore important dimensions of the decision.
72. Tribe, "The 'Fundamental Right' that Dare Not Speak Its Name," 1911.

CHAPTER 12

Why *Lawrence v. Texas* Was Not Expected

A Critique of Pragmatic Legalist and Behavioral Explanations of Supreme Court Decision Making[1]

RONALD KAHN

Introduction

Other contributors to this volume have emphasized that *Lawrence* is truly a landmark decision. H. N. Hirsch states in the introduction that *Lawrence* was truly revolutionary because it was broadly based, made clear that fundamental rights were involved, and overturned *Bowers v. Hardwick* (1986), a relatively recent decision. John D'Emilio argues that it was a landmark decision because it puts closure on a long history not only of criminalization, but also of the stigma and related liabilities that grow out of criminalization.

In this chapter, I argue that the significance of *Lawrence* lies in the fact that in reasoning about the case, while the Court's "originalist" justices rejected a social construction process, the Court's non-originalist justices wholeheartedly embraced such an approach to constitutional reasoning.[2] As such, the Court's decision in *Lawrence* did not simply overturn *Bowers*, but rather eviscerated it. In doing so, it sidestepped a number of less transformative options open to it, such as deciding the case on equal protection grounds, or distinguishing, on minimalist grounds, the laws at issue in *Bowers* and *Lawrence*. *Lawrence* also is a landmark decision because it set in motion the continuation of a social construction process involving the meaning of liberty that began decades ago and provided the jurisprudential bases for expanding homosexual rights in the near future and decades to come.

This transformative decision, I emphasize, cannot be explained by scholars of a legal realist bent, whether they be pragmatic legalists, judicial minimalists, or behavioral political scientists. The primary reason why these scholars and legalists could not anticipate the *Lawrence* decision is their failure to recognize the importance of the "social construction process" in Supreme Court decision making. This process is engaged in by all non-originalist Supreme Court justices, whether they are conservatives, moderates, or liberals.[3] Among the most prominent recent theories of judicial decision making that *Lawrence* refutes is the judicial minimalism of Cass Sunstein, the focus of my analysis in this chapter.[4]

The Social Construction Process and *Lawrence v. Texas*

Lawrence v. Texas (2003) provides a textbook analysis of non-originalist justices engaging in the social construction process.[5] At the core of Supreme Court decision making is the construction, or the justices' picture of the social, political, and economic world outside the Court as it applies polity and rights principles. A primary role of the Supreme Court is to define the nature of rights and the social context in which they are embedded.[6]

When it confronts the practice of homosexual intimacy, the Supreme Court must not only define where privacy comes from as part of liberty, under the Constitution, and in case law, but it must also set inner and outer limits or boundaries for that right. It does so through a historically informed consideration of prior social construction processes, by considering which polity and rights principles are at issue in a case and how they have been applied in the past. Although it has been heretofore overlooked, these prior social constructions become important features of legal precedents. By the process of analogy, the Court considers a new social construction in light of prior constructions in a particular doctrinal area.[7] As such, the social construction of a classification is central to the development of law.[8]

Social constructions are at the core of what the Court means when it says a right exists. Social constructions form the central elements of the "cocoon" or rights entitlements that surround each person under the Constitution. They include prominent constructions such as those involving privacy and personhood. It is the social construction process which inculcates individual rights with their life and solidity.

Social constructions are informed by adduced social "facts" but are not the social facts themselves.[9] In *Plessy*, for example, blacks, and not the state, were construed to be responsible for their feelings of inferiority in response to government-enforced segregation of races. By the time of *Brown*, however, this social construction was undercut by social facts that led to the belief that such feelings of inferiority were plainly the product of state action and not individual interpretation. By centering on the relative strength of these social constructions in precedents and lines of cases, one can better understand the place of *stare decisis* in particular doctrinal areas.[10]

If we take social constructions into account in our analysis of Supreme Court opinions, we come to appreciate the degree to which the constitutional text is both inward- and outward-looking.[11] As it is lived across time in political life, the principles and meanings that the words of the text, as well as the social constructions that the Court has created to help define those words, inform the Court's understanding of the meaning of constitutional principles. As such, the text and the world outside the text mutually construct each other in what I have called the social construction process. An appreciation for the place of social constructions in the law moves us away from explaining court action in terms either of only narrow legalisms or external events and (social, political, or economic) structures. It helps us move beyond the distorting dualities that posit a sharp distinction between one and the other.

Supreme Court decision making is rule-governed behavior because it occurs in terms of individuals understanding both the norms they are following, including fidelity to the constitutional text, and their activity of following norms. Supreme Court justices live in the world constituted by the Constitution.[12] This is a world that can be seen as an institution comprised not merely of regulative rules, but, more fundamentally, of constitutive rules, which we must know to understand that institution.[13] These inter-subjective meanings on the Court, or in any institution, are in the minds and practices themselves, which cannot be conceived as a set of individual actions. They are modes of social relations or mutual action.[14] This means that all justices agree to follow precedent, to consider polity and rights principles, and to engage in analogical reasoning, and to do so as they participate in the social construction process.

Social constructions foster the transformative nature of law as new social facts allow justices to build on past social constructions. Social constructions force the Court to ask what is different and the same in society from the past, when it must decide what constitutes a just decision. By engaging in this process, the Court demonstrates a conscious regard for the necessity of reconciling conflicting values in a non-static, non-consensual, liberal political culture.[15]

Justice Kennedy's Majority Opinion

Justice Kennedy's majority opinion in *Lawrence* evinces a robust engagement in the social construction process. We see it when Justice Kennedy castigates the *Bowers* Court for failing to engage in *stare decisis*, for misapprehending what history has to tell us about proscriptions against homosexual conduct, and for misapprehending the liberty claims in the case.[16] We also see it when he links the above faults in *Bowers* to post-*Bowers* decisions, such as *Planned Parenthood of Southeastern Pa. v. Casey* (1992) and *Romer v. Evans* (1996), which he views as casting *Bowers's* holding into even more doubt.[17] The *Casey* decision was crucial in breathing meaning into the abstract concepts of liberty and privacy; it shifted the construction of abortion rights from a passive notion of privacy to a more forceful concept of personhood, placing women in closer proximity to the social and economic world in which they live. Kennedy then linked this analysis to questions of homosexual rights.[18]

The conditions for the social construction process are set when the majority announces its non-originalist starting point—that decisions about rights do not start and stop at the time of the founding of the Constitution, or the Fourteenth Amendment, or even at the time *Bowers* was decided. Neither history, tradition, nor the views of political majorities about morality provide sufficient reason to deny rights to individuals. If that were so, after all, anti-miscegenation laws would still be constitutional. The definition of rights requires a process of looking at past principles, history, and social constructions of those rights as compared to principles and the social world outside the Court today, and in light of the future. When this is done, the Court concludes that *Bowers* was wrongly decided in 1986, and would be even more wrong if it were allowed to continue as the law of the land. The final paragraph of the *Lawrence* decision includes a ringing affirmation of the importance of a continuous and continuing social construction process when the Court interprets the Constitution. Kennedy writes,

> Had those who drew and ratified the Due Process Clauses of the Fifth Amendment or the Fourteenth Amendment known the components of liberty in its manifold possibilities, they might have been more specific. They did not presume to have this insight. They knew times can blind us to certain truths and later generations can see that laws once thought necessary and proper in fact serve only to

oppress. As the Constitution endures, persons in every generation can invoke its principles in their own search for greater freedom.[19]

Although the *Lawrence* majority chooses to invalidate *Bowers* on due process rather than equal protection grounds, its analysis provides evidence that the social construction process and the rights that are at issue with regard to homosexual rights are actually not all that different.

Justice O'Connor's Concurrence and Justice Scalia's Response

Both the majority opinion and O'Connor's concurring opinion suggest that at the core of each is a concept that the state may not impute the inferiority of homosexuals. Justice O'Connor's equal protection analysis is a close kin to the imputations of inferiority arguments found in *Brown* and *Loving,* and also found in the *Lawrence* majority opinion. Also, like the majority, she was highly sensitive to the fact that the law's effect meant that being homosexual meant being viewed as a criminal.[20] This is not a minimalist decision; it is a maximalist argument in agreement with many of the substantive conclusions about privacy rights for gays that are at the core of the majority's opinion.[21] Scalia recognizes this similarity in pointing out that the logic of her argument suggests that bans on same-sex marriages would be unconstitutional—despite what he characterizes as her disingenuous suggestion that moral disapproval alone is a sufficient constitutional grounding for not allowing the practice.[22]

The social construction process O'Connor engages in places her in sharp disagreement with Justice Scalia's originalist dissent, which rejects the social construction process as a legitimate part of constitutional decision making.[23] The social construction process does not play a major role in the development of doctrine for originalists because they picture polity and rights principles, and their construction, as fixed at the time of the establishment of the Constitution and its amendments.

Scalia understands that the most effective way of blunting the future effects of the landmark *Lawrence* decision with regard to an expansion of privacy rights and gay rights is to attack the non-originalist social construction process that produced the line of cases from *Griswold,* through *Casey,* to *Lawrence.* Scalia views this process as result-oriented, unprincipled, and not following a disciplined rule of *stare decisis.*[24]

Scalia is opposed to this because he refuses to allow the liberty interest to be defined substantively over time, or to evolve under a non-originalist social construction process.[25] Scalia simply cannot accept the substantive rights talk as law, and he cannot accept the development of social constructions as part of the process through which the Supreme Court decides new cases. For Scalia, this would involve backward- and forward-looking rights-talk, rather than what he favors: defining rights based on what laws the state legislatures have passed, court convictions of homosexuals, federal and state court reliance on *Bowers*, and the status of such rights at the time of the framing of the Fourteenth Amendment and the Constitution itself. He scoffs at the assertion that there is "an *emerging awareness* that liberty gives substantial protection to adult persons in deciding how to conduct their private lives *in matters pertaining to sex.*"[26] For Scalia, an "emerging awareness" does not establish a fundamental right; moreover, state laws and arrests for homosexual sodomy offer clear evidence that protection of such acts are not "deeply rooted in the nation's history and traditions."[27] Scalia objects to the forward-looking and aspirational qualities of a social construction process which defines what constitutes an emerging awareness.[28] For Scalia, conditions for the overturning of *Bowers* (and *Roe*), that is, his reliance test, rests upon quite different notions of the role of the Supreme Court, compared to legislatures, in our constitutional regime. The fact that homosexual sodomy is opposed morally by a number of states seventeen years after *Bowers* is the key for him.[29]

For the non-originalists, evidence as to workability and settled expectations is not about majority votes in legislatures or arrests. Rather, such evidence is to be used as part of a process of social construction that looks at principles, such as privacy and personhood, and the redefinition of those principles in light of the social, economic, and political system in which citizens live today and in the future. For the non-originalists, the law at issue in *Lawrence* is not viewed as unworkable because legislatures support or oppose it. It is unworkable because when jurists engage in the social construction process, the rights at issue in considering the validity of anti-homosexual sodomy laws and the acts themselves are not different from those that the Court has affirmed for heterosexuals, whether married or not, as part of their rights of intimacy, privacy, and personhood.

Interestingly, however, Scalia is willing to accept the social construction process in *Loving v. Virginia*, which he distinguishes from that in *Bowers*.[30] He believes that the law at issue in *Loving* was in effect to support the superordination of whites over African Americans. However, Scalia argues that this is not the case with regard to laws against homosexual sodomy.[31] Scalia refuses to accept O'Connor's point that because sodomy as conduct is closely correlated with being a homosexual, such laws are targeted at more than conduct; they are targeted against gay persons as a class. Scalia's willingness to support the Court's social construction process in some cases, but not others, supports the view of scholars of hermeneutics that no judge or justice, even originalists, can refuse to engage in the interpretive turn.[32]

Legal Pragmatists' and Behavioral Political Scientist's Failure to Expect *Lawrence v. Texas*

Few legal pragmatists and judicial minimalists predicted that *Bowers* would be overturned, and even fewer predicted that *Lawrence* would place the Court on the threshold of declaring new constitutional rights for homosexuals. Nor are they accepting of the transformative nature of the rights defined in *Lawrence*. Sunstein writes, "For the majority [in *Lawrence*], a central problem was to develop a rationale that would strike down the Texas statute without producing the unintended revolution in the law."[33] However, when the overturning of *Bowers* is viewed in light of previous landmark cases which were overturned, such as *Plessy* and *Lochner,* as well as *Casey* where the Court chose not to overturn *Roe v. Wade,* the *Lawrence* decision should not have been unexpected.

Exploring the reasons for this failure to predict the outcome in *Lawrence* has implications for the way scholars do constitutional theory and how the wider society is asked to envision Supreme Court decision making and the place of the Supreme Court in American political development. If any theory redefining the rights of subordinated groups is to have legitimacy in the interpretive community and the wider society, it must be meaningful to people as a description of the world they see about them and how the world might look in the future. Any transformative theory of constitutional change must involve a concern for changes in meanings as to what constitutes structural inequalities and how they should be linked to denials of rights. There is a linkage between the definition of social constructs and whether legal classifications which refer to specific subordinated groups are to be subjected to close Court scrutiny. Again, social constructions are not simply facts from social scientists, nor do social constructions necessarily change with social reality, as we saw in *Lochner.* Social constructions have within them images of superordination and subordination that become constitutionally recognized as precedent: for example, the relationship between women and their spouses in *Casey* with regard to spousal notification. As these social constructions change, so do our visions of the denial of equal protection and due process, and what constitutes public and private action. Through case analysis that considers the construction of the social, economic, and political world outside the Court, we can identify when the Court is changing the translation of constitutional principles to take in the new realities of life, which result in new concepts of what is just.

Legalist Sunstein's Pragmatism

I use Sunstein's scholarship as a springboard for exploring some central questions about how the process for reconceptualizing the rights of subordinated groups might be undertaken. It builds on a central assumption that the Supreme Court is constitutive, not instrumental. To a lesser degree, Sunstein is arguing that constitutional law, and the definition of the rights of subordinated groups, is at its core a product of the polity principles as to Court and elected official and institutional power. What I am arguing is that the nature of individual rights is derived from the application of rights principles through the Court constructing the world outside the Court. They do not and cannot flow primarily or simply from polity principles, such as Sunstein's value of the need for more political deliberation. Nor can rights flow from Bruce Ackerman's faith in major and minor constitutional moments external to the Court, as intergenerationally synthesized by the Court. They have come in the past, and continue to come, from a constitutive Supreme Court decision-making process whose decisions are the product of both internalist rights and polity principles (and Court institutional norms) and the construction of the external social, political, and economic order outside the Court—a mutual construction process that is far more critical than would result from a process such as Sunstein and Ackerman envision under their civic republican blinders. We need to document these patterns of doctrinal change, using models of the decision-making process which respect the fact that the Supreme Court has to bring the outside world into its consideration of cases. Only then can we be more specific about the structure of a new theory of subordinated rights.

The Supreme Court Must Not Accept the Status Quo as Neutral

Sunstein's concept of judicial minimalism mischaracterizes how and on what bases the Supreme Court makes its decisions; therefore it is an inaccurate model for understanding that process and the place of the Supreme Court in American political development. The cause of Sunstein's error is in part traceable to the theoretical break that his *One Case at a Time: Judicial Minimalism on the Supreme Court* makes with his genuinely seminal theoretical contribution, *The Partial Constitution*, a book which emphasized the need for the Supreme Court not to accept the status quo as neutral. Moreover, in *One Case at a Time*, Sunstein does not clearly explain the role of rights principles in constitutional choices as he describes whether cases are or are not minimalist decisions, and whether they should be. He fails to specify the place of rights principles in his constitutional theory in relationship to the conditions under which the polity principle of judicial minimalism should be honored. Nor is it clear when polity principles, such as respect for political deliberation and minimalism, should trump rights principles or when rights principles should trump polity principles, in precedents, particular cases, and in a line of cases. Therefore, the moral justifications for protecting rights become secondary to the objective of reducing conflict and securing stability. When this occurs, Cass Sunstein joins many other scholars whose constitutional theories support judicial restraint as a good in itself, rather than basing his theory on the actual constitutive process of Supreme Court decision making.

The call for judicial minimalism is many things, the most important of which is a call to inhibit the articulation of social constructions. This call is made, ironically, as contemporary justices find that they should continue to engage in the construction process, as seen in the *Lawrence* case. Justices have little choice if the Supreme Court is to meet the institutional role that the founders had laid out for it in 1787, in the post-Civil War period, and in the nineteenth and twentieth centuries.

Ironically, although Sunstein's notion of judicial minimalism is pragmatic and instrumental, the Rehnquist-era Supreme Court today, as it has for many decades, continues to be constitutive in its decision making, not simply pragmatic and instrumental, nor dominated by the value premises inherent in Sunstein's concept of judicial minimalism. The Court's process respects the notion that the Constitution consists of both polity and rights principles that need protection through their redefinition as our nation's social, economic, and political structures change.

Social constructions played a central role in *The Partial Constitution*. At the core of *The Partial Constitution* was an argument for the importance of the Supreme Court not viewing the status quo as neutral. Sunstein argued that the Supreme Court is uniquely positioned, especially compared to electorally accountable institutions, to make decisions which are principled and do not simply allocate resources and values based on the raw power of factions and interest groups. While it is correct to say that Sunstein wanted the Supreme Court to foster democratic deliberation in electorally based institutions, in *The Partial Constitution* there is also a strong argument that the Court must make decisions to stop abuses by the government and private institutions that are creatures of government regulation.

In *The Partial Constitution* Sunstein emphasized the qualitatively different abilities of the Supreme Court, and federal courts in general, compared to electorally accountable institutions, to consider what the rights principles mean in the Constitution, and how they should be protected. It was not simply polity considerations inherent in Federalist 10 principles, the concepts of separation of powers and federalism, and the institutional structures that the founders placed in the Constitution, that were to ensure that individual rights were protected. The Bill of Rights and other rights principles, including background rights such as natural rights to person and property, were on an equal footing with institutional principles when the Court was to make constitutional choices. For Sunstein, in *The Partial*

Constitution, constitutional theory must maintain a critical balance among polity and rights principles if it is to provide the moral energy to make a substantive critique of politics, and not let faction, private-regarding values and politics overwhelm the public-regarding values and individual rights in the Constitution.

The theory of Supreme Court decision making in *The Partial Constitution* is correctly based on the Court having to construct the social, economic, and political world when deciding individual rights; that is, the Court is to be explicit about the assumptions and views of the world upon which they based their decisions. To understand why this is so, we need to look more deeply at Sunstein's call for the Supreme Court to reject the status quo as neutral. In doing so Sunstein is asking us to be careful not to transform the existent into the normative, i.e., that the existent, what is, should not be the measure against which the constitutionality of government action is to be evaluated.[34] Sunstein's constitutional theory in *The Partial Constitution* is based on a critique of interest group liberalism and a recognition of what Edward Purcell notes are the two most important characteristics of American intellectual thought in the twentieth century: the tendency to view America as the ultimate form of human society and the related inclination to view existing social and political institutions as expressions of those positive moral and political norms. Purcell writes:

> On the ethical level, reality becomes the standard to evaluate ideals, rather than the ideals the standard by which to judge reality. It was almost as if many social scientists had purposely accepted an operationalist theory of meaning: democracy was defined as the way in which the American government worked in practice.[35]

Throughout *The Partial Constitution* modern democratic and constitutional theory is critiqued as being suffused with methodological and theoretical assumptions that transform the status quo (whether that refers to the American political system or to the makeup of American society) into the criterion or the ideal against which decisions are evaluated. Sunstein argues that naturalizing the status quo removes the possibility of morally substantive criticism of the political system and societal arrangements. Moreover, the search to see whether the status quo is neutral requires "criticizing the widely held view that a democracy should always respect the preferences of its citizenry, and base its decisions on existing desires and beliefs," especially because preferences themselves may be the result of social and economic structures and legal rules that violate substantive norms in the Constitution and institutional principles.[36] Thus, the acceptance of the status quo as neutral may naturalize distributions that are, in fact, products of raw political power.

I am not making an argument here for or against court power relative to electorally accountable institutions; I am making the argument that the social construction of the wider political, economic, and social world in which we live is required if we are to determine whether the status quo is neutral. Once we have seen that it is not neutral, that is, that it is created by government actions, we need to ask whether those actions violate the polity and rights principles in the Constitution. Through such a process, Sunstein argues in *The Partial Constitution* that the Supreme Court has an affirmative responsibility to see whether such a violation has occurred. Moreover, this process is not simply deferential to deliberation by electorally accountable institutions; it requires severe limitations on those institutions when they do not respect rights and polity principles. There is a substantive rights element and role for the Supreme Court to protect rights in *The Partial Constitution*. I say this even though it is possible to argue that there is too great an emphasis on faith in politics and civic deliberation, and too great a call for the Supreme Court to foster that deliberation, rather than to analyze critically whether the status quo is neutral and apply substantive rights in such a way that calls upon courts to define new rights.[37] Since the government has made legal rules, policies, and practices that have structured private and public action, when making constitutional choices the Court must consider the degree to which the government has structured private action, and must intervene to ensure such private actions do not violate the Constitution.

Such considerations are at the core of why *Plessy v. Ferguson* (1896) and *Lochner v. New York* (1905) were wrongly decided and overturned in later cases.[38] As seen in his critiques of *Plessy* and *Lochner* in *The Partial Constitution*, Sunstein is arguing that the Supreme Court must construct a vision of the social, political, and economic world in which the Court acts with particular regard to how government structures that reality. The Supreme Court must not accept the social, political, and economic order as a given. If the status quo had not been viewed as neutral by the state, then segregation of the races would not have been allowed in *Plessy*, and state maximum hours laws would have been permitted in *Lochner*. It was the misguided construction of social relations in *Plessy* and economic relations in *Lochner*, not simply a misstatement of the nature of rights which are protected in the Equal Protection and Due Process Clauses of the Fourteenth Amendment, which constitute the central failure by the Supreme Court in these two landmark cases which were to be overturned in subsequent decisions.

In *The Partial Constitution*, Sunstein emphasized that the Supreme Court must assess the existing distributions of wealth, status, and entitlements to see whether there is a denial of the basic rights and interests of citizenship.

Accepting the status quo as neutral shuts off the process of improvement for deliberative democracy and takes from the Supreme Court its rightful place in the American political system—which is to interpret the open-ended language of the Constitution in a way that ensures full participation in a process of deliberative democracy. This requires that all choices be based on stated public-regarding values. Sunstein correctly argues in *The Partial Constitution* that the Supreme Court must construct the political, economic, and social world in making constitutional choices because such constructions are necessary if the Court is to reject the status quo as neutral.

This does not mean that *The Partial Constitution* is not without its faults. There is no affirmative, clear theory or analysis of the place of social constructions in the Supreme Court's development of constitutional law, when it is to determine whether the status quo is neutral. Nor is there a clear theory or analysis of the place of social constructions in the determination of such rights as liberty and person. Because of such absences, one is forced to tease out the substantive rights elements in Sunstein's theory of judicial review as he argues for a deliberative democracy in which there are no second-class citizens.[39] All rights seem to be linked to the role of citizenship in the post-New Deal administrative state, with new entitlements such as education viewed as rights because of their link to citizenship. There is less written about the role of individuals as private citizens. There is little or no discussion of the rights of persons, not linked to the rights of citizen and public-regarding deliberation. Sunstein is brilliant at showing that a political system viewed as one of interest group liberalism is a static and simplistic vision. However, political institution or polity principles are at the core of his constitutional theory. Fundamental individual rights take a secondary place, and they are not clearly linked to his vision of a more open deliberative nation, whose government is continually forced by the Supreme Court to discuss public policy in public-regarding rather than simply private-regarding terms. The heightened Court scrutiny that results from not accepting the status quo as neutral involves a consideration of substantive values which call for rooting out the "naked" preferences that result from raw political power, rather than the consideration of public-regarding values, some of which might be fundamental rights.

More specifically, Sunstein argues that at the core of the New Deal revolution was the notion that the economy was a structure of government action and thus not natural. In contrast to the Lochner era, economic distribution was not taken as a given, nor were economic markets viewed as natural and simply private. If this is the case, then government can pass laws to change the power of economic institutions and protect workers through government regulations. When the Court begins to reject existent social, economic, and political orderings as natural, that is, when it does not view them as pre-political, there is a better chance that the substantive values in the Fourteenth Amendment and the Bill of Rights can be protected. This is particularly so, as our nation's social, economic, and political systems and our knowledge of causation become more complex. For example, if the relationship between blacks and whites is seen as the result of past government acts, legal rules, and failures to act, one can argue for an effects standard, rather than an intent standard, in cases involving race discrimination by government. Through more complex social constructions, the greater failure rate among blacks compared to whites in police entrance examinations in *Washington v. Davis* (1976) would not be viewed as natural. Moreover, the notion that the social, economic, and political systems should be viewed as a product of state action raises serious questions as to whether differences between *de facto* and *de jure* causes of outcomes should play as great a role in race discrimination law, as is called for in *Washington v. Davis* (1976) and in 1990s congressional districting cases.

If we do not accept the status quo as neutral, we are required to ask what effect government action has on the lives of its citizens. In *The Partial Constitution*, Sunstein argues that the Equal Protection Clause requires us to revise the existing distribution of power, status, and governmental benefits between whites and blacks, if the present distribution is the result of past actions, conscious and unconscious, that treated blacks as second-class citizens. To reject the status quo as neutral means that the Equal Protection Clause is more likely to be interpreted in aspirational terms, so that all citizens will have the resources to engage in the more demanding requirements of a deliberative democracy, which requires debate over public-regarding reasons prior to government action. The Equal Protection Clause is aspirational in another sense. The nation expands its view as to what the government must provide to ensure equal citizenship. Moreover, it must be active in ensuring that castes do not exist for reasons extraneous to the actions of each individual, such as due to race, gender, sexual orientation, religion, or ethnicity. The Equal Protection Clause does more than simply require formal equality of access to government; it opposes the social dependency of subordinated groups on the wider public for reasons that are constitutionally suspect, as we see in the ringing language of the *Lawrence* decision.

In *The Partial Constitution*, Sunstein notes that because of the endowment effect (that most people believe that past economic, political, and social choices are natural and thus good) we should pay less attention to present biases, choices, and values of the people. Since all preferences are contextual, the allocation of those preferences at any given time should not be the baseline of Court action. Both acts and failures to act may be subject to Court scrutiny. Preferences result from shifting legal rules, social priorities and practices, consumption patterns, and are backward-looking. Deliberative democracy requires a questioning of what exists, and of what the state does, in light of constitutional principles such as liberty and autonomy. Thus, *Plessy*'s adherence to custom and its view that legislatures cannot change the views of citizens is rejected, in part because of the endowment effect, and in part because they reflect private-regarding values in the Constitution.

It follows from Sunstein's theory in *The Partial Constitution* that liberty and autonomy values mean that we do not accept private preferences as simply private, random, and made on the basis of public-regarding choices by political institutions and lower courts, even if based on a dialogue with each other. At the core of our constitutional values is the principle that public officials must refuse to simply accept preferences when making public policy, especially if they are private-regarding. Preferences do not necessarily respect public-regarding interests, and they may deny the rights of all citizens. Sunstein's constitutional theory demonstrates his faith in democratic deliberation and the Supreme Court as a primary agent to foster that deliberation.

However, Sunstein's call for the Supreme Court to reject the status quo as neutral does not fully appreciate the qualities and dimensions of the social construction process. Sunstein's call to reject the status quo as neutral is a call for affirmative constructions that are usually linked directly to polity principles, but also may refer to weak conceptions of rights in the Constitution. However, Sunstein favors the role of the Court as one of fostering public-regarding deliberation in political institutions, with the underlying premise or hope that to do so will produce what the Founders wanted by way of the political process and rights values in the Constitution.

Instead of jumping ahead to this premise, we need to study systematically the role of constructions in Supreme Court decision making. We need to ask what makes constructions aspirational, forward-looking, and what makes them backward-looking with regard to changes in the social, economic, and political world in which they are made. We need to study the patterns of construction by the Supreme Court to see which patterns lead to new concepts of individual and/or group rights and which patterns lead to the overturning of landmark cases. Sunstein seems to place his emphasis on the Supreme Court's goal of ensuring deliberative democracy rather than on the goal of defining fundamental rights and their place in the process of construction and the rejection of the status quo as neutral.

Sunstein Rejects the Social Construction Process

The Cass Sunstein of *One Case at a Time* is a very different scholar; in this later book, we see the following tenets of minimalism emphasized: courts should leave most fundamental questions undecided; they should settle the case before them and leave many things undecided; courts should be alert to the existence of reasonable disagreement in a heterogeneous society, and thus realize that there is much they do not know, especially the unintended consequences of their actions; and cases should be decided on narrow grounds and avoid clear rules and final resolutions. Minimalism sees itself as a part of the system of democratic deliberation and thus sees its major objective as fostering the democratic ideals of participation, responsiveness, and democratic reflection from Congress and the states. Courts should accommodate new judgments about facts and values by deferring to elected bodies and democratic deliberation and, to the extent possible, should provide rulings that can attract support from people with diverse theoretical commitments. Minimalism is not simply a call for judicial self-restraint in that Sunstein argues that minimalist judges are willing to invalidate some laws while not committing to majority rule in all contexts. However, judges should be cautious of imposing their own views on the rest of society and thus they should not favor broad rules which would draw a wide range of democratically enacted legislation into question.

Sunstein argues for incompletely theorized agreements by courts because they allow a diverse people to live together in productive ways with mutual respect. Behind this assumption is the belief that people agree on more abstract ideas, like freedom and equality. Sunstein's chapter 4, "Minimalism's Substance," offers (his) list of the nine propositions that form the "core" of our nation's commitments under liberalism today.

Sunstein suggests when minimalism is and is not warranted. He emphasizes that it is clearly warranted when the Court agrees on an outcome in a case but cannot agree on the right on which the outcome is based. The Court should provide reasons, yet not be conclusionary with regard to such reasons, thus not closing off the growth of the law. Sunstein even supports what he calls sub-minimalism, as in *Romer v. Evans* (1996), when the Court outlawed Colorado's requirement that homosexuals (and their supporters) must amend the state constitution when they seek protective legislation. Sub-minimalism allows democratic politics to work out homosexual rights while avoiding the intense conflicts produced by non-minimalist or maximalist decisions, such as *Roe v. Wade* (1973).[40]

To get a better picture of minimalist Court decision making, Sunstein provides four possible Court choices as to the results of the use of minimalist and maximalist methods of crafting Court decisions. A court can use maximalist or minimalist methods of crafting decisions either to validate or invalidate laws and government actions. Maximalist validations of government actions, including post-New Deal Commerce Clause cases, such as *Ferguson v. Skrupa* (1963), offer the widest scope for democratic judgments.

However, such validation may be too wide because, rather than allowing government deliberation of public-regarding values, the validation by the Court of such actions may permit too many "naked preferences" by government, that is, decisions made based on raw political power in an interest group pluralist system, rather than through democratic deliberation based on public-regarding values.

Another possible method of decision making is maximalist invalidation. Sunstein views *Miranda v. Arizona* (1966), *Roe v. Wade* (1973), *Loving v. Virginia* (1967), and Justice Scalia on affirmative action as prime examples of maximalist invalidation of laws and government actions. Here the Court invalidates government actions drawing on the broadest principles covering the broadest range of cases. Sunstein cautions the Court to avoid maximalist invalidation unless it is confident in its reasons for invalidation because such decisions close off democratic deliberation. Justices Black and Scalia are viewed as rule-bound maximalists whose methods of interpretation foreclose democratic deliberation. Maximalist invalidation promotes deliberation, but it is futile as a forum for change unless an amendment to the Constitution is made, or there is a significant change in the make-up of the Court.

Sunstein favors minimalism. He offers the following cases as classic examples of minimalist invalidation of laws and government actions: *Romer v. Evans* (1996), *United States v. Lopez* (1995), *United States v. Virginia* (1996), *Kent v. Dulles* (1958), *City of Cleburne v. Cleburne Living Center* (1985), and *Hampton v. Mow Sun Wong* (1976). Each of these cases invalidated a law or government action but did so on narrow grounds without using bright-line principles and without affecting a wide range of cases and future situations. Minimalist invalidation spurs the democratic process and allows case-by-case determinations in situations where Court agreement on larger principles is lacking. It also promotes political accountability by political institutions, while signaling to political leaders and institutions which level of government should make choices of constitutional significance.

Sunstein argues that there is a long tradition of minimalism on the Court. It was the primary form of decision making on the Rehnquist Court, especially in the 1990s. It was used less frequently during the eras of the Supreme Court headed by Chief Justices Earl Warren and Warren Burger. Justices O'Connor, Breyer, Ginsberg, Stevens, and Souter are viewed as minimalists by Sunstein because they are cautious about broad rulings and usually like to decide cases on the narrowest possible grounds. Justices Scalia and Thomas, as originalists, are not minimalist, with Justices Kennedy and Rehnquist less clearly placed.

At the core of Sunstein's argument for minimalism is his pragmatic view of Supreme Court decision making. Sunstein argues that making constitutional choices on broad-based constitutional theories constrain further inquiry and close off deliberative democracy. Sunstein opposes broad-based theories advocated by originalists, such as Robert Bork, as well as rights-oriented theorists, such as Ronald Dworkin or Richard Epstein.[41] Sunstein praises Justices Ginsberg, Souter, O'Connor, Breyer, and Kennedy, whom Sunstein calls "the analytic heart of the current Court," because they have not adopted "a unitary theory of constitutional interpretation."[42] Sunstein argues that these justices avoid broad rules and abstract theories and attempt to focus on the disputes before them. All are minimalists for reasons connected to "their conception of the role of the Supreme Court in American government."[43]

As in *The Partial Constitution*, in *One Case at a Time* Sunstein's main concern is improving deliberative democracy. He writes, "One of my principal goals is to identify the distinctive kinds of minimalism that serve to improve political deliberation; the underlying conception of democracy thus places a high premium on both deliberation (in the sense of reflection and reason-giving) and accountability (in the sense of control by the voters)."[44] Through minimalism, the Court can hint that equal protection values may be at issue in a policy area by invalidating a single instance of constitutional violation, as in *Romer v. Evans* (1996). This compels the states to deal with the issue of homosexual rights, having been given a signal that there are equal protection values at stake. In so doing, the Court will foster the exchange of reasons, values, and information, and, perhaps, increased knowledge of why citizens should not fear homosexuals or allowing them basic rights. Given the social, religious, class, and racial pluralism of the nation, the Supreme Court should foster innovation in the states rather than impose a constitutional regime on them, with the many unintended consequences which will result.

Sunstein feels that cautious justices can promote democratic deliberation with more minimalist strategies designed to bracket some of the deeper questions; this ensures accountability and reflection. Sunstein argues that there are democracy-promoting, democracy-foreclosing, and democracy-permitting outcomes. One promotes, the other limits, and third permits.[45] He emphasizes that the Court must use minimalist methods of inquiry, which require government to give public-regarding reasons for their action. These methods include opposing laws for vagueness; using the non-delegation doctrine; requiring clear statements by Congress on bureaucratic power; and desuetude, which is to forbid government reliance on old non-used laws which do not have public support.[46]

Sunstein argues that although *One Case at a Time* devotes more space to the procedural components of minimalism, substance still is important.[47] In a chapter titled "Minimalism's Substance," these individual rights are listed: protection against unauthorized imprisonment; protection of polit-ical dissent; the right to vote; religious liberty; protection against physical invasion of property; protection against police abuse of person or prop-erty; the rule of law, which includes clear, general public rules of criminal law laid down in advance, conformity between law on the books and law in the world, and hearing and appeal rights; no torture, murder, or physi-cal abuse by the government; protection against slavery or subordination on the basis of race or sex; and substantive protection of the human body against government invasion.[48] He writes, "American constitutional law now embeds a distinctive set of underlaying commitments" about individual rights.[49] Constitutional debates operate with these fixed points in the back-ground. These commitments are held by minimalists and maximalists, who would, of course, disagree at times as to the constitutional bases for these rights. For Sunstein, at any given time constitutional law will consist of a set of widely shared propositions about rights together with a list of more contentious ones. The list he offers is a minimal one which commands substantial current agreement, though not consensus, in the current legal culture.[50] All are evaluated, with regard to application, primarily on the ideal of fostering deliberative democracy. He writes,

> In keeping with the minimalist spirit, I have suggested that one of the purposes of a well-functioning system of constitutional law is to support the internal morality of democracy. That morality calls for political equality, participation, reason-giving (or deliberation), and accountability (in the sense of responsiveness to the multiple voices of the public).[51]

He notes that "outside the area of deliberative democracy ... I will argue that courts should play a cautious role—because they may make mistakes, and because when democracy is working well, there is far less reason to suppose that the political process should be disrupted."[52]

Minimalism is most attractive: (1) when judges are operating in the midst of constitutionally relevant factual or moral uncertainty and rapidly changing circumstances; (2) when any solution will be confounded by future cases; (3) when there is no insistent need for advance planning; (4) when preconditions for democratic self-government are not at stake and demo-cratic goals are not likely to be promoted by a rule-bound judgment; and (5) "when the area involves a highly contentious question not receiving sus-tained democratic attention," like *Dred Scott v. Sanford* (1857) and *Lochner*.[53] In such situations, even if courts base decisions on deep-held beliefs, they may make a mistake.

Maximalism, the reliance on deep principles, in contrast, is most attrac-tive: (1) when judges have confidence in the merits of that solution; (2) when the solution reduces costly uncertainty for future courts and litigants; (3) when advance planning is important; and (4) when a maximalist approach will promote democratic goals either by creating the precondi-tions for democracy or by imposing good incentives on public officials to which they will respond. Sunstein notes, "It would be foolish to suggest either that minimalism is generally a good strategy or that maximalism is generally a blunder. Everything depends on contextual considerations. The only point that is clear ... is that sometimes the minimalist approach is the best way to minimize the sum of error costs and decision costs."[54] Even though Sunstein makes this disclaimer, it is clear that in *One Case at a Time* he believes that minimalism is the best strategy for the Supreme Court.

A Critique of Judicial Minimalism

There are numerous grounds on which to critique Sunstein's vision of judi-cial minimalism. I will concentrate on the following: (1) Sunstein's views on the Supreme Court and political system as forums for deciding issues of constitutional importance; (2) the place of fundamental rights principles in Sunstein's approach to Supreme Court decision making; (3) the role of social constructions in the application of polity and rights principles in Supreme Court decision making; and (4) the lack of clear guiding princi-ples as to what constitutes minimalist and maximalist Supreme Court deci-sion making.

Sunstein has a very conservative view of the role of the Supreme Court's process of constitutional interpretation, arguing that the Supreme Court should be humble in its making of constitutional choices. The Court is to work case-by-case incrementally, rather than make maximalist decisions and thus encourage incompletely theorized decisions. The Supreme Court is viewed as having limited capacities and information when compared to legislatures and bureaucracies. The Court should slowly and incrementally develop judicial standards; clearly they should not be developed before the long-term fact specifications are clear. The Court is to work out constitu-tional problems with political institutions, not on its own. Analogical case-by-case incremental reasoning is favored over deciding cases on broad constitutional principles. This process will allow more pragmatic decision making by future courts that, because of prior minimalist decisions, will be able to read prior dicta as holdings and holdings as dicta, thus allowing more change in the future as new problems and fact situations arise. This process will allow the Supreme Court, which consists of justices of differ-ent viewpoints, to search for relevant similarities and low-level principles on which they can agree. It will also allow more people and groups outside the Court to agree with the decisions of the Court. The key components of Sunstein's minimalism are stability, incremental change, reducing conflict, and working with political institutions, primarily by getting them to deliberate about constitutional questions and make decisions—rather than having the Court make wide-ranging constitutional choices.

In supporting minimalism, Sunstein is supporting what Alexander Bickel has called the passive virtues of courts, and especially the Supreme Court. Narrow decisions and incompletely theorized agreements, i.e., agreements of low-level principles and oriented to incremental outcomes, allow the Court to be humble about its capacities, especially since in most complex constitutional questions they are not sure about substance and methods, and are not sure that they are right.[55] The Supreme Court should develop judicial "standards" that are not "rules," which for Sunstein constitute before-the-fact specification of legal outcomes.[56] These "standards" would allow the Court and political institutions to work out constitutional problems on a case-by-case basis, and thus support Sunstein's view that the key role for the Supreme Court is to foster democratic deliberation and to allow most constitutional choices to be made by political institutions.

One obvious problem here is that having placed the Supreme Court in a secondary role to the political system results in a strong—perhaps too strong—foot-on-the-scale for trusting politics. This approach places the protection of fundamental rights and principles in the Constitution in a secondary position to civic republican values in support of trusting politics—when the structure of government in the Constitution is based on not trusting politics. Sunstein is advocating what he calls "reasonable pluralism," which is not simply support for interest group pluralism, but also for social stability. In arguing for judicial minimalism, Sunstein writes, "reasonable pluralism mak[es] agreement possible when agreement is necessary, and mak[es] agreement unnecessary when agreement is impossible. This goal is associated both with promoting social stability and with achieving a form of mutual respect."[57] There is less advocacy here for the Supreme Court and lesser courts to push political institutions to promote public-regarding values and to provide clear reasons for their actions and less of a call for Court opposition to raw political power than in his earlier scholarship.

Moreover, the rights principles and their relationship to polity principles in Sunstein's vision of judicial minimalism is blurred even further by his assumption that minimalist (sub-minimalist) or maximalist Court responses to constitutional questions are clearly identifiable. In all likelihood, sub-minimal, minimal, and maximal are not separable categories of analysis. Part of the problem is that arguments for minimalism are built on Sunstein's case-by-case analysis, which is mostly informed by his views of the role of the Supreme Court, electorally accountable political institutions, and the overall process of deliberation in and out of public bodies, rather than by rights principles.

Notions of fundamental rights and justice, which seem to be involved in the triggering of arguments for minimalism and maximalism, are never discussed in detail when Sunstein entertains questions of whether the Court should engage in minimalism or maximalism. The place of core rights principles in deciding cases is not clearly stated in the analysis of particular cases and their place in a line of cases. Nor is it clear when rights principles should trump the polity principles which are emphasized in his concept of judicial minimalism. One can see this, ironically, most clearly in Sunstein's support of maximalism in *Brown v. Board* (1954). When discussing *Brown v. Board* (1954), Sunstein admits some of the dangers of minimalism at any cost. He concedes that *Brown v. Board* (1954) is the best argument against minimalism; the nation was sharply divided on moral and political grounds, and there was doubt that democratic deliberation would bring out new facts. When Supreme Court decision making is dedicated to judicial minimalism there simply are far fewer avenues for substantive rights questions, and whether they should trump polity principles.

Judicial minimalism's basic principles favor Court deference to political institutions and oppose a strong look at whether the status quo is neutral. That is, the Court is not to construct the social, economic, and political world to ensure that public-regarding values are being protected. The Court is to be a partner with political institutions in forcing out facts and issues in a constitutional debate, rather than imposing choices on legislatures and government officials. The call for the Court to no longer forcefully consider whether the status quo is neutral has a devastating affect on the critical bite of Sunstein's constitutional theory. Most importantly, it understates the place that the social construction process plays in Supreme Court decision making.

By not accepting the present order as natural and by asking how it affects the nature of citizenship and deliberative democracy, constitutional interpretation could be forward-looking. In rejecting the status quo as neutral, the Court must take into its decision-making process newly created definitions of property, liberty, and entitlements. The notion that social, economic, and political power is the result of state action and not simply the result of individual agency, as the rejection of the status quo as neutral implies, says that the Supreme Court must construct the nature of the social, political, and economic world outside the Court. Only in this way can open-ended constitutional concepts of equal protection, liberty, and equality have meaning as our nation changes with each decade. To favor the values of judicial minimalism and reject the importance of the court rejecting the status quo as neutral, as Sunstein does in *One Case at a Time,* trumpets the view that social and political stability is a more important value than fundamental rights. It undermines the transformative and aspirational aspects of Sunstein's prior constitutional theory.

A Misconception of Supreme Court Decision Making

There are many problems with judicial minimalism. For the purposes here, I emphasize the limitations of judicial minimalism in relation to the process of constitutive Supreme Court decision making and the place of social constructions in that decision making. The problem is that Sunstein asks the Supreme Court to foster conservative polity principles rather than to continue his (former non-robust) quest to discover whether the status quo is neutral. Moreover, he provides no clear guidelines for when the Court should be minimalist or maximalist in its orientation to a case.[58] Evaluation is on a case-by-case basis. *Roe v. Wade* (1973) is criticized as maximalist jurisprudence at its worst. Throughout the book, rights, principles, moral questions and issues of justice are mentioned, usually as background factors as he argues for judicial minimalism. At no time are we provided a theory or set of standards of evaluation as to when minimalism, with the conservative polity principles on which it is based, should be chosen by the Supreme Court over maximalism, with its more robust application of rights principles and social construction.

This is a severe drawback, especially since when the Supreme Court applies polity and rights principles in deciding cases, it must engage in the process of social construction; social constructions are significant components of precedents and lines of Court doctrine, and must be considered by the Court as it engages in deciding each new case, through the application of polity and rights principles. Therefore, to fully explain constitutive Supreme Court decision making, or even to fulfill the more limited task of advocating a political and legal strategy (such as support of judicial minimalism), a scholar must explain the relationships among the advocated polity and rights principles and the process of social construction. Sunstein fails to do so.

Moreover, viewing fundamental rights principles as secondary to polity norms, as Sunstein does in his concept of judicial minimalism, will result in less protection of individual rights. Also, Sunstein's trust of political institutions, which is at the core of his judicial minimalism, is unwarranted. For example, without maximalist Court decisions, why would states and the national government just fail to act, that is, stonewall, and thus limit even minimalist privacy rights, as they did on racial segregation? There is little evidence that political institutions would take cues for increased rights protection should the Court make minimalist decisions. Would they not cave in to the naked preferences of whatever group has power in a state or the national government to stop the protection of rights?

I also question whether it is best for the Supreme Court to have a minimalist approach in an argument for a right. While it is correct that minimalism may foster a decision for a new right because justices can agree on the right for different reasons, I am not sure that it is best for the development of constitutional law, particularly with regard to the contribution of constitutional theorists to that development and to the clarification of what rights and government powers the nation can expect. Minimalism may stifle a full discussion of legal arguments in later cases. Also, there is no discussion as to whether the legitimacy of the Supreme Court will be helped or hurt by minimalism, or whether it has been helped or hurt by it over the years.[59] Institutional values, like deliberation and political and social stability, in the short run seem more important to Sunstein than are clear definitions of individual rights. The needs of subordinated groups are sacrificed to the value of stability. Finally, if constructions that mirror the complexity of structural inequalities in our nation are only possible in the world of judicial maximalism, with its more filigreed, in-depth arguments and wider breadth of application, and more open-ended defining of rights principles, then there is reason to believe that the rights of subordinated groups can best be protected by maximalism.

Desuetude as an Explanation for *Lawrence, Griswold,* and Rights of Privacy

In *The Supreme Court Review* Sunstein analyzes *Lawrence v. Texas* (2003).[60] He makes an argument for desuetude as an explanation for not only *Lawrence,* but for *Griswold* and for the development of substantive due process cases over the decades. This article provides additional evidence for the problems with judicial minimalism as a method for interpreting Supreme Court decision making and as a basis for constitutional law. Sunstein refuses to view such cases as based on maximalist fundamental rights grounds, whether under the Due Process Clauses, such as liberty or autonomy, or even on equal protection grounds. Rather, *Lawrence* can be explained by an American expression of desuetude.[61] He writes,

> This particular kind of sex—homosexual sex between consenting adults—counts as fundamental. It does so because of major changes in social values in the last half-century. On this view, *Lawrence* finds a fundamental right as a result of existing public convictions, with which the Texas statute cannot be squared, simply because sodomy prosecutions are so hopelessly out of step with them ... the Court's decision was less about sexual autonomy, as a free standing idea, and

closer to a kind of due process variation on the old common law idea of desuetude.[62]

However, throughout the article Sunstein seems stunned by the possible maximalist implications of *Lawrence*. He writes, "Even if my argument [for desuetude] is correct, it must be acknowledged that the Court's remarkably opaque opinion has three principle strands. Each of those supports a different understanding of the Court's holding and the principle that supports it."[63] These are due process autonomy and liberty, equal protection rational basis analysis, and the principle he favors, desuetude, American style, a quite narrow reading of due process principles. Sunstein admits that there is a fourth possible ground, one that is a subtext for the decision but cannot be characterized as the Court's holding: equality.

Sunstein links desuetude to procedural, not to big principle "substantive" due process analysis. Sunstein specifically asks us to reject the notion of "emerging awareness" as an emerging "right," which for Sunstein is an "attempt to define the idea of liberty, and the legitimacy of intrusions on it, by reference to an evaluative account that is independent of whatever views now happen to prevail. ... A more critical approach, from the Court, should not be accepted so readily."[64]

He argues that if due process is to be the rationale in overturning the anti-sodomy law at issue in *Lawrence*, desuetude is the method for understanding it. He likes desuetude because it can claim a strong foundation in the rule of law. Most importantly, it emphasizes the procedural not substantive aspects of due process: the lack of fair notice and the invitation to arbitrary and unpredictable enforcement.[65]

Moreover, desuetude can be linked to emphasizing democratic values as a component of judicial review. He writes, "Such a law also lacks a democratic pedigree. It is able to persist only because it is enforced so rarely."[66] Here Sunstein is saying that democracy is working; the Court is merely recognizing the citizenry's choice not to enforce sodomy laws in practice. By using desuetude as an interpretive scheme, the Court is simply recognizing the wishes of the majority, as seen in the enforcement of laws, not their presence on the books. Moreover, a decision based on desuetude does not require the Court to formally overturn *Bowers* or to define in a maximalist way the fundamental rights for homosexuals in the future.[67]

This argument rejects Sunstein's admonition in *The Partial Constitution* that the key to Supreme Court decision making is that the Court not view the status quo as neutral. It assumes that the Court should simply accept the decision by society, as indicated the government's failure to enforce its anti-sodomy laws against homosexuals. Therefore, the Court is to confirm the actions of government, law enforcement, and the criminal justice process;

it should not engage in a searching analysis of whether the political, social, and economic status quo is equal for homosexuals with regard to rights and polity principles in the Constitution.

Sunstein's approach has many drawbacks. It assumes the status quo is neutral—there are not many convictions under the anti-sodomy laws. This view rejects the place of law as providing important signals as to whether all citizens are to be viewed with equal respect by the wider community. It assumes that the Court is not supposed to get into whether there is a structure of superordination and subordination with regard to sexual orientation. It assumes that discriminatory laws on the books, whether they are enforced, do not add to the subordinate status of homosexuals. Ironically, like Scalia, this view rejects aspiration, the forward-looking nature of rights and the social construction process through which rights are defined. It rejects the fact that the social construction process has within it the notion that government is not to have laws which have a chilling affect on rights, even if such laws are rarely enforced.

The justifications for a minimalist reading of *Lawrence,* rather than a critical "rights as truths" approach, are quite similar to those enunciated in *One Case at a Time.* These include the "simple risk of judicial error;" "unmoored from public convictions ... a risk that the Court's conception of liberty will be confused or indefensible"; and "the danger of unintended bad consequences." The greatest consequence that Sunstein fears is "large-scale social backlash." [68] He writes,

> Even if the Court has the right conception of liberty, it may not do much good by insisting on it when the nation strongly disagrees. If the Court had held in 1980, that the Due Process Clause requires states to recognize same-sex marriage, it would (in my view) have [been] responding to the right concept of liberty. But it would undoubtedly have produced a large-scale social backlash, and very likely a constitutional amendment, that would have made same sex marriage impossible. [69]

Such justifications for judicial minimalism become a self-fulfilling prophecy as to limited rights definitions by the Court and deference to politics by the Supreme Court, even up to the point that laws are not enforced. Should our nation have waited for the lack of enforcement of racial segregation laws and laws discriminatory of women before the Supreme Court defined rights in these areas?

We see the linkage of the call for desuetude to court respect for democratic principles and changing moral claims of the majority. Sunstein argues the Court's refusal to permit criminal convictions, under these conditions of desuetude, is not radically inconstant with democratic ideals. He notes that the fact that the Texas law was enforced rarely "stemmed from the particular fact that the moral claim that underlay it could no longer claim public support."[70]

We see a back door, very limited social construction process at work under the desuetude method of judicial minimalism when Sunstein argues that in such cases (where the interests at stake are similar to those in prior cases) the state needs more justification than "a moral position that no longer fits with public convictions."[71] Here, there is recognition that even he must engage in a social construction process. But Sunstein's social construction process is a second-order one, which is triggered by desuetude, not the rights principles at issue in a case. Moreover, Court action is triggered by procedural due process principles, such as the randomness of arrest, rather than primarily on the liberty or rights interests at issue in the case.

Sunstein supports a "narrow American-style version of the idea of desuetude—not because broader readings [of *Lawrence*] are entirely implausible, but because the Court would have been extremely unlikely to rule as it did if not for its perception that the Texas law could not claim a plausible foundation in widely shared moral commitments."[72] He also admits that broader due process and equal protection readings of *Lawrence* would make it difficult for government to find a compelling justification for refusing to recognize same sex marriage. He writes,

> If we emphasize an equality rationale, the subtext of *Lawrence*, then bans on same-sex marriages are in serious constitutional trouble. On the other hand, the ban on same sex marriages cannot, at this point in time, be regarded as an anachronism, or as conspicuously out of touch with emerging social values; on the contrary, the ban on same-sex marriage continues to have widespread public support. In any case, there are strong prudential reasons for the Court to hesitate in this domain and to allow democratic processes much room to maneuver. The marriage issue, more than any other, will test the question whether *Lawrence* is this generation's *Griswold*—or the start of something more ambitious.[73]

The problem with Sunstein's minimalist analysis is that *Griswold* was not about desuetude; neither is *Lawrence*, given the expansion of rights of privacy and personhood by the Supreme Court over the decades since *Griswold*. Moreover, it would not be "the start of something more ambitious" for the Supreme Court after *Lawrence* to define a right of civil union for homosexuals under the Constitution, or, perhaps, the separation of the religious and civil nature of marriage as the basis for the right to same-sex marriage.

By moving the standard of evaluation to something as nebulous as social values, or actual convictions under law, when "liberty interests are involved," is to make law and Court cases unprincipled. No evidence is presented by Sunstein as to what moral values are, or what is anachronistic. It is assumed the Court is following public opinion. This is not much different than behavioral political scientists assuming that the Court follows politics. It is a strong externalist and weak internalist argument. It is the misguided recognition of a distorted concept of Supreme Court decision making, with a foot on the scale for externalist values as explanations of Court action, rather than a social construction process through which the internal and external mutually construct each other. Since there is no evidence of the attitudes of the majority or elites for that matter about homosexual rights, or the act of sodomy, or on the basis of clear constitutional principles, the argument is being made primarily on prudential grounds. This is not very principled; it is outcome-oriented. It is a total rejection of the role of the Court in society and the nature of its decision making. It is a rejection of key elements of *The Partial Constitution*.

Sunstein not only failed to predict the maximalist *Lawrence* decision; he also urges us (and the Court) to view *Lawrence* in its most minimalist way with regard to future homosexual rights cases. Thus, he assumes that Supreme Court justices are pragmatists, when the case's maximalist opinions, with their robust social construction processes, suggest that they are not pragmatists or minimalists.[74] Finally, throughout the 2003 article, Sunstein demonstrates how *Lawrence* can be read as a case decided on maximalist grounds, and argues that it may be so interpreted in the future.

Legalist Pragmatism May Not Be So Different from Behavioral Political Science

Sunstein, like the behavioralists, emphasizes external factors in explaining Court action rather than a mutually constitutive Supreme Court decision-making process. There is a close fit between the call for desuetude and a call for the Court to follow society. For Sunstein, the Court is to invalidate laws that are not enforced because the lack of enforcement means that moral claims that underlie the intrusion into the personal and private life of the individual have "become hopelessly anachronistic," and there is a "ludicrously poor fit between the sodomy prohibition and the society in which justices' live."[75] This is an externalist argument in that the Court is urged to follow the actions of institutions in making its constitutional choices. We see the externalist foundation of Sunstein's minimalism when Sunstein writes,

If I am correct, *Lawrence* will have broad implications only if and to the extent that those broad implications receive general public support. For example, the Supreme Court may or may not read *Lawrence* to require states to recognize gay and lesbian marriages. But if and when it does so, it will be following public opinion, not leading it. Political and social change was a precondition for *Lawrence,* whose future reach will depend on the nature and extent of that change.[76]

The Court is viewed as an institution whose rights and decisions follow public opinion. Sunstein rejects the notion that Supreme Court decision making is a mutually constitutive process in both directions, that is, from a strong internal basis of rights principles and the rule of law, to the world outside, as well as from the social, political, and economic world outside the Court back to those principles and institutional norms. Emphasis on desuetude, the lack of arrests and convictions, is a rejection of Sunstein's former call that the Court must not accept the status quo as neutral. Sunstein's legalist pragmatism leads to a most deferential Supreme Court in practice, as well as the expectation for Court action by constitutional theorists and the wider public in the future. The status quo is defined by the acts of society, not by what the rights of citizens and subordinated groups should be, after a robust social construction process. Moreover, Sunstein's judicial minimalism is based not on a deep discussion of the substance of liberty and rights. A right is now justified on the notion that non-enforcement, or arbitrary enforcement, violates primarily the procedural, not the substantive value in the Due Process Clause—even though Sunstein admits that weak substantive considerations are present when the Court decides questions of due process in the form of his procedural concept of desuetude, American style.

Behavioral political science and externalist historians, like legal pragmatists, are unable to explain Court action. Constitutional choices cannot be explained simply by such externalist reasons as the agreement in policy terms between justices and the presidents who appointed them, election returns, majority coalitions in power at a specific time, or the attitudes and policy proclivities of justices before they came to the Court.[77] Externalist historical and "revolution" theorists try to make a link directly between specific historical events, such as a critical election or the "growth of the administrative state," and Court decision making—with no great success.[78] Supreme Court decision making is not about protecting the policy choices of the framers in the law, which (ironically) can be viewed as an externalist argument. Rather, it is to apply the words of the Constitution, in light of their interpretation through time in all ages.[79] Externalists refuse to give credence to the long-term process of Supreme Court decision making built on a social construction process which is both internal and external and normative and empirical in character.

Sunstein's pragmatic legalist approach is similar to that of behavioral political scientists. Both approaches reject the importance of internal factors in Supreme Court decision making, such as institutional norms of *stare decisis*, and the place of polity and rights principles in Supreme Court decision making as causative factors in doctrinal change.[80] Both behavioralists and pragmatic legalists emphasize external factors in explaining doctrinal change. For behavioral political scientists, and for externalist historians, the Court follows elections, specific events in politics and history, and policies already under way in society. For Sunstein, the Court follows patterns of non-arrest under anti-sodomy laws in the short run and public opinion in the long run.

Both behavioralists and legal pragmatists reject the importance of the inter-subjective and constitutive nature of Supreme Court decision making, which provides the process with an objectivity that is independent of the sum total of subjective opinions held by participants on the Court and those outside the Court.[81] Because of this, constitutive Supreme Court decision making is not reducible to the sum total of individual private preferences of justices, in contrast to what the attitudinalists argue; nor can the act of constituting be reducible to explanations based on historical and political events external to the Court; nor is it based on counting the number of arrests for anti-sodomy laws.

Because the process is at the same time "normative" and "empirical," it has an ontological character of its own that is not reducible to either polity or rights principles or the social construction of them. It is the ontological nature of Supreme Court decision making that results in the Court defining new rights, with a moral force not found when the President or Congress acts, or as a direct result of those acts. Moreover, because "the text and world are mutually constitutive," the study of the Supreme Court and individual rights "situates itself within the general paradigm of interpretive social science counter-posed to behavioral social science."[82] Because the process is public, and includes oral argument, written opinions, and what scholars can glean from justices' notes and writings, and because the social construction process is both inward- and outward-looking, it adds a democratic element to American politics.[83]

Moreover, the dual normative and empirical constitutive Supreme Court decision-making process is neither simply (or only) foundational, as legalists emphasize. Nor is it simply legal realist at its core, only influenced by the world outside and not influenced by internal institutional norms and doctrinal principles, as externalists emphasize. The fact that the process is simultaneously internal and external is to be expected if we view our system of Supreme Court decision making as having common law aspects, in which it is expected that legal principles would be applied in light of the changing economic, social, and political world outside the Court.[84]

A model of Supreme Court decision making which emphasizes the mutual construction of the internal and external that occurs in the social construction process provides a better understanding of the development of the rights of subordinated groups and the long-term process of doctrinal change. However, pragmatic legalists and behavioral political scientists reject the importance of the mutual construction of the internal and external by the Court in its decision making. They seek to explain Court actions by primarily external factors. In so doing, both behavioral political scientists and legal pragmatists, who argue for judicial minimalism, did not expect a landmark decision in *Lawrence v. Texas* (2003).[85]

Moreover, Court decisions, which fail to be both internal- and external-looking, which fail to engage in the social construction process, or whose social constructions become viewed as anachronistic in terms of society and principles that have subsequently been developed, are most likely to either be overturned or disregarded in the future. The process through which rights are seen as anachronistic is quite different from that provided by Sunstein. This difference has much to do with whether the Court is viewed as properly having a transformational impact on society.

By centering on social constructions in precedents and lines of cases, one moves beyond the idea of constructions as simple social facts and beyond questions of the use of facts or social science data in one case at a time. One can study the progression from a social construction in a case to a social construction which becomes central to a doctrinal area, to which later Courts must give obeisance if the rule of *stare decisis* is to be honored.

Social constructions become clearer as lines of cases develop. They become benchmarks, as important as polity and rights principles, in the process of analogy which is at the core of legal decision making. However, in the first case in a line of cases, the nature of the rights questions may not be clear because social constructions have yet to be developed. This is evident in *Reed v. Reed* (1971), the first in a long line of cases as to what constitutes gender discrimination under the Equal Protection Clause. It is also clear with regard to *Bush v. Gore* (2003). As the line of cases develops, social constructions remain in place and are added to, discussed, and given more filigree, as rights are extended. Social constructions serve as benchmarks, adding solidity to how each case is decided. Perhaps the most dramatic example of this was the *Casey* decision, a case which did not simply uphold the central tenets of the right of abortion choice that were first enunciated in *Roe v. Wade* (1973), but expanded them. It is this process that explains why *Lawrence v. Texas* (2003) was decided in a way that made it a landmark decision.

Conclusion: The Future of Homosexual Rights

We should expect additional landmark decisions in the area of homosexual rights in the future, as long as there is not an originalist majority on the Supreme Court. Because all non-originalists, whether they be conservative, moderate, or liberal, believe in the centrality of the social construction process, because the central element of that process is not simply to follow politics and public opinion but rather to respect institutional and legal norms such as *stare decisis*, and because that process is simultaneously inward- and outward-looking, as rights principles are applied, we can expect increased homosexual rights from the Court in the future. This does not mean that in a few years the Court will necessarily declare a fundamental right to marry. It does mean that civil union laws, and laws that treat homosexuals and lesbians differently from heterosexuals for no reason other than majority prejudice, will fall by the wayside.

This conclusion results from more than counting the now six votes on the Court that are for the right of sexual intimacy. It results from the fact that the underlying rights principles at the core of the *Lawrence* decision are so powerful, and the social constructions that lie behind those rights are so stunning in their depth and in their rejection of majority prejudice against homosexuals. All but the most originalist of justices will respect the *Lawrence* decision because unlike *Bowers* it fits with a rich line of cases since *Griswold v. Connecticut*, and since *Bowers* itself. Moreover, belief in the rule of law and the institutional interests of the Court as separate from politics in support of that principle will mean that the Court, as has happened numerous times in the past, will continue to be ahead of politics and the people on the most challenging of social questions.

Unfortunately, behavioral political scientists and pragmatic legalists will continue to tell their students, the legal academy, and the wider public to lower their expectations as to the expansion of individual rights in general and homosexual rights in particular, in the future, for reasons I have explored in this chapter. Fortunately, the methods of interpretation employed by non-originalist justices, especially with regard to the importance of the social construction process, do not comply with the predictions or the assumptions of such scholars.

Notes

1. The author would like to thank Harry Hirsh and Ken Kersch for their comments and criticisms. Research assistance was provided by Sara Chatfield.

2. Originalism, roughly defined, is the belief that interpretations of the Constitution should follow the original intent of the constitutional framers. Non-originalists believe it is legitimate to veer from such original meanings.

3. See Cass R. Sunstein, *One Case at a Time* (Cambridge: Harvard University Press, 1999), and Mark Tushnet, *Taking the Constitution Away from the Courts* (Princeton: Princeton University Press, 1999). Tushnet is even more trusting of politics and more dedicated to a minimalist role for the Supreme Court than Sunstein is. See Mark Graber, "Commentaries on Mark Tushnet, 'Taking the Constitution Away from the Courts: The Law Professor as Populist,'" *University of Richmond Law Review* 34 (May, 2000): 373–413, for a superb analysis of this book.

4. See Christopher J. Peters, "Assessing the New Judicial Minimalism," *Columbia Law Review* 100 (October, 2000): 1454–1537, 1457, for a superb overview of the concept of judicial minimalism with particular regard to the justifications offered by Sunstein and other scholars in support of judicial minimalism. Peters writes, "The case for the new minimalism significantly fails in crucial respects, because it significantly underestimates both the legitimacy and the competence of the judiciary in making decisions about individual and minority rights." This chapter uses the concept of judicial minimalism in order to demonstrate that it is built on a misguided conception of Supreme Court decision making. Most importantly, it understates the ability of the Supreme Court to bring the outside world into its decision making through a disciplined process of constructing the social, political, and economic world outside the Court.

5. See Ronald Kahn, "Social Constructions, Court Reversals, and Path Dependence: *Lochner, Plessy, Bowers,* But Not *Roe,*" in *The Supreme Court and American Political Development,* eds. Ronald Kahn and Ken I. Kersch (Lawrence: The University Press of Kansas, in press), for a detailed analysis of *Lawrence v. Texas* (2003), with respect to the place of the social construction process in Supreme Court decisions to overturn landmark cases.

6. See Ian Hacking, *The Social Construction of What?* (Cambridge: Harvard University Press, 1999): 7–37, 10, for the concept of social constructions as part of an ideational matrix. Ian Hacking writes, "Ideas do not exist in a vacuum. They inhabit a social setting. Let us call that the *matrix* within which an idea, a concept or kind, is formed." For example, the social construction "woman refugee" refers first of all to the woman refugee as a kind of person, the classification itself, and the matrix within which the classification works. Such classifications matter; if a person fails to be classified by the government as a woman refugee, she may be deported, or go into hiding, or marry to gain citizenship.

7. See Edward H. Levi, *An Introduction to Legal Reasoning* (Chicago: University of Chicago Press, 1949), for the classic statement about legal reasoning, which emphasizes that as the rule of law is applied in later cases, the nature of the rule itself changes. Reasoning is by example, ideas rejected in prior cases become acceptable in later cases, and this process allows courts to shift course doctrinally.

8. See Peter L. Berger and Thomas Luckmann, *The Social Construction of Reality: A Treatise in the Sociology of Knowledge* (New York: Anchor Books, 1966): 19–24. In using the term social construction, I am not using it as Berger and Luckmann did in their path breaking work. Social construction used here is not "the social construction of our sense of, feel for, experience of, and confidence in, commonsense reality." It is not the social construction "of various realities that arise in the complex worlds we inhabit." In studying the role of social constructions I am not concerned about examining everyday reality or experience of people, but rather how the Court uses that reality in defining social constructions that inform the development of individual rights.

9. See H. N. Hirsch, *A Theory of Liberty: The Constitution and Minorities* (New York: Routledge Press, 1992), for a filigreed and pointed critique of the Supreme Court for failing to adequately take information about real people's lives into its rights of liberty jurisprudence; also see Howard Gillman, "Sociological Jurisprudence Revisited or Why Facts Can't Serve as Foundations for Constitutional Theory," William Haltom, "Facts of Political Life," and Michael McCann, "As a Matter of ("Social") Fact," in "Symposium on Social Facts, Constitutional Theory, and Doctrinal Change," ed. Ronald Kahn, *Law and Courts,* Vol. 5, Number 2 (Summer, 1995): 3–15. These scholars raise important questions about whether sociological facts themselves can be the basis for constitutional theory. For some scholars, the concept of social construction is particularly suspect when we talk of law and the rule of law, which is

not supposed to be relativistic but solid and timeless. For other scholars, describing the social construction process presents an opportunity for raising consciousness about inequalities in society and the contingent nature of how we view race and gender politically in terms of social forces. Much social construction scholarship is critical of the status quo; scholars want to change what they dislike in the established order of things. It is not my purpose to engage in these larger controversies of contextualism versus essentialism.

10. In the *Casey* decision, for example, non-originalist justices emphasize the importance of the veracity and continued viability of social constructions in their earlier rights-protective precedents.

11. See Ronald Kahn, *The Supreme Court and Constitutional Theory, 1953–1993* (Lawrence: University Press of Kansas, 1994), 89–96. Elsewhere I have argued that the introduction of constitutional theories and ways of looking at problems from the interpretive community make their way into Court cases. The Court listened to the interpretive community and replaced the right to abortion choice in *Roe v. Wade* (1973), which was based on a relatively hollow definition of privacy as the right to be left alone, and replaced it in *Planned Parenthood Southeastern Pennsylvania v. Casey* (1992) with a more vibrant notion of personhood for women. However, the social construction process is more than the Court's discussion with the interpretive community. It is a process in which the Court brings the social, political, and at times, even the economic world into its scholarship, as we shall now explore in *Lawrence v. Texas* (2003), as the Court continues the process of defining the liberty interests of homosexuals.

12. See Dennis Goldford, *The American Constitution and the Debate over Originalism* (New York: Cambridge University Press, 2005): 263–280.

13. Ibid., 275.

14. Ibid., 284–285.

15. See J. David Greenstone, "Against Simplicity: The Cultural Dimensions of the Constitution," *University of Chicago Law Review* 55 (1988): 428–49, on the place of republican, reformed liberal, and humanist liberal strands of American political culture in theories of constitutional interpretation; see also Ronald Kahn, "Liberalism, Political Culture, and the Rights of Subordinated Groups: Constitutional Theory and Practice at a Crossroads," in *The Liberal Tradition in American Politics: Reassessing the Legacy of American Liberalism*, eds. David F. Ericson and Louisa Bertch Green, (New York: Routledge Publishing, Inc., 1999): 171–197, for how the conflict among these strands of American political culture play themselves out through the Court's engaging in the social construction process. This conflict helps produce the transformative quality of American constitutional law. Also see Rogers Smith, *Civic Ideals: Conflicting Visions of Citizenship in U.S. History* (Cambridge: Harvard University Press, 1997), for the alternative argument that the American liberal tradition is built on multiple traditions which are less supportive of the needs of subordinated groups.

16. 539 U.S. 558 (2003), 567.

17. Ibid., 573.

18. Ibid., 574.

19. Ibid., 578–79.

20. Ibid., 581–82.

21. O'Connor is not minimalist in her analysis of the substantive rights at issue in *Lawrence*. She is a minimalist only in her conclusion to base this decision on equal protection rather than due process grounds. That is, O'Connor engaged in a social construction process which did not shy away from criticizing key substantive elements of the *Bowers* decision, including its key premise that moral disapproval of gays by government is a rational basis for denying rights.

22. 539 U.S. 558 (2003), 601–602.

23. We have evidence of the centrality of the social construction process in due process and equal protection jurisprudence in Scalia's vocal opposition to the social construction process in his *Lawrence* dissent, which builds on his arguments against the social construction process in *Casey* and *Romer*. Support for the social construction process among non-originalists and opposition to it as an aspect of Court interpretation by originalists is the key fault line on the mature Rehnquist Court, not differences among conservatives, moderates, and liberals.

24. 539 U.S. 558, (2003), 592.

25. Part of the opposition by Scalia and the other originalists on the Court to the *Casey* decision, and now to the *Lawrence* decision, is that the right to privacy itself is not found in the Constitution. For them *Griswold*'s right of privacy was a misinterpretation of the Constitution, as was *Roe*. Therefore, the right of homosexual sodomy as part of the right of privacy is not a right protected in the Constitution. Therefore, any social construction process which follows *Roe*, including the social construction process outlined in *Casey*, is illegitimate. Originalists refuse to consider the impact on such rights of changes in the social, economic, and political world outside the Court since *Griswold* in 1965, and *Roe* in 1973. However, the attack by originalists on the non-originalist social construction process takes quite direct forms. Moreover, Scalia cannot rest his case against homosexual rights on the view that rights not specifically stated in the Constitution may not be fundamental rights. Scalia leaves the door ajar, conceptually, for the Court at times to define such implied fundamental rights when government is so abusive of its citizens. Scalia must engage in a social construction process in the rare times such abuse is found.
26. 539 U.S. 558 (2003), 597.
27. Ibid., 590.
28. Ibid., 588. In *Lawrence*, Scalia admits *Roe v. Wade* (1973) recognized abortion of an unborn child as a "fundamental right" protected by the Due Process Clause (Ibid., 595). However, he sees *Casey* as undermining this fundamental right since no longer "must regulations of abortion ... be narrowly tailored to serve a compelling state interest." (Ibid.) In so doing, Scalia rejects the non-originalists' expanded definition of personhood in *Casey*, and the application of those expanded rights in *Lawrence*, and any subsequent social constructions of rights that might follow these cases.
29. For the joint opinion in *Casey*, the reliance on *Roe*'s right to abortion choice (as a back-up to failed contraception) and its link to liberty rights defined in *Roe* and the twenty-nine years since *Roe*, is based on the relationship of social facts to the rights defined. That is, the social facts are part of the conception of liberty.
30. 539 U.S. 558 (2003), 600.
31. Ibid.
32. See Goldford, *The American Constitution and the Debate over Originalism*, for a subtle, forceful, and filigreed argument about why this is so. However, when the process of interpretation is so radically different as it is between originalists and non-originalists on the mature Rehnquist Court, it is valid to argue that such a difference in the interpretive turn between originalists and non-originalists as to how and when to engage in the social construction process constitutes, for all intent and purposes, a rejection of the legitimacy of the social construction process itself.
33. See Cass Sunstein, "What Did *Lawrence* Hold?: Of Autonomy, Desuetude, Sexuality, and Marriage." *The Supreme Court Review* 2003: 27–74, 34.
34. See Kahn, *The Supreme Court and Constitutional Theory, 1953–1993*, 69–104, where I explore how this transformation of the existent into the normative has deep roots in much of American political and constitutional theory, and in the social sciences and the humanities, and how it has shaped how we view the Supreme Court's use of its power of judicial review.
35. Edward A. Purcell, *The Crisis of Democratic Theory: Scientific Naturalism and the Problem of Value* (Lexington: University Press of Kentucky, 1973), 262.
36. Sunstein, *The Partial Constitution*, 11.
37. See Hirsch, *A Theory of Liberty: The Constitution and Minorities*, 5, for the argument that American Constitutionalism, the Supreme Court, and judicial review was meant by the founders of the Constitution and the Civil War amendments to be counter-majoritarian. Clearly Sunstein's deliberative democracy does not meet Hirsch's vision.
38. See Ronald Kahn, "Social Constructions, Court Reversals, and Path Dependence: *Lochner, Plessy, Bowers*, But Not *Roe*," in Ronald Kahn and Ken I. Kersch, eds., *The Supreme Court and American Political Development*.
39. This problem is even more prevalent in Sunstein's *One Case at a Time*.
40. See Sunstein, "Sexual Orientation and the Constitution."
41. Sunstein, *One Case at a Time: Judicial Minimalism on the Supreme Court*, 9.
42. Ibid.
43. Ibid.
44. Ibid., xiv.

45. Ibid., 26.
46. Ibid., 27.
47. Ibid., ix.
48. Ibid., 63–68.
49. Ibid., 63.
50. Ibid., 70
51. Ibid.
52. Ibid., 71.
53. Ibid., 57–59.
54. Ibid., 50.
55. Ibid., 40.
56. See Theodore J. Lowi, *The End of Liberalism: The Second Republic of the United States, Second Edition* (New York: Norton, 1979), chapter 5, "Liberal Jurisprudence: Policy without Law," 92–130, for the classic statement of why policy made without prior clear principles to limit the discretion of policy makers leads to government actions that are favorable to the most politically powerful. Judicial minimalism has similar drawbacks, but now they are encouraged for the Supreme Court and lesser courts.
57. Sunstein, *One Case at a Time: Judicial Minimalism on the Supreme Court,* 50.
58. See Sunstein, *One Case at a Time: Judicial Minimalism on the Supreme Court,* chapter 4, "Minimalism's Substance," 61–72.
59. We do have *Dred Scott* as a horrible example of maximalism, but there are lists of horribles on both sides.
60. Cass Sunstein, "What Did *Lawrence* Hold?: Of Autonomy, Desuetude, Sexuality, and Marriage." *The Supreme Court Review* 2003: 27–74.
61. This is not the first time that Sunstein has called for minimalism on questions of homosexual rights. In "Sexual Orientation and the Constitution: A Note on the Relationship between Due Process and Equal Protection," *The University of Chicago Law Review* 55 (1988): 1161–79, 1163, Sunstein argues that *Bowers* was a due process case while *Watkins* v. *U.S. Army* 847 F2nd 1329 (9th Circuit 1988) reh'g granted, en banc 847 F2nd 1362 (1988) was an equal protection case. Most importantly, one can see Sunstein's rejection of a deeper support for a robust social construction and against due process foundations for homosexual rights when he argues the Due Process Clause looks backward and the Equal Protection Clause looks forward, "serving to invalidate practices that were widespread at the time of ratification and that were expected to endure." This view understates the degree to which the social construction process requires the interpretation of both clauses as backward- and forward-looking, and a rejection of the view accepted by the *Lawrence* Court, that the substantive issues (and social construction processes) involved in due process and equal protection analysis may not be so different.
62. Ibid., 48–49.
63. Ibid., 29.
64. Ibid., 55–56.
65. Ibid., 54.
66. Ibid.
67. Ibid., 37. This is very similar to O'Connor's hopes about future political action. Sunstein will either wait for society to get rid of laws that treat similar acts in different ways to groups of citizens under the Equal Protection Clause, or the Court, after a long period of significant enforcement by society, will declare the law void for reasons of the procedural due process type principles that are central to Sunstein's concept of desuetude, American style.
68. Ibid., 56.
69. Ibid.
70. Ibid., 59.
71. Ibid.
72. Ibid., 73.
73. Ibid., 73–74.
74. Ibid., 34.
75. Ibid., 31.
76. Ibid.

77. See Jeffrey Segal and Harold J. Spaeth, *The Supreme Court and the Attitudinal Model* (New York: Cambridge University Press, 1993), and *The Supreme Court and the Attitudinal Model Revisited* (New York: Cambridge University Press, 2002) for classic statements of the attitudinal model.

78. See Barry Cushman, *Rethinking the New Deal Court: The Structure of Constitutional Revolution* (New York: Oxford University Press, 1998), for the most comprehensive critique of arguments made by historians that external political events can explain *West Coast Hotel,* and the judicial "revolution" of 1937. Also see Howard Gillman, "The Collapse of Constitutional Originalism and the Rise of the Notion of the 'Living Constitution' in the Course of American State-Building," *Studies in American Political Development* 11 (1997): 191–247, for an insightful discussion of the debate in the early twentieth century over whether the Constitution should be changed by evolution through interpretation or by amendment. However, in this discussion, Gillman tends to continue the traditional reification by externalist scholars of the importance of 1937 as the key dividing line between the Court following originalist thinking and one in which the Constitution is to be defined as a "living" document.

79. Dennis Goldford, *The American Constitution and the Debate Over Originalism,* 105.

80. The call for minimalism seems to be based on premises about Court decision making and the wider political system that are at the core of Gerald Rosenberg, *The Hollow Hope: Can Courts Bring About Social Change?* (Chicago: University of Chicago Press, 1991). However, see Michael McCann, *Rights at Work: Pay Equity Reform and the Politics of Legal Mobilization* (Chicago: University of Chicago Press, 1994), where he argues that the unintended consequences of maximalism in rights definitions by the Court actually expands the rights of citizens because institutions fear future court cases. Also, Sunstein argues that minimalist justices act strategically to get votes in cases, while maximalist justices are less likely to do so. Does this mean that Justice Brennan was a minimalist because he put together voting coalitions? However, I thought his decisions included deep reasoning and an attempt to have decisions apply to as many instances in the world outside the Court. There needs to be more discussion of minimalism in Court eras defined as maximalist, and visa-versa.

81. See Goldford, *The American Constitution and the Debate Over Originalism,* 348. Thus, the Constitution, in principle (and as constitutive practice) is distinct from whatever anyone says about it, including the founders. The Constitution can be invoked as a critical standard against current practices which are alleged to be unconstitutional.

82. Ibid, 268. Supreme Court decision making is both subjective and objective at the same time; and we as social scientists must explain that process, not simply argue for this or that rights or polity principles.

83. See Christopher L. Eisgruber, *Constitutional Self-Government* (Cambridge: Harvard University Press, 2001), and Randy E. Barnett, *Restoring the Lost Constitution: The Presumption of Liberty* (Princeton: Princeton University Press, 2004), for recent scholarship as to why the formally undemocratic Supreme Court makes the overall political system more democratic and more inclusive.

84. See David A. Strauss, "Common Law Constitutional Interpretation," *University of Chicago Law Review,* 63 (Summer, 1996): 877–935; Ronald Kahn, "*Marbury v. Madison* as a Model for Understanding Contemporary Judicial Review," in *Marbury v. Madison: Documents and Commentary,* eds. Mark A. Graber and Michael Perhac (Washington, D.C.: CQ Press, 2002): 155–179; and Edward Levi, *An Introduction to Legal Reasoning.*

85. Political scientists need not accept the externalist stance of behavioralists or of legalist pragmatists. See Mark Graber, "The Clintonification of American Law: Abortion, Welfare, and Liberal Constitutional Theory," *Ohio State Law Journal* 58 (1997): 731–818, 802, for the argument that "if the right to abortion and the right to engage in homosexual sodomy both follow logically from a more general right of privacy, then a society whose constitution is interpreted as protecting that general right of privacy should not keep abortion legal and ban homosexual sodomy. At the very least, Supreme Court justices in gay rights cases should not reject general constitutional rights to privacy without explaining why they are still protecting abortion."

CHAPTER 13

To What Extent Should We Be Looking Abroad for Guidance in Interpreting the United States Constitution?

SANFORD LEVINSON

To what extent should those charged with interpreting national constitutions take into account the lessons that might be taught by foreign experience? This question took on special importance after Justice Kennedy's path-breaking opinion in *Lawrence v. Texas*,[1] in which he cited foreign legal materials even as he interpreted the United States Constitution to invalidate a Texas law criminalizing same-sex sodomy. In asking this question, I do not mean to confine myself to the relevance of such foreign materials as cases from other courts; there is no reason to confine oneself to such material if one is seriously interested in learning more about comparative approaches to similar problems.

Although the question of looking to foreign sources can obviously arise with those charged with interpreting *any* of the more than 150 written constitutions around the world, I will approach this issue from the context of someone charged only with interpreting the U.S. Constitution. The principal reason is, of course, that this is the system that I know best; a second reason is that the issue is now the subject of an unusually heated debate among justices of the United States Supreme Court.

The question, I might point out, is not the potential *authority*—i.e., obligatory nature—of non-U.S. law with regard to the decision of American cases, an authority that could derive from treaties entered into by the United States or, most controversially, from the reception of international law into U.S. law. One obviously need not believe that there is an *obligation* to be bound by foreign legal materials in order to believe that it is simply prudent practice to become knowledgeable about and to apply the lessons one finds there to comparable dilemmas facing us here in the United States.

In order to set the stage for the debate here in the United States, it is helpful to look at the practices of at least one other American country, just north of us. In an examination of the citation practices of the Supreme Court of Canada, three political scientists note the frequency with which that court has looked to foreign cases, especially following the adoption of the Canadian Charter of Rights in the early 1980s. Almost 45 percent of the 858 decisions that were decided between 1984 and 1995 contained at least one citation to a British case, though some might dispute whether this really counts as a "foreign" citation, given the particular historical relationship of Canada to the United Kingdom. Consider, then, that 30 percent had at least one citation to a U.S. case, with 58 percent of these citations being to cases decided in the United States after 1970. This suggests, among other things, an interest in how such courts are confronting similar problems in the present. (Another 18 percent were citations to cases decided between 1950 and 1970; only 24 percent were to "old cases," including presumably classic chestnuts of American constitutional law.)[2]

Citations per se obviously provide only limited, albeit suggestive, information. Consider, then, two representative comments from Canadian judges. In a concurring opinion in a case involving self-incrimination and right-to-counsel claims by someone charged with child molestation and sexual assault, Justice L'Heureux-Dube wrote that "the case before us presents the ideal opportunity to look south and learn from the experience of the United States. ... [G]iven what appears to me to be the overly cumbersome and obtrusive position which has developed in Canada, the American position might well offer a compromise between the two conflicting rights which is worthy of our attention."[3]

To be sure, in another case Justice LaForest expressed some caution about looking southward:

> While it is natural and even desirable for Canadian courts to refer
> to American Constitutional jurisprudence in seeking to elucidate the
> meaning of the Charter guarantees that have counterparts in the

United States Constitution, they should be wary of drawing too ready a parallel between constitutions born to different countries in different ages and in very different circumstances. ... American jurisprudence, like the British, must be viewed as a tool, not as a master.[4]

Surely, though, no reasonable person could object to these cautionary notes; Justice L'Heureux-Dube certainly did not believe that American (or any other non-Canadian) law should be put in the position of "mastery." The very use of the conditional "might well offer a compromise" suggests only the hope that our experiences in the United States might provide a potentially useful "tool" to the solution of common problems.

Canada is obviously not unique in citing foreign, including American, sources. A splendid, indeed seminal, article by Sujit Choudhry, aptly entitled *Globalization in Search of Justification,* notes the copious use of foreign materials by the South African Constitutional Court.[5] This has been justified in part by such comments as that of Justice Albie Sachs, who calls on South African constitutional jurisprudence to acknowledge "its existence as part of a global development of constitutionalism and human rights."[6] As part of a global community, Justice Sachs is arguing, South Africa should look to the decisions of courts around the world for the insight that they cast on the solution of common problems. South Africa, to be sure, might be viewed as occupying a very special position inasmuch as its pre-1996 legal traditions are so dismal concerning issues involving social justice or human rights. Still, there ought to be no country, most certainly including our own, that should regard its own instantiated commitment to social justice or human rights as absolutely pristine, in need of no wisdom that might be provided by external sources. After all, slavery was absolutely legal in the United States until 1865, and a serious commitment to dismantling its successor, the Jim Crow legal system of segregation, did not get underway until after World War II. Indeed, historians increasingly agree that one factor that encouraged both the Truman and Eisenhower administrations to call for the dismantling of segregation was the beating the United States was taking from its Communist enemies abroad because of the patent injustice of American racial practices.[7]

Thus, from my perspective—and, I suspect, from many of your own—the sentiments expressed by both Canadian justices are so obvious as to sound banal. So let us now turn to justices of the U.S. Supreme Court, some of whose comments might allow us to realize how non-banal are our friends to the North.

I begin with the most recent manifestation of the debate, which took place in a June 2003 decision involving the constitutionality of a Texas statute criminalizing sodomy.[8] Justice Kennedy, in his opinion for the Court striking down the legislation, took into account not only the British Wolfenden Report of 1957, but also, and far more significantly, decisions by the European Court of Human Rights, including *Dudgeon v. UK*.[9] "Authoritative in all countries that are members of the Council of Europe (21 countries then, 45 nations now)," Kennedy wrote, "the decision is at odds with the premise in *Bowers* that the claim put forward was insubstantial in our Western civilization."[10]

I should note, incidentally, that Kennedy was referring primarily to the "premise" enunciated in Chief Justice Burger's *concurring* opinion in that case. Burger wrote that "[d]ecisions of individuals relating to homosexual conduct have been subject to state intervention throughout the history of Western civilization. Condemnations of those practices is firmly rooted in Judeao-Christian moral and ethical standards."[11] This was a quite brilliant rhetorical move on Kennedy's part, since he could argue that it was, after all, Burger who opened up the question of "Western civilization"—and "Judeao-Christian moral and ethical standards"—and, therefore, allowed the possibility of rebuttal. As a matter of fact, Justice White's majority opinion did not rely on the general teachings of Western civilization but, instead, argued only that one could not legitimately understand the specifically *American* tradition of protected spheres of autonomy to include what White repeatedly called "homosexual sodomy." I shall have more to say about the relevance of the difference between the White and Burger opinions below.

In any event, Kennedy's reference to European materials led Justice Scalia to respond as follows:

> Constitutional entitlements do not spring into existence. ... because *foreign nations* decriminalize conduct. ... The Court's discussion of these foreign views (ignoring, of course, the many countries that have retained criminal prohibitions on sodomy) is therefore meaningless dicta. Dangerous dicta, however, since "this Court ... should not impose foreign moods, fads, or fashions on Americans."[12]

This was, of course, not Justice Scalia's first foray into denunciation of what might be termed jurisprudential cosmopolitanism, i.e., looking abroad for possible wisdom. An earlier exchange took place between Justices Scalia and Breyer on the occasion of Breyer's dissenting from a Scalia opinion that had ruled unconstitutional the "commandeering" of state officials in order to implement federal policies—in this case "commandeering" was the duty of a local sheriff to engage in relatively minimal checks of the possible criminal record of someone wishing to buy a gun. Justice Breyer, who, like Scalia, had taught administrative law at a major American law school before being appointed to the judiciary, pointed to what might be learned by looking at the experience of European countries operating within federal systems:[13]

> [T]he United States is not the only nation that seeks to reconcile the practical need for a central authority with the democratic virtues of more local control. At least some other countries, facing the same basic problem, have found that local control is better maintained through application of a principle that is the direct opposite of the principle the majority derives from the silence of our Constitution. The federal systems of Switzerland, Germany, and the European Union, for example, all provide that constituent states, not federal bureaucracies, will themselves implement many of the laws, rules, regulations, or decrees enacted by the central "federal" body.[14] They do so in part because they believe that such a system interferes less, not more, with the independent authority of the "state," member nation, or other subsidiary government, and helps to safeguard individual liberty as well.[15]
>
> Of course, we are interpreting our own Constitution, not those of other nations, and there may be relevant political and structural differences between their systems and our own.[16] But their experience may nonetheless cast *an empirical light* on the consequences of different solutions to a common legal problem—in this case the problem of reconciling central authority with the need to preserve the liberty enhancing autonomy of a smaller constituent governmental entity.[17]

All of this was prefatory to Breyer's altogether correct conclusion that "there is neither need nor reason to find in the Constitution an absolute principle, the inflexibility of which poses a surprising and technical obstacle to the enactment of a law that Congress believed necessary to solve an important national problem."

Justice Scalia blithely, almost insultingly, dismissed the relevance of Breyer's argument and, more to the point, the evidence on which it was based:

> Justice Breyer's dissent would have us consider the benefits that other countries, and the European Union, believe they have derived from federal systems that are different from ours. We think such comparative analysis inappropriate to the task of interpreting a constitution, though it was of course quite relevant to the task of writing one.[18]

Scalia did not deny the obvious truth that "[t]he Framers were familiar with many federal systems, from classical antiquity down to their own time."

But, according to Scalia, the principal point is that Madison and Hamilton studied these other federal systems only to reject them. Thus, said Scalia, the principal lesson to be drawn from 1787 is that "our federalism is not Europe's." It is apparently *sui generis*, "the *unique* contribution of the Framers to political science and political theory."[19] Scalia's argument appears to be that the eighteenth-century rejection, after full study, of the various models of federalism then prevalent in Europe entails a similar rejection of even the possibility of learning from contemporary models of European federalism some two centuries later. I confess that I find this argument illogical. I simply do not understand why even a hard-core originalist might not draw from Madison and Hamilton—and their essays in *The Federalist*—the message that "experience" is indeed important. One obviously might find the specifics of foreign experience repellant, as Scalia argues was the actual case, but this scarcely seems to entail a *permanent* closing off from the potential of future enlightenment. That eighteenth-century analysts might have decided, altogether correctly, that most doctors had no idea what they were doing, and that one therefore was well-advised to stick with self-medication instead of submitting to the ministrations of quacks and charlatans does not, I presume, entail that we should be equally dismissive of contemporary medical science.

I turn now to a final quotation from Justice Scalia, this one from his angry 2002 dissent in *Atkins v. Virginia*,[20] where a five-Justice majority had the temerity to declare that the execution of the mentally retarded was unconstitutional because it was violative of the prohibition by the Eighth Amendment of "cruel and unusual punishment." The key debate between the majority and the dissenters concerned the presence of a sufficient "national consensus" to justify limiting the autonomy of states like Virginia (and Texas), who find executing the retarded perfectly legitimate. According to Scalia,

> the Prize for the Court's Most Feeble Effort to fabricate 'national consensus' must go to its appeal (deservedly relegated to a footnote) to the views of assorted professional and religious organizations, members of the so-called "world community," and respondents to opinion polls. I agree with [Chief Justice William Rehnquist] that the views of professional and religious organizations and the results of opinion polls are irrelevant. *Equally irrelevant are the practices of the "world community," whose notions of justice are (thankfully) not always those of our people.* "We must never forget that it is a Constitution for the United States of America that we are expounding. ... [W]here there is not first a settled consensus among our own people, the views of other nations, however enlightened the Justices of this

Court may think them to be, cannot be imposed upon Americans through the Constitution.

It should be obvious from what I have said so far that I am no fan of Justice Scalia. I find the militant provincialism suggested by these quotations embarrassing; I much prefer the cosmopolitanism expressed by the Canadian justices and by Justice Breyer. This being said, I want to explore in the remainder of my remarks the question of whether there is *anything* at all to be said for at least some of Scalia's views, and I think the answer is yes.

I begin by making a distinction that, whatever its theoretical difficulties, is one that we cannot in fact do without: that is, the distinction we commonly draw between *facts* and *values*, between *empirical* and *normative* arguments. Recall Scalia's altogether correct emphasis on the fact that other countries, including a quite mythic "world community," may possess "notions of justice [that] are (thankfully) not always those of our people." Although this is, in form, an empirical proposition based on study of different notions of justice, its real importance is with regard to the fact that "justice" itself is a *normative* concept. To call something "just" or "unjust" is to evaluate it, as against, for example, describing something as mineral or vegetable. And, of course, the central question of Western philosophy for at least 2,500 years has been the foundation, if any, of such evaluations.

One obvious possibility is the presence of "right reason" that teaches us, through disciplined methods of rational analysis, what the truth is as to propositions of morality. Scalia's own Roman Catholic Church is the primary institutional articulator of such a view. Or, of course, if one is what might be called an anthropological naturalist, one might look to the presence of *convergence* in the moral views and practices of otherwise diverse communities as evidence of moral truths.

What is interesting about Scalia, though, is that as a Justice he almost ruthlessly rejects the legal relevance of Thomism or of any socio-anthropological inquiry into general cultural practices. Indeed, a careful analysis of his comment in *Atkins* reveals that he is a thoroughgoing conventionalist in terms of deciding what legal norms operate within the United States. Whether or not he would agree with Thrasymachus in *The Republic* that any given society's notion of justice is only ideological, reflecting the interests of the strongest within that society, it is clear that Scalia is totally unwilling, in terms of his conception of judicial role, to adopt what might be called a "critical" stance toward conventional morality, unless he can root such a stance in the text of the Constitution or in its original understanding. Thus Justice Scalia joined in the Court's two decisions striking down the criminalization of burning the American flag[21] as clear violations of the

First Amendment, even though it is almost undoubtedly the case that most contemporary Americans support such laws. Generally speaking, though, he is much like Lord Devlin's famous passengers in the Clapham omnibus, whose untutored collective views about morality—and, interestingly enough, what sparked the classic debate between Devlin and H. L. A. Hart was precisely the legal rights that should be accorded homosexuals[22]—were more important than any consensus that might be present, say, at All Souls College at Oxford, the Sorbonne, or Harvard.[23] Devlin insisted that his version of "the reasonable man" whose views about social morality are entitled to prevail "is not to be confused with the rational man. He is not expected to reason about anything and his judgment may be largely a matter of feeling. It is the viewpoint of the man in the street—or to use an archaism familiar to all lawyers—the man in the Clapham omnibus." I have no doubt that Scalia would agree with Devlin. In other opinions, indeed, Scalia has sounded like a populist demagogue in his zealous attacks on colleagues he views as dedicated to advancing the philosophy of "elites."[24]

However much I disagree with Scalia on the particulars of given cases, I think that in certain ways he is correct in his basic analysis. That is, I do not interpret the American constitutional tradition as one that necessarily privileges the "refined" moral views of professional philosophers over the untutored intuitions of the majority. As a descriptive matter, I certainly do not believe that the Court has ever deviated in any truly significant way from the dominant sensibility. As a normative matter, I find it difficult to argue that the judge *should* ignore the dominant sensibility and declare that an inchoate notion of "justice" requires something radically different, especially if the notion is derived from what might be termed "purely" philosophical arguments.

One might reject the Clapham omnibus per se as the source of authoritative guidance because one has suspicions of the degree to which that particular bus is representative of the population at large or concerns about their ability to engage in even the most primitive level of analysis of the implications of their ostensible views. But even Ronald Dworkin himself cannot entirely escape *some* omnibus insofar as his ideal-type Herculean judge is charged with developing a coherent portrait of the values of his or her own particular society rather than, say, simply interpreting the Constitution to instantiate the teachings of some universalistic system of natural justice. This is why, for example, Dworkin has an embarrassingly difficult time answering the question whether Hercules would necessarily have been an anti-slavery judge or would necessarily validate, as a constitutional matter, Lincoln's taking of private property that we also know as the Emancipation Proclamation.[25]

In many ways, these debates go back to a classic 1798 exchange between Justices Chase and Iredell, in which Iredell sharply rejected the relevance of "natural law" to constitutional interpretation. The Court ought not to invalidate legislation, said Iredell, "merely because it is, in their judgment, contrary to the principles of natural justice. The ideas of natural justice are regulated by no fixed standard; the ablest and the purest men have differed upon the subject; and all that the Court could properly say, in such an event, would be, that the Legislature, possessed of an equal right of opinion, had passed an act which, in the opinion of the judges, was inconsistent with the abstract principles of natural justice."[26] Iredell's argument can be viewed as a rejection of the *epistemological* ability to comprehend natural law in a sufficient manner to justify legal decisions. Other, more contemporary critics might be *ontological* skeptics, i.e., deny the very reality of natural law in the first place, so that our failure to comprehend them is not evidence merely of our human limitations, but, rather, of the fact that there is literally nothing to comprehend. (It would be like comprehending the internal body parts of unicorns.)

There are, to be sure, critics of such skepticism, the most prominent, like Professor John Finnis, identified with Scalia's own Roman Catholic Church, though my colleague Richard Markovits has also presented a powerful challenge to such skeptical arguments.[27] As I've already suggested, though, one might even agree with Finnis as to the ontological and epistemological reality of norms of natural justice without going to agree that they are automatically part of the American Constitution. Instead, as Scalia (and many others) would argue, they become part of the Constitution only when affirmatively adopted by "we the people" through legislative action or, even if one accepts the notion of "fundamental rights," when accepted by enough passengers on the Clapham omnibus to allow us to say that they have indeed become part of the operative consensus of American opinion. This is, of course, simply to reiterate the central tenet of positivism, which is the analytical separation of law and morality. And, as I have argued elsewhere, one can simply not understand a constitutional tradition that includes the legitimacy of chattel slavery as one that privileges morality over legal conventions.[28]

This means, I regret to say, that Scalia may be right when he describes as "irrelevant" "the practices of the 'world community,'" at least insofar as their "notions of justice are (thankfully [or not]) not always those of our people." If, obviously, their notions are similar to "those of our people," they are irrelevant in the specific reason that it makes no difference whether one takes them into account, since the outcome is presumably the same. We may be encouraged to learn that other presumably enlightened countries agree with us, but otherwise it is hard to see what difference it would make. Only differences present potentially interesting dilemmas.

Ironically or not, Justice Scalia's views of the basis of what we call *legal* "justice" are identical to those expressed by contemporary post-modernists, whom I suspect the Justice would otherwise profess to disdain; one of the principal assertions of post-modernists (with whom I am often identified), is that our notions of "reality" are "socially constructed." As already suggested, there is not anything necessarily chronologically modern about such views; they can easily be traced back to participants in Platonic dialogues, including *The Republic* and that most legally significant of all dialogues, *The Gorgias.*

The other way that Scalia overlaps with post-modernism is his adoption of a type of "identity politics." This term is usually applied to assertions of racial or ethnic community. There is, however, no reason why the analysis doesn't apply as well to nationalism, which is, after all, the assertion that the world is sorted into separate nations whose separateness is constituted, in part, precisely by commitments to different notions of justice. From this perspective, what distinguishes Albanians from Zimbabweans is not only color, religion, or cuisine; it may also include quite different conceptions of justice as well. And the deepest premise of "separate identity" is that it is indeed impossible to engage in the truly impersonal assessment of one or another aspect of the culture. This would require a "view from nowhere," but a central premise of much contemporary philosophy is that all of us look at the world from situated perspective rooted in "somewhere." Scalia the judge roots himself in an America whose values he purports to be able to identify. If the job of the judge is to identify and then apply these distinctive values, why would it be relevant to study how other cultures approach similar questions? To learn that Orthodox Jews put hats on when entering holy places is totally and utterly irrelevant with regard to what counts as acceptable "hat behavior" when entering Catholic churches.

The same is true with regard to identifying an explicitly *American* community, as distinguished from a European one. Indeed, it is not clear why anyone interested in describing what constitutes *Texas* as a distinctive subcommunity within the United States would spend much, if any, time in the study of New Hampshirites or Montanans, except by way of noting that (most, though not all) Texans seem to have a taste not only for fajitas and barbecue, but also for putting convicted criminals, including the mentally retarded, to death and stigmatizing non-heterosexual forms of sexual expression. Both of these tastes are now unconstitutional, but only because the Supreme Court has decided that there is a sufficient "American" consensus to trump what is now perceived as a truly idiosyncratic set of Texas values. The possibility that local values will in fact be trumped by national ones is the price one pays for entering into a federal union. But this obviously does not entail that one looks beyond the borders of the federal union in order to find out whether what Marshall once called, sincerely or not, a "sovereign State"[29] is subject to constraints because it is, of course, also a member of a nation with its own supreme norms. Justice Scalia is, to be sure, parochial, but it is not clear that that isn't required by the presuppositions of the American legal system insofar as it rejects the existence (or relevance) of natural law or "international human rights" that, in effect, dominate more local norms and cultures.

So, with regard to the death penalty and regulation of gay and lesbian sexual expression, one must, for better and worse, take Justice Scalia's position with some seriousness, at least, *and this is a crucial point,* if one views such issues only within the context of expressing basic social values about the importance of retributive punishment, on the one hand, and condemning "unconventional" sexual expression, on the other. Things get far more complicated if one views either the death penalty or suppression of gay and lesbian sexuality in more instrumental terms, including, for example, the deterrent effect of capital punishment or the effects, say, on military cohesion of accepting open gays or lesbians into the armed forces. These latter assertions are not merely *expressive;* they are *empirical,* and they call for an entirely different response. There is no reason in the world, quite literally, to ignore the experience of other countries with regard to the death penalty or integration of gays and lesbians into their national militaries.

In the original version of this chapter, I wrote, "It is Justice Scalia's failure to appreciate this point that makes his response to Justice Breyer not only (typically) ill-tempered, but almost truly irrational."[30] Although I think that his rather flamboyant style lent credence to this conclusion, I now believe that his position is in fact more nuanced and is in some significant measure congruent with the approach taken here. Thus in a spring 2004 speech to the American Society on International Law (ASIL),[31] Justice Scalia clearly distinguished between looking to foreign sources for help in what might be termed "first-order" interpretation of the Constitution (forbidden) and more limited consultation for certain empirical purposes (legitimate). Actually, he even offers an example when foreign materials could be helpful even for first-order interpretation: to the extent that the Framers of the Constitution looked to British law to define the 1791 meaning of "due process of law," then he would indeed be willing to look at such foreign law himself. But this is obviously a very limited concession, and no one who does not share his originalist premises would be much impressed. More important are his examples of legitimately looking to contemporary materials. He offers two:

> I suppose foreign statutory and judicial law can be consulted in assessing the argument that a particular construction of an ambiguous provision in a federal statute would be disastrous. If foreign courts have long been applying precisely the rule argued against, and disaster has *not* ensued, unless there is some countervailing factor at work the argument can safely be rejected. This is perhaps more precisely described not as using foreign law but as using the product of foreign experience.[32]
>
> What about *modern* foreign legal materials? Do I ever consider *them* relevant to constitutional adjudication? To tell you the truth, I cannot say *never.* Only *hardly ever.* Just as with a case involving statutory construction, so also with a case involving constitutional interpretation; the argument is sometimes made that a particular holding will be disastrous. Here, as there, I think it entirely proper to point out that other countries have long applied the same rule *without* disastrous consequences. ... I have also joined an opinion dealing with the question of whether there is a constitutional right to assisted suicide that discussed, in a footnote, the fact that "[o]ther countries are embroiled in similar debates"—citing materials from Canada, England, New Zealand, Australia, and Colombia.[33] I have no problem with reciting such interesting background, so long as the laws of those countries are not asserted to be relevant to the interpretation of our Constitution.[34]

In the case cited by Justice Scalia, Chief Justice Rehnquist's majority opinion rejected a claim that the Constitution, correctly understood, protects what has come to be called "assisted suicide," i.e., the ability of a doctor to provide terminally ill patients with drugs that might be used to end their lives. He wrote that "[t]he State's assisted suicide ban reflects and reinforces its policy that the lives of terminally ill, disabled, and elderly people must be no less valued than the lives of the young and healthy, and that a seriously disabled person's suicidal impulses should be interpreted and treated the same way as anyone else's. *This concern is further supported by evidence about the practice of euthanasia in the Netherlands,*" and he goes on to present some interesting information about those practices in the Netherlands.[35]

One might interpret Rehnquist's argument as follows: *All* of us are united by a commitment to valuing "the lives of terminally ill, disabled, and elderly people." Supporters of assisted suicide believe that offering them practical ways to end their lives, should they wish to, honors their autonomy. Many opponents do not reject the value of autonomy as such; rather, they argue that the actual realities of life make it more likely that assisted suicide will end up dishonoring that value than honoring it. Evidence for this argument is ostensibly found by analysis of what has happened in the Netherlands, the country that has gone furthest to allow assisted suicide as a legal possibility. Among other things, there seem to have been incidents of what can more accurately be described as euthanasia than genuinely autonomous decisions to end one's life. One may or may not agree with Rehnquist's interpretation of the data. The point is that it seems impossible to deny that what has gone on in Holland should be of interest to any judge called upon to determine whether the vague contours of the Constitution, which *is* committed to *some* notion of autonomy, embrace something like assisted suicide.

As noted, Justice Scalia seems quite happy with Rehnquist's references to foreign practices inasmuch as they demonstrate the lessons of experience. I think that he should have been similarly supportive with Justice Breyer's reference to European materials in his *Printz* dissent, even if Scalia ultimately most certainly did not find them dispositive. After all, Breyer is not attacking the value of federalism per se or suggesting that the Framers were simply wrong in valuing some measure of state autonomy. Rather, he is arguing that a look at the European experience reveals that federalism can easily be maintained, perhaps even strengthened, by allowing a certain amount of "commandeering" of state officials to enforce national policy. I believe that Scalia's summary rejection of Breyer's data *in toto* is in contrast with the more nuanced views expressed in his ASIL address and does not follow at all from his dismissals of comparative law in *Lawrence* and *Atkins,* which can be viewed as debates about fundamental values.

Indeed, it is worth noting one aspect of Justice Scalia's dissent in a recent case, *Locke v. Davey*.[36] It is actually Scalia who invokes foreign developments by way of criticizing the majority for its seeming disdain of the rights of the religious to full participation in the benefits of the modern welfare state. "Today's holding," says Scalia, "is limited to training the clergy, but its logic is readily extendable, and there are plenty of directions to go. What next? ... [R]ecall that France has proposed banning religious attire from school, invoking interests in secularism no less benign than those the Court embraces today."[37] I must say that this seems to be a clear case where the values of France, however understandable in terms of their own rich cultural history of anti-clericalism and concern to maintain a relentlessly secular state, is quite out of line with our own values as a nation committed to a considerably greater degree of pluralism in the public square. Given the toleration by the European Court of Human Rights of headscarf laws arising from Switzerland and Turkey, one can easily imagine that the French law will pass muster in Strasbourg. But so what? How many American analysts would say that the quite different European approach toward what is in this country called "free exercise" should lead us to modify our own understandings?

It is worth considering the argumentative practices of Scalia's presumptively more cosmopolitan opponents. To be sure, they cite foreign materials, especially when they are in accordance with what one suspects are preexisting views. What seems strikingly lacking, though, is any real analysis of them or explanation, beyond the ostensible force provided by their very existence, of why we should be impressed by them. Scalia notes, for example, that if Europe is tolerant of sodomy, this is not the case in Africa, where thirty-three of fifty-one countries prohibit it, or the Middle East, where eleven out of fourteen countries are similarly intolerant. Perhaps it suffices to say that "our tradition" is European and not African or Middle-Eastern (or Asian), though, as a matter of fact, such assertions become ever more controversial as the United States becomes ever more truly "multi-cultural" in terms of the ethnic background of immigrants and new citizens.[38] But even if one maintains a more "Eurocentric" view of what constitutes "our" heritage, then one must consider the fact that among the countries with less tolerant abortion laws than our own are the United Kingdom, Finland, Iceland, Ireland, Luxembourg, Germany, New Zealand, Portugal, Spain, and Switzerland.[39] Scalia describes the use of foreign materials by their devotees as "selective," and he is surely correct.

Edward Rubin has coined the wonderful term "puppy federalism" to refer to the infatuation of the present Supreme Court with restoring federalism to its pride of place in the constitutional pantheon.[40] "Like puppy love," says Rubin, "it looks somewhat authentic but does not reflect the intense desires that give the real thing its inherent meaning."[41] I wonder if there is something similarly "puppyish" about the invocation of foreign materials by members of the Supreme Court (who tend, of course, to be on the opposite side from the purported federalism devotees).

As Choudry's superb article demonstrates, there are courts elsewhere—South Africa's apparently being the primary, but not unique, example—that not only cite foreign materials but also, and far more importantly, actually discuss them and grapple with their arguments, especially when they choose in a different direction. Justice Kennedy, however, tells us nothing interesting about the European case that he cites. The citation is mere ornamentation, like a trill in a cadenza. Should we want to know anything more, we must go ourselves to the library (or log on to the Internet) and track the case down. Justice Breyer is a bit better, but he, too, at the end of the day, does little more than provide some bibliographical help for someone interested in reading about European experience administering modern states or the European Union.

This is not to say, incidentally, that Breyer is necessarily correct and that Scalia is necessarily wrong with regard to the instrumental relationship between commandeering and preserving the agreed-upon values of federalism, which include, among other things, respect for diversity and the virtues of a less alienated form of popular governance. As Vicki Jackson and my colleague Ernie Young have both suggested, it may be that federalism is actually more robust in Europe than in the United States, so that European states can "afford" some degree of "commandeering." In contrast, American states might lose what little significance they truly possess if courts allow their officials to be commandeered. I personally suspect that Breyer is correct in all respects and that Scalia and my esteemed colleague are both too fearful about the health of American federalism. But the point is that at least Young and I might agree that facts really count. And the relevant facts, I believe, are not those of eighteenth-century federalism, any more than we would particularly be interested in discussing eighteenth-century notions of medical care (think of leeches, for example) when trying to figure out what contemporary Americans are entitled to. Instead, they are precisely the experiences of other countries *today.*

In any event, the challenge facing those of us who self-identify with the cosmopolitanism of Justice Breyer and lament the parochialism of Justice Scalia is to articulate exactly why it is worth becoming genuinely familiar with—which means really discussing and not simply tipping our hats to—foreign materials. This discussion is especially important if we find Scalia's account persuasive of what it means to be faithful to *this* Constitution, in all of its decided imperfection.

Notes

1. 539 U.S. 558 (2003).
2. C. L. Ostberg, Matthew E. Wetstein, and Craig R. Ducat, "Attitudes, Precedents and Cultural Change: Explaining the Citations of Foreign Precedents by the Supreme Court of Canada," *Canadian Journal of Political Science* 34 (2001): 377, 387–87.
3. *The Queen v. Elshaw* (1991), 3 SCR 24, 57.
4. *Rahey v. The Queen* (1987), 1 SCR 588.
5. See generally Sujit Choudhry, "Globalization in Search of Justification: Toward a Theory of Constitutional Interpretation," *Indiana Law Journal* 74 (1999): 819.
6. *State v. Mhlungu,* (1995), 3 South African Law Reports 867, 917 (Constitutional Court).
7. See, e.g., Michael Klarman, *From Jim Crow to Civil Rights: The Supreme Court and the Struggle for Racial Equality* (New York: Oxford University Press, 2004), 184; ("The importance of the Cold War imperative for racial change is hard to overstate.") For the initial statement of this thesis, see generally, Mary Dudziak, "Desegregation as a Cold War Imperative," *Stanford Law Review* 41 (1988): 61. Dudziak further elaborated her argument in *Cold War Civil Rights: Race and the Image of American Democracy* (Princeton, NJ: Princeton University Press, 2000).

8. *Lawrence v. Texas*, 539 U.S. 558 (2003). Although *Lawrence* was indeed the most recent relevant case when I drafted this chapter, the debate that I am describing certainly erupted once more on March 1, 2005, when a sharply divided Supreme Court, in *Roper v. Simmons*, invalidated capital punishment as applied to persons who were under eighteen years of age when the crime for which they were sentenced was committed. See http://caselaw.lp.findlaw.com/scripts/getcase.pl?court=US&vol=000&invol=03-633. Justice Anthony Kennedy devoted a section of his majority opinion to international legal developments: "Our determination that the death penalty is disproportionate punishment for offenders under eighteen finds confirmation in the stark reality that the United States is the only country in the world that continues to give official sanction to the juvenile death penalty." He immediately went on to acknowledge that "[t]his reality does not become controlling. ..." But foreign legal materials are nonetheless "instructive for their interpretation of the Eighth Amendment's prohibition of cruel and unusual punishments." What follows are three paragraphs referring to various international and foreign materials. Kennedy then concludes that "the opinion of the world community, while not controlling our outcome, does provide respected and significant confirmation for our own conclusions."

    As one could readily predict, Justice Scalia, in dissent, was savagely critical, with, I believe, some good reason. He is particularly adept at noting the selective nature of the Court's assimilation of foreign views, a topic discussed later in this chapter. "The Court should either profess its willingness to reconsider all [of] these matters [including abortion] in light of the views of foreigners, or else it should cease putting forth foreigners' views as part of the *reasoned basis* of its decisions. To invoke alien law when it agrees with one's own thinking, and ignore it otherwise, is not reasoned decision making, but sophistry." In any event, it is clear that the question spelled out in the title of this chapter continues to be a source of lively (and bitter) debate in the Supreme Court, not to mention law reviews and newspaper editorials.

9. See *Lawrence v. Texas*, 573, discussing 4 European Human Rights Reports (1981) 149, 164–65.

10. *Lawrence v. Texas*.

11. 478 U.S., 196 (1986).

12. 539 U.S., 598, citing *Foster v. Florida*, 537 U.S. 990 (2002) n.* (Justice Thomas, concurring in denial of certiorari).

13. *Printz v. United States*, 521 U.S. 898 (1997; emphasis added in quotations).

14. *Printz v. United States*, 976–77, citing Kurt Lenaerts, "Constitutionalism and the Many Faces of Federalism," *Am. J. Comp. L.* 38 (1990) 205, 237; David P. Currie, *The Constitution of the Federal Republic of Germany* (Chicago: University of Chicago Press, 1994), 66, 84; Lord MacKenzie-Stuart, "Foreword" in *Comparative Constitutional Federalism: Europe and America* (Mark Tushnet ed., Westport, Conn.: Greenwood Publishing Group, 1990), ix; Cliona, J. M. Kimber, "A Comparison of Environmental Federalism in the United States and the European Union," *MD. L. REV.* 54 (1995): 1658, 1675–1677.

15. "A Comparison of Environmental Federalism in the United States and the European Union," citing Council of European Communities, European Council in Edinburgh, 11–12 December 1992, Conclusions of the Presidency (1993), 20–21, http://www.europarl.eu.int/summits/edinburgh/default_ue.htm; Dominik Asok and K. P. E. Bridge, *Law and Institutions of the European Union* (London: Butterworths, 1994), 114; David P. Currie, "Integration and the Federal Experience in Germany and Switzerland," *The Constitution of the Federal Republic of Germany* (Chicago: University of Chicago Press, 1994), 68, 81–84, 100–101; Jochen Abr. Frowein, *Integration through Law*, 573, 586–587 (M. Cappelletti, M. Seccombe, and J. Weiler eds., Berlin: W. de Gruyter, 1986); Lenaerts, 232, 263.

16. Cf. *The Federalist No. 20*, 134–138 (C. Rossiter ed., New York: Penguin Books, 1961), 134–138 (rejecting certain aspects of European federalism).

17. Cf. *The Federalist No. 42*, 268 (J. Madison) (looking to experiences of European countries); *The Federalist No. 43*, 275, 276.

18. *Printz v. United States*, 921 n. 11.

19. *Printz v. United States*, quoting *United States v. Lopez*, 514 U.S. 549, 575 (1995) Justice Kennedy, concurring, citing Friendly, "Federalism: A Forward," *Yale Law Journal* 86 (1977): 1019 (emphasis added).

20. 536 U.S. 304, 321 (2002) (Justice Scalia, dissenting).

21. See *Texas v. Johnson*, 491 U.S. 397 (1989); Eichman, 496 U.S. 310 (1990).
22. See H. L. A. Hart, *Law, Liberty, and Morality* (Stanford, CA: Stanford University Press, 1963).
23. Patrick Devlin, The Enforcement of Morals 15 (New York: Oxford University Press, 1965), 15 (reprinting Devlin's 1959 Maccabean Lecture in Jurisprudence).
24. See, e.g., Scalia's dissent in *Romer v. Evans*, 517 US (1996) 620, 636.
25. See Sanford Levinson, "Hercules, Abraham Lincoln, The United States Constitution, and the Problem of Slavery," in *Essays on Ronald Dworkin*, Arthur Ripstein, ed. (Cambridge University Press, forthcoming).
26. *Calder v. Bull*, 3 U.S. (3 Dall.) (1978) 386, 399 (1798).
27. Markovits responded to the original version of this essay in "Learning from the Foreigners: A Response to Justice Scalia's and Professor Levinson's Professional Moral Parochialism," *Texas International Law Journal* 39 (2004): 367. His full-scale arguments are spelled out in Richard S. Markovits, *Matters of Principle: Legitimate Legal Argument and Constitutional Interpretation* (New York: New York University Press, 1998).
28. See e.g., "Constitutional Rhetoric and the Ninth Amendment," 64 *Chi.-Kent L. Rev.* (1988): 131, reprinted in Randy E. Barnett, ed., *The Rights Retained by the People: The History and Meaning of the Ninth Amendment, Vol. 115*, 2nd vol. (Fairfax, Va.: George Mason University Press, 1993).
29. See *McCulloch v. Maryland*, 17 U.S. (4 Wheat.) (1819) 316, 400 (1819).
30. See Sanford Levinson, "Looking Abroad When Interpreting the U.S. Constitution: Some Reflections," *Texas International Law Journal* 30 (2004): 353, 364.
31. Antonin Scalia, *Keynote Address: Foreign Legal Authority in the Federal Courts.* ASIL Proceedings 2004 (Washington, D.C.). I am grateful to Justice Scalia for making this text available to me and for a very helpful conversation during a conference in Banff, Canada, in July 2004.
32. *Keynote Address: Foreign Legal Authority in the Federal Courts*, 2.
33. *Washington v. Glucksberg*, 521 U.S. (1997) 702, 718 n. 16.
34. *Keynote Address: Foreign Legal Authority in the Federal Courts*, 2–3.
35. Emphasis added.
36. 124 S.Ct. 1307, (2004) 1315–20 (Justice Scalia, dissenting).
37. Id. at 1320 (citing Elaine Sciolino, "Chiric Backs Law to Keep Signs of Faith out of School," *New York Times*, Dec. 18, 2003, A17).
38. For a decidedly negative view of such developments, see Samuel P. Huntington, *Who Are We: The Challenges to America's National Identity* (New York: Simon & Schuster, 2004).
39. *Keynote Address: Foreign Legal Authority in the Federal Courts*, 5.
40. See generally Edward L. Rubin, "Puppy Federalism and the Blessings of America," *ANNALS American Academy of Political and Social Science* 37 (2001).
41. "Puppy Federalism and the Blessings of America," 38.

PART **III**
The Future

CHAPTER 14

Liberal with a Twist

Queering Marriage

H. N. HIRSCH

I spent many years teaching pre-law courses in the political science department at the University of California, San Diego. There I met (among many lesbian, gay, bisexual and transgendered [LGBT] students) a lesbian, whom I also got to know through our involvement in the same community theater organization. Let's call her Jane.

Jane was what most people would call a butch dyke (if they were familiar with such categories). Indeed, she acted on the stage part-time, and played a butch dyke—one who repaired motorcycles, no less—in our production of "Street Theater," a play about the Stonewall Rebellion.

I remember to this day a casual but startling conversation with Jane in which she told me she had always wanted to get married, to have a wedding. "It's just something I've wanted since I was a little girl," she said wistfully. This was during rehearsals for the play in 1994, the twenty-fifth anniversary of Stonewall—eleven years ago.

Jane also readily referred to herself as "queer."

As of this writing, same-sex couples have been legally married in Massachusetts. I can honestly say that, as a fifty-three-year-old gay man, I never expected to see this in my lifetime. Never mind whether other states will recognize such unions, and the (perhaps) decades of legal wrangling over that question that lie ahead. Never mind the brouhaha over a proposed constitutional amendment. This is every bit as stunning an event as *Brown v. Board of Education*, the fiftieth anniversary of which the Massachusetts court cleverly chose as the first day of legal gay marriages.

Same-sex couples, legally married. An earthquake. Jane is, if she wishes, on her way to the altar (and probably on her way from California to Massachusetts).

What strikes me now about Jane, though, is the extent to which recent scholarly and popular discourse would lead us to believe that these two parts of her identity—her self-described queerness, and her desire to be married—are contradictory. Queers aren't supposed to want marriage, at least according to most queer theorists—those radical theorists dedicated to "resistance to regimes of the normal."[1] And gays and lesbians who want to get married are usually labeled as assimilationists—that is, they are supposed to be interested in fitting into straight society to the maximum extent possible—with "appropriate" behavior and dress, a picket fence or the urban equivalent (most likely a gentrified townhouse), and, usually, children.

In this chapter I want to examine critically the major positions within the gay community on the marriage question, and to suggest that reality is more complicated than recent commentators would have us believe. To support this point, I use empirical data from a study of political attitudes among gay citizens in four American cities.[2]

Liberals, Queers, and Neocons

There are three major positions on marriage within recent gay commentary: the liberal (or civil libertarian), the queer, and the neo-conservative. I will briefly examine each, though it should be remembered that these are ideal types; many individual writers blend elements of more than one of these positions in their writing.

The liberal position is the most familiar and most simple: All should be equal before the law. The decision to marry is fundamental, and it cannot be circumscribed by the gender of the parties in question.

For the liberal, sex is private; what happens behind closed doors between consenting adults is not the business of the state or anyone else.

The liberal legal position has been presented most persuasively by Andrew Koppelman, who argues that the prevention of same-sex marriage is a form of sex discrimination,[3] and by Evan Gerstmann, who focuses on the fundamentality of the right to marry.[4] As Gerstmann states it, his fundamental premise is straightforward: "*The Constitution guarantees every person the right to marry the person of his or her choice.*"[5]

This is the logic of the majority of the Massachusetts Supreme Judicial Court in *Goodridge v. Department of Public Health*.[6] Chief Justice Marshall's opinion is quick to speak of the "common human dignity protected by the Fourteenth Amendment to the United States Constitution," and the "deeply personal realms of consensual adult expressions of intimacy and one's choice of an intimate partner."[7] In line with the standard liberal jurisprudence that began with the definition of a right to privacy in *Griswold v. Connecticut* in 1965 and continued through *Roe v. Wade* and its progeny, the Massachusetts court characterizes marriage as a private "decision," a decision that "shape[s] one's identity."[8]

The emotional appeal of the liberal argument has perhaps been best presented by legal scholar Barbara Cox, who writes movingly of her desire to wed her same-sex partner:

> Yes, I know that weddings can be "heterosexual rituals" of the most repressive and repugnant kind. Yes, I know that weddings historically symbolize the loss of the woman's self. … [but] …
>
> When my partner and I decided to have a commitment ceremony, we did so to express the love and caring we feel for one another, to celebrate that love with our friends and family, and to express that love openly and with pride.[9]

Cox continues, "It angers me when others, who did not participate or do not know either of us, condemn us as part of a mindless flock accepting a dehumanizing ceremony."[10] Cox goes on to discuss the "radical aspects of lesbian marriage," and the "transformation" her ceremony had on people around her, from her sister's children to her law students.[11]

The liberal argument often points to the literally hundreds of legal benefits that accrue to a spouse, from hospital visitation to survivor benefits under Social Security. Along those lines, gay philosopher Richard Mohr posits that gay and lesbian couples do, in fact, already live together "as married people do," and presents a powerful anecdote supporting gay marriage and the importance of the rights attached to it:

> On their way back from the neighborhood bar to the Victorian which, over the years, they had lovingly restored, Warren and Mark stopped along San Francisco's Polk Street to pick up milk for breakfast and for Sebastian, their geriatric cat. Just for kicks, some wealthy teens from the Valley drove into town to "bust some fags." Warren dipped into a convenience store, while Mark had a smoke outside. As Mark turned to acknowledge Warren's return, he was hit across the back of the head with a baseball bat. Mark's blood and vomit splashed across Warren's face. In 1987, a California appellate court held that under no circumstance can a relationship between two

homosexuals—however emotionally significant, stable, and exclu-sive—be legally considered a "close relationship," and so Warren was barred from bringing any suit against the bashers.[12]

The liberal argument often rests on the unarticulated premise that gays and lesbians are just like everyone else—that their sexual orientation is but one small and irrelevant difference between them and their neighbors. As such, the liberal argument often reduces to an argument of "no difference"—there is no real, substantial difference between gay people and everyone else, and thus no difference between a gay or lesbian marriage and a heterosexual marriage. We are all alike, fundamentally; the gender of one's partner, or one's spouse, is irrelevant to the life one leads.

In the hands of mainstream national gay organizations, this argument quickly becomes an argument for assimilation. A recent pamphlet published by the Human Rights Campaign (HRC), for example, opens with a personal letter from Cheryl Jacques, the organization's then president:

> When I kiss my children good night after a long day's work, I some-times wonder what they will learn in school about this moment in history—when Americans are wrestling, once again, with questions about who should have access to one of the most cherished, joyful freedoms in the world, the freedom to marry.[13]

My children are just like your children, Jacques is saying to straight America; my family is just like yours:

> I am confident that in the end, my sons will learn that the American people did right by all our nation's families, including their own.[14]

The next page of the pamphlet features a large picture of a male couple (both white and Hollywood gorgeous, of course) with two handsome children on their shoulders. It then recites "10 facts," including:

> One of three lesbian couples is raising children. One out of every five gay male couples is raising children.
> Between 1 million and 9 million children are being raised by gay, lesbian and bisexual parents in the United States today.
> At least one same-sex couple is raising children in 96 percent of all counties nationwide.[15]

And, for good measure:

> The highest percentage of same-sex couples raising children live in the South.[16]

All of this "normal family" appeal, this attempt to join the mainstream on the basis of fundamental legal and constitutional rights, is rejected by queer theorists. The queer critique of marriage has been argued most cogently by Michael Warner, who states forthrightly that "marriage is unethical," and that the queer ideal is not normalcy, but rather "sexual autonomy."[17]

Chapter one, page one of Warner's *The Trouble with Normal,* his most extended discussion of marriage to date, begins with the claim that "sooner or later, happily or unhappily, almost everyone fails to control his or her sex life."[18] For Warner, and for most queer theorists, sex is no longer a mere private matter, and is not to be covered over with liberal discretion; sex is central to politics and identity, and to be embraced and celebrated in all of its wild uncontrollability—so long as relations are between consenting adults:

> It might as well be admitted that sex is a disgrace. We like to say nice things about it: that it is an expression of love, or a noble endowment of the Creator, or liberatory pleasure. But the possibility of abject shame is never entirely out of the picture.[19]

"If the camera doesn't cut away at the right moment"—as it does for the liberal, Warner would say, "or if the door is thrown open unwontedly, or the walls turn out to be too thin, all the fine dress or piety and pride will be found tangled around one's ankles."[20]

For Warner, the contemporary mainstream gay movement has been reduced to a "desexualized identity politics … becoming more and more enthralled by respectability."[21] As such, groups such as HRC have led the gay movement to "increasingly narrow its scope to those issues of sexual orientation that have least to do with sex."[22] What queerness stands for, according to Warner, is that "one doesn't pretend to be above the indignity of sex."[23]

For queers, according to Warner, marriage discriminates. It "sanctifies some couples at the expense of others."[24] Warner argues that queers should resist "any attempt to make the norms of straight culture into the standards by which queer life should be measured," and should especially resist "the notion that the state should be allowed to accord legitimacy to some forms of consensual sex and not others."[25] Gay men, especially, have cultivated "nonstandard intimacies" that will be discriminated against in the rush to embrace respectable marriage.[26] Thus, "marrying has consequences for the unmarried."[27] Marriage confers a status, and will divide the world into the good gay who marries and the bad queer who does not, who will continue to enjoy "nonstandard intimacies."[28]

For Warner, coming out as gay or queer "exposes you to being defined by desire," and this "always implies some impropriety"—an impropriety he believes should be celebrated.[29] Marriage, on the other hand, privatizes and sanitizes gay sexuality. And, he adds, "the gap between gay and queer" is growing.[30]

Neo-conservatives within the gay movement are at the opposite end of the political spectrum from queer theorists such as Warner, but, intriguingly, they (sometimes implicitly) share one of the central premises of queers: that (especially male) sexuality is often uncontrollable, anti-social, and dangerous. For queers, that danger is to be embraced and celebrated; for neo-conservatives, that danger is precisely what marriage would be best at ameliorating.

The most prominent spokesmen for the neo-conservative position on marriage within the gay community have been journalist Andrew Sullivan and legal scholar William Eskridge.

Sullivan, a prolific author and the former editor of the *New Republic*, has been tireless in his promotion of the cause of gay marriage. Along with the right to serve openly in the military, he considers it the only right really worth pursuing. He writes that "surprisingly … one of the strongest arguments for gay marriage is a conservative one."[31] If gays were to marry, they would make "a deeper commitment to one another and to society."[32] Marriage, for Sullivan, "provides an anchor … in the maelstrom of sex and relationships to which we are all prone."[33] Marriage "provides a mechanism for emotional stability and economic security."[34]

And marriage, Sullivan asserts, "would also be an unqualified social good for homosexuals."[35] Marriage would provide "role models for young gay people, who, after the exhilaration of coming out, can easily lapse into short-term relationships and insecurity with no tangible goal in sight."[36] Marriage would also "help bridge the gulf often found between homosexuals and their parents"; it "could bring the essence of gay life—a gay couple—into the heart of the traditional family."[37]

Above all, says Sullivan,

> As gay marriage sank into the subtle background consciousness of a culture, its influence would be felt quietly but deeply among gay children. For them, at last, there would be some kind of future; some older faces to apply to their unfolding lives, some language in which their identity could be properly discussed, some rubric by which it could be explained—not in terms of sex, or sexual practices, or bars, or subterranean activity, but in terms of their future life stories, their potential loves, their eventual chance at some kind of constructive happiness.[38]

Similar arguments are offered by Eskridge, who says that marriage would "civilize" gays.[39] It would remove the need for gays to be "outlaws"; it would further their increasing integration into "larger society."[40] Same-sex marriage, says Eskridge, "will likely contribute to the public acceptability of homo-sexual relationships. The interpersonal commitments entailed by same-sex marriage ought to help break down the stereotypes straights have about gays, especially about gay and bisexual men." [41]

Eskridge writes approvingly of the "domestication" that marriage would entail, for "it should not have required the AIDS epidemic to alert us to the problems of sexual promiscuity and to the advantages of committed relation-ships." [42] Although conceding that male promiscuity "may be a consequence of biology," Eskridge claims that "sexual variety has not been liberating to gay men," for

> in addition to the disease costs, promiscuity has encouraged a cult of youth worship and has contributed to the stereotype of homosexu-als as people who lack a serious approach to life. (Indeed, a culture centered around nightclubs and bars is not one that can fundamen-tally satisfy the needs for connection and commitment that become more important as one grows older.) [43]

Sexual liberation—which can take many forms, including multiple partners—is thus celebrated and embraced by the queer theorist, and exco-riated by the neo-conservative. But clearly, sexuality, especially male sexu-ality, is at the center of the theorizing of both groups.

Empirical Fndings

To what extent are the attitudes of the liberal, the queer, and the neo-conservative shared by everyday members of LGBT communities? In part to answer that question, a colleague and I have been engaged in a long-range study of the attitudes of LGBT individuals toward politics and law in four "average" American cities—Albany, New York; San Diego, California; Minneapolis, Minnesota; and Nashville, Tennessee. [44] The results are instructive.

There is virtually no support whatever for the neo-conservative position on marriage—and this despite the fact that the sample contained a good number of gay Republicans and despite the fact that the sample as a whole is somewhat biased toward the well-to-do.

Virtually every respondent in the sample agrees with the statement that "it is important for gay and lesbian people to fight for the right to marry," and, at the same time, there is strong support for turning to law and the legal system to redress grievances. Only 10 percent of the sample self-identify as queer (and, not surprisingly, queers are somewhat less likely to support the fight for the right to marriage). At first glance, then, it would seem that these respondents wholeheartedly support the liberal position.

At the same time, though, there are intriguing indications of both political radicalism and what might be called sex positivity in the sample, and, as such, there are clearly queer elements mixed in. For example, a huge majority (74 percent) claim that LGBT couples are not "imitating heterosexual patterns." A large majority (60 percent) claim that being gay has changed their ideas about politics. A healthy majority (58 percent) believe that sex clubs should not be closed, even in the midst of the AIDS pandemic. Half of the sample is unwilling to condemn two men for having sex without a condom, and only a third of the sample is willing to say they disapprove of two men doing so.

A large majority (56 percent) claim that they want to change society, rather than simply being left alone to live their own lives. The younger a respondent, the more likely he or she is to support the fight for the right to marry, and, perhaps most intriguingly, those who report having experienced some form of discrimination as a result of being gay are more likely to support the idea of gay marriage.[45]

Although there is clearly some radicalism on issues of sex and politics in these numbers, the sample is, on the whole, not militant, angry at the straight world, or separatist.

What Goes on Here?

Buried in these survey responses, we believe, is strong evidence that there is more to being gay than the gender of one's chosen sexual partner or partners. There *is* something about being gay that gives one a different attitude about sex; and there *is* something about being gay in a homophobic society that is inherently politicizing. As loyal Americans, strongly believing in the law, not angry or militant, our respondents do nevertheless want to change society, and they believe people who want to have anonymous, promiscuous, or dangerous sex should be free to do so.

In other words, queer theory is definitely onto something in its sex positivity; it is accurately reflecting the mores of the LGBT community, even when only a small portion of that community will label themselves "queer." But it is wrong—spectacularly wrong—when it simultaneously rejects gay marriage. On this score, liberals are clearly more accurately reflecting the desires of the community about which they speak.

This data also seem to be strongly hinting that gay citizens are able to separate sex and love. Love, emotional and financial commitment, cohabitation—these elements of marriage are replicated and sought in gay couplings. But it is generally more widely accepted, at least among gay men, that sexual fidelity is a separate matter, and is not a required element of a strong and lasting emotional bond.[46]

If this is true, and if in fact the march toward gay marriage continues to gain momentum across the country, it could well be the case that this sort of honesty and realism about sexuality will have a profound impact on the institution of marriage more generally. A great many heterosexual marriages falter over the issue of sexual exclusivity; a great many gay "marriages" incorporate non-monogamy into their explicit self-understanding. It is hard to imagine that the legal and social recognition of the latter will not profoundly influence the former.

Thus, paradoxically, gay marriage—which queer theorists condemn as assimilationist—may in fact be a radicalizing institution for American heterosexuality. Modern conservatives are therefore on to something when they worry that gay marriage may, in fact, challenge and change the institution. In its majority opinion in *Goodridge*, the Massachusetts court defines civil marriage "to mean the voluntary union of two persons as spouses, to the exclusion of all others."[47] It is this exclusivity, and the sexual ethics, living arrangements, and child-rearing customs it implies, that gay marriage will challenge as it continues to gain acceptance.

Mohr comments that "people at the margins of society have frequently provided the beacon for reform in family law."[48] For example, the law slowly accepted the rights of "bastard" children and the legitimacy of extended families, both developments reflecting social realities in African-American families. A similar evolution in the law may well follow the recognition of same-sex marriages. As one of our survey respondents put it, "We should not foreclose the option of recognizing a wider range of relationship types."

What this data also suggests is that liberal theorists need to think seriously about sexuality. The standard liberal assumption—that (voluntary, adult) sexuality is a wholly private matter, and that this constitutes everything one needs to know about it—is not sufficient. We cannot, and should not, assume that gay sexuality is "no different" from heterosexuality; we cannot, and should not, assume that male sexuality is no different from female sexuality. And we cannot and should not assume that the sexuality in any given relationship is fixed forever at the point of marriage.

Notes

1. Donald E. Hall, *Queer Theories* (New York: Palgrave Macmillan, 2003), 15.
2. Joe Rollins and H. N. Hirsch, "Sexual Identities and Political Engagements: A Queer Survey," *Social Politics* 10, no. 3 (2003): 290–313.
3. Andrew Koppelman, *The Gay Rights Question in Contemporary American Law* (Chicago: University of Chicago Press, 2002), 53–71.
4. Evan Gerstmann, *Same-Sex Marriage and the Constitution* (New York: Cambridge University Press, 2004), 67–114.
5. Ibid., 67 (emphasis in original).
6. *Goodridge v. Department of Public Health*, 798 N.E. 2d 941 Mass., Nov. 18, 2003.
7. *Goodridge*, 948.

8. *Goodridge*, 948.
9. Barbara J. Cox, "A (Personal) Essay on Same-Sex Marriage," in *Same-Sex Marriage: The Moral and Legal Debate*, eds. Robert M. Baird and Stuart E. Rosenbaum (Amherst, MA: Prometheus Books, 1997), 27–29.
10. Ibid., 28.
11. Ibid., 28–29.
12. Richard D. Mohr, "The Case for Gay Marriage," in *Same-Sex Marriage: The Moral and Legal Debate*, eds. Robert M. Baird and Stuart E. Rosenbaum (Amherst, MA: Prometheus Books, 1997), 85–86.
13. Human Rights Campaign, *Answers to Questions about Marriage Equality* (Washington, D.C.: FamilyNet Project, 2004), 1.
14. Ibid.
15. Ibid., 3.
16. Ibid.
17. Michael Warner, *The Trouble with Normal: Sex, Politics, and the Ethics of Queer Life* (New York: Free Press, 1999).
18. Ibid., 1.
19. Ibid., 2.
20. Ibid.
21. Ibid., 24.
22. Ibid., 25.
23. Ibid., 35.
24. Ibid., 82.
25. Ibid., 88.
26. Ibid., 94.
27. Ibid., 108.
28. Ibid., 94.
29. Ibid., 133.
30. Ibid., 145. For a relatively early and quite similar critique of marriage, written from a lesbian point of view, see Paula L. Ettelbrick, "Since When Is Marriage a Path to Liberation," *OUT/LOOK National Gay and Lesbian Quarterly* 6 (1989), who writes:

> marriage will not liberate us lesbians and gay men. In fact, it will constrain us, make us more invisible, force our assimilation into the mainstream, and undermine the goals of gay liberation. … The thought of emphasizing our sameness to married heterosexuals … terrifies me. It rips away the very heart and soul of what I believe it is to be a lesbian in this world. It robs me of the opportunity to make a difference. We end up mimicking all that is bad.

31. Andrew Sullivan, "Virtually Normal," in *Same-Sex Marriage: The Moral and Legal Debate*, eds. Robert M. Baird and Stuart E. Rosenbaum (Amherst, MA: Prometheus Books, 1997), 127.
32. Ibid., 128.
33. Ibid.
34. Ibid.
35. Ibid.
36. Ibid.
37. Ibid., 129.
38. Ibid.
39. William N. Eskridge, Jr., *The Case for Same-Sex Marriage: From Sexual Liberty to Civilized Commitment* (New York: Free Press, 1996), 8.
40. Ibid.
41. Ibid., 9.
42. Ibid.
43. Ibid., 10.
44. Joe Rollins and H. N. Hirsch, "Sexual Identities and Political Engagements: A Queer Survey," *Social Politics* 10, no. 3 (2003): 290–313. Includes a description of sampling techniques and the survey instrument.
45. H. N. Hirsch and Joe Rollins, "Beating Up Queers: Discrimination, Violence, and Political Attitudes in Sexual Minority Communities," in *Coming Out Around the World*, eds. Lee

Badgett and Jeff Frank (New York: Routledge, 2006). This piece offers an analysis of the effect of discrimination on the political attitudes of the sample.

46. This finding has been replicated in other research on gay couples; see David P. McWhirter and Andrew M. Mattison, *The Male Couple: How Relationships Develop* (Englewood Cliffs: Prentice Hall, Inc., 1984). They found that no couple in existence for longer than five years incorporated sexual monogamy into its self-understanding.

47. *Goodridge* , 798 N.E.2d 941, 969 Mass., Nov. 18, 2003.

48. Mohr, "The Case for Gay Marriage," 96.

CHAPTER 15

The Polite Thing to Do

KEITH J. BYBEE

In the final debate of the 2004 presidential election, the Democratic candidate John Kerry was asked whether homosexuality was a choice. "We're all God's children," Kerry answered. "And I think if you were to talk to Dick Cheney's daughter, who is a lesbian, she would tell you that she's being who she was. She's being who she was born as. I think that if you talk to anybody, it's not a choice."[1] Following the debate, the Bush campaign attacked Kerry's answer as a "crass, below-the-belt" effort to alienate conservative voters from the Bush-Cheney ticket by outing Mary Cheney as a homosexual. Kerry dismissed the criticism and argued that he was simply "trying to say something positive about the way strong families deal with the issue." Elizabeth Edwards, the wife of Kerry's running mate, went further and suggested that the Republicans' criticism was an overreaction rooted in a "certain amount of shame with respect to [Mary Cheney's] sexual preference."

For those interested in the future of LGBT rights in the United States, the controversy over Kerry's remarks is instructive—not because of the accusations of homophobia and gay baiting that were slung back and forth, but because these accusations were exchanged over a question of good manners. Basic rules of campaign etiquette in the United States place the candidates' families outside the bounds of political debate. A candidate's spouse or children may be mentioned by a political opponent, but only in a positive, apolitical way. To breach this rule of campaign etiquette is to be politically impolite, to convert an otherwise legitimate political disagreement into an illegitimate personal attack by raising private issues that are not of public concern. The Bush campaign claimed that Kerry had been politically impolite in precisely this way. In their heated reactions to Kerry's comments, Vice President Cheney and his wife, Lynne, described themselves, respectively, as an "angry father" and as an "indignant mom," lashing out in response to a personal insult.[2] The Kerry campaign did not deny that campaign etiquette required the Democrats to draw a line between the rough-and-tumble of political debate and the candidates' families. On the contrary, the Kerry campaign claimed that this particular rule of campaign etiquette had been suspended because the Cheneys had previously made use of their daughter's sexual orientation for political purposes. Mary Cheney's homosexuality was fair game for Kerry, Democratic vice-presidential candidate John Edwards argued, because the Cheneys "had themselves brought it up."

Ultimately, then, the controversy over Kerry's remarks was about how issues of sexual orientation are to be handled relative to the courtesies that govern political discussion. In this particular instance, rules of etiquette were invoked to head off an open debate about homosexuality and to focus attention instead on the issue of appropriate candidate behavior. This oppositional relationship between sexual orientation and good manners is instructive because it is not just an artifact of presidential elections. As Randall Kennedy has noted, the political efforts of marginalized groups are frequently bound up with questions of courtesy.[3] Codes of courtesy typically mark-off and counter-pose the groups that comprise a given polity, providing a means of reinforcing existing hierarchies across classes. Thus, in order to win an equal standing in society, marginalized groups must often call into question accepted standards of politeness.

We can see examples of this in many different areas of LGBT political action. In their efforts to spur stronger governmental responses to the AIDS crisis, members of ACT UP self-consciously contested the prevailing norms of courtesy that disparaged public displays of anger and treated LGBT sexuality as an object of shame.[4] Similarly, a variety of activists have agitated against the U.S. military's comprehensive "Don't Ask, Don't Tell" code of etiquette that skews speech and action in a decidedly heterosexual direction.[5]

Less obviously perhaps, proponents of same-sex marriage have also found themselves bedeviled by manners. Numerous individuals resist the idea of same-sex marriage on the basis of religious conviction, while others object to the extension of material benefits enjoyed by opposite-sex married couples, and still others reject same-sex marriage because of anti-homosexual prejudice. Yet, for many Americans, same-sex marriage is something that simply is not done: Polite society attaches a special degree of respect and a distinctive set of expectations to husbands and wives that are not extended to unmarried couples, regardless of whether such couples are same-sex or opposite-sex. The idea of same-sex marriage consequently strikes many as a kind of rudeness, a violation of the code of accepted behavior that should be met with indignant disapproval. This polite understanding of marriage helps explain the passage of same-sex marriage bans by large margins in states throughout the country.

These examples suggest that, beyond the repeal of restrictive laws and the winning of favorable judicial decisions, the expansion of LGBT rights requires engagement with and re-appropriation of the prevailing practices of courtesy. What might this look like? It is tempting to see the process of engagement and re-appropriation as a straightforward crusade against an artificial and unjust hierarchy. But LGBT efforts must be more nuanced than that because courtesy is not simply a system of rules manufactured to serve the interests of the powerful.

First of all, the very "fakeness" of courtesy makes it useful to everyone in society.[6] Rather than unrealistically attempting to reconcile stubborn conflicts or romantically wishing away deep differences, courtesy attempts to achieve social peace and smooth interaction among people by requiring them to conform to an artificial code of decent behavior whether they actually like or respect one another. The artificial code enforced by courtesy is not neutral between all groups in society. But the lack of symmetry does not mean that courteous interactions are without some benefit for all parties involved. Although it has its inequities, courtesy also has the virtue of making agreement possible when it is necessary and of making agreement unnecessary when it is impossible.[7] It is a kind of organized hypocrisy that allows all sorts of "false friends" to make mutually beneficial arrangements without requiring deep agreement or genuine affinity.[8]

Second, the rules of courtesy are not only generally useful, but also generally normative. For all its thinness and artificiality, courtesy is not typically experienced as a mere *modus vivendi*. In part, this is because the basic elements of courtesy are introduced to most people when they are young. The method of introduction is not based on persuasion; on the contrary, children are usually habituated to courteous behavior through a prolonged program of repetition enforced by the inflexible say-so of parents. The continuous drill of courtesy lessons during childhood produces adults who are disposed to follow the conventions of etiquette and who can be shamed whenever they stray from the path of courtesy. Adults thus schooled need not be truly virtuous; they are committed to particular forms of conduct and need not actually accept the substantive notions of concern and respect behind these forms.[9] In this sense, courtesy remains artificial and thin. The properly trained adult is nonetheless attached to courtesy as a routine for negotiating social interaction. Manners are habits of action and such habits cannot be lightly set aside.

The sense that one ought to be polite is further bolstered by pleasure. Courtesy serves as an agreed-upon means for granting respect and giving praise to truly deserving individuals, providing a way of satisfying the legitimate desire to recognize and reward exemplary individuals. Courtesy also serves to gratify the desires of the undeserving. The artificial rituals and fake pleasantries of courtesy appease vanity in a thousand small ways, allowing everyone in polite society to feel more honorable and worthy of respect than they actually may be. By appealing to pleasure, the reciprocal practice of courtesy progressively binds the heart of every individual in polite society to the conventions of good manners. As a result, it is not only useful to be polite, but it also positively feels like the right thing to do.

With this fuller portrait of courtesy in hand, it is possible to draw a few general conclusions about the LGBT struggle for more equitable standards of appropriate behavior. First, the effort to reconstruct courtesy on a new basis cannot succeed merely by pointing out that existing courtesies are artificial and inconsistent with the facts of contemporary life. It is true, for example, that the prevailing polite view of marriage is belied by the high rates of domestic violence and divorce in the United States. This does not mean, however, that the polite view of marriage is loosely held. To some extent all conventions of courtesy are artificial and disregarded either by boors who do not know any better or by free spirits attempting to fashion their own personal style of manners. Nonetheless, well-mannered individuals perpetuate and defend the rules of courtesy by drumming the rudiments of good behavior into their children and by disapproving the antics of the rude. The general utility of artificial rules, coupled with the force of habit and the pleasures of politeness, make manners resistant to criticism based solely on facts and figures.

Second, in order for LGBT rights to be advanced, the average American need not be genuinely convinced that every sexual orientation is deserving of equal treatment. Personal intentions matter a great deal in morality, but they hardly matter at all in manners. A person performing a moral action for the wrong reasons is considered to be immoral. By contrast, a person acting courteously is considered to be courteous regardless of her motives. Politeness is as politeness does. The practice of courtesy will change when Americans, for whatever reason, act as if the committed relationships of heterosexuals and non-heterosexuals deserve the same measure of respect, just as they currently act as if all husband and wives deserve respect. A revolution in manners will not erase the underlying differences in belief and identity that divide us, but it can substantially re-structure the way in which those differences are managed.

Finally, to the degree that the expansion of LGBT rights depends on the alteration of courtesy, the process of expansion is likely to take significant time. In some ways, the rules of courtesy are quite malleable. The very artificiality of manners means that codes of courtesy can be drawn up in any number of ways. Moreover, there is no reason why the pleasures of politeness cannot be derived from many different schemes of etiquette (though the gratification of vanity will undoubtedly be higher for specific individuals in a system that clearly privileges small elites). Habit, to the contrary, places stubborn limits on the malleability of courtesy and, at least in the near-term, commits people to the prevailing modes of behavior. The surest way to weaken the hold of old habits is to instill new habits by gradually exposing people to alternative practices that can form a new basis for social interaction. In this vein, the most lasting benefit of Massachusetts's experience with same-sex marriage may be that it creates the opportunity for individuals to become habituated to different marital arrangements and, in doing so, lays the groundwork for a more inclusive common courtesy.

Will LGBT efforts finally succeed? Change is certainly possible. The statutes that set up the basic terms of Jim Crow segregation were surrounded and sustained by well-established rules of racial etiquette. The civil rights movement of the 1960s, among other things, engaged in a series of "rude" actions like lunch-counter sit-ins that contravened the prevailing etiquette and initiated a transition toward a less hierarchical form of civility between the races. The transformation in racial etiquette is arguably incomplete, but a shift has undeniably occurred. The fact of this shift gives reason to hope that in some future presidential debate the discussion of sexual orientation will not be deemed impolite.

Notes

1. All of the quotations in this paragraph are drawn from "Cheneys Indignant About Kerry Remark," CNN.com, October 14, 2004, http://www.cnn.com/2004/ALLPOLITICS/10/14/lynne.cheney.ap (accessed November 19, 2004).
2. All of the quotations in this paragraph are drawn from "Cheneys Indignant about Kerry Remark."
3. Randall Kennedy, "The Case Against Civility," *The American Prospect* 9 (November 1, 1998–December 1, 1998), http://www.prospect.org/print/V9/41/kennedy-r.html (accessed November 19, 2004).
4. Deborah B. Gould, "Life during Wartime: Emotions and the Development of ACT UP," *Mobilization* 7 (2002), 177–200. As Gould notes, contestation is not the only response that AIDS activists have had to the prevailing norms of courtesy. Prior to the rise of ACT UP, AIDS activists adopted a more accomodationist "politics of respectability," attempting to remove the shame attached to LGBT sexuality by actively embracing conventional rules of acceptable behavior.
5. Aaron Belkin and Geoffrey Bateman, eds., *Don't Ask, Don't Tell: Debating the Gay Ban in the Military* (Boulder, CO: Lynne Rienner Publishers, 2003).

6. The leading works on courtesy are by Norbert Elias: *The History of Manners*, Vol. 1 of *The Civilizing Process*, trans. Edmund Jephcott (New York: Urizen, 1978, originally published 1939); *Power and Civility*, Vol. II of *The Civilizing Process*, trans. Edmund Jephcott (New York: Pantheon, 1982, originally published 1939); and *The Court Society*, trans. Edmund Jephcott (New York: Pantheon, 1983, originally published 1969). See also Erving Goffman, *The Presentation of Self in Everyday Life* (Garden City, NY: Doubleday Anchor Books, 1959). For very useful first-hand accounts of courtesy, see Lord Chesterfield, *Letters*, ed., David Roberts (New York: Cambridge University Press, 1992) and the following works by Judith Martin (also known as Miss Manners): *Common Courtesy: In Which Miss Manners Solves the Problem that Baffled Mr. Jefferson* (New York: Athenaeum, 1985) and *Miss Manners Rescues Civilization from Sexual Harassment, Frivolous Lawsuits, Dissing, and Other Lapses of Civility* (New York: Crown Publishers, 1996). For my take on the subject, see Keith J. Bybee, "Legal Realism, Common Courtesy, and Hypocrisy," *Law, Culture and the Humanities*, 1 (2005) 75–102.

7. For the expression of the same idea in a different context, see Cass R. Sunstein, *One Case at a Time: Judicial Minimalism on the Supreme Court* (Cambridge: Harvard University Press, 1999), 50; and Edward Levi, *An Introduction to Legal Reasoning* (Chicago: University of Chicago Press, 1949).

8. The term comes from Ruth W. Grant, *Hypocrisy and Integrity: Machiavelli, Rousseau, and the Ethics of Politics* (Chicago: University of Chicago Press, 1987), 20–21. This is not to say that only hypocrites are courteous; after all, polite behavior may be the genuine expression of a truly gracious soul. Even so, courtesy functions without requiring each individual to cultivate personal grace.

9. It may be, of course, that the practice of polite conduct will occasionally encourage the development of genuine virtue. As Martin writes, it may be that "if you write enough thank-you letters, you may actually come to feel a flicker of gratitude" (*Common Courtesy*, 11–12).

Contributors

John Brigham is Professor of Political Science, University of Massachusetts, Amherst.

Keith J. Bybee holds the Michael O. Sawyer Chair of Constitutional Law and Politics at the Maxwell School of Citizenship and Public Affairs, Syracuse University. He is currently completing a book manuscript, *Legal Courtesy: A Study of Courts, Politics, and Hypocrisy* (to be published by Stanford University Press).

Sean Cahill is Director of the National Gay and Lesbian Task Force Policy Institute.

Dale Carpenter is Associate Professor of Law at the University of Minnesota.

Jo Ann Citron is Visiting Assistant Professor in the Women's Studies Department at Wellesley College and practices law with the firm of Altman & Citron, LLP, in Boston, Massachusetts.

John D'Emilio is Professor of Gender and Women's Studies and Professor of History at the University of Illinois, Chicago. He is the author of *Lost Prophet: The Life and Times of Bayard Rustin* (Free Press, 2003) and *The World Turned: Essays on Gay History, Politics, and Culture* (Duke University Press, 2002).

David O. Erdos is a Ph.D. candidate at Princeton University.

H.N. Hirsch is Professor of Politics and Dean of the Faculty of Arts and Sciences at Oberlin College.

Ronald Kahn is James Monroe Professor of Politics and Law at Oberlin College.

Ethel D. Klein is President of EDK Associates, Inc. She is the author of *Gender Politics* (1984) and the lead author of *Ending Domestic Violence: Changing Public Perceptions/Halting the Epidemic* (1997).

Andrew Koppelman is Professor of Law and Political Science at Northwestern University. He is the author of *Antidiscrimination Law and Social Equality* (Yale University Press, 1996) and *The Gay Rights Question in Contemporary American Law* (University of Chicago, 2002).

Sanford Levinson is Professor at the University of Texas Law School and Department of Government.

Joe Rollins is Associate Professor of Political Science at Queens College, City University of New York, and the author of *AIDS and the Sexuality of Law: Ironic Jurisprudence* (Palgrave Macmillan, 2004).

Mary Lyndon (Molly) Shanley is Margaret Stiles Halleck Professor of Social Science at Vassar College. She is the author of *Making Babies, Making Families: What Matters Most in an Age of Reproductive Technologies, Surrogacy, Adoption, and Same-Sex and Unwed Parents* (Beacon, 2001) and a contributor to *Just Marriage* (Oxford, 2004).

Kenneth Sherrill is Professor and Chair of the Department of Political Science, Hunter College, City University of New York.

Anna Marie Smith is Associate Professor of Government at Cornell University.

INDEX